# Hands-On Artificial Intelligence with Unreal Engine

Everything you want to know about Game AI using Blueprints or C++

**Francesco Sapio**

**BIRMINGHAM - MUMBAI**

# Hands-On Artificial Intelligence with Unreal Engine

**Acquisition Editor:** Larissa Pinto
**Content Development Editor:** Akhil Nair
**Technical Editor:** Ralph Rosario
**Copy Editor:** Safis Editing
**Project Coordinator:** Kinjal Bari
**Proofreader:** Safis Editing
**Indexer:** Manju Arasan
**Graphics:** Alishon Mendonsa
**Production Coordinator:** Jisha Chirayil

First published: April 2019

Production reference: 1240419

Published by Packt Publishing Ltd.
Livery Place
35 Livery Street
Birmingham
B3 2PB, UK.

ISBN 978-1-78883-565-7

www.packtpub.com

To all of the game developers out there who are bold enough to travel and create magical worlds and dedicate their life and soul for the joy of others.

*– Francesco Sapio*

`mapt.io`

Mapt is an online digital library that gives you full access to over 5,000 books and videos, as well as industry leading tools to help you plan your personal development and advance your career. For more information, please visit our website.

# Why subscribe?

- Spend less time learning and more time coding with practical eBooks and Videos from over 4,000 industry professionals

- Improve your learning with Skill Plans built especially for you

- Get a free eBook or video every month

- Mapt is fully searchable

- Copy and paste, print, and bookmark content

# Packt.com

Did you know that Packt offers eBook versions of every book published, with PDF and ePub files available? You can upgrade to the eBook version at `www.packt.com` and as a print book customer, you are entitled to a discount on the eBook copy. Get in touch with us at `customercare@packtpub.com` for more details.

At `www.packt.com`, you can also read a collection of free technical articles, sign up for a range of free newsletters, and receive exclusive discounts and offers on Packt books and eBooks.

# Contributors

## About the author

**Francesco Sapio** received his Master of Science in Engineering in Artificial Intelligence and Robotics degree from Sapienza University, Rome, Italy, a couple of semesters in advance, graduating with summa cum laude; he is currently a researcher at the same university. He is an Unreal and Unity 3D expert, skilled game designer, and an experienced user of major graphics programs. He helped the development of many games (both educational and commercial). He is also an active writer on the topic of game development. Finally, Francesco loves math, philosophy, logic, and puzzle solving, but most of all, creating video games—thanks to his passion for game designing and programming.

*I'm thankful to my love for her infinite patience, enthusiasm, and support. I do love you. Moreover, I'm thankful to the rest of my family, in particular to my parents and grandparents for their constant encouragement to do better in my life with the Latin expressions "Ad maiora" and "Per aspera ad astra".*
*Finally, a huge thanks to all the special people around me whom I love, but that this acknowledgment is too short to properly mention them.*

# About the reviewers

**Lauren S. Ferro** has a Ph.D. in player profiling and modeling. She is currently an Adjunct Professor and researcher at Sapienza University, in Rome. Lauren is also the co-organizer of the Unreal Engine Meetup in Rome. In addition, she created the game design resource Gamicards, which is a prototyping tool for game experiences. At heart, she is intrigued by how we interact with the world and those in it.

> *Packt Publishing – For the opportunity to review this book.*
> *Francesco Sapio – for providing a great contribution to the world of artificial intelligence and game development with this book.*
> *My family – for their motivation, patience, support, and encouragement in everything that I do.*

**Katax Emperor** is originally from Melbourne, Australia. He received bachelor's degree in Computer Hardware Engineering and two master's degree in Multimedia at Swinburne University of Technology in 2012.

Katax is involved in particle system programming, developing web-based interactive applications such as games, making animation with 3D applications for use in Unreal Engine, and also doing VJ performance with real-time improvisation style.
Katax started programming with Commodore 64 and started making digital art works with Commodore Amiga 500. After Windows 98 was released, he switched to PC. He expanded his experience with 3D applications, fractal and graphic design, and video editing programs. Today, he has a wide range of experience in a number of applications for artists, designers, and developers.

> *I am grateful to John Carmack from id Software for his great work on 3D graphic programming. What he developed in the 90's was the beginning of the wonderful genre of first-person shooter games. Also, I would like to thank Westwood Studios for introducing the Command and Conquer (C&C) series. This game pioneered many aspects of the modern real-time strategy games, which later powered many sub-genres in this area as well.*

# Packt is searching for authors like you

If you're interested in becoming an author for Packt, please visit authors.packtpub.com and apply today. We have worked with thousands of developers and tech professionals, just like you, to help them share their insight with the global tech community. You can make a general application, apply for a specific hot topic that we are recruiting an author for, or submit your own idea.

# Table of Contents

# Section 3: Debugging Methods

# Preface

Learning how to apply AI is crucial and can take the fun factor to the next level when developing traditional, educational, or any other kind of game. Unreal Engine is a powerful game development engine that allows you to create 2D and 3D games. If you want to use AI to extend the life of your games and make them challenging and more interesting, this book is for you.

The book starts with breaking down **artificial intelligence (AI)** into simple concepts to get a fundamental understanding of it. Using a variety of examples, you will work through actual implementations designed to highlight key concepts and features related to game AI in UE4. You will learn how to work through the built-in AI framework to build believable characters for every genre (e.g. RPG, Strategic, Platform, FPS, Simulation, Arcade, and Educational games). You will learn how to configure *Navigation*, *Environmental Querying* and *Sensory* systems for your AI agents and couple it with *Behavior Trees*, all with practical examples. You will then explore how the engine handles dynamic crowd. In the concluding chapters, you will learn how to profile, visualize and debug your AI systems, to correct the AI logic, and increase performance.

By the end of the book, your AI knowledge of the built-in AI system in Unreal will be deep and comprehensive, allowing you to build powerful AI agents within your projects.

## Who this book is for

This book is for you if you are a game developer with a bit experience in Unreal Engine, and now want to understand and implement believable game AI within Unreal Engine. The book will be both in Blueprint and C++, allowing people from every background to enjoy the book. Whether you're looking to build your first game or to expand your knowledge as a Game AI Programmer, you will find plenty of exciting information and examples of game AI in terms of concepts and implementation, including how to extend some of these systems.

## What this book covers

Chapter 1, *Moving the First Steps in The AI World*, explores the prerequisites to becoming an AI game developer and how AI is used in the game development pipeline.

Chapter 2, *Behavior Trees and Blackboards*, introduces you to two principal structures used within the Unreal AI framework, which are used to control most AI agents in games. You will learn how to create a *Behavior Tree* and how these can store data within *Blackboards*.

Chapter 3, *Navigation*, teaches you how an agent can navigate or find a path through a map or the environment.

Chapter 4, *Environment Query System*, helps you get to grips with making an *Environmental Query*, which is a subsystem of the Unreal AI Framework for spatial reasoning. Mastering them is key in implementing believable behaviors within Unreal.

Chapter 5, *Agent Awareness*, deals with how an AI agent can sense the world and the surrounding environment. These include sight, sound, and potentially any sense you might imagine (by extending the system).

Chapter 6, *Extending Behavior Trees*, takes you through the task of extending behavior trees with Unreal by using Blueprint or C++. You will learn how to program new *Tasks*, *Decorators*, and *Services*.

Chapter 7, *Crowds*, explains how to handle crowds within the Unreal AI Framework that offer some functionality.

Chapter 8, *Designing Behavior Trees – Part I*, focuses on how to implement a Behavior Tree so that the AI agent can chase our player in the game (both in Blueprint and C++). This chapter, along with the next two, explores this example from designing to implementation.

Chapter 9, *Designing Behavior Trees – Part II*, is a continuation of the previous chapter. In particular, we will build the last missing piece of the puzzle (a custom *Service*) before we build our final *Behavior Tree* in the next chapter.

Chapter 10, *Designing Behavior Trees – Part III*, is a continuation of the previous chapter and is the final part of *Designing Behavior Trees*. We will finish what we started. In particular, we will build the final *Behavior Tree* and make it run.

Chapter 11, *Debugging Methods for AI – Logging*, examines a series of methods that we can use to debug our AI systems, including console logging, on-screen messages in Blueprint, and many more. By mastering the art of logging, you will be able to easily keep track of your values and which part of the code you are executing.

Chapter 12, *Debugging Methods for AI – Navigation, EQS, and Profiling*, explores a number of more specific tools for the AI systems that are incorporated within Unreal Engine. We will see some more tools for analyzing performance related to AI code, as well as tools to visualize *Environmental Queries* and the *Navigation Mesh*.

Chapter 13, *Debugging Methods for AI – the Gameplay Debugger*, gets you to explore the most powerful debugging tool and the best friend of any Unreal AI developer—Gameplay Debugger. This chapter will take you even a step further, by teaching how to extend this tool so to customize it to your needs.

Chapter 14, *Going Beyond*, concludes with some suggestions on how to explore the concepts presented (and others) beyond this book and some thoughts regarding AI.

# To get the most out of this book

Being comfortable with using Unreal Engine 4 is an important starting point. The objective of this book is to take those who work with the technology to a level where they are comfortable enough with all aspects to be a leader and driver of that technology on a project.

# Download the example code files

You can download the code bundle for this book from here: `https://github.com/PacktPublishing/Hands-On-Artificial-Intelligence-with-Unreal-Engine`.

We also have other code bundles from our rich catalog of books and videos available at `https://github.com/PacktPublishing/`. Check them out!

# Download the color images

We also provide a PDF file that has color images of the screenshots/diagrams used in this book. You can download it here: `https://www.packtpub.com/sites/default/files/downloads/9781788835657_ColorImages.pdf`.

# Conventions used

There are a number of text conventions used throughout this book.

`CodeInText`: Indicates code words in text. Here is an example: "The next event to implement is `OnBecomRelevant()`, and it is only fired when the *Service* becomes relevant"

A block of code is set as follows:

```cpp
void AMyFirstAIController::OnPossess(APawn* InPawn)
{
  Super::OnPossess(InPawn);
  AUnrealAIBookCharacter* Character = Cast<AUnrealAIBookCharacter>(InPawn);
  if (Character != nullptr)
  {
    UBehaviorTree* BehaviorTree = Character->BehaviorTree;
    if (BehaviorTree != nullptr) {
      RunBehaviorTree(BehaviorTree);
    }
  }
}
```

When we wish to draw your attention to a particular part of a code block, the relevant lines or items are set in bold:

```cpp
void AMyFirstAIController::OnPossess(APawn* InPawn)
{
  Super::OnPossess(InPawn);
  AUnrealAIBookCharacter* Character = Cast<AUnrealAIBookCharacter>(InPawn);
  if (Character != nullptr)
  {
    UBehaviorTree* BehaviorTree = Character->BehaviorTree;
    if (BehaviorTree != nullptr) {
      RunBehaviorTree(BehaviorTree);
    }
  }
}
```

**Bold**: Indicates a new term, an important word, or words that you see on screen. For example, words in menus or dialog boxes appear in the text like this. Here is an example: "Select **BT_MyFirstBehaviorTree** from the drop-down menu within the **Behavior Tree** variable."

 Warnings or important notes appear like this.

 Tips and tricks appear like this.

# Get in touch

Feedback from our readers is always welcome.

**General feedback**: If you have questions about any aspect of this book, mention the book title in the subject of your message and email us at customercare@packtpub.com.

**Errata**: Although we have taken every care to ensure the accuracy of our content, mistakes do happen. If you have found a mistake in this book, we would be grateful if you would report this to us. Please visit www.packt.com/submit-errata, selecting your book, clicking on the Errata Submission Form link, and entering the details.

**Piracy**: If you come across any illegal copies of our works in any form on the internet, we would be grateful if you would provide us with the location address or website name. Please contact us at copyright@packt.com with a link to the material.

**If you are interested in becoming an author**: If there is a topic that you have expertise in, and you are interested in either writing or contributing to a book, please visit authors.packtpub.com.

# Reviews

Please leave a review. Once you have read and used this book, why not leave a review on the site that you purchased it from? Potential readers can then see and use your unbiased opinion to make purchase decisions, we at Packt can understand what you think about our products, and our authors can see your feedback on their book. Thank you!

For more information about Packt, please visit packt.com.

# Section 1: The Unreal Framework

In this section, we are going to explore in depth the built-in Unreal AI Framework. We will start from what are Behavior Trees and Blackboard, and we will proceed in learning about the Navigation System, the Environmental Querying System and the Perception System. Towards the end of this section, we will also understand how Unreal handles large Crowds, and how we can extend (both in Blueprint and C++) our Behavior Trees, by creating custom Tasks, Decorators and Services.

The following chapters will be covered in this section:

# Making the First Steps in the World of AI

1

*From the bronze giant Talos, to Symbolic Systems and Neural Networks: how AI has been shaped and used in video games.*

Welcome, reader, to the beginning of our journey in Artificial Intelligence, or AI for short. Have you ever wondered about how those hard-working peons in *Warcraft* explore complicated maps? Or, how those perky ghosts in *Pac-Man* can get you wherever you are? Or perhaps how your opponents in *Final Fantasy* optimize their attacks to slaughter your team?

A screenshot from Final Fantasy XV [Square Enix, 2016] during a battle.

Then you've come to the right place!

In this chapter, we will explore the prerequisites to becoming an AI game developer and how AI is used in the game development pipeline. Then, we will take a look at the history of AI in general and in video games, and learn how the conjunctive effort of many brilliant minds built AI as we know it today. Afterwards, we will discuss the AI Framework underneath the Unreal Engine, since this book will focus on Unreal.

Finally, we will plan our journey and get a general overview of the topics that the different chapters in this book deal with.

# Before starting...

... I'd like to reply to some questions that some of you might already have.

**Does this book take into account Blueprint or C++?**

This book will explain both, so don't worry.

If you don't know C++, you can follow along with the Blueprint part of this book, and if you so wish, you can try the C++ one.

If, on the other hand, you are a programmer that prefers C++, then don't worry! This book will explain how to deal with AI in Unreal using C++.

**There are so many books around about AI, why should I choose this one?**

Different books explain different aspects of AI, and often they are not mutually exclusive, but rather they complement each other.

However, the major point of interest of this book is that it is a good compromise between the theory of the different AI systems that are present in Unreal and practical applications, since the whole book is full of concrete examples.

**Does this book provide a test project/materials to work on?**

Absolutely, yes. You will be able to download the content for this book from the following link: `http://hog.red/AIBook2019ProjectFiles` (the link is case-sensitive).

**I am already using the Unreal Engine for Artificial Intelligence, is this book good for me?**

This all depends on your level of knowledge. In fact, in the first part of this book, we will talk mainly about the AI framework that's built into the Unreal Engine and how to use it. This is probably the part you are more familiar with if you have had some experience with Unreal for AI. However, this book will dive deep in these topics, that even an expert could find some useful tips. The second part, instead, will discuss some debugging methods for Game AI and will also explain how to extend them (mainly with C++). Feel free to have a look at the outline, and decide if this book suits you.

**I am already using another game engine, is this book still good for me?**

Well, as much as I'd like to say that this is a general book about AI, it isn't—at least not completely. Although the main focus will still be toward the main concepts of AI, we will look at implementing them in Unreal. However, this book will heavily rely on the built-in AI framework in Unreal. Thus, I encourage you to read more generalized books about AI to get a better understanding. On the other hand, you can always try. Maybe, by understanding some concepts here, other books will be easier to read and you will be able to transfer this knowledge into the game engine of your choice.

**I'm a student/teacher, is this book suitable for teaching in class?**

Absolutely, yes. I know how important it is to find good resources when teaching a class, and I'm writing this book with this intention in mind. As a result, regardless of whether you are a student or a teacher, you will find a section at the end of each chapter with some exercises that you can improve your skills this (or propose them to your students, if you are a teacher). Also, you can find some more integrative material here: `http://hog.red/AIBook2019LearningMaterial` (the link is case-sensitive).

**Is this book going to cover everything, everything, and everything about AI in Unreal and all its systems?**

Well, despite my best efforts to describe each of the systems in great detail, covering everything is an impossible task, due also to the complexity of such big engine. However, I'm confident to say that this book covers most of the aspects related to each AI system within the Unreal Engine, including how to extend the built-in systems and how to efficiently perform debugging. Thus, I can certainly say that this book is very comprehensive.

# Prerequisites

Since this book is targeted at people who are getting started with AI in game development, I will not assume any prior/background knowledge in AI. However, please take the following into account:

- *Blueprint users*: You should be familiar with Blueprint programming, and know how a Blueprint graph works in general.
- *C++ users*: You should be familiar with programming, especially with the C family languages (such as C, C#, C++, or even Java), and in particular with C++, since it's the language that Unreal Engine uses. Being familiar with the Unreal Engine C++ API is a great bonus, although not strictly required. So, even if you are not a master, don't worry—follow along and you will learn.

Also, it would be great if you had some knowledge about vector math and physical kinematic principles – at least the ones commonly used in video games. Either way, in case you are rusty on those, don't worry too much, since it is not required for this book; however, it is *nice to have* if you're looking for a job as an AI Developer.

# Installing and preparing the software

Before you continue reading, let's install the software we need. In particular, we will need Unreal Engine and Visual Studio.

# Unreal Engine

Let's talk about Unreal Engine. After all, this is a book about how to develop game AI within this wonderful game engine.

*Unreal Engine* is a game engine that was developed by *Epic Games*. It was first released in 1998, and nowadays it is one of the most used (open) game engines (alongside Unity) due to its powerful features. The following screenshot shows the main interface of Unreal Engine:

Screenshot of the main interface of Unreal Engine

We need to have the latest version of Unreal Engine installed. You can find it by visiting `https://www.unrealengine.com/en-US/what-is-unreal-engine-4` . Unless you took Unreal Engine from the source code (`https://docs.unrealengine.com/en-us/Programming/Development/BuildingUnrealEngine`), you will have the *Epic Launcher* installed. If you are a Blueprint user, and do not intend to use C++, then this is enough for you. If, on the other hand, you will be using C++, you will need to perform a couple of extra steps.

When installing the Engine, you will need to check some options (if you are using C++). In particular, we need to check that we have both "*Engine Source*" and "*Editor symbols for debugging*", as shown in the following screenshot:

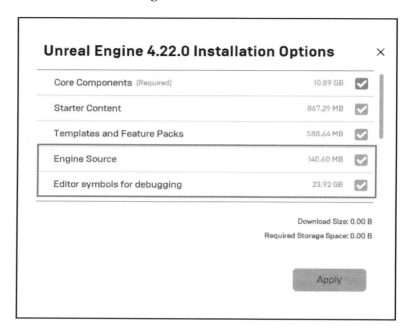

By doing so, we will be able to navigate through the C++ Engine Source and also have a full stack of calls in the case of a crash (so you will know what went wrong).

# Visual Studio

You won't need this if you are using Blueprint—this is for C++ users only.

In fact, we will need an IDE to edit our C++ code. We are going to use *Visual Studio*, since it's well-integrated with Unreal. You will be able to download *Visual Studio Community Edition* for free through the official website, https://www.visualstudio.com, or from https://visualstudio.microsoft.com/vs/.

You may also find this short guide on how to set up *Visual Studio* so that it works with Unreal Engine useful: https://docs.unrealengine.com/en-us/Programming/Development/VisualStudioSetup.

Once you have everything installed and ready to go, we can continue with the rest of this chapter.

 If you are a *MacOS* user, there is a version of *Visual Studio* for *MacOS*. You can use that one. Alternatively, you might be able to use *XCode*.

# Becoming an AI Game Developer

Ever dreamed of becoming an AI Game Developer? Or maybe just be able to write *"intelligent"* programs? Then this book is for you!

However, I need to advise you that this is no easy task.

Game development and design are some of the most extensive works of art around. This is due to a large amount of expertise that is required to bring a game to life. You can get an idea of this by just looking at the final credits in a game. They are endless and contain names of people who have dedicated a lot of their time to the game in various roles. AI development is a central part of this big process, and it requires years to master it, like most things in life. As such, iteration is key, and a great place to get started in this book.

# What it means to be an AI Game Developer

First of all, you will need to master maths, physics, and coding. Also, you will mostly probably work in an interdisciplinary team, which includes artists, designers, and programmers. In fact, you will probably work with existing proprietary software technology, and it's required that you are able to build new technology to fulfill the project's technical requirements. You will be asked to research coding techniques and algorithms so that you keep yourself up to date on technological developments and advancements in the game industry and to identify technical and developmental risks/obstacles and generate solutions to overcome identified risks.

On the other hand, you will be able to give life to characters and entities in video games. After all the frustrations that you might go through, you will be the first one to assist, or better, generate an intelligent behavior in games. It takes time and is quite challenging, so don't be too hard on yourself in the early stages. Once you achieve some real AI in your game that can think on its own, this is an achievement worthy of rewarding yourself for.

For beginners in AI, this book will help you set the first stones toward that goal. For experts, this book will provide a useful guide to refresh the different AI systems in Unreal, and explore in-depth features that might help you in your work.

# AI in the game development process

The game development pipeline might vary a lot, depending on which studio you visit, but all of them lead to the creation of a video game. This is not a book about pipelines, so we won't explore them, but it's important to have a rough idea of where AI is collocated.

In fact, AI intersects with many parts of the game development pipeline. Here are some of the main ones:

- **Animation**: It might surprise some of you, but there is a lot of research going on regarding this topic. Sometimes, animation and AI overlap. For instance, one of the problems that developers need to solve consists of how we can procedurally generate hundreds of animations for characters, which can behave realistically, and also how they interact with each other. In fact, solving the inverse kinematic (IK) is a mathematical problem, but which of the infinite solutions to choose to achieve a goal (or just to provide a realistic look) is an AI task. We won't face this specific problem during this book, but the last chapter will provide pointers to places where you can learn more about this.

- **Level Design**: If a game automatically produces levels, then AI plays an important role in that game. *Procedural Content Generation* (PCG) in games is a hot topic at the moment. There are games that are entirely based on PCG. Different tools to procedurally generate height maps can help Level Designers achieve realistic looking landscapes and environments. This is indeed a wide topic to explore.

- **Game Engine**: Of course, inside the game engine, there are many AI algorithms that come into play. Some of these are specific for agents, while others just improve the engine's features and/or tasks. These represent the most vast category, in which they can vary from simple algorithms to adjust a Bezier curve based on the context, to implementing behavior trees or finite state machines for animations. Under the hood, there is a lot going on here. We will explore some of these concepts in this book, but the message to take home is that an algorithm can be adapted to solve similar problems in different fields. In fact, if Finite State Machines (FSMs) are used to make decisions, why not use them to "*decide*" which animation to play? Or why not even handle the whole game logic (i.e. the blueprint visual scripting in Unreal Engine)?

- **Non-Player Characters** (**NPCs**): This is the most visible example of using AI in games, and this is also the most obvious AI to the Player (we will explore more about the relationship between the AI and the player in Chapter 14, *Going Beyond*). This is what most of this book is focused on; that is, from moving the character (for instance, with a Pathfinding Algorithm) to making decisions (i.e. with Behavior trees), or collaborate with other NPCs (multi-agent systems).

Unfortunately, we don't have the space to deal with all of these topics in this book. Therefore, we will just be focusing on the last part (NPCs), and explore the AI Framework that's built into Unreal.

# A bit of history

Before venturing on our journey, I believe that having a general overview of the history of AI and AI in games might be beneficial. Of course, you can skip this part if you are a more hands-on type of person who cannot wait to getting down to programming AI.

# What is AI?

This is a very interesting question, which doesn't have a unique answer. In fact, different answers lead to different aspects of AI. Let's explore some (of many) definitions that have been given by different scholars (in chronological order).

Actually, Russell and Norvig, in their book, organized these specific definitions into four categories. Here is their schema:

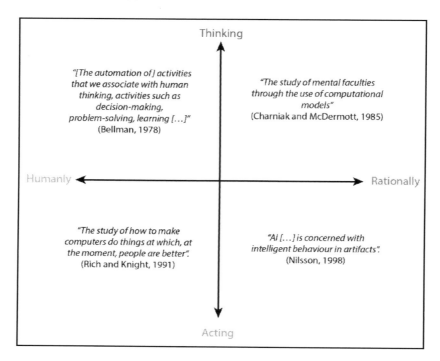

Russell and Norvig's four categories. Top-left: "Systems that think like humans". Top-Right: "Systems that think rationally". Bottom-Left: "Systems that act like humans". Bottom-Right: "Systems that act rationally".

We don't have the time to go into detail about the question "*What is AI?*", since this could fill up another book on its own, but the last chapter of this book will also include some philosophical reference where you can expand your knowledge on this topic.

# A glance into the past

It might come unexpected to some of you, but the story of AI started well before computers. In fact, even ancient Greeks hypothesized the existence of intelligence machines. A famous example is the bronze giant Talos, who protected the city of Crete from invaders. Another is the golden helpers of Hephaestus, who helped God in his volcano forge along with the Cyclops. In the XVII century, René Descartes wrote about automatons that could think, and believed that animals were do different from machines, which could be replicated with pulleys, pistons, and cams.

However, the core of this story starts in 1931, when the Austrian logician, mathematician, and philosopher Kurt Gödel proved that all the true statements in the first-order logic are derivable. On the other hand, this is not true for higher order logics, in which some true (or false) statements are unprovable. This made first-order logic a good candidate to automate derived logical consequences. Sounds complicated? Well, you can imagine how that sounded to the ears of his traditionalist contemporaries.

Photo of Alan Turing at the age of 16

In 1937, Alan Turing, an English computer scientist, mathematician, logician, cryptanalyst, philosopher, and theoretical biologist, pointed out some of the limits of "*intelligent machines*" with the halting problem: it is not possible to predict a-priori if a program will terminate unless it is actually run. This has many consequences in theoretical computer science. However, the fundamental step happened thirteen years later, in 1950, when Alan Turing wrote his famous paper "*Computing Machinery and Intelligence*", in which he talked about the imitation game, nowadays mostly known as "*The Turing Test*": a way to define what an intelligent machine is.

In the 1940s, some attempts were made to emulate biological systems: McCulloch and Pitts developed a mathematical model for a neuron in 1943, and Marvin Minsky created a machine that was able to emulate 40 neurons with 3,000 vacuum tubes in 1951. However, they fell into the dark.

From the late 1950s through to the early 1980s, a great portion of AI research was devoted to "*Symbolic systems*". These are based on two components: a knowledge base made out of symbols and a reasoning algorithm, which uses logical inference to manipulate those symbols, in order to expand the knowledge base itself.

During this period, many brilliant minds made significant progresses. A name worth quoting is McCarthy, who organized a conference in Dartmouth College in 1956, where the term "*Artificial Intelligence*" was first coined. Two years later, he invented the high-level programming language *LISP*, in which the first programs that were able to modify themselves were written. Other remarkable results include Gelernter's *Geometry Theorem Prover* in 1959, the *General Problem Solver* (GPS) by Newell and Simon in 1961, and the famous chat-bot *Eliza* by Weizenbaum, which was the first software that, in 1966, could have a conversation in natural language. Finally, the apotheosis of symbolic systems happened in 1972 with the invention of *PROLOG* by the French scientist Alain Colmerauer.

Symbolic systems led to many AI techniques, which are still used in games, such as blackboard architectures, pathfinding, decision trees, state machines, and steering algorithms, and we will explore all of them throughout this book.

The trade-off of these systems is between knowledge and search. The more knowledge you have, the less you need to search, and the faster you can search, the less knowledge you will need. This has even been proven mathematically by Wolpert and Macready in 1997. We will have the chance to examine this trade-off in more detail later in this book.

At the beginning of the 1990s, symbolic systems became inadequate, because they proved hard to scale to larger problems. Also, some philosophical arguments arose against them, maintaining that symbolic systems are an incompatible model for organic intelligence. As a result, old and new technologies have been developed that were inspired by biology. The old Neural Networks were dusted off from the shelf, with the success of Nettalk in 1986, a program that was able to learn how to read aloud, and with the publication of the book "*Parallel distributed processing*" by Rumelhart and McClelland in the same year. In fact, "*back-propagation*" algorithms were rediscovered, since they allow a Neural Network (NN) to actually learn.

In the last 30 years of AI, research took new directions. From the work of Pearl on *"Probabilistic reasoning in intelligent systems"*, probability has been adopted as one of the principal tools to handle uncertainty. As a result, AI started to use many statistical techniques, such as Bayesian-nets, Support Vector Machines (SVMs), Gaussian processes, and the Markov Hidden Model, which is used widely to represent the temporal evolution of the states of a system. Also, the introduction of large databases unlocked many possibilities in AI, and a new whole branch named *"Deep Learning"* arose.

However, it's important to keep in mind that, even if AI researchers discover new and more advance techniques, the old are not to be discarded. In fact, we will see how, depending on the problem and its size, a specific algorithm can shine.

# AI in games

The history of AI in video games is as interesting as what we talked about in the previous section. We don't have the time to go through it in detail and analyze every single game and how each one of them contributed to the field. For the most curious of you, toward the end of this book, you will find other lectures, videos, and books where you can dive deeper into the history of AI in games.

The first form of AI in video games was rudimental and used in games like **Pong** [*Atari*, 1972], **Space Invaders** [*Midway Games West, Inc., 1978*], and so on. In fact, beyond moving a paddle to try and catch a ball, or moving aliens toward the player, there wasn't much more we could do:

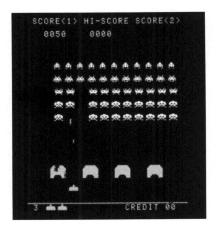

A screenshot of **Space Invaders** Midway Games West, Inc., 1978], in which a rudimental form of AI is used to control the aliens

The first renowned game that used a noticeable AI was **Pac-Man** [*Midway Games West, Inc.,* 1979]. The four *monsters* (later named *ghosts* due to a flickering port in the Atari 2600) used an FSM to chase (or flee from) the player:

A screenshot from the game **Pac-Man** Midway Games West, Inc., 1979], in which the four monsters use an FSM trying to catch the player

During the 1980s, AI in games didn't change much. It was only with the introduction of **Warcraft: Orcs & Humans** [*Blizzard Entertainment*, 1994] that a pathfinding system was successfully implemented in a video game. We will explore the Navigation system in Unreal in Chapter 3, *Navigation:*

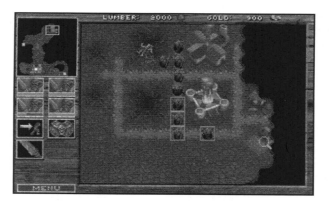

A screenshot from **Warcraft: Orcs Humans** Blizzard Entertainment, 1994], in which the units (orc peons and grunts in this screenshot) use pathfinding algorithms to move in the map

The game that probably started to sensitize people about AI was **Goldeneye 007** [*Rare Ltd.,* 1997], which showed how AI could improve gameplay. Although it was still relying on FSMs, the innovation was that characters could *see* each other, and act accordingly. We will explore *agent-awareness* in Chapter 5, *Agent Awareness*. This was a hot topic at the time, and some games made it the main game mechanic, such as **Thief: The Dark Project** [*Looking Glass Studios, Inc.*, 1998]:

A screenshot from **Goldeneye 007** Rare Ltd., 1997], which has changed how people perceive AI in video games

and **Metal Gear Solid** [*Konami Corporation*, 1998]:

A screenshot from **Metal Gear Solid** [*Konami Corporation*, 1998].

Another hot topic was modeling a soldiers' emotions during battles. One of the first games that implemented an emotional model was **Warhammer: Dark Omen** [*Mindscape*, 1998], but it was only with **Shogun: Total War** [*The Creative Assembly*, 2000] that these models were used with extreme success with a large number of soldiers without performance issues:

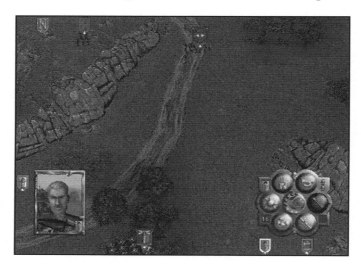

A screenshot from **Warhammer: Dark Omen,** one of the first games that used an emotional model for soldiers

and

A screenshot from Shogun: Total War. The emotional model of the soldiers were more sophisticated than the one in Warhammer: Dark Omen, and yet it was used successfully with many soldiers

Some games even made AI the core of the gameplay. Although one of the first games to do so was **Creatures** [*Cyberlife Technology Ltd., 1997*], the concept is more evident in games like **The Sims** [*Maxis Software, Inc., 2000*] or **Black and White** [*Lionhead Studios Ltd., 2001*]:

A screenshot from The Sims. A Sim (the character) is cooking, which is part of a complex behavior piloted by AI in the game.

In the last 20 years, many AI techniques have been adopted and/or developed. However, if the game doesn't require an advanced AI, you will probably find FSMs, still being broadly used, along with Behavior trees, which we will start exploring soon in `Chapter 2`, *Behavior Trees and Blackboards*.

# AI in games – Industry and Academia

When it comes to comparing AI that's applied to video games, both in Academia and in the Industry, there is a big discrepancy. I would say that there was almost a fight between the two. Let's have a look at the reasons behind this. In fact, they have very different goals.

Academia wants to *create AI agents for games that* **think intelligently** *to act in the environment and interact with the player.*

On the other hand, the game industry wants to *create AI agents for games that* **seem to think intelligently** *to act in the environment and interact with the player.*

We can clearly notice that the first leads to a **more realistic AI**, whereas the second leads to a **more believable AI**. Of course, commercial games are more worried about the latter rather than the former.

We will explore this concept in more detail in Chapter 14, *Going Beyond*, when we talk about the psychology and game design involved in creating an AI system for games. In fact, to achieve a believable behavior, you often need to try and be realistic as well.

However, in more formal terms, we can say that game AI falls in the category of *weak AI* (opposite to *strong AI*), which focuses on solving a specific task or problem *intelligently*, rather than develop a consciousness behind it. In any case, we won't venture further into this.

# Planning our journey

It's finally time to start planning our journey, before jumping into the next chapter.

# Technical terminology

Since, for some of you, this is your first journey into AI, it's important that you have a small glossary of the technical terms that are used throughout this book (and in general, in AI). We have already encountered some of these in the past few pages:

- **Agents** are systems that are capable of autonomous reasoning toward solving a specific set of goals.
- **Backward Chaining** is the process of tracing the cause of a problem by working backwards.
- **Blackboard** is an architecture for exchanging data between different agents, and sometimes even within the agent itself (especially in Unreal).
- **Environment** is the world where an agent lives. For instance, the game world is the environment of an NPC from the same game. Another example is a chess board, which represents the environment of a system that plays chess against humans (or other systems).

- **Forward Chaining**, opposite to Backward Chaining, is the process to work forward to find the solution to a problem.
- **Heuristic** is a practical approach to problem-solving, which does not guarantee to be optimal, nor sufficient for immediate goals. Heuristic methods are used when finding the optimal solution to a problem is impractical (if not impossible), in order to find a satisfactory solution. They can be thought of as mental shortcuts to lighten cognitive load during a decision-making process. Sometimes, it can represent the knowledge of an agent based on his/her past experience (although this is often given a-priori). The term "*Heuristic*" derives from ancient Greek, with the meaning of "*find*" or "*discover*".

 For a more extensive glossary, you can have a look at the one on Wikipedia. Here is the link: `https://en.wikipedia.org/wiki/Glossary_of_artificial_intelligenc e`.

# The bottom-up approach

Usually, when a system is built or studied, there are two main approaches: top-down and bottom-up. The former starts from the high-level structures of the system and proceeds gradually into the granular details of the system. The latter starts from the basics and proceeds to create more complex structures that depend on the previous ones. Both approaches are valid, but, as a matter of preference, I chose the bottom-up approach to introduce the topics of this book.

In fact, we will start with how an agent can move, then understand how it can perceive, and finally use this data to make an informative decision or even come up with a plan. This is reflected in the structure of this book and its parts.

# The agent schema

Since, during this book, we will be going through the different parts of how an AI agent can perceive, move, plan, and interact with its surroundings, it will be useful to draw a schema for this. Of course, there can be many other schemas, and they are all equally valid, but I believe that this one is particularly useful for getting started with *AI Game Development*:

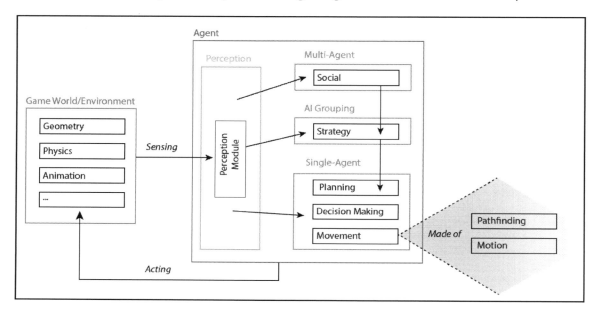

The Agent model that we are going to use in this book

Since we chose a bottom-up approach, we should read the schema from the bottom. We will refer to this in more formal terms as our *agent model*.

First, we can see that the agent always exchanges information with the Game World, which includes geometry, physics, and animations, but also abstractions of it. This information is used at all the levels of our agent model.

From the bottom, we can see that our first concern is how to move in the environment. This is a process that can be split into Motion and Pathfinding (chapter 3, *Navigation*). Going up the chain, we can see that the agent perceives the world (chapter 4, *Environment Query System, and 5, Agent Awareness*), and, based on this perception, the agent can make a decision (chapter 2, *Behavior Trees and Blackboards*). Sometimes, making the best decision at that moment in time, might not lead to a better result in the long run, and so the agent should be able to plan ahead. Often, in video games, an AI system (which is not necessarily an NPC) can control more than one character, and, as a result, it should be able to coordinate a group of characters. Finally, the agent might need to collaborate with other agents. Of course, we won't be able to go deep into each topic in this book, but feel free to take a look online so that you can dive deeper into certain topics.

One final remark: Often, AI in games doesn't use all of these levels at once; some implement just one of them, or mix them up. However, it's important to keep in mind how things are structured before you start playing with them.

# Unreal Engine AI Framework

Despite other game engines, which just give you rendering capability, Unreal Engine comes with many things implemented (and extended through plugins). This doesn't mean that making a game is easier, but rather that we have more tools to develop one.

As a matter of fact, Unreal implements many tools for Artificial Intelligence as well. While we explore them, we can create a schema of these tools and how they correlate to each other. So, let's try to just understand at which level we are going to operate. This means scratching the surface of the **Unreal Game Play Framework** (you can find more information about this here: https://docs.unrealengine.com/en-us/Gameplay/Framework).

There is a Controller Class, which can be divided into two subclasses. The first one is a Player Controller; as the name suggests, it offers an interface between the game and the player (of course, it is not covered in this book, since we will focus on AI and not general Gameplay). The second class is the AIController, which, instead, offers an interface between our AI algorithms and the game itself.

The following diagram shows these and how they interact with one another:

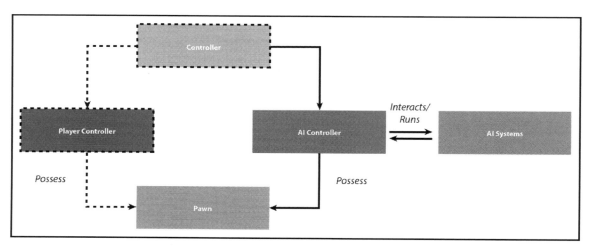

Both kinds of controllers can possess a Pawn, which can be considered a virtual avatar. For the player, this may be the main character; for an AIController, a Pawn can be the enemy who wants to defeat the player.

In this book, we will focus only on the AIController, and all the tools around and beneath it to bring our AI to life (we will not cover the dotted sections in the preceding diagram). We will understand what I mean by this at a later stage, but the key concept is that we are going to operate at the level of an *AIController*.

 If you are already a bit familiar with C++ and Unreal, you can have a look at its class, which is defined in the *AIController.h* file, to learn a bit more about this controller.

# A sketch of our journey

Now that we have a rough idea of the schema we are going to use, let's break down what we will cover in this book, more or less in the order we will face the topics (I said more or less, because some topics are spread over more than one chapter, and they need to iterate once our knowledge of AI has been expanded).

However, you can think of this book as being divided into three parts:

- *Chapters 2-7*: A description of the different built-in AI systems
- *Chapters 8-10*: A concrete example of how to use the AI systems we explored in the previous chapters
- *Chapters 11-13*: A description of the different debugging methods for Game AI (since I believe that this part is equally important that knowing the systems themselves)

Let's talk about what we will be covering in this book in detail.

# Decision-making with Behavior Trees (chapters 2, 6, 8, 9, and 10)

Once the agent can perceived the world around it, it needs to start making decisions, which have consequences. Some decision-making processes might become so complicated that the agent needs to come up with a proper plan to successfully achieve a goal.

The built-in Unreal Engine framework for AI rotates around Behavior Trees, which occupy a significant part of this book. Of course, this doesn't preclude the possibility to implement other AI systems on your own for decision-making in Unreal, but, by choosing Behavior Trees, you will have a strong set of tools ready to go, which we will explore in detail in this book.

# Navigation (chapters 3 and 7)

Unless the game is discrete or turn-based, each AI agent needs to move around its own environment in a continuous fashion. Unreal provides a strong Navigation System that lets your AI Agents navigate easily within the environment, from falling to jumping, from crouching to swimming, to different kind of areas and different types of agent.

This system is so huge that it will be hard to cover it all, but we will do our best to cover everything you need to get started in Chapter 3, *Navigation*.

# Environment Query System (chapters 4 and 12)

The *Environment Query System (ESQ)* can gather information from the environment surrounding the agent, thus allowing the agent to make decisions accordingly. This book dedicates a whole chapter to this system. In fact, it lies between Chapter 5, *Agent Awareness*, and *Decision Making*, and it is a great resource that's already built into Unreal.

# Agent Awareness (chapters 5 and 12)

*Agent Awareness* (or *Perception*) deals with the capacity to give senses to the AI agents. In particular, we will cover sight, which is the most common and widely used, but also hearing and smell.

Moreover, we will start to explore how this data will be used in higher level structures so that the agent can act accordingly.

# Crowds (chapter 7)

When you have many AI agents within your map, the environment becomes easily overcrowded, and the various agents might interfere with each other. Crowds Systems allow you to control large sets of AI Agents (while they can keep an individual behavior) so that they can avoid each other.

# Designing Behavior Trees (chapters 8, 9, and 10)

It is not enough for an AI developer to know how a Behavior Tree works: he/she needs to know how to design them. In fact, most of your job is about creating an abstract system that coordinates all your AI agents, and only after that will you spend the rest of the time implementing it. Therefore, we will cover a single and large example of how to design, create single pieces, and build a whole *Behavior Tree* from scratch.

# Debugging methods for Game AI (chapters 11, 12, and 13)

Once you have learned about all the different AI systems, you can start to experiment on those or program a game, but how do you understand if your AI is doing what you have planned and/or is performing well? Debugging methods are key in any software, but in Game AI, you will also need visual debugging. As such, Unreal Engine comes with many debugging methods (including some that are specific for AI), and I strongly believe that being knowledgeable of those is very important. You will not only learn the tools, but also how to extend them as per your needs.

# Going beyond (chapter 14)

This last section of this book will explore some exciting ideas and innovation that's currently going on in the AI world, and will give you the inspiration to continue your wonderful journey. I will introduce some of the ongoing research on AI that's being applied to games, and how this can ultimately benefit your game. Being aware of new technologies and algorithms is key in this field so that you are always up to date.

# Enabling AI for C++ users

In case you are following this book as a C++ user, when you write C++ code within your project (or a specific module of your project or plugin), you will need to ensure that you add the right dependencies so that you have access to the AI systems, otherwise you will end up with compilation errors. We will look at this in more detail in the next chapter when we create a project for inserting all the code we will produce in this book. However, here is the line of code to insert/modify code in the `.cs` project file (the part of code in bold is required for AI to work):

```
PublicDependencyModuleNames.AddRange(new string[] { "Core", "CoreUObject",
"Engine", "InputCore", "HeadMountedDisplay", "GameplayTasks", "AIModule"
});
```

# Summary

In this chapter, we have seen how wonderful the world of AI in video games is. We explored the history behind video games, both in Academia and in the industry. We have planned our journey in this book and explained what it will look like.

Now, it is time to prepare ourselves because, starting from the next chapter, we are going to get our hands dirty and jump straight into Unreal Engine.

# 2
# Behavior Trees and Blackboards

*A tree to decide how we should behave, a blackboard to remember it!*

Welcome to `Chapter 2`, *Behavior Trees and Blackboards*. This is where things start to get a bit more interesting because we will learn how to use the two main Unreal AI Framework structures. First, we will look at *Behavior Trees* and learn all about their principal components, such as tasks, decorators, and services. Next, we will learn about *Blackboards* and how to integrate them with *Behavior Trees*. After we have covered this, will be able to set up AI controllers that use *Behavior Trees*, which is key in implementing the rest of the techniques in this book.

As you may notice, there is a pattern in which we first learn a little bit about the theory, and then we jump straight into practice to understand how it all works. This is a pattern that we will follow in each chapter. So, let's get going.

In the field of *Decision-Making*, there are many mathematical structures that can be used. **Finite State Machines** (**FSM**s) are an easy, yet powerful example of systems that are able to make complex decisions. However, in the world of Artificial Intelligence for games, there is another structure that can also be used by non-AI experts: *Behavior Trees*.

As a result, one of the design choices of Unreal Engine is that it has built-in support for Behavior Trees, and is actually part of the main core of the AI Framework. This does not imply that you cannot implement other decision-making processes or structures, but using the built-in support for Behavior Trees will greatly benefit your team's budget (in terms of time). So, before you implement a different Decision-Making structure in Unreal, think twice about whether that is a good decision (of course, a Behavior Tree might not be optimal for your game, but keep in mind that they have built-in support and might be a great time-saver). Nonetheless, you can still implement sub-structures within the *Behavior Tree* to extend its functionality, but do not rush too much; first, let's learn about the basics of *Behavior Trees*.

In particular, in this chapter, we will learn about the following topics:

- What a *Behavior Tree* is, both in broader terms and within the Unreal Context.
- How a *Behavior Tree works* within Unreal, including its different components and how they interact with the tree
- What a *Blackboard* is and how it can be used to store data for the Behavior Tree
- How to *start running a Behavior Tree* by using the AI Controller, both in Blueprint and C++

So, let's dive in!

# How Behavior Trees work

The easiest way to think about the role that a Behavior Tree assumes within our AI Agent is to imagine it as a brain. It makes decisions and, as a consequence, acts on them. It is the processor for the artificial intelligence within our agent. Before we get started, if you have any experience with Behavior Trees in other contexts, it is important to understand that they differ in the context of Unreal.

 If you want to learn more about how they are different, you can do so by visiting the following link: `https://docs.unrealengine.com/en-US/Engine/AI/BehaviorTrees/HowUE4BehaviorTreesDiffer`.

It is, however, important to highlight one key difference here: ***Unreal Behavior Trees*** are read from the top to the bottom, and nodes will be executed from left to right. In other contexts, you might have found this to the other way around, in which the tree is read from left to right, and the nodes are executed from top to bottom.

If this is the first time you have encountered a Behavior Tree, then this will make sense when you read the next section.

# The structure of a Mathematical Tree

Alright, it's time to understand how a *Behavior Tree* works. First of all, as the name suggests, it is a tree, mathematical speaking.

If you are interested to learn more about trees in graph theory, you can consult the following Wikipedia page: `https://en.wikipedia.org/wiki/Tree_(graph_theory)`. Alternatively, if you want to get even more technical, you can consult the following page: `http://mathworld.wolfram.com/Tree.html`. However, the definitions that are found at both the links are pretty mathematical, and you don't need them to understand Behavior Trees.

It is important to specify that a (mathematical) tree expresses relationships between nodes. In this sense, the same relationship that describes a family (e.g. parent, child, sibling) has been adopted in technical terms. To simplify the understanding of a tree, you can imagine your genealogical tree: each node is a person, and the branches (that connect people) are the relationships between the various people. However, the structure is still slightly different.

So, what is a tree? It is a graph that describes relationships between different nodes.

In particular, there is a "**Root**" node, which is *the only node without a parent*. From there, *every node can have one or more children, but only one parent*. The end nodes, which are the ones that do not have any child, are called **leaves**. Here is a simple diagram to help you understand the basic structure of a *Mathematical Tree* in general:

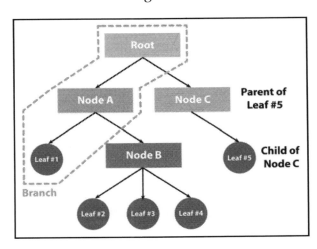

It might sound complicated, but it really isn't. Things will start getting interesting as we move on and talk about BehaviorTrees.

# Behavior Tree components

If you go through the official documentation, you will find that there are five types of nodes (*Task*, *Decorator*, *Service*, *Composite*, and *Root*) available to use, depending on the type of behavior that you're trying to create (and subsequently, how the AI should act in the world). However, I'd like to reformulate this to you in order to make it easier to understand and hopefully more practical.

Besides the *Root* node, the only kind of nodes (that are not leaves) are the *Composites* nodes. Leaves are called *Tasks*. *Decorators* and *Services* are *add-ons* for either a *Composite* node or a *Task* leaf. Although Unreal lets you leave a *Composite* node as a leaf, you shouldn't, because it means that you can remove that node and the Behavior Tree will still work in the same way. Here is an example of a tree showing all the different types of node (actually, we will build this *Behavior Tree* later in this book):

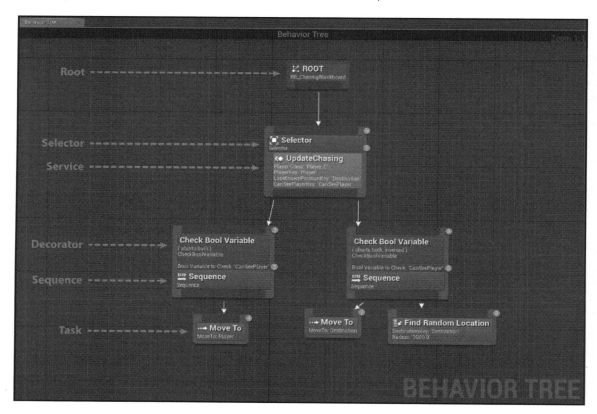

When a tree is executing, you need to start following from the root node and go down the tree, reading the nodes from left to right. You traverse all the different branches (*Composite* nodes) in a specific way (we are going to see this in a little while), until we reach a leaf, which is a *Task*. In this case, the AI performs that *Task*. It is important to note that a *Task* can fail, for instance, if the AI is unable to complete it. The fact that a *Task* can fail will be useful for understanding how Composite nodes work. After all, a decision-making process is just choosing which task to perform to achieve a goal in a better way (e.g. killing the player). Thus, based on which task failed to execute (or, as we will see, a Decorator can make a task or a whole branch fail), the Composite nodes will determine the next tasks in the tree.

In addition, when you create your *Behavior Tree*, each node can be selected, and some settings to adjust the behavior of the node/leaf can be found in the *Detail Panel*. Moreover, since the order is important, the nodes in the Behavior Tree have numbers (in the top-right corner) to help you understand the ordering of the node (although it is always from top to bottom, left to right). The following screenshot shows where you can find these numbers:

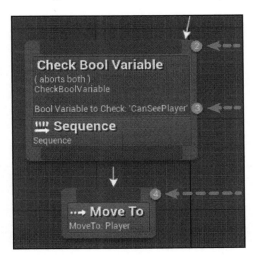

A value of "-1" means that the node will never be executed in any order, and the color around the node will be a bit darker. This might be due to the fact that the node is not connected in some way to the root, and so it is isolated:

Let's look at these components in detail and pay particular attention to *Composite* nodes.

# Root

There isn't much to say about the *ROOT* node. The tree needs to begin somewhere, so the Root node is just where the tree starts its execution. Here is what it looks like:

Please note that the *Root* node can have only one child, and this must be a *Composite* node. You cannot attach any *Decorator* or *Service* to the *Root*. If you select the *Root* node, it doesn't have any property, but you will be able to assign a *Blackboard* (which we will cover later in this chapter), as shown in the following screenshot:

# Tasks

When we think of a tree, we often picture a large trunk with branches, and on those branches are leaves. In the context of UE4, those *"leaves"* are what we call *"Tasks"*. These are nodes that perform various actions, such as moving an AI, and can have *Decorator* or *Service* nodes attached to them. However, they do not have an output, which means that they do not play a role in the decision-making process itself, which is left entirely to Composite nodes. Instead, they define what an AI should do if that task needs to be executed.

Please note that *Tasks* can be as complex as you like. They can be as simple as waiting an amount of time, to being as complex as solving a puzzle while shooting at the player. Huge tasks are hard to debug and maintain, while small tasks can make the **Behavior Tree** easily overcrowded and huge. As a good AI Designer, you should try to find a balance between the size of the task and write them in such a way that they can be reused in different parts of the tree (or even in other trees).

A *Task* can either **Fail** (report **Failure**) or **Succeed** (report **Success**), and it will not stop its execution until one of these two results is reported. *Composite* nodes are responsible for taking care of this result and deciding on what to do next. Thus, a Task might need several frames to executed, but it will end only when it reports either *Failure* or *Success*. Keep this in mind when you move on to `Chapter 6`, *Extending Behavior Trees*, where you will create your own Tasks.

*Tasks* can have parameters (which you will be able to set in the *Details Panel* once a *Task* has been selected), and usually, they are either hard-coded values or *Blackboard Key references* (more on *Blackboards* later in this chapter).

Within the Behavior Tree editor, a Task appears as a purple box. In the following screenshot, you can see some examples of Tasks and how they look within the Editor:

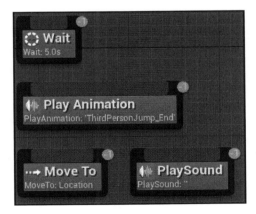

Unreal comes with some built-in Tasks that are ready to be used. They are general and cover the basic cases that you will probably need. Obviously, they cannot be specific to your game, so you will need to create your own *Tasks* (we will look at this in Chapter 6, *Extending Behavior Trees*).

Here is the list of the built-in tasks in Unreal:

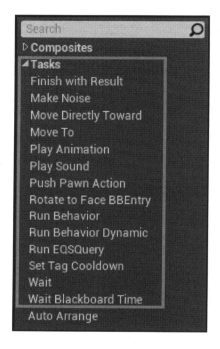

- *Finish with Result*: Forces the Task to return a *Finish Result* (either *Fail* or *Succeed*) for this task immediately.
- *Make Noise*: Produces a noise stimulus, which is used by the *Perception System* (this will be explored in Chapter 5, *Agent Awareness*).
- *Move Directly Toward*: Like the following node, but it disregards the *Navigation System*.
- *Move To*: Moves the Pawn (by using the *Navigation System*, which we will explore in Chapter 3, *Navigation*) to a location that's specified from the *Blackboard* (we will explore *Blackboards* later in this chapter).

- *Play Animation*: As the name suggests, this node plays an animation. However, exceptions aside (and this is the reason why this node exists), it is good practice to separate animation logic and behavior logic. Therefore, try not to use this node, and instead improve your Animation Blueprint.
- *Play Sound*: As the name suggests, this node plays a sound.
- *Push Pawn Action*: Performs a *Pawn Action* (unfortunately, we will not cover them in this book).
- *Rotate to face BBEntry*: Rotates the AI pawn to face a specific key that's been memorized inside the Blackboard (we will look at what *Blackboards* are later in this chapter).
- *Run Behavior*: Runs another *Behavior Tree* as a whole sub-tree. As a result, it is possible to nest *Behavior Trees* to create and compose very complex behaviors.
- *Run Behavior Dynamic*: Like the previous node, but it is possible to change which (*sub-*)*Behavior Tree* to execute at runtime.
- *Run EQSQuery*: Performs an *EQS Query* (we will see what they are in `Chapter 4`, *Environment Querying System*) and stores the result within the *Blackboard*.
- *Set Tag Cooldown*: Sets the timer (by using a tag) for a specific *Cooldown* node (which is a decorator that we will look at later in this chapter).
- *Wait*: Stops the behavior for a specific amount of time. Arandom deviation can be specified to make the amount of time to wait different each time.
- *Wait Blackboard Time*: Like the previous node, but the amount of time is retrieved from the *Blackboard* (more on *Blackboards* later in this chapter).

Now that we have looked at how a *Task* node works, let's explore *Composite* nodes, which make decisions based up whether a *Task* returns Failure or Success.

# Composite

Composite nodes are at the core of the decision-making capabilities of **Behavior Trees** in Unreal, and understanding how they work is key.

There are three kinds of Composite nodes: *Selector*, *Sequence*, and *Simple Parallel*. The last one has been added recently, and you will find that by using a combination of *Selectors* and *Sequences*, you will be able to cover most of your cases. Here is how they work:

**Selector**: This kind of node will try to find one of its children to execute, which means it tries to find either a branch (so another *Composite* node attached as a child) or a *Task* (another child, but it is a leaf) to execute. So, the *Selector* starts from the left-most child node and tries to execute it. If it fails (either the *Task* failed to be executed, or the whole branch failed), then it tries the second left-most, and so on. If one of the children returns *Success*, which means that either the Task has been completed or a whole branch has been completed, then the *Selector* reports *Success* to its parent, and stop executing other children. On the other hand, if all the children of the *Selector* report a *fail*, then the *Selector* reports a *fail* to its parent as well. In the following screenshot, you can see what the *Selector* node looks like:

**Sequence**: This kind of node works a bit like the opposite of the *Selector*. To report a success to its parent, all of the Sequence's children must report a success. This means that the Sequence will start executing the left-most child node. If it is a success, it carries on with the second left-most, and so on if it is successful as well. If all the children until the right-most are a success, then the *Sequence* reports a *Success* to its parent. Otherwise, if just one the children fail, then the *Sequence* will stop executing its children, and report a *fail* to the parent. In the following screenshot, you can see what the *Sequence* node looks like:

**Simple Parallel**: This is a particular kind of *Composite* node, which is used in specific cases. In fact, it can only have two children. The left-most child must be a *Task*, whereas the right-most child can be either a *Task* or a *Composite* (thus giving birth to a sub-tree). The *Simple Parallel* starts to execute both its children in parallel, although the left-most is considered the main one. If the main one fails, it reports a fail, but if the main one succeeds, then it reports a success. Based on its settings, the Simple Parallel, once it has finished executing the main task, can either wait until the end of execution of the sub-tree or directly report success or fail the main one to its parent and stop executing the sub-tree. In the following screenshot, you can see what the *Simple Parallel* node looks like. Please note that it is possible to drag only two children, in which the left-most must be a *Task* (the purple block is the draggable area):

In this way, *Composite* nodes can "*decide*" which tasks to execute, based on what their children report (fail or success), and the *Composite* node reports back (either fail or success) to their parent. Even if the only-child of the root (which is a *Composite* node) reports back a success to the **Root**, then the tree has been executed with success. A good **Behavior Tree** design should always allow for success.

# Decorators

*Decorator* nodes (also known as conditionals) are attached to either a *Composite* or *Task* node. *Decorator* nodes make decisions on whether a branch in the *Behavior Tree*, or even a single node, can be executed. In their essence, they are a condition; they check whether something should be occurring. In other words, a **Decorator** can check whether it is worthwhile continuing on that branch and can report a preventive F*ailure* if, based on a condition, we know for sure that the *Task* (or the sub-tree) will fail. This will avoid the Decorator trying to perform a *Task* (or sub-tree) that is impossible (for any reason: lack of information, the goal is no longer relevant, etc...).

In general, Decorator nodes can assume the role of a **Gate** between the parent and the rest of the sub-tree. Thus, Decorators have the power to loop the sub-tree until a certain condition is met, or to not make execute within that sub-tree until a specific timer has expired, or even change the return result of the *Sub-Tree*.

For a (simple) example, imagine that there is a sub-tree dedicated to killing the player (it will make decisions so that the Agent will try and kill the player). Checking if the player is in range (and not from the other side of the map), or even if the player is still alive, might give us a preventive fail without us even having to execute that sub-tree. Consequently, the tree can continue with other events or parts of the tree, for example, in another sub-tree, which will be responsible for the wander behavior.

*Decorators* can have parameters (which you will be able to set in the *Details Panel* once a *Decorator* has been selected), and usually they are either hard-coded values or *Blackboard Key references* (more on *Blackboards* later in this chapter).

Almost every *Decorator* has a checkbox in its parameters that allows you to invert the conditions (as a result, you will have more freedom, and you can use the same decorator on two different parts of the tree to execute different conditions).

The following screenshot shows how a decorator can be attached to a *Composite* node. Note that it is possible to have more than one Decorator per node:

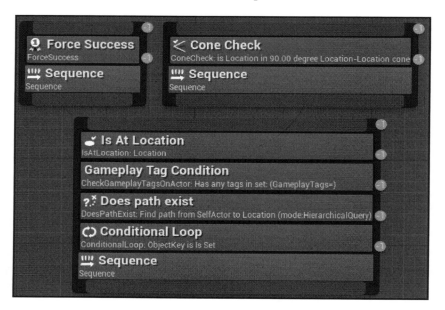

 For those who are familiar with Conditional nodes in other Behavior Tree systems, it is important not to confuse them with Task leaf nodes in Unreal Engine. More information can be found at `https://docs.` `unrealengine.com/en-us/Engine/AI/BehaviorTrees/` `HowUE4BehaviorTreesDiffer`.

Like Tasks, Unreal comes with some built-in Decorators that are ready to be used. They are general and cover the basic cases that you will probably need, but obviously, they cannot be specific for your game or application, and so you will need to create your own *Decorators* (we will look at this in detail in `Chapter 6`, *Extending Behavior Trees*).

Here is the list of the built-in tasks in Unreal:

- *Blackboard*: Checks if a specific key on the *Blackboard Is Set* (or *Is Not Set*).
- *Check Gameplay Tags on Actor*: As the name suggests, it checks if there is a specific Gameplay Tag(s) on an Actor that's been specified by a Blackboard value.
- *Compare BBEntries*: Compares two Blackboard values and checks if they are equal (or not equal) to each other.
- *Composite*: This allows you to compose different *Decorators* at once with boolean logic. Once you have placed this *Decorator*, you can open its editor by double-clicking on it. From there, you will be able to build a graph with boolean operators and other *Decorators*.
- *Conditional Loop*: As long as the condition is satisfied (whether a *Blackboard Key Is Set* or *Is Not Set*), it will keep looping through the sub-tree.

- ***Cone Check***: This checks if one point (usually another Actor) is within a cone, starting from another point (usually the AI agent); the cone angle and direction can be changed. An example of its use is if you want to check whether the Player is in front of the enemy or not—you could use this code to determine this condition.

- ***Cooldown***: Once the execution exits from the branch containing this *Decorator*, a *Cooldown timer* will start, and this *Decorator* doesn't allow the execution to enter again until this timer has expired (it reports *Failure* immediately). This node is used so that you don't repeat the same sub-tree too frequently.

- ***Does Path Exist***: This uses the Navigation System (more on this in Chapter 3, *Navigation*) to determine (and check) whether or not a Path exists for a specific point.

- ***Force Success***: As the name suggests, it forces the Success of the sub-tree, regardless of whether a *Failure* (or a *Success*) has been reported from below. This is useful for creating optional branches in a Sequence.

> Note that Force Failure doesn't exist, since it wouldn't make sense. If this were to be placed on a Selection, this would make it a Sequence, and if it were placed on a Sequence, it would only make one child execute.

- ***Is at Location***: As the name suggests, it checks if the Pawn is (near or) at a specific Location (optionally, using the *Navigation System*).

- ***Is BBEntry of Class***: As the name suggests, it checks if a specific Blackboard Entry is of a specific Class. This is useful when the Blackboard Entry is of type Object, and you need to check if the reference within the Blackboard is of a specific class (or inherits from one).

- ***Keep in Cone***: Similar to *Cone Check*, this *Decorator* (continuously) checks if the *Observer* is within a *Cone*.

- ***Loop***: As the name suggests, it loops within the sub-tree for a specific number of times (or even an infinite number of times; in this case, something else is needed to stop the behavior of the sub-tree, e.g. another *Decorator*).

- ***Set Tag Cooldown***: Similar to its homonym *Task*, when this *Decorator* becomes relevant (or if you imagine it as a gate, when it is traversed), it will change the *Cooldown* timer for a specific *Tag* (see the following node).

- ***Tag Cooldown***: This is the same as the *Cooldown* node, but it has a timer associated with a *Tag*. As a result, this timer can be changed by the "*Set Tag Cooldown*" Task and by the "*Set Tag Cooldown*" Decorator.

- *Time Limit*: As the name suggests, it provides a time limit for the sub-tree to finish its execution. Otherwise, this Decorator will stop execution and return a *Failure*.

Now that we have seen how *Decorator* nodes work, let's explore the last type of nodes of the Behavior Tree, *Service* nodes, which will continuously update and provide information in real time.

# Service

*Service* nodes attach to *Composite* or *Task* nodes and will execute if their branch is being executed. This means that as long as a node below the node is attached, it doesn't matter how many levels of parent-children are being executed—the Service will run as well. The following screenshot will help you visualize this:

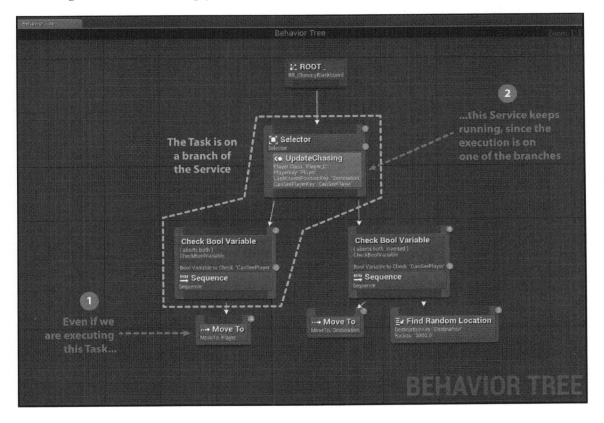

This means that Service nodes are the eyes on the Behavior Tree's execution. In fact, they run continuously (if the sub-tree is active) and can perform checks and/or update *Blackboard* (see later) values in real-time.

*Service* nodes are really specific for your *Behavior Tree* application, so there are only two default ones. An example of their usage might be providing/updating information to the sub-tree. For instance, imagine a situation where a sub-tree (the enemy) is trying to kill the player. However, it would be dumb (well, it depends of the enemy type, trolls might not be so smart) to pursue this objective, even when the player isn't shooting back at the enemy. Thus, while the sub-tree is trying to kill the player, the sub-tree needs to find cover to reduce the damage the enemy takes. However, the enemy might be moving in the map, or the player might destroy the cover where our AI is hiding. Thus, the sub-tree needs information regarding the location of the nearest and safest cover, which is still in range of the player (an *EQS Query* can calculate that). A service can update this information in real-time so that when the sub-tree needs to use the data regarding the cover, they are ready. In this particular example, to find cover, running an *Environment Query* on the Service is a dynamic way to handle the task (we will look at this topic in Chapter 4, *Environmental Querying System*). Otherwise, the *Service* might check certain specified points in the map that have been placed by a designer and evaluate which one is the best for its given action.

As you can see, **Service** nodes can be really powerful, but they are also specific to the application you are using them for. Thus, they really depend on the AIs you are programming for your game.

The following screenshot shows a couple of examples of Services. Please notice that *Services* can be used along with *Decorators*, and that a *Composite* node can have more than one **Service**:

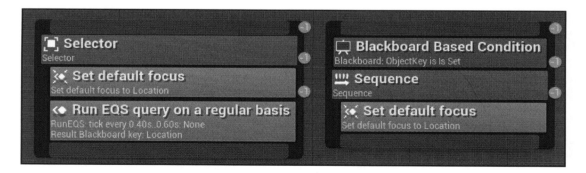

*Service nodes* replace traditional *Parallel nodes* in other *Behavior Tree systems.*

The only two available default *Services* (since you will need to program your own for your game, which we will do in `Chapter 6`, *Extending Behavior Trees*) are shown in the following screenshot:

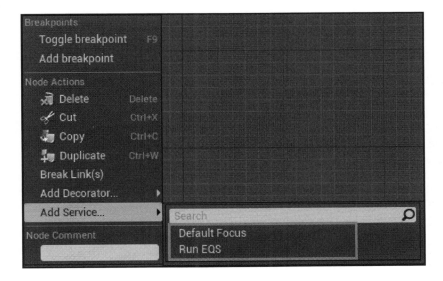

- *Set Default Focus*: When this node becomes active, it automatically sets the *Default Focus* for the *AI controller*.
- *Run EQS (Query on a regular basis)*: As the name suggests, it runs an *Environmental Query* (check out `Chapter 4`, *Environment Querying System*, for more information) on a regular basis to check for specific locations or actors. This was the kind of service that we needed in our example of finding cover for the enemy.

You will learn more about *Environmental Queries* in Chapter 4, *Environment Querying System*. However, for now, all you need to know is that this is a system for spatial reasoning, and running these queries can find locations (or actors) within the space with specific properties (in the example of finding cover for the enemy, the one that maximizes these properties: the nearest, the safest, and still in rage to shoot to the player).

Now, we have learned about the different kind of nodes that compose a *Behavior Tree*. Now, it is time to explore Blackboards!

# Blackboards and their integration with Behavior Trees

Considering the *Behavior Tree* as a brain, we can think of a **Blackboard** as its memory—more specifically, the memory of the AI. The **Blackboard** stores (and sets) key values for the *Behavior Tree* to use.

They are called blackboards because, in a classroom, the blackboard is a place where a lot of information is conveyed, but most of it is shared among students; the single notes that are given out to students are personal. You can imagine the students as the different tasks (and nodes) of the *Behavior Tree*, and the **Blackboard** as a shared place for data.

*Blackboards* are fairly simple to understand, since they are only a little more complex than a data structure. The only difference lies in the possibility to assign to a *Behavior Tree* to a particular **Blackboard**, which is shared by every node of the tree. As a result, each node can read and/or write back to the *Blackboard*.

For those of you who are familiar with the ***Design Pattern of Blackboards***, within the context of Unreal, they just cover the role of holding the memory for a *Behavior Tree*.

It works like a *dictionary* (the data structure), in which a key corresponds to a specific value type (e.g. a vector, a float, an actor, etc..., even another *Blackboard Key*). So, by using or recalling the key, it is possible to write or read the associated value.

Another cool feature of **Blackboards** is that they can be extended through inheritance. This means that another **Blackboard** can be a parent, and the child will inherit all the parent's pairs key-value, plus some specific ones that are contained in the child itself.

Now that we have covered the theory, let's look at how we can create a *Behavior Tree* and make it run. To do that, let's start by creating a new project.

# Creating our AI project

From now on, we will get our feet wet by creating a project, and get a gist of what we have learned about **Behavior Trees**. In this section, we are going to create a simple tree, but as we learn more about other topics in the following chapters, we will iterate over the tools for **Behavior Trees**. As a result, this will provide you with a better understanding of the tools that are required to create awesome **Behavior Trees**. Then, in Chapter 8, *Designing Behavior Trees - Part I*, Chapter 9, *Designing Behavior Trees - Part II*, and Chapter 10, *Designing Behavior Trees - Part III*, we will be focusing on how to *create and design* a **Behavior Tree** from scratch that chases the player, which will give you a practical approach to **Behavior Trees**.

So, to be able test the techniques that we are going to explore in this book, we need to create a project. By doing this, you will be able to follow the practical aspects that will be covered throughout this book.

You can create a new project from a template. The Third Person template works particularly well. In fact, it already has a character set up inside it, which can be easily possessed by an AI. This means that you don't have to worry too much about non-AI related details, such as animations. You can choose either the Blueprint version or the C++ one. I'll explain the concepts that we'll cover in both Blueprint and C++ terms throughout, but do note that some techniques in this book will work better if they're programmed in C++. As a result, I'm choosing the C++ version of the Third Person template, although this initial choice doesn't affect us much (we are programming AIs, not a Player or Gameplay).

Finally, I'm naming my project `UnrealAIBook`, as shown in the following screenshot. Once again, you will be able to find the project files at the following link: `http://hog.red/AIBook2019ProjectFiles` (the link is case-sensitive):

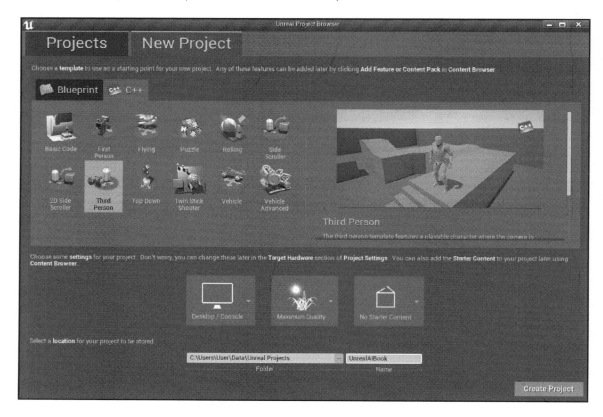

# Starting Behavior Trees from AI Controllers

Now that we have covered the basics of what Behavior Trees are and what they consist of, let's create our own. Recall from the previous chapter, the class in charge of possessing a Pawn and controlling it is the AI Controller. Thus, our *Behavior Trees* should run on *AI Controllers*.

We have two ways we can do this. The first one is by using Blueprints. Usually, even if you are a programmer, it is best to create a *Behavior Tree* using Blueprints, since the logic is really easy and the controller is simple. On the other hand, if you are a C++ fan and you want to use it as much as possible, even for small tasks, don't worry—I'll recreates the same logic we will do in Blueprint again, but this time in C++. In any case, *Behavior Tree* assets should be created and modified within the editor. What you will eventually program are different nodes than the ones that are available by default (we will see this later in this book), but the tree itself is always made in the editor.

# Creating the Behavior Tree and the Blackboard

To begin, we will need to create four Blueprint Classes: *AI Controller, Character, Behavior Tree*, and *Blackboard*. We will cover the AI controller later. If you chose one of the two Third Person templates, you should already have a *Character* ready to go. Thus, you just need to create a *Behavior Tree* and a *Blackboard*.

In the *Content Browser*, create a new folder and name it Chapter2. This will help keep things organized. Then, create a sub-folder and name it AI. As a result, we can keep our project tidy and ensure that we don't mix up items from this chapter with other *non-AI-related* classes and/or objects we might create. We will put all the assets we are going to create for the AI in this folder.

## Creating the Blackboard

Now, we need to add a *Blackboard,* which should always be within the AI folder. To do this, go to the **Content Browser** and select **Add New** > **Artificial Intelligence** > **Blackboard**.

For now, we will call our Blackboard BB_MyFirstBlackboard. Here, I'm using the naming convention to prefix all Blackboards with BB_. Unless you have a specific reason to not follow this naming convention, please use it. By doing this, you will be in sync with the rest of this book.

Since it is not possible to have multiple Blackboards on the same *Behavior Tree*, you can use inheritance with Parent and Child within the **Blackboard Details** panel, as shown in the following screenshot on the right):

# Creating the Behavior Tree

Let's add a *Behavior Tree* by going to the **Content Browser** and selecting **Add New** > **Artificial Intelligence** > **Behavior Tree**, as shown in the following screenshot:

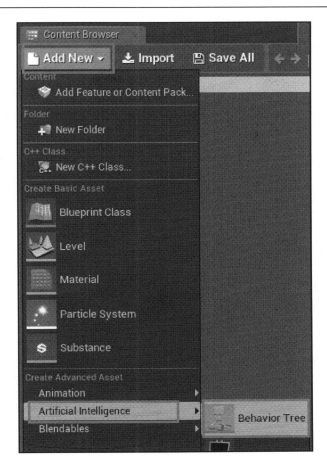

For now, we will call our Behavior Tree BT_MyFirstBehaviorTree. Again, here, I'm using a specific naming convention to prefix all Behavior Tree assets with BT_. Once again, please follow the naming convention, unless you have a specific reason not to.

When you open the *Behavior Tree* window, you will see a single node called **Root**, as follows:

The **Root** is where the execution of your *Behavior Tree* begins (from top to bottom and left to right). The Root itself only has one reference and that is the Blackboard, so it cannot be connected to anything else. It is the tip of the tree, and all subsequent nodes are below it.

If you drag from the *Root* Node, you will be able to add *Composite* nodes:

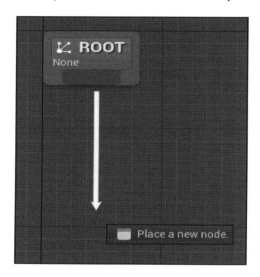

For this, the *Behavior Tree Editor* is very intuitive. You can keep dragging out from the nodes to add *Composite* or *Tasks* nodes. To add a *Decorator* or a *Service*, you can right-click on a node and select "*Add Decorator...*" or "*Add Service...*", respectively, as shown in the following screenshot:

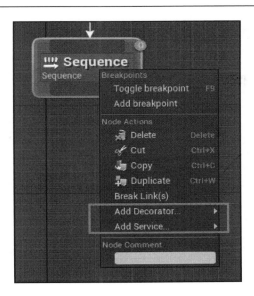

Finally, if you click on a node, it is possible to choose its parameters in the *Details Panel* (the following screenshot shows an example of a *Move To Node*):

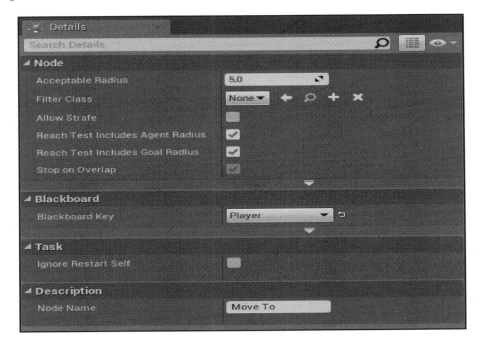

# The AI Controller to run a Behavior Tree

The next step is to run the *Behavior Tree* from an *AI Controller*. Usually, this is an easy task that it is implemented in Blueprint (in which it is possible to directly refer to a specific Behavior Tree). Even if we have a complex C++ *AI Controller*, we can extend the controller in Blueprint and *Run* the *Behavior Tree* from Blueprint. In any case, if a hard reference doesn't work (e.g. you are using C++ or because you want to have more flexibility), then you can store the *Behavior Tree* in the *Character/Pawn* that needs to run that specific *Behavior Tree*, and retrieve it when the *AI Controller* possesses the *Pawn*.

Let's explore how we can do this both in Blueprint (we will reference the *Behavior Tree* in a variable, in which we can decide on the default value) and in C++ (in which we will store the *Behavior Tree* in the *Character*).

## AI Controller in Blueprint

We can create a Blueprint AI Controller by clicking on **Add New** | **Blueprint Class** | **AI Controller.** You will have to click **All Classes** and search for **AI Controller** to access it. You can see an example of this in the following screenshot:

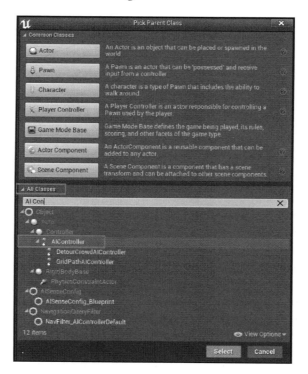

For now, we will call our **AI Controller** `BP_MyFirstAIController`. Double-click on it to open the *Blueprint Editor*.

First, we need to create a variable so that we can store our ***Behavior Tree***. Although it's not necessary to keep reference of the *Behavior Tree*, it's good practice to do so. To create a variable, we need to press the *+ Variable* button in the *My Blueprint* panel, next to the ***Variables*** tab, as shown in the following screenshot (keep in mind that your cursor needs to be on the Variables tab for the button to show up):

Then, as a variable type, you need to select *Behavior Tree* and give it a name, such as ***BehaviorTreeReference***. This is how what your variable should look like:

Then, in the *Detail Panel*, we will set the Default value (remember that to set the default value, the Blueprint needs to be compiled):

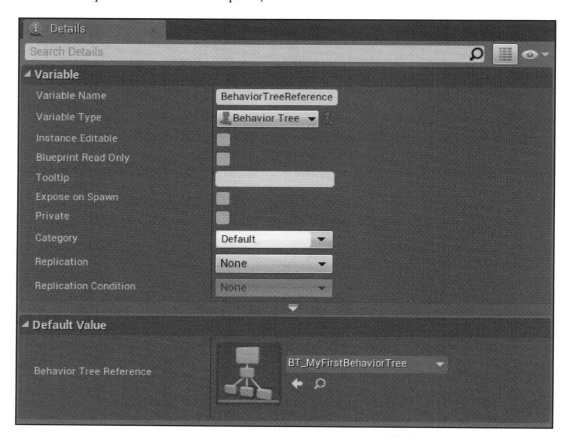

Then, we need to override the *On Possess* function, as shown in the following screenshot:

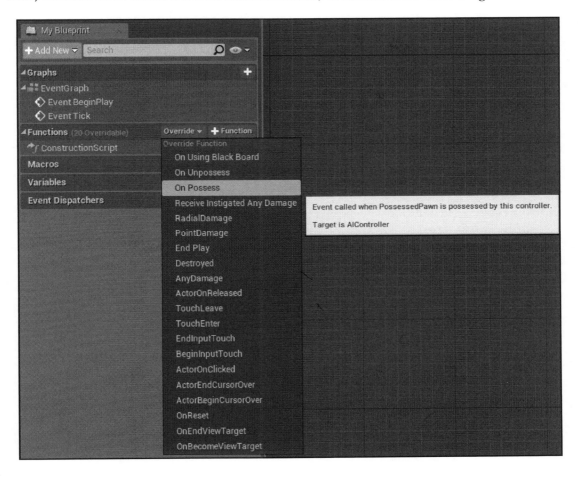

Finally, in the ***Event On Possess*** of the *AI Controller*, we need to start running/executing the *Behavior Tree*. We can achieve this by using the following simple node, named ***Run Behavior Tree***:

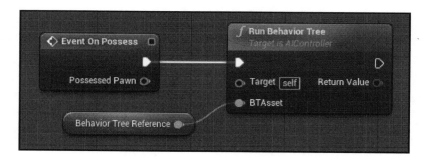

As a result, your AI controller will be able to execute the *Behavior Tree* that's stored within the ***BehaviorTreeReference***.

# AI Controller in C++

If you have decided to create this simple AI controller in C++, let's get started. I'm assuming that your Unreal Editor is already set up to work in C++ (e.g. you have Visual Studio installed, symbols for debugs, etc.... Here is a reference link so that you can get started: https://docs.unrealengine.com/en-us/Programming/QuickStart) and that you have basic knowledge of how C++ works in Unreal. Here is a link for the naming convention so that you understand why some classes are prefixed with letters in the code: https://docs.unrealengine.com/en-us/Programming/Development/CodingStandard.

 Before you start, remember that in order to work on AI in C++, you need to add the public dependencies in your your .cs file (in this case, *UnrealAIBook.cs*), and add **GameplayTasks** and **AIModule** as public dependencies, like in the following code:
PublicDependencyModuleNames.AddRange(new string[] { "Core", "CoreUObject", "Engine", "InputCore", "HeadMountedDisplay", **"GameplayTasks", "AIModule"** });
This will ensure that your code will compile without problems.

Let's create a new C++ class, as shown in the following screenshot:

The class needs to inherits from the ***AIController*** class. You might need to check the *Show All Classes* checkbox in the right-top corner and then use the search bar, as shown in the following screenshot:

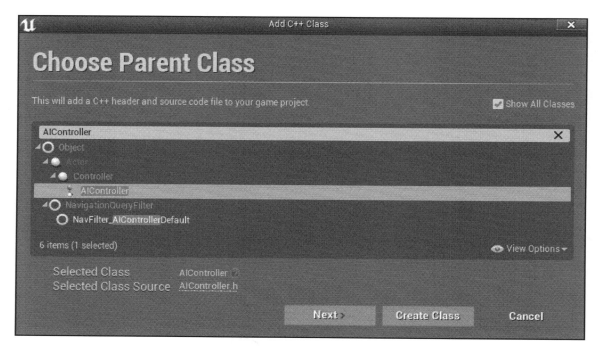

Click on *Next* and name the class ***MyFirstAIController***. Moreover, I'd suggest that you keep our project tidy. Thus, click on the ***Choose Folder*** button. Unreal will prompt you to go to your system folder explorer. Here, create a folder named Chapter2, and within it a sub-folder named AI. Choose this folder as the place where you are going to store the piece of code we are going to create. This is what the dialogue box should look like, just before you click on *Create*:

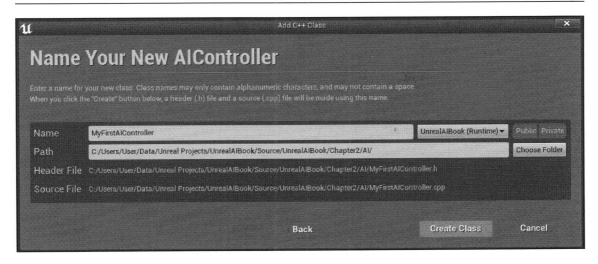

Now, click on *Create* and wait for your editor to load. You might see something like this:

The structure of our code will be slightly different compared to the Blueprint version. In fact, we cannot assign a ***Behavior Tree*** directly from the AI Controller class (mainly because it would be hard to reference it directly); instead, we need to take it from the Character. As I mentioned previously, this is a good approach when you're working with Blueprints too, but since we have chosen a C++ project, we should look at some code. In Visual Studio, open the `UnrealAIBookCharacter.h` file, and just below the public variables, add the following lines of code:

```
//** Behavior Tree for an AI Controller (Added in Chapter 2)
UPROPERTY(EditAnywhere, BlueprintReadWrite, category=AI)
UBehaviorTree* BehaviorTree;
```

For those who are still unfamiliar, here is a larger chunk of code so that you can understand where to place the preceding code within the class:

```
public:
    AUnrealAIBookCharacter();
```

```
     /** Base turn rate, in deg/sec. Other scaling may affect final turn
rate. */
     UPROPERTY(VisibleAnywhere, BlueprintReadOnly, Category=Camera)
     float BaseTurnRate;

     /** Base look up/down rate, in deg/sec. Other scaling may affect final
rate. */
     UPROPERTY(VisibleAnywhere, BlueprintReadOnly, Category=Camera)
     float BaseLookUpRate;

     //** Behavior Tree for an AI Controller (Added in Chapter 2)
     UPROPERTY(EditAnywhere, BlueprintReadWrite, category=AI)
     UBehaviorTree* BehaviorTree;
```

Moreover, to compile the preceding code, we also have to include the following statement at the top of the class, just above .generated:

```
#include "CoreMinimal.h"
#include "GameFramework/Character.h"
#include "BehaviorTree/BehaviorTree.h"
#include "UnrealAIBookCharacter.generated.h"
```

Close the *Character class*, since we have finished with it. As a result, every time we have an instance of that character placed in the world, we will be able to specify a *Behavior Tree* from the *Details* panel, as shown in the following screenshot:

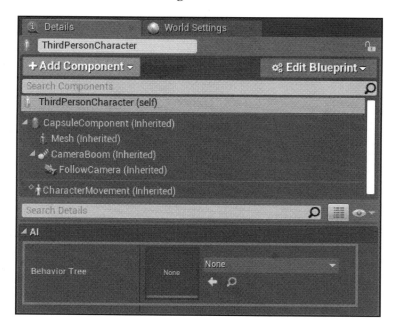

Let's open the header (.h) file of our newly created AI controller (it should already be open in *Visual Studio* if you are using it as an *IDE*). In particular, we need to override a function of the AI Controller class. The function we are going to override is called Possess(), and it allows us to run some code as soon as this AI Controller possess a new Pawn (that is, when it takes control of the character, which is a Pawn). Add the following code in bold (within a protected visibility):

```
UCLASS()
class UNREALAIBOOK_API AMyFirstAIController : public AAIController
{
    GENERATED_BODY()

protected:

    //** override the OnPossess function to run the behavior tree.
    void OnPossess(APawn* InPawn) override;


};
```

Next, open the implementation (.cpp) file. Once again, to use *Behavior Trees*, we have to include both *Behavior Trees* and the UnrealAIBookCharacter class:

```
#include "MyFirstAIController.h"
#include "UnrealAIBookCharacter.h"
#include "BehaviorTree/BehaviorTree.h"
```

Next, we need to assign a functionality to the Possess() function. We need to check whether the *Pawn* is actually an ***UnrealAIBookCharacter***, and if so, we retrieve the *Behavior Tree* and run it. Of course, this is surrounded by an if statement to avoid our pointers being nullptr:

```
void AMyFirstAIController::OnPossess(APawn* InPawn)
{
  Super::OnPossess(InPawn);
  AUnrealAIBookCharacter* Character = Cast<AUnrealAIBookCharacter>(InPawn);
  if (Character != nullptr)
  {
    UBehaviorTree* BehaviorTree = Character->BehaviorTree;
    if (BehaviorTree != nullptr) {
      RunBehaviorTree(BehaviorTree);
    }
  }
}
```

If, for any reason, you cannot get the code to work, you can just use a Blueprint controller to start the *Behavior Tree*, or just inherit the C++ controller, and make sure that all rest of the code runs, and make a call to the `RunBehaviorTree()` function in Blueprint.

Once we have compiled our project, we will be able to use this controller. Select our AI character from the Level (if you don't have it, you can create one) and this time, in the *Details* panel, we can set our C++ controller, as follows:

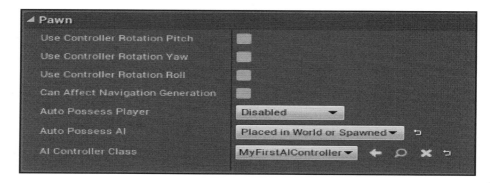

Also, don't forget to assign the *Behavior Tree* as well, which we always do in the *Details Panel*:

As a result, once the game starts, the enemy will start executing the Behavior Tree. At the moment, the tree is empty, but this gives us the structure we need so that we can start working with *Behavior Trees*. In the following chapters, we are going to explore *Behavior Trees* more in detail, especially in chapters 8, 9, and 10, where we will look at a more practical approach to designing and building *Behavior Trees*.

# Summary

In this chapter, we have covered what a *Behavior Tree* is and some of the things that they consist of, including *Tasks, Decorators,* and *Services.* Next, we learned about **Blackboards** and how to integrate them with *Behavior Trees.* Then, we created a *Behavior Tree* and learned how to make it start from an *AI Controller* (both in Blueprint and C++). By doing this, we have developed a solid foundation that has provided us with key knowledge so that we can tackle the other parts of this book.

As a result, we will meet more **Behavior Trees** throughout this book, and you will have a chance to master them. But before that, there are certain topics we need to learn about first. Once we have a solid foundation of navigation and perception (including EQS), we can iterate over **Behavior Trees** to understand the role of *Composite* nodes, along with *Decorator* and *Tasks.* Moreover, we will be able to create our own. Chapters 8, 9, and 10 will guide you through the process of creating a Behavior Tree from scratch, from the designing phase to realization.

But until then, let's move on to the next chapter, in which we are going to discuss *Navigation* and *Pathfinding*!

# 3
# Navigation

*The problem behind pathfinding is as old as the Labyrinth at Knossos: how do I get from point A to point B using the shortest route and avoiding all obstacles in-between?*

Many algorithms have been developed to solve pathfinding problems, including those related to the A* algorithm, which was first introduced in computer science during the 1960s (section 2).

Pathfinding routines are typical components of many video games, with Non-Player Characters (NPCs) having the task of finding optimal paths on the game maps, which can constantly change. For example, passageways, gates, or doors can change their statuses during gameplay.

There are quite a lot of problems when it comes to pathfinding, and unluckily for us, there isn't a one-solution-fits-all approach. This is because each problem will have its own solution, depending on the type of problem it is. Not only this, it will also depend on the type of game that you are developing. For example, is the final destination for the AI a static building (stationary), or do they need to jump on top of a floating raft (dynamic)? You also need to take the terrain into consideration – is it flat or rocky, and so on? To add an additional layer of complexity, we also need to consider whether there are obstacles present, as well as whether these objects are static (fire hydrant) or if they can be moved (e.g. boxes). Then, we need to think about the actual path itself. For example, it might be easier to travel along the road, but running across rooftops will get you where you need to be quicker. Following the same train of thought, the AI might not even have a final destination, in the sense that they don't have to be somewhere specific. For example, they might just wander around as someone who is part of a village. However, I have only highlighted a few issues and considerations that are related to pathfinding. As you experience different situations that use pathfinding, you are likely to encounter other issues. Remember to be patient and to consider all the variables that I have mentioned here and others that are specific to your situation.

Fortunately for us, Unreal has incorporated a navigation system that can be used for the most common of situations. As a result, we don't need to re-implement everything from scratch. The main goal of this chapter is to ensure that you understand how to use it, and ensure that you have some idea of how you can expand on it.

In this chapter, we will cover the following topics:

- What to expect from a *Navigation System*

- The *Unreal Navigation System*, and how it works

- How to *Generate the Navigation Mesh* for a level, and its available settings

- How to *Modify the Navigation Mesh*, by using the following:

    - *Navigation Areas*, to change the weight associated with a part of the Navigation Mesh
    - *Navigation Links*, to connect two parts of the Navigation Mesh that would otherwise be separated
    - *Navigation Filters*, to perform a slight change to the Navigation Mesh while executing a specific query on the *Navigation System*

Let's dive in!

# What to expect from a Navigation System

First of all, before we explore the *Unreal Navigation System*, it is useful to define what we would expect from a generic *Navigation System*. The following is required from the *Navigation System*:

- It needs to determine if a path (that can be traversed by the agent performing the query) exists between two generic points on the map
- If such a path exists, return the one that is the most convenient for the agent (usually the shortest)

However, while searching for the best path, there are many aspects to take into consideration. A good navigation system should not only consider these, but also perform the query in a relatively short period of time. Some of these aspects are as follows:

- Is the AI agent who's performing the query able to pass through a specific portion of the map? For instance, there might be a lake, and the AI character may or may not know how to swim. Similarly, can the agent crouch and move into a ventilation tunnel?
- The AI agent might want to avoid (or prefer) certain paths, which aren't necessarily the shortest ones. For instance, if a building is on fire, the agent should try to avoid this, or risk of getting burned. As another example, let's say there are two paths: one is covered from enemy fire, but it's long, while the other one is short but exposed to enemy fire; which one should the AI choose? Although this might be part of the decision-making process, some heuristics can be implemented at the level of pathfinding, and a navigation system should support them.
- A map might be dynamic, which means that obstacles, objects, roads, cliffs, and so on, change during gameplay. Is the navigation system able to handle these changes in real time while they happen, and correct the generated paths?

Now, it's time to see how Unreal implements all of these features.

# Unreal Navigation System

The Unreal navigation system is based on a *Navigation Mesh* (*Nav Mesh* for short). It entails dividing the navigable space into areas – in this case, polygons – which are subdivided into triangles for efficiency. Then, to reach a certain place, each triangle is considered a node of a graph, and if two triangles are adjacent, then their respective nodes are connected. On this graph, you can execute a pathfinding algorithm, such as A* with a Euclidean distance heuristic, or even something more complicated (e.g. variants of A* or systems that take into consideration different costs). This will produce a path among these triangles where the AI character can walk.

In reality, this process is a little bit more complicated, because considering all the triangles as nodes of a giant graph will produce a good result, but it is inefficient, especially since we have access to the information that's stored in the polygons and how these are connected. Moreover, you might need extra information about specific triangles, which might have different costs, different abilities required to traverse them, etc... However, unless you need to change the underlying structure of the *Navigation System*, you don't need to work/operate at this level of detail. Being able to understand that all of the triangles form a graph in some way, in which pathfinding algorithms can run, is more than sufficient to master the tool itself.

To be able to use the *Navigation System*, let's understand the main process of setting up the navigation system. At this stage, we will no longer worry about how the system is structured underneath, but rather how we can use all of its features. The system will do the rest. In the same way, we need to provide information about the map to the navigation system (e.g. specify special areas). Usually, it's the AI programmer in your team who takes care of this, but if your team is small, a level designer might take care of this task. Although there is not a specific process, but, rather an iterative procedure, let's explore the different steps – or tools, if you prefer – that you can use to define the *Nav Mesh* in Unreal. We will examine them in detail throughout this chapter:

- **Generation of the Navigation Mesh**: This is the first step. Before you'll be able to use the following tools, it is important to start generating a *Nav Mesh*. This step includes defining how to generate the polygons, the triangles, the precision of the *Nav Mesh*, and even which kind of agents will traverse this specific *Nav Mesh*.
- **Navigation Mesh Modifiers**: Not all the parts of the *Nav Mesh* are created equal, and this is a tool to specify which parts of the *Nav Mesh* should behave differently. In fact, as we have seen before, there might be a zone with poisoned gas, and the agent would like to avoid this part, unless they really have to traverse it. The Nav Mesh Modifier allows you to specify that the area containing the gas is special. However, the type of behavior within the area (e.g. this path should not be traversed, or should only be traversed by agents with swimming abilities) is specified within a Nav Area.
- **Navigation Areas**: This allows you to specify how a specific type of area should behave, whether it should be avoided, etc. These are key when performing *Nav Filtering* to determine which areas the agent can traverse.

- **Navigation Links**: These can connect two different parts of the *Nav Mesh*. Suppose you have a platform ledge. By default, the AI agent will find another way. If you have in mind the Third Person map template, the agent that needs to get down from platform will go around the area to use the stairs, rather than just falling/jumping off the platform. A *Nav Link* allows you to connect the part of the *Nav Mesh* that's on top of the platform with the part below it. As a result, the agent will be able to fall off the platform. However, note that *Nav Links* can connect two generic portions of the *Nav Mesh*, thus allowing pathfinding to find its way through jumps, teleports, etc.
- **Nav Filtering**: We don't necessarily want to find a path in the same way on every occasion. *Nav Filtering* allows us to define specific rules on how to perform the pathfind for that specific instance (for that specific time that the pathfind is invoked to seek a path).

Let's break these points down and talk about them in more detail.

# Generating the Navigation Mesh

Generating a simple *Navigation Mesh* is pretty straightforward in Unreal. Let's look at how we can do it. From the *Mode* panel, in the *Volume* tab, you will be able to find the **Nav Mesh Bounds Volume**, as shown in the following screenshot:

Drag it into the world. You will notice that the volume is quite small in respect to the map. Everything inside that volume will be taken into consideration to generate a *Nav Mesh*. Of course, a *Nav Mesh* has many parameters, but for now let's keep thing simple.

If you press the *P* button on your keyboard, you will be able to see the *Nav Mesh* in the *Viewport*, as shown in the following screenshot:

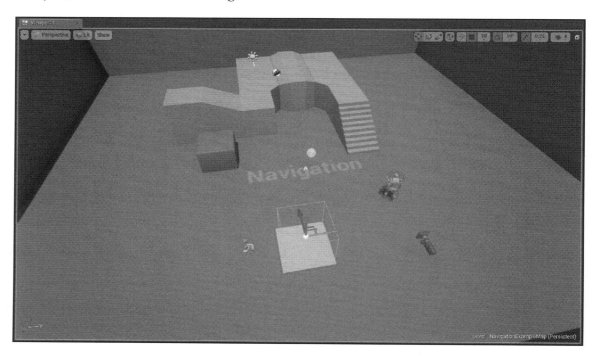

As you can see, it is limited to the area that's contained in the volume of *Nav Mesh Bounds Volume*. Let's scale the *Nav Mesh Bounds Volume* to fit all the level we have. This is what your level should look like:

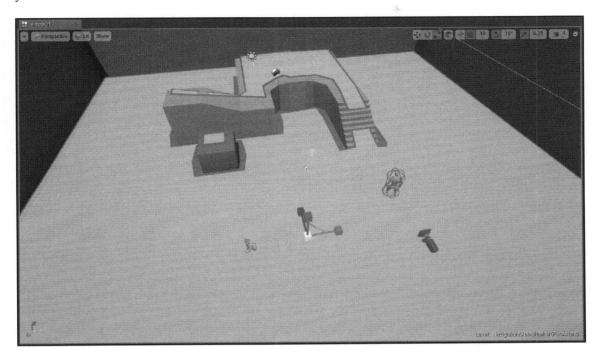

Did you notice how, while you were scaling your volume, the *Nav Mesh* was updating automatically? This is because, in Unreal, the *Nav Mesh* is generated every time something that impacts the *Nav Mesh* moves.

While updating, the part of the *Nav Mesh* that's affected (that is, updated) should turn red, as shown in the following screenshot:

This is how easy is to generate a *Nav Mesh*. However, to be able to master the tool, we need to learn more about how to refine the *Nav Mesh* and how it is used by the AI.

# Setting parameters for the Nav Mesh

If you click on the **Nav Mesh Bounds Volume**, you will notice that there are no options for the generation of the *Nav Mesh*. In fact, some parameters are at the project level, while others are at the map level.

Let's navigate to the *World Outliner*, where you will find that a *RecastNavMesh-Default* actor has been placed in the scene, as shown in the following screenshot:

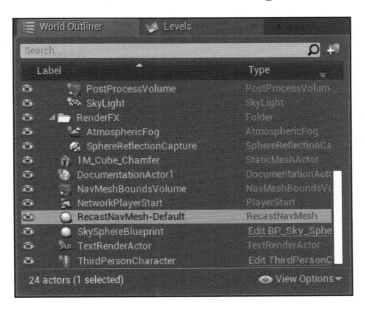

In fact, when you drag a *Nav Mesh Bounds Volume*, if the map doesn't have a *RecastNavMesh-Default*, one will be created. If we click on it, we will be able to change all of its properties in the *Details Panel*.

As you can see, there are a lot of default values. These can be changed in the *Project Settings* (under the *Navigation Mesh* tab). Let's break down every section, and try to grasp the main concepts around them.

# Display settings

As the name suggests, these are settings that are related on how we can visualize the *Nav Mesh* that we have generated in detail. In particular, we will be able to see the generated Polygons, the triangles, and how the polygons are connected. We will go through these in more detail in Chapter 12, *Debugging Methods for AI - Navigation, EQS, and Profiling*, when we will talk about debugging tools:

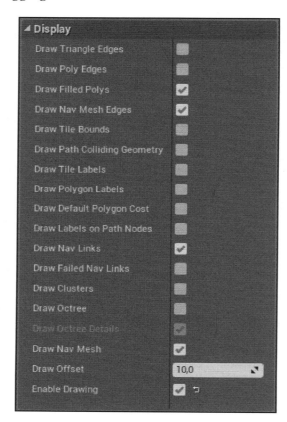

# Generation settings

These settings concern the generation of the *Nav Mesh*. Usually, the default values are more than perfect to start with, and so you should only touch these values if you know what you are doing. The following screenshot shows these settings:

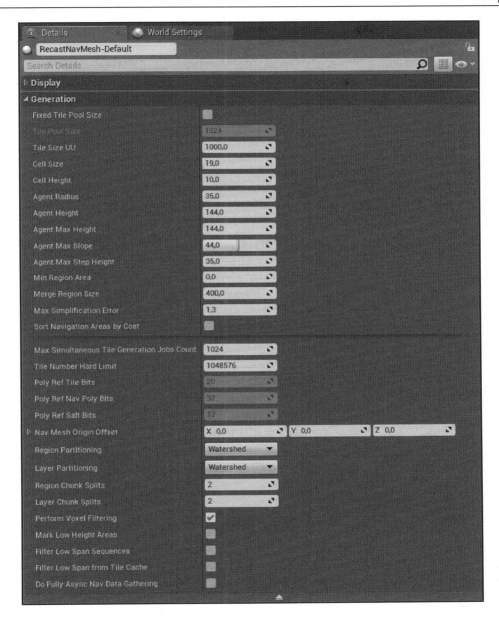

The best way to learn about these settings is by playing with their parameters, first in an example map, then in your own maps. After that, you need to check the results of doing this (especially with the visual debugging tools that are presented in `Chapter 12`, *Debugging Methods for AI - Navigation, EQS, and Profiling*). To get you started, let's look at the main ones:

- **Tile Size UU**: This parameter defines how fine the polygons that are generated are. Lower values mean a more precise navigation mesh, with more polygons, but also a slower generation time (and potentially more memory usage). You can see the effect of this parameter by turning on the **Draw Triangle Edges** in the display settings that are shown in the preceding screenshot.
- **Cell Height**: This determines how high the generated cells are from the floor (which might result in connecting areas at a different height, so be careful).
- *Agent settings* (**Radius**, **Height**, **Max Height**, **Max Slope**, **Max Step Height**): These settings are specific to your agents and should be specified appropriately. In particular, these are the minimum values an agent should have to traverse this *Nav Mesh*. As a result, the *Nav Mesh* will not be able to navigate with agents with smaller values than this, because the *Nav Mesh* is generated only for agents with these requirements. These settings are useful to generate an appropriate *Nav Mesh* for your agents, without wasting resources on a *Nav Mesh* with areas that your agents will never be able to navigate.
- **Min Region Area**: This gets rid of certain artifacts of the *Nav Mesh Generation* that are too insignificant to navigate.

Many of the remaining settings are about optimization, and they can be overwhelming, especially for newcomers in AI Programming. Therefore, I decided to not include these details in this book. However, once you are confident about using the Navigation System, you can check the tool-tips of these settings and experiment with them so that you can learn about what they do.

# Project Settings

It is worthwhile mentioning, even if we don't go through them in details, that same *Navigation* settings can be changed from the *Project Settings*; there is a specific tab for that, as shown in the following picture:

Interesting to notice is the last tab about *Agents*. Here it is possible to create an *Array* of **Supported Agents**, so that different agents can have different ways to navigate the *Nav Mesh*. For instance, a mouse might have a very different *Navigation Mesh* than a Giant Troll. In fact the mouse can also go in small holes, whereas the Troll can't. Here you will be able to specify all the different kinds of agents you have:

You cannot assign directly which kind of *agents* your character will follow, but, based on the *Character Movement Component* (or *Movement Components* in general), a kind of agent is assigned to the *Character/AI Agent*.

# Settings on the Character Movement Component

As we have seen from the previous section, the agents, which are its abilities, its shape, etc... influence a lot how it navigates the *Nav Mesh*. You will be able to find all of these settings on the *Character Movement Component*.

However, this component is outside the scope of this book, and we will not see it.

# Modifying the Navigation Mesh

So far, we have seen how is it possible to generate a Navigation Mesh. However, we would like to modify this so that it suits our needs better. As we mentioned previously, there might be different areas that can be costly to traverse, or there might be a connection between two points of the *Nav Mesh* that seem to be separated (e.g. by a ledge).

As a result, this section explores the different tools that Unreal has to modify the *Nav Mesh* so that it can be adapted to the level.

# Nav Modifier Volume

Alright – it's time to look at how we can start modifying the *Nav Mesh*. For instance, there might be a part of the *Nav Mesh* that we don't want to be crossable, or another section that we want to have different properties. We can do this by using a ***Nav Modifier Volume***.

You can find this setting by going to the *Mode* panel, under the *Volumes* tab, and then by going to the *Nav Mesh Bounds Volume*:

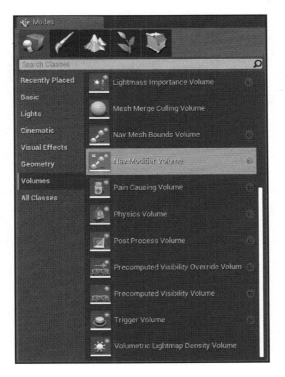

Once this volume has been placed in the map, the default value is to remove the part of the *Nav Mesh* within the volume, as shown in the following screenshot:

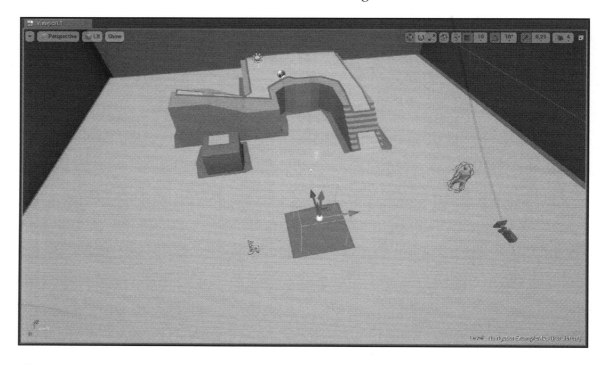

This is useful when you have areas that you don't want your AI to go in, or fix up artifacts of your navigation mesh. Although the *Nav Modifier Volume* specifies a part of the map, the behavior is specified in the *Nav Mesh Areas*. This means that, if we look at the settings of the *Nav Mesh Modifier Volume*, we can find only one related to the *Navigation*, named *Area Class*:

As a result, this volume can only specify a portion of the map in which a specific *Area Class* is applied. By default, the *Area Class* is *NavArea_Null*, which "*removes*" the *Nav Mesh* in that portion of the map that's overlapping this volume. We'll explore how *Nav Mesh Areas* work in the next section.

# Nav Mesh Areas

In the previous section, we talked about how not all parts of the navigable area of the map are created equal. If there is a zone that it is considered dangerous, the AI should avoid it. Unreal's built-in navigation system is able to handle these different areas by using costs. This means that the AI will evaluate the path to take by summing all the costs along the path, and it will select the one with the minimal cost.

Also, it is worth specifying that there are two types of costs. For each area, there is an initial cost for entering (or leaving) the area and a cost for traversing the area. Let's look at a couple of examples to clarify the difference between the two.

Imagine that there is a forest, but at each entrance of the forest, the AI needs to pay a toll to the indigenous living in the forest. However, once inside, the AI can move freely, as if they were outside the forest. In this case, entering the forest has a cost, but once inside, there is no cost to pay. As a result, when the AI needs to evaluate whether to traverse the forest or not, it depends on whether there is another way to go and how long it would take them to do so.

Now, imagine that there is an area with poison gas instead. In this second scenario, the cost for entering the area might be zero, but the cost for traversing it is high. In fact, the longer the AI stays in the area, the more health it loses. Whether it is worth entering or not only depends on whether there is an alternative way and how long that alternative way will take to traverse (like in the previous case), but also how long, once entered, the AI needs to traverse the area.

In Unreal, costs are specified inside the class. If you click on a *Nav Modifier Volume*, you will notice that you need to specify an *Area Class*, as shown in the following screenshot:

As you may have guessed, the default value is *NavArea_Null*, which has an infinite cost for entering, resulting in the AI never going into that area. The Navigation system is smart enough to not even bother generating that area, and treats it as a non-navigable area.

However, you can change the *Area Class*. By default, you will be able to access the following *Area Classes*:

- *NavArea_Default*: This is the default area that is generated. It is useful to have it as a modifier in case you want to have more than one of these modifiers in the same spot.
- **NavArea_LowHeight**: This indicates that the area is not suitable for every agent, since the height is reduced (for example, in the case of a ventilation tunnel, not all the agents can fit/crouch).
- **NavArea_Null**: This makes the area non-navigable for all the agents.
- **NavArea_Obstacle**: This assigns a higher cost to the area, so the agent will want to avoid it:

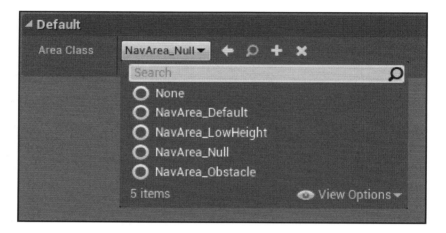

 You will notice that if you create a new Blueprint, or even when you open the source code in Visual Studio, there will be **NavArea_Meta** and a child of it, **NavArea_MetaSwitchingActor**. However, if you look at their code, they mainly have some deprecated code. Therefore, we won't be using them in this book.

However, you can extend the list of the different areas (and potentially add more functionalities) by extending the *NavArea Class*. Let's see how we can do this, both in Blueprint and C++. Of course, as we did in the previous chapter, we are going to create a new folder named *Chapter3/Navigation*, in which we will place all our code.

# Creating a NavArea class in Blueprint

Creating a new *NavArea* class in blueprint is quite straightforward; you just need to create a new Blueprint that inherits from the *NavArea* class, as shown in the following screenshot:

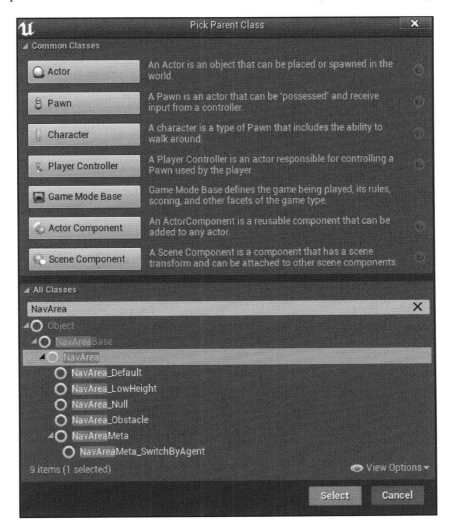

By convention, the name of the class should start with "*NavArea_*". We will rename it to **NavArea_BPJungle** here (I added BP to signify that we have created this with Blueprint, since we are repeating the same task both in Blueprint and in C++). This is what it should look like in the *Content Browser*:

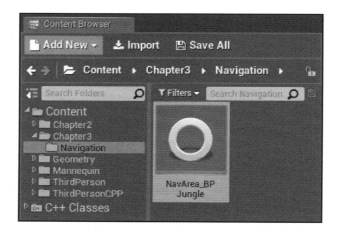

Then, if you open the blueprint, you will be able to assign the custom costs to the area. You can also specify a specific color for your area so that it is easy to recognize when you build your *Nav Mesh*. This is what the *Details* panel looks like by default:

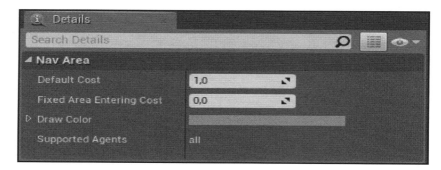

Now, we can customize as per our needs. For example, we might want to have a cost to enter the *Jungle,* and a slightly higher cost to traverse it. We are going to use a bright green for the color, as shown in the following screenshot:

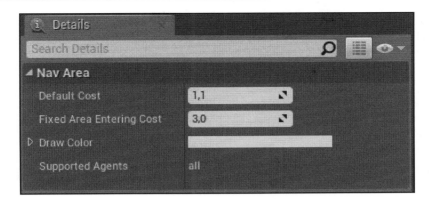

Once compiled and saved, we can assign this newly created area to the **Nav Modifier Volume**, as shown in the following screenshot:

This is what our finished class looks like in our level (if the *Navigation Mesh* is visible):

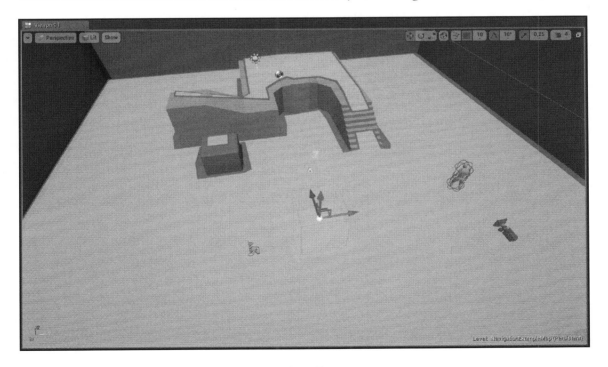

## Creating a NavArea class in C++

It's easy to create a *NavArea* class in C++ as well. First of all, you need to create a new C++ class that inherits from the *NavArea* class, as shown in the following screenshot:

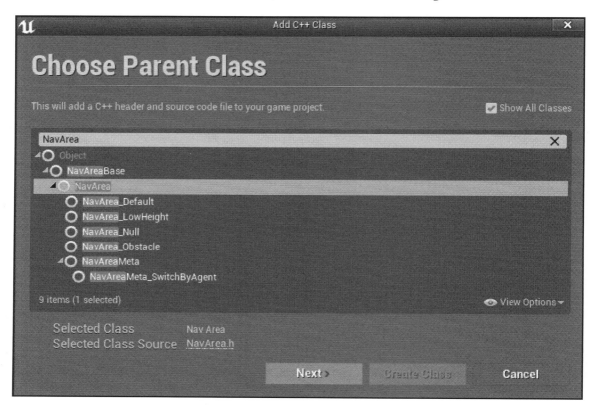

By convention, the name should start with "*NavArea_*". Therefore, you can rename it **NavArea_Desert** (just to vary which kind of terrain the AI can face, since we created a *Jungle* previously) and place it in "***Chapter3/Navigation***":

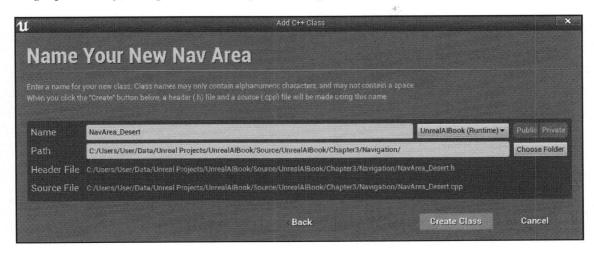

Once you have created the class, you just need to assign the parameters in the constructor. For your convenience, here is the class definition in which we declare a simple constructor:

```cpp
#include "CoreMinimal.h"
#include "NavAreas/NavArea.h"
#include "NavArea_Desert.generated.h"

/**
 *
 */
UCLASS()
class UNREALAIBOOK_API UNavArea_Desert : public UNavArea
{
  GENERATED_BODY()

  UNavArea_Desert();
};
```

Then, in the implementation of the constructor, we can assign the different parameters. For instance, we can have a high cost for entering and a higher cost for traversing (with respect to the *Default* or the *Jungle*). Furthermore, we can set the color to *Yellow* so that we remember that it is a desert area:

```
#include "NavArea_Desert.h"

UNavArea_Desert::UNavArea_Desert()
{
  DefaultCost = 1.5f;
  FixedAreaEnteringCost = 3.f;
  DrawColor = FColor::Yellow;
}
```

 You can always play with these values to see which one works best for you. For instance, you can create an area with a very high entering cost, but a low traversal cost. As a result, you will have an area that, should be avoided if it's only going to be traversed for a little while, but if the agent traverses it for a long period of time, it might be more convenient than the shorter route.

Once you have created the class, you can set it as part of the *Nav Modifier Volume*, as shown in the following screenshot:

As a result, you will be able to see your custom area in the *Nav Mesh* (in this case, with a *Yellow Color*):

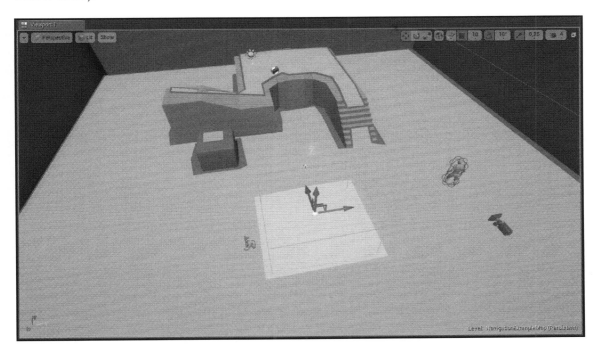

# Nav Link Proxy

By default, if there is a ledge, the AI will not fall through it, even if it would be the shortest path they could take to get to their destination. In fact, the *Nav Mesh* on top of the ledge is not (directly) connected with the *Nav Mesh* at the bottom. However, the *Unreal Navigation System* provides a way to connect two arbitrary triangles in the *Nav Mesh* through what is called a *Nav Link Proxy*.

 Although the regions are connected, and the pathfinder will find the correct road, the AI cannot go against the rules of the game, both in terms of physics or game mechanics. This means that if the AI is unable to jump or traverse a magic wall, the character will get stuck since the pathfinder returned a path, but the character cannot execute it.

Let's explore this tool in more detail.

# Creating a Nav Link Proxy

To connect two regions with a link, we need to go to the *Mode* panel in the *All Classes* tab and select *Nav Link Proxy*, as shown in the following screenshot:

Alternatively, you can search for it in the *Modes* panel to find it more quickly:

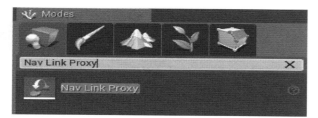

Once the link has been placed in the level, you will see an *"arrow/link"*, and you will be able to modify the start and end points of the link. They are called *Left* and **Right**, and the easiest way to set their location is by dragging (and placing) them in the *Viewport*. As a result, you will be able to connect two different parts of the *Nav Mesh*. As we can see in the following screenshot, if the *Nav Mesh* is visible (enabled with the *P* key), you will see an arrow connecting the **Right** and *Left* nodes. This arrow is pointing in both directions. This will result in the link being bidirectional:

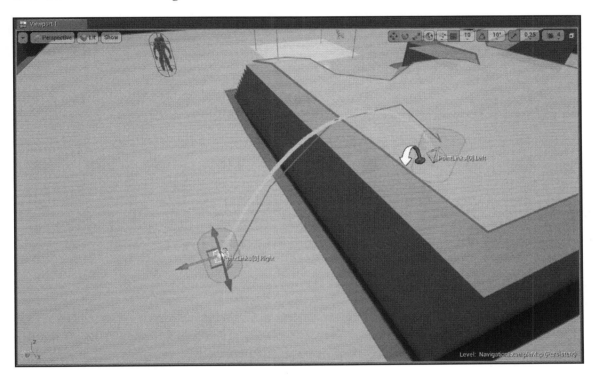

You might notice that there are two arrows, one with a darker shade of green. Also, this second *arrow/arc/link* might not be exactly where you placed your *Right* end, but rather attached to the *Nav Mesh*. You can see this second arrow more clearly in the following screenshot:

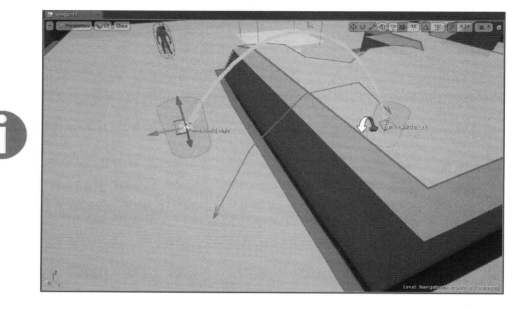

This is actually how the *Nav Mesh* is connected, due to the *Projection Settings* of the *Link*. We will explore this setting in the next section.

If you want to make the link go only in one direction, we can change this setting in the *Details Panel*. However, to explore these settings, we first need to understand that there are two different types of *Links*: **Simple** and **Smart**.

# Simple Links and Smart Links

When we create a *Nav Link Proxy*, it comes with an array of *Simple Links*. This means that with a single *Nav Link Proxy*, we can connect different parts of the *Nav Mesh* together. However, the *Nav Link Proxy* comes with a single *Smart Link* as well, which is disabled by default.

Let's learn about the similarities and difference between a *Simple Link* and a *Smart Link*.

## Both Simple and Smart Links

*Both Simple and Smart Links* behave in a similar fashion, in the sense that they connect two parts of the *Nav Mesh* together. Moreover, Both type of links can have *Direction* (*Left to Right*, *Right to Left*, or *Both Ways*) and a *Nav Area* (which kind of navigation area the link is in; for instance, you might want to have a custom cost when using this link).

## Simple Links

*Simple Links* exists in the *Point Links Array* within the *Nav Proxy Link*, which means that multiple simple links in a single *Nav Proxy Link* are possible. To create another *Simple Link*, you can add an additional element to the array of *Simple Nodes* from the *Details* panel, as shown in the following screenshot:

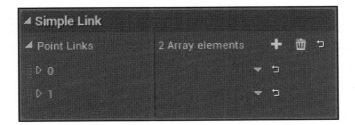

Once we have more *Simple Links*, we can set the **Start** and **End** positions, like we did for the first one (by selecting them and moving them within the *Viewport* as any other actor). The following screenshot shows where I placed two *Simple Links* on the same *Nav Proxy Link* next to each other:

Every time we create a *Nav Link Proxy*, it comes with one *Simple Link* within the array.

For every **Simple Link** we have in the *Point Links Array*, we can access its settings by expanding the item. The following screenshot shows the Settings for the first *Simple Link*:

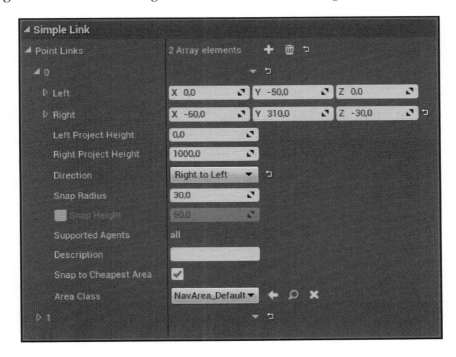

Let's understand these various settings:

- *Left* and *Right*: The position of the *Left* and *Right* ends of the Link, respectively.
- *Left Project Height* and *Right Project Height*: If this number is greater than zero, then the link will be projected down to the navigation geometry (using a trace with the maximum length specified by this number) for the *Left* and *Right* end of the *Link*, respectively. You can see this projected link in the following screenshot:

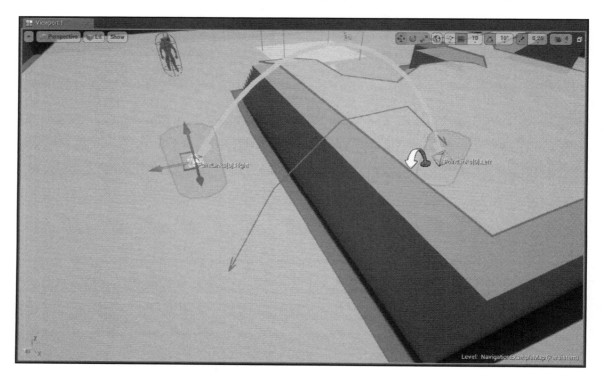

- *Direction*: This specifies in which direction the link works. Also, the arrow in the *Viewport* will update accordingly. The possible options for this are as follows:
    - *Both Ways*: The link is bidirectional (remember that the AI needs to be equipped to traverse the Link in both directions; e.g. if we're going over a ledge, the agent needs to be able to fall from it (one direction of the link) and jump (the other direction of the link).
    - *Left to Right*: The link is only crossable from the Left end to the Right one (the agent still needs to have the ability to go in that link direction).

- **Right to Left**: The link is only crossable from the Right end to the Left one (the agent still needs have the ability to go in that link direction).

- **Snap Radius** and **Height Radius**: You may have noticed a cylinder that attaches the end of each link. These two settings control the Radius and the Height of that cylinder. Check *Snap to Cheapest Area* for more information about the use of this cylinder. The following screenshot shows that the first link has a bigger cylinder (both a bigger radius and higher):

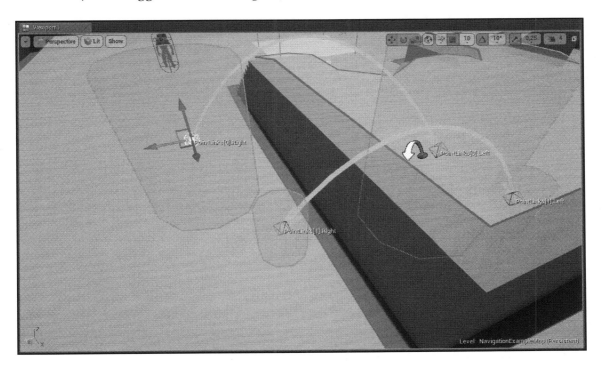

- **Description**: This is just a string in which you can insert a description for your convenience; it has no impact on the *Navigation* or on the *Link*.

- **Snap to Cheapest Area**: If enabled, it will try to connect the link ends to the cheapest area among the available triangles within the cylinder that's specified by the *Snap Radius* and the *Height Radius*. For instance, if the cylinder intersects both the *Default Nav Area* and the *BPJungle* Nav Area (that we created earlier), the link will be connected directly to the *Default Nav Area*, rather than the jungle.

- **Area Class**: The *Link* might have a cost to traverse, or be of a specific *Nav Area*. This parameter allows you to define which kind of *Nav Area* the *Link* is when traversed.

This concludes all the possibilities for the **Simple Links**. However, this is a very powerful tool that lets you shape the *Nav Mesh* and achieve amazing AI behavior. Now, let's dive into *Smart Links*.

## Smart Links

Smart Links can be enabled and disabled at *runtime* using the "**Smart Link Is Relevant**" boolean variable. You can also notify surrounding actors of this change. By default, it is not relevant (it isn't used in the sense that the link is not available), and there is only a single **Smart Link** per *Nav Proxy Link*.

 **Please note, and don't get confused**: The *Smart link* can be in two states: Enabled and Disabled. However, if the link is actually "present/exists" (for the Navigation Mesh), that is another property (*Smart Link Is Relevant*), which in other words means that the link is "*active*" for the Navigation System (but it can still be in the Enabled or Disabled state).

Unfortunately (at least for the current version of the Engine), these are not visible in the Editor, which means that the **Start** and **End** positions need to be set manually.

However, let's go through the settings of a *Smart Link*:

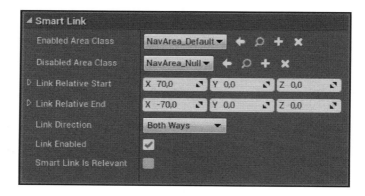

- **Enabled Area Class**: This is the *Nav Area* that the Link assumes when it is enabled. The default is *NavArea_Default*.
- **Disabled Area Class**: This is the *Nav Area* that the Link assumes when it is disabled. This means that, when the Link is disabled, it can still be traversed if a crossable area is assigned (e.g. when the link is disabled, we might want to have a very high cost to cross, but we still want it to be possible to traverse it. Of course, the default is *NavArea_Default*, which means that it is not crossable.

- *Link Relative Start*: This represents the Start point of the link, relative to the position of its *Nav Link Proxy*.
- *Link Relative End*: This represents the End point of the link, relative to the position of its *Nav Link Proxy*.
- *Link Direction*: This specifies in which direction the link works. The possible options are as follows:
    - *Both Ways*: The link is bidirectional (remember that the AI needs to be equipped to traverse the Link in both directions; e.g. over a ledge, the agent needs to be able to fall from it (one direction of the link) and jump (the other direction of the link).
    - *Left to Right*: The link is only crossable from the Left end to the Right one (the agent still needs to have the ability to go in that link direction).
    - *Right to Left*: The link is only crossable from the Right end to the Left one (the agent still needs to have the ability to go in that link direction).

> Although the options of this parameter label the end points of the link as *Left* and *Right*, they refer to the *Start* and *End* point of the link. Alternatively (this may be better since the link can be bidirectional), *Link Relative Start* and *Link Relative End* refer to *Left* and *Right*.

- *Link Enabled*: This is a boolean variable that determines whether the *Smart Link* is enabled. This value can be changed at runtime, and the link can "*notify*" surrounding agents/actors that are interested in such information (see later for more info). The default value is true.
- *Smart Link Is Relevant*: This is a boolean variable that determines whether the *Smart Link* is actually "*active*", that is, if it is relevant or whether we should ignore it. The default value is false.

These are the main settings regarding a Smart Link.

It's worth mentioning that *Smart Links* can actually do more than just connect Nav Meshes. They have a series of functions to handle agents that are traversing the Link. For instance, by opening the `NavLinkProxy.h` file, we can find the following functions:

```
/** called when agent reaches smart link during path following, use
ResumePathFollowing() to give control back */
    UFUNCTION(BlueprintImplementableEvent)
    void ReceiveSmartLinkReached(AActor* Agent, const FVector& Destination);

    /** resume normal path following */
```

```
UFUNCTION(BlueprintCallable, Category="AI|Navigation")
void ResumePathFollowing(AActor* Agent);

/** check if smart link is enabled */
UFUNCTION(BlueprintCallable, Category="AI|Navigation")
bool IsSmartLinkEnabled() const;

/** change state of smart link */
UFUNCTION(BlueprintCallable, Category="AI|Navigation")
void SetSmartLinkEnabled(bool bEnabled);

/** check if any agent is moving through smart link right now */
UFUNCTION(BlueprintCallable, Category="AI|Navigation")
bool HasMovingAgents() const;
```

Unfortunately, these functions are outside the scope of this book, but I invite you to read the code to learn more about them.

Previously, we mentioned that the *Smart Link* can broadcast information regarding its status change at runtime to nearby agent/actors. You can change how the *Smart Link* broadcasts this information with the **Broadcast** settings, which are just below the *Smart Link* ones:

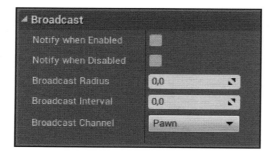

These settings are quite intuitive, but let's go through them quickly:

- **Notify when Enabled**: If true, the Link will notify agents/actors when it gets *Enabled*.
- **Notify when Disabled**: If true, the Link will notify agents/actors when it gets *Disabled*.
- **Broadcast Radius**: This specifies how far the broadcast should go. Every agent that is outside this radius will not get notified about the change of the Link.
- **Broadcast Interval**: This specifies after how long the Link should repeat the broadcast. If the value is zero, the broadcast is repeated only once.
- **Broadcast Channel**: This is the trace channel for broadcasting the change.

This concludes our discussion on *Smart Links*.

## Other settings of the Nav Link Proxy

Finally, it's just worth mentioning that the *Nav Link Proxy* can create an *Obstacle Box* when the *Nav Mesh* is generated. You can find these settings in the *Details Panel* of the *Nav Link Proxy*, as shown in the following screenshot:

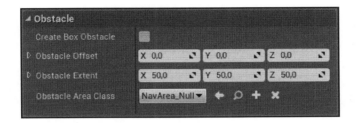

These settings allow you to decide whether the *Obstacle Box* is active/used, its *dimension/extent* and its offset, as well as the type of *Nav Area*.

## Extending the Nav Link Proxy

If you are wondering whether it is possible to extend *Links* or include them within more complex actors, the answer is *"Of course, Yes! But you can only extend them in C++"*.

Since this book cannot cover everything, we don't have the time to deal with this in detail. However, some of the reasons why you may want to extend the *Nav Link Proxy* are to have a better control over the characters that enter your Link. For instance, you might want to have a *Jump Pad* that pushes the character through the Link. This isn't very complicated to do, and if you search for this online, you will find plenty of tutorials on how to do this using *Navigation Links*.

Just keep in mind that to be a good AI programmer in Unreal, you will eventually need to master this part of *Nav Links* as well, but for now, we are covering enough.

# Navigation Avoidance

Navigation Avoidance is a very broad topic, and Unreal has some subsystems that do this for us. Therefore, we will deal with this topic in `Chapter 6`, *Crowds*.

# Navigation Filtering

We don't want to find a certain path in the same way every time. Imagine that our AI agent uses a power up and it is able to move through the jungle twice as fast. In this case, the Navigation System is not aware of this change, nor is it a permanent change to the shape or weights of the *Nav Mesh*.

*Nav Filtering* allows us to define specific rules on how to perform the pathfind for that specific period of time. You may have noticed that every time we perform a navigation task, either in Blueprint or C++, there is an optional parameter for inserting a *Nav Filter*. Here are some examples of Blueprint nodes (the same goes for C++ functions) that have this optional filter parameter:

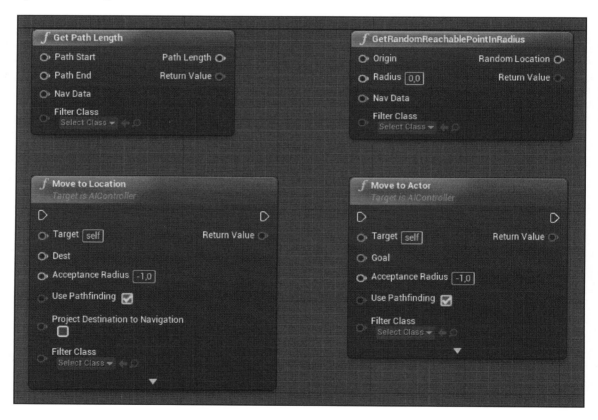

Even the *Move To* nodes of *Behavior Trees* have the *Navigation Filter* option:

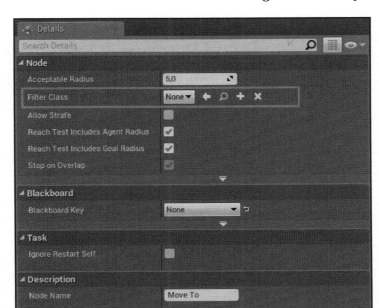

Of course, once you have inserted a filter, the pathfinding will behave accordingly. This means that using *Nav Filters* is pretty straightforward. However, how can we create *Nav Filters*? Let's find out, both in Blueprint and C++.

## Creating a Navigation Filter in Blueprint

Previously in this chapter, we created a Jungle area in Blueprint. Thus, this seems like a good example that we can use to create a *Nav Filter* that allows the AI Agent to travel through the Jungle faster – even faster than it takes to traverse the *Default Area* of the *Nav Mesh*. Let's imagine that the AI Agent has some power or ability that allows it to move faster in Jungle type areas in the level.

To create a *Nav Filter* in Blueprint, we need to start creating a new Blueprint that inherits from *NavigationQueryFilter*, as shown in the following screenshot:

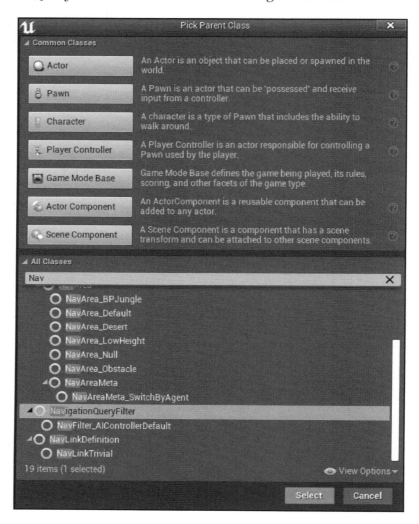

By convention, the name of the class should start with "*NavFilter_*". We will rename it to *NavFilter_BPFastJungle* (I added BP so that I can remember that I created this with Blueprint, since we are repeating the same task in Blueprint and in C++). This is what it should look like in the *Content Browser*:

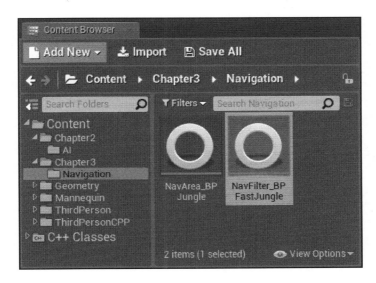

Once we open the Blueprint, we will find its options in the *Details* panel:

As you can see, there is an **Array of Areas** and two sets for *Including and Excluding (Nav) Flags*. Unfortunately, we didn't cover *Nav Flags* since they are out of the scope of this book, and they can only be assigned in C++ at the time of writing. However, the **Array of Areas** is quite interesting. Let's add a new Area and use our **NavArea_BPJungle** for the **Area Class**, as shown in the following screenshot:

Now, we can override the **Travel Cost** and the **Entering Cost** for the Jungle Area, which will be used instead of the costs we specified in the Area Class if this filter is used. Remember to tick the checkbox next to the option's name to enable editing. For example, we could have a **Travel Cost** of **0.6** (since we can move through the Jungle quickly without any issues) and an **Entering Cost** of *zero*:

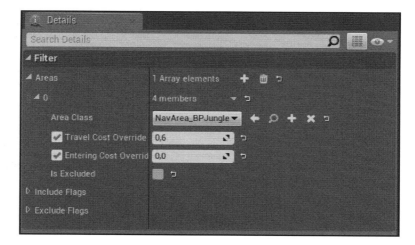

Now, we are all good to good. The filter is ready for if you prefer traveling in the Jungle!

 **Changing the Travel Cost for a Nav Area DOESN'T make the AI agent go faster or slower in that area**, it just makes pathfinding prefer that path over another. The implementation that the agent becomes faster in that area is left out from the *Navigation System*, and so you will need to implement that when the AI character is in the jungle.

If you also followed the C++ part for the *Nav Areas*, then you should also have the Desert area in your project. As an optional step, we can add a second area to the filter. Imagine that by using the power-up or ability to move faster in the Jungle, our character has become very sensitive to the sun and very prone to sunburns, which decreases their health significantly. As a result, we can set a higher cost for the *Desert Area* if this filter is used. Just add another Area, and set the **Area Class** to **NavArea_Desert**. Then, override the costs; for instance, a **Travel Cost** of **2.5** and an **Entering Cost** of **10**:

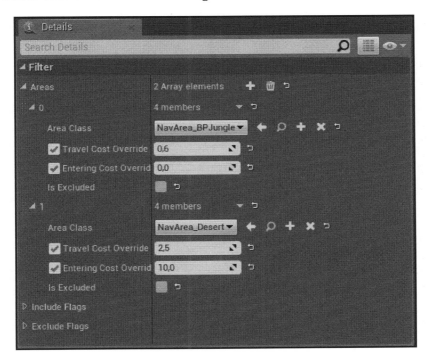

Once you have finished editing the settings, save the Blueprint. From now on, you will be able to use this filter within the *Navigation System*. This concludes how to create a *Nav Filter* in Blueprint.

# Creating a Navigation Filter in C++

In a similar way to Blueprint, we can create a C++ *Nav Filter*. This time, we can create a filter that slightly lowers the cost for the Desert Area. You can use this filter on certain animals that live in the desert and will be less prone to its effects.

To start, we need to create a new C++ class that inherits from *NavigationQueryFilter*, as shown in the following screenshot:

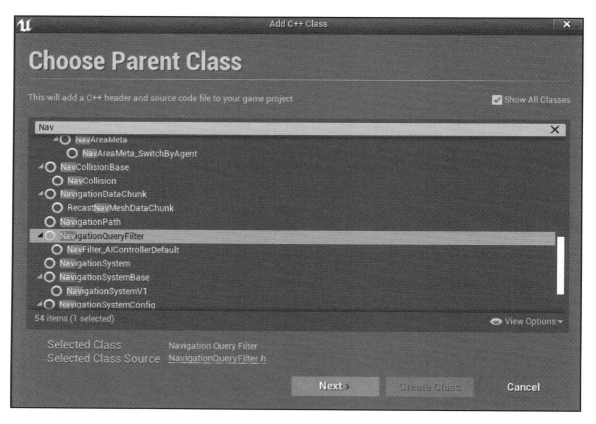

By convention, the name of the class should start with "*NavFilter_*". Hence, we will rename it to *NavFilter_Desert Animal* and place it in "*Chapter3/Navigation*":

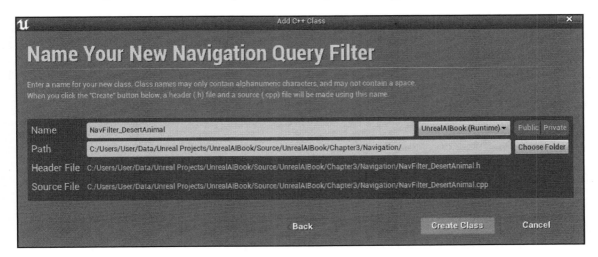

To set its properties, we need to create a default constructor. Write the following in the header (.h) file:

```
#include "CoreMinimal.h"
#include "NavFilters/NavigationQueryFilter.h"
#include "NavFilter_DesertAnimal.generated.h"

/**
 *
 */
UCLASS()
class UNREALAIBOOK_API UNavFilter_DesertAnimal : public
UNavigationQueryFilter
{
    GENERATED_BODY()

    UNavFilter_DesertAnimal();
};
```

For the implementation (.cpp file), we need to do a bit more work. First of all, we need to have access to the *Nav Area* that we need, which, in this case, is the Desert. Let's add the following #include statement:

```
#include "NavArea_Desert.h"
```

Then, in the constructor, we need to create a ***FNavigationFilterArea***, which is a class that contains all the options for filtering a specific class. In our example, we can store this new *Filter Area* inside a variable named Desert:

```
UNavFilter_DesertAnimal::UNavFilter_DesertAnimal() {

    //Create the Navigation Filter Area
    FNavigationFilterArea Desert = FNavigationFilterArea();

    // [REST OF THE CODE]
}
```

Next, we need to fill the Desert variable with the options that we want to override for that class, including which ***Nav Area*** we are modifying:

```
UNavFilter_DesertAnimal::UNavFilter_DesertAnimal() {

    // [PREVIOUS CODE]

    //Set its parameters
    Desert.AreaClass = UNavArea_Desert::StaticClass();

    Desert.bOverrideEnteringCost = true;
    Desert.EnteringCostOverride = 0.f;

    Desert.bOverrideTravelCost = true;
    Desert.TravelCostOverride = 0.8f;

    // [REST OF THE CODE]
}
```

Finally, we need to add this *Filter Area* in the ***Areas*** array:

```
UNavFilter_DesertAnimal::UNavFilter_DesertAnimal() {

    // [PREVIOUS CODE]

    //Add it to the the Array of Areas for the Filter.
    Areas.Add(Desert);
}
```

For your convenience, here is the full .cpp file:

```cpp
#include "NavFilter_DesertAnimal.h"
#include "NavArea_Desert.h"

UNavFilter_DesertAnimal::UNavFilter_DesertAnimal() {

  //Create the Navigation Filter Area
  FNavigationFilterArea Desert = FNavigationFilterArea();

  //Set its parameters
  Desert.AreaClass = UNavArea_Desert::StaticClass();

  Desert.bOverrideEnteringCost = true;
  Desert.EnteringCostOverride = 0.f;

  Desert.bOverrideTravelCost = true;
  Desert.TravelCostOverride = 0.8f;

  //Add it to the the Array of Areas for the Filter.
  Areas.Add(Desert);
}
```

Compile this code and you will be able to use this filter next time you need to use the *Navigation System*. This concludes our discussion on *Navigation Filters*.

# Overriding the Navigation System

From the *Mode Panel*, you are able to drag into the level a special actor called *Nav System Config Override*.

This actor allows you to override the built-in *Navigation System* by using another one. Of course, you will have to develop it first, and this would need a lot of effort.

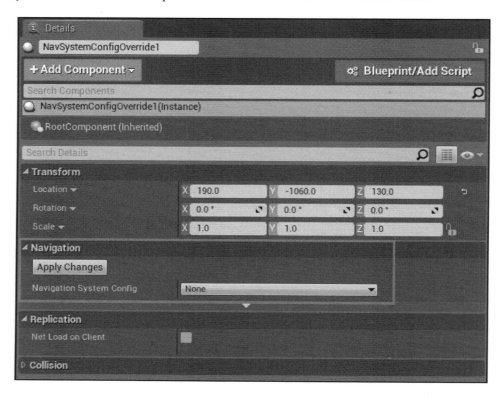

Reasons why you should substitute the default Navigation System (or maybe used along with another one) is mainly due to overcome limitations. What about air-units; how can they do a 3D Pathfinding? How about spiders who have a surface pathfinding?

# Summary

In this chapter, we looked at how we can set up the *Navigation System* so that our AI character can move around the map. In particular, we have learned how we can shape the *Nav Mesh* with *Modifier Volumes*, *Nav Link Proxies*, and *NavMesh Areas*.

As a result, our AI agents can smoothly navigate through the map, efficiently finding a path between two points that is optimized based on their capabilities (e.g. using *Navigation Filters*) by respecting the varies types of "*terrains*" of the map (e.g. using *Navigation Areas*). Moreover, they can fall over ledges or jump between platforms (e.g. by using *Nav Link Proxies* and a bit of coding for jumping).

In the next chapter, we are going to learn about a more advanced AI feature in the Unreal Framework, that is, the *Environment Querying System*, which allows the agent to "*query*" the environment so that they can find locations (or actors) with specific requisites.

# Environment Querying System 4

*A good leader knows which place is good, and EQS knows better!*

Welcome to `Chapter 4`, *Environment Querying System*. In this chapter, we are going to use a specific, yet very powerful, system within the Unreal AI Framework. I'm talking about the **Environment Querying System (EQS)**. We will explore the system and will understand not only how it works, but how to use it effectively in our games.

Once again, **EQS** falls into the realm of *Decision-Making*, and, in particular, evaluating which is the best place (or actor, in the context of Unreal) to satisfy certain conditions. We will see how it works in detail through this chapter, but as an anticipation of what we will cover, know that the system filters offer different possibilities, and the remaining ones assign a score. The choice that has the highest score is selected.

In particular, we will cover the following topics:

- How to enable the *Environment Querying System (EQS)*
- Understanding *how EQS works*
- Learning about *Generators*, *Tests*, and *Contexts*
- Exploring the *built-in Generators*, *Tests*, and *Contexts* of *EQS*
- *Extending EQS* with custom *Generators*, *Tests*, and *Contexts*

So, let's dive in!

# Enabling the Environment Querying System

EQS is a feature that was introduced way back to Unreal 4.7, and improved a lot in 4.9. However, in version 4.22, EQS is listed as an experimental feature, despite it being successfully used in many games, thus revealing that EQS is robust.

As a result, we need to enable it from the *Experimental* features settings. From the top menu, go to **Edit | Editor Preferences...**, as shown in the following screenshot:

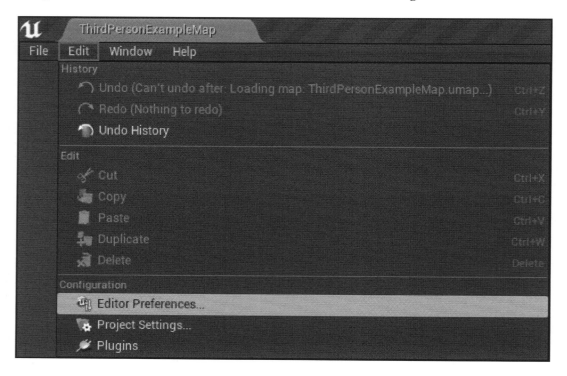

 Be careful that you don't get confused with the *Project Settings*. From the top menu, above the *Viewport*, you only have access to the *Project Settings*. However, from the top menu of the whole editor, you will be able to find *Editor Preferences*. The preceding screenshot should help you locate the right menu (that is, the *Edit* drop-down menu).

From the lateral menu, you will be able to see a section named **Experimental** (under the **General** category), as highlighted in the following screenshot:

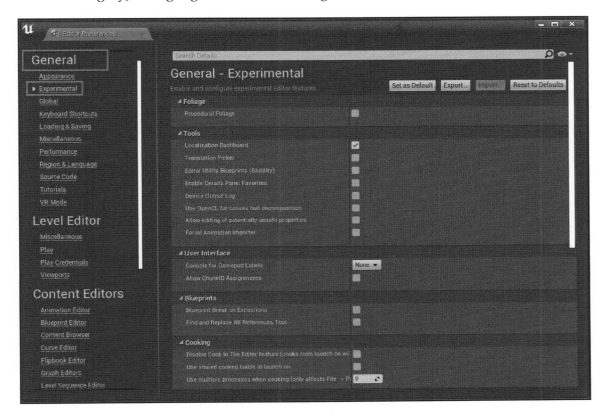

If you scroll down through the settings, you will find the AI category, in which you are able to enable the **Environment Querying System**:

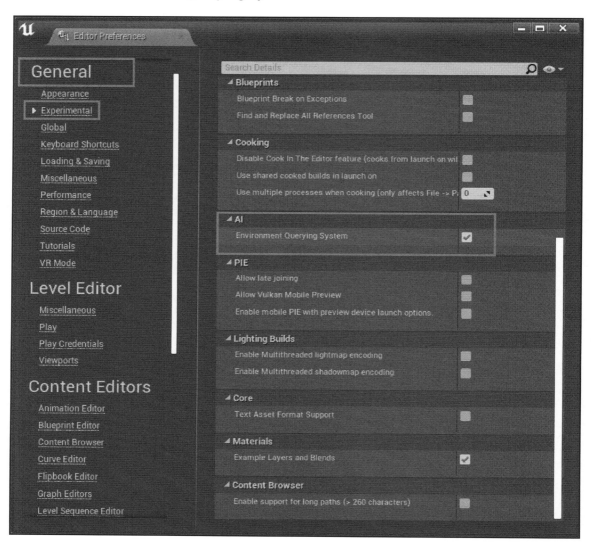

Check the box next to this option and, as a result, the *Environment Querying System* will be activated in the whole project. Now, you will be able to create assets for it (as well as extend it) and call it from a *Behavior Tree*.

> In case you are unable to see the *Environment Querying System* checkbox within the *AI category*, it's likely you are using a recent version of the engine in which (finally) *EQS* is not experimental anymore, and so it is always enabled within your project. If this is your situation, then skip this section and move on to the next one.

# Understanding the Environment Querying System

When people face EQS for the first time, it might seem overwhelming, especially because it is unclear how the different parts of the system work and why. The aim of this section is to improve your understanding of the system by getting you familiar with the underlying workflow of EQS, which will help you with the actual workflow when you create a query.

## The general mechanism of EQS

Imagine that, at a certain point, our AI agent is under fire, and it needs to evaluate different places for cover. One place might be far but well protected, whereas another one might be very close but not well protected. What should we do?

One way to solve this problem is by using *Utility Functions* and solving equations in time (we will discuss them in more detail in `Chapter 14`, *Going Beyond*). Actually, this produces very good results, and it is successfully implemented in many games. However, Unreal offers another possibility: EQS. This being said, it's not mandatory to use EQS instead of utility functions, but EQS as part of the AI framework makes it easy to evaluate such decisions since it is a built-in system.

So, coming back to our agent in need of a cover, a *Behavior Tree* will run an EQS query, which will give the final result of the place where the agent should get cover. Now, how does an Environment Query work?

First of all, a component (called a Generator, which we will look at in a moment) will generate a series of locations (or agents, which we will look at later in this chapter) according to some criteria specified in the Tests (we will get to them in a moment). For instance, we can take different positions on a uniform grid, which is very handy when we don't know which kind of locations we are searching for in advance (before evaluation).

Then, there is a filtering process for possible locations (or actors), in which it eliminates all that do not satisfy a certain criteria. In our cover example, any place that is still exposed to direct fire should be discarded.

The remaining places are evaluated (the system assigns them a score), based on other criteria. Again, in our cover example, this might be the distance from the agent, how much cover they offer, or how close to the enemy the place is. The system assigns a score by taking into consideration all of these factors (and, of course, some will be weighted more than others; e.g. protection from fire might be more important than the distance from the enemy's location).

Finally, the location (or actor) with the highest score is given from the query to the *Behavior Tree*, which will decide what to do with it (e.g. flee quickly to that place to take cover).

# The components of an Environment Query

Based on the mechanism we described in the previous section, let's dig deeper into how the actual implementation of the EQS in Unreal works.

At a high level, we have *Environment Queries*, *Contexts*, *Generators*, and *Tests*.

## Environment Queries

As the name suggests, an **Environment Query** is a data structure (similar to a *Behavior Tree*) that holds information regarding how the query should be performed. In fact, it is an asset that you can create and find within your *Content Browser*.

You can create a new **Environment Query** by right-clicking on your *Content Browser* and then **Artificial Intelligence | Environment Queries,** as shown in the following screenshot:

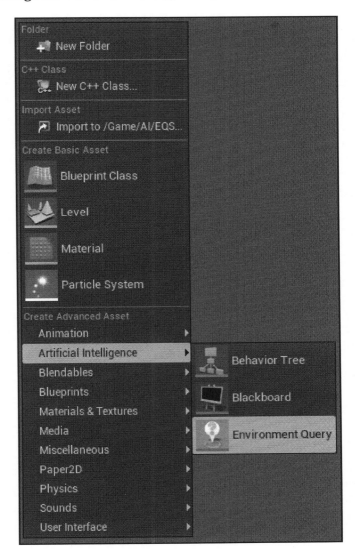

 Keep in mind that this option will not appear if EQS is not enabled.

This is what it looks like in the *Content Browser*:

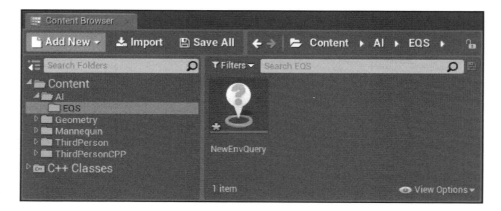

If we double-click on it to open it, Unreal opens a specific and **dedicated editor** for *Environmental Queries*. This is what the Editor looks like:

Editor view

As you can see, it is very similar to a *Behavior Tree*, but you can only attach a Generator node to the *Root* node (only one), which results to be a leaf as well. Therefore, the whole "*tree*" will be just the *Root* node with a *Generator*. In fact, by using a *Behavior Tree*-like editor, you can easily set up an *Environmental Query*. On the (unique) *Generator* node, you can attach one or more *Tests*—either the Generator itself, or Contexts. Here is an example:

Editor view

We will understand what this means in the next section.

# Contexts

Contexts are children of a particular and handy class that retrieves information. You can create/extend a *Context* either through Blueprint or by using C++.

The reason why they are called contexts is because they provide a context to either a Generator or to a Test. By having a context, the Generator (or the Test) is able to perform all the calculations, starting from that point. If you prefer, a context can be thought of as a special (and very articulated) variable that is able to procedurally pass a set of interesting Actors and/or locations.

Let's look at an example so that we're clear about what **Contexts** are. While performing a *Test*, you usually know where the **Querier** (e.g. the agent who needs the cover) is located (under the hood, even if the *Querier* is a default context). However, our test might need the location of our enemies (e.g. to check whether a cover spot is under fire or not, since it depends on the position of the enemies of our agent). **Contexts** can provide all of this information, and can do so in a procedural way: for instance, the agent might not be aware of every enemy of the map, so the **Context** might return only the enemies that the agent is currently aware of, so it only finds cover from those. Therefore, if there is a hidden enemy where it's chose to take cover, then it's tough luck for our agent!

Understanding **Contexts** is not easy, so stick through this chapter, and maybe re-read the previous paragraph at the end, when you have a better idea of what Generators and Tests are, as well as how to build an *EQS* in our project.

## Generators

*Generators*, as the name suggests, generate an initial set (or array) of locations (or actors). This set will be filtered and evaluated by Tests.

The way to generate the initial set is completely free. If you have some important information regarding the place you are looking for before the evaluation stage, then you can create a custom **Generator** (for example, don't check places with water if the agent is unable to swim, or don't consider flying enemies if the only available attack is melee).

Like *Contexts*, **Generators** are children of a specific class. You can create Generators in Blueprint as well as in C++.

 Usually, the most used generator is the grid one, which will generate a uniform grid around a context (e.g. around the agent). By doing this, the agent will check more or less all of its surroundings.

# Tests

*Tests* are responsible to both *Filtering* and *Assigning a Score (Evaluating)* to the different locations (or actors) that are generated by the *Generator*. A single *Test* can filter and score on the same criteria, as well as just one of the two.

In the case of *Tests* that use *Filtering,* they try to identify which locations (or Actors) are not suitable for our criteria. EQS is optimized, so it performs the *Tests* in a specific order to try and detect unsuitable places early on. It does this so that it doesn't assign a score that won't be used.

Once all of the locations (or Actors) have been filtered out, the remaining ones are evaluated. Thus, *each Test* that *is able to assign a score* is called (*executed*) on the location (or Actor) to report the evaluation in the form of a score (which can be positive or negative).

As a side note, *Tests* need (at least) a *Context* to properly *filter* and *evaluate.*

Let's look at an easy example of a Test to understand how they work. One of the most common Tests is *Distance,* that is, how far is this place (the generated we are evaluating) from a *Context*? The *Context* can be the *Querier,* or the enemy that it is attacking, or anything else. Thus, we can (for instance) filter places above or below a certain distance threshold (e.g. we might not want perfect cover places if they are too far from the Player). The **same** *Distance Test* can assign a score, depending on the distance, which can be positive (or negative) if the context is far (or close).

Moreover, a **Test** has a **Scoring Factor** that represents **the weight** of the *Test*: how important the Test is, and much influence this *Test* needs to have when calculating the final score of the currently evaluated location (or actor). In fact, you will run many different *Tests* on the locations that are generated by the *Generator*. The *Scoring Factor* allows you to easily weigh them to determine which Test has a higher impact on the final score of the location (or actor).

Each *Test* has the following structure for its options in the *Details* panel:

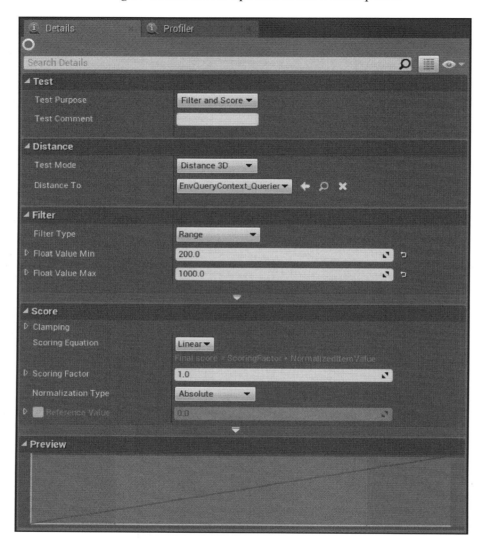

- **Test**: Here, you can select whether the **Test Purpose** is to **Filter and Score**, or just one of the two, and add a description (has no impact on the Test, but you can see it as a comment to recall what this test was about). Additionally, there might be other options, such as *Projection Data* that you can use with the *Navigation System* (for those tests that rely on the *Navigation System*).

- **Specific Test**: This is the place where the specific options for the Test are held. This varies from test to test.

- **Filter**: Here, you can select how the *Filter* behaves. This varies from test to test, but usually you are able to select a **Filter Type**, which can be a *range* (or *minimum* or *maximum*) in case the tests valuate a float as a return value; otherwise, it can be a *boolean* in the case of conditional *Tests*. This tab doesn't appear if the **Test Purpose** is set to **Score Only**.

- **Score**: Here, you can select how the *Scoring* behaves. This varies from test to test. For float return types from tests, you can select an equation for scoring, along with a normalization. Moreover, there is **Scoring Factor**, which is the weight of this test compared to the others. For boolean return values, there is just the Scoring Factor. This tab doesn't appear if the **Test Purpose** is set to **Filter Only**.

- **Preview**: This gives you a preview of what the filter and scoring function look like.

As you can see, these options are very easy to grasp, and you will understand them even better if you practice with EQS.

# Visual representation of the components

These components might not be super intuitive at the beginning, but once you get used to EQS, you will realize how they make sense, and why the system has been designed in this way.

To summarize the components and their importance, as well as to give you a visual representation, here is a diagram that you can reference:

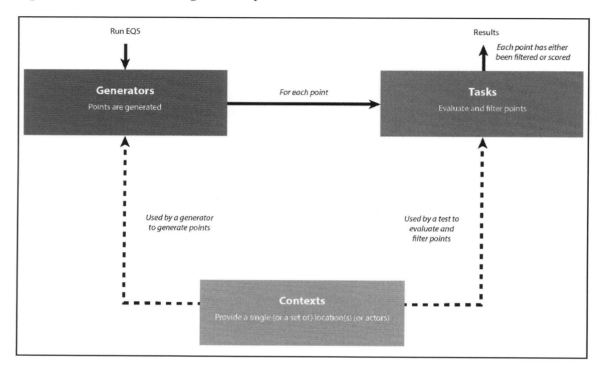

# Running an Environmental Query within a Behavior Tree

Finally, the last step to fully understanding how an *Environmental Query* works is to see how it can be run within a *Behavior Tree*.

Thankfully, we have a node named run EQS, which is a built-in Behavior Tree Task. In looks as follows in a hypothetical *Behavior Tree Editor*:

The possible settings, which can be found in the **Details** panel, are as follows:

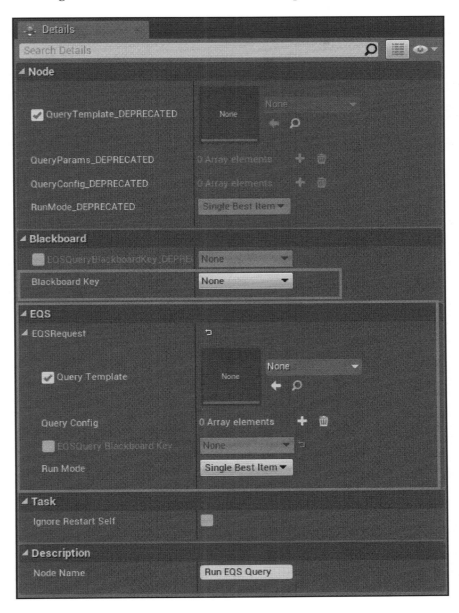

As you can see, many are deprecated (so just ignore them), but I have highlighted the ones that are the most important. Here's an explanation of them:

- **Blackboard Key**: This is the Blackboard Key Selector that references a *Blackboard Variable*, in which the result of the EQS will be stored.
- **Query Template**: A specific reference to the EQS we want to run. Otherwise, we can deactivate this option to activate an *EQSQuery Blackboard Key*.
- **Query Config**: These are optional parameters for the query (unfortunately, we won't be looking at them in detail in this book).
- **EQSQuery Blackboard Key**: A *Blackboard Key Selector* that references a *Blackboard Variable* containing an *EQS*. If activated, the *EQSQuery* contained in the *Blackboard Variable* will be executed, and not the *Query Template* one.
- **Run Mode**: This shows results of the query we are going to retrieve. The possible options are as follows:
  - **Single Best Item**: This retrieves the point (or actor) that scored the best
  - **Single Random Item from Best 5%**: This retrieves a random point among the best 5% scoring locations (or actors)
  - **Single Random Item from Best 25%**: This retrieves a random point among the best 25% scoring locations (or actors)
  - **All Matching**: This retrieves all the locations (or actors) that match the query (they haven't been filtered out)

This concludes how we can run an EQS and retrieve its result so that it can be used within a *Behavior Tree*.

 Of course, there are other ways to trigger an EQSQuery, which are not necessarily done within a *Behavior Tree*, even though this is the most common use of the EQS. Unfortunately, we will not cover other methods to run an EQSQuery in this book.

# Not only Locations, but also Actors!

I emphasised a lot when I said "…evaluating a location **(or Actor)…** ".

In fact, one of the coolest features of EQS is the possibility to evaluate not only locations, but actors as well!

Once again, you can use EQS as a decision-making process. Imagine that you need to choose an enemy to attack first. You might want to take into consideration various parameters, such as the remaining life of that enemy, how strong it is, and how much it is considered a threat in the immediate future.

By carefully setting an EQS, you are able to assign a score to each of the enemies, depending on which one is the most convenient to attack. Of course, in this situation, you might need to put in a little bit of work to create the proper Generator, along with Contexts and the proper Tests, but in the long run, it makes EQS a very good choice when the agent needs to make these kinds of decisions.

# Exploring the built-in nodes

Before we create our own Generators, Contexts, and Tests, let's talk about built-in nodes. Unreal comes with a handful of useful built-in, general-purpose nodes. We are going to explore them in this section.

 Keep in mind that this section is going to analytically explain how each of the built-in nodes of EQS works, like documentation would. So, please use this section as a reference manual if you wish, and skip sections if you are not interested in them.

## Built-in Contexts

Since we started explaining EQS by looking at *Contexts*, let's start from *built-in Contexts*. Of course, making general-purpose *Contexts* is almost a paradox, since a Context is very specific to the "*context*" (situation).

However, Unreal comes with two built-in Contexts:

- *EnvQueryContext_Querier*: This represents the Pawn that is asking the query (to be precise, it isn't the Pawn asking the Query, but the Controller that is running the *Behavior Tree* that is asking the query, and this context returns the controlled Pawn). Therefore, by using this *Context*, everything will be relative to the **Querier**.

 As I mentioned previously, under the hood, the *Querier* is indeed a *Context*.

- *EnvQueryContext_Item*: This returns all the locations that are generated by the *Generator*.

# Built-in Generators

There are many built-in *Generators*, and most of the time, these will be more than enough so that you can do most of the EQS you want. You would use *custom Generators* only when you have a specific need, or when you want to optimize the EQS.

Most of these Generators are intuitive, so I'm going to explain them in brief, and provide (when necessary) a screenshot showing the kinds of points they are generating.

 The following screenshots use a special Pawn that is able to visualize an Environment Query. We will learn how to use it later in this chapter.

This is the list of available built-in *Generators*, as you find them in the *Environmental Query Editor:*

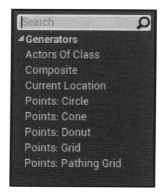

To organize this information, I'm going to split each Generator into a subsection, and I'm going to order them as they are listed in the preceding screenshot (alphabetically).

 When I refer to the Settings of a Generator, I mean, once a specific Generator has been selected, the available options for it in the *Details Panel*.

# Actors Of Class

This Generator takes all of the actors of a specific class and returns all their locations as generated points (if these actors are within a certain radius from the Context).

This is what it looks like in the *Environmental Query Editor*:

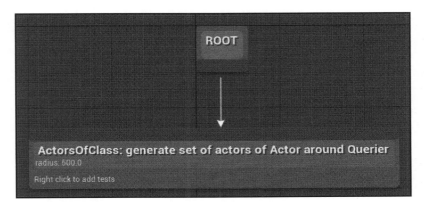

The possible options are the **Searched Actor Class** (obviously) and the **Search Radius** from the **Search Center** (which is expressed as a *Context*). Optionally, we can retrieve all the actors of a certain class and ignore whether they are within the *Searched Radius*:

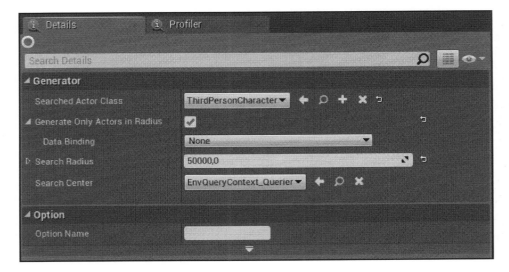

In the preceding screenshot, I used the **Querier** as the **Search Center**, a **Search Radius** of **50000**, and the **ThirdPersonCharacter** as the **Searched Actor Class**, since it is already available in the project.

By using these settings (and placing a couple of **ThirdPersonCharacter** actors), we have the following situation:

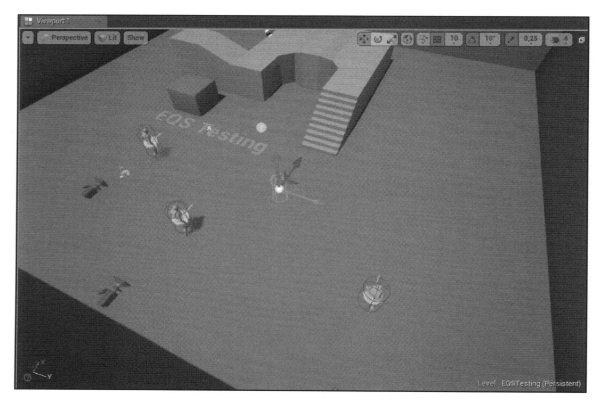

Note the (blue) sphere around the three **ThirdPersonCharacter** actors.

# Current Location

The **Current Location Generator** simply retrieve the location(s) from the *Context* and uses it (or them) to generate the points.

This is what it looks like in the *Environmental Query Editor*:

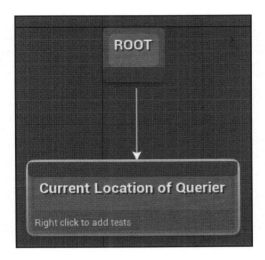

The only setting that's available for this *Generator* is **Query Context**:

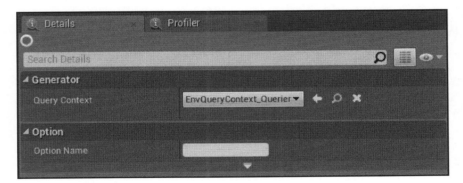

Thus, if we use the **Querier** as the **Query Context**, then we just have the location of the **Querier** itself, as shown in the following screenshot:

## Composite

The **Composite Generator** allows you to mix multiple Generators so that you have a vaster selection of points.

This is what it looks like in the *Environmental Query Editor*:

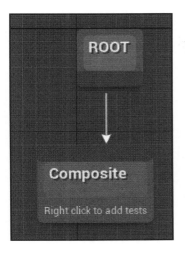

In the *Settings*, you can set an array of **Generators**:

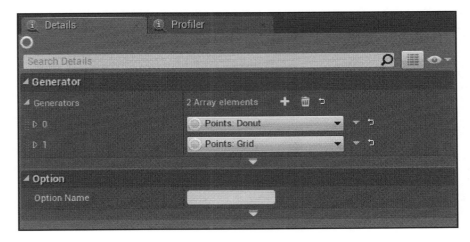

Since we don't have the time to go through everything in detail, I won't cover this Generator further.

# Points: Circle

As the name suggests, the *Circle Generator* generates the points around a circle of a specified radius. Moreover, options for interacting with the *Navmesh* are available (so that you don't generate points outside the *Navmesh*).

This is what it looks like in the *Environmental Query Editor*:

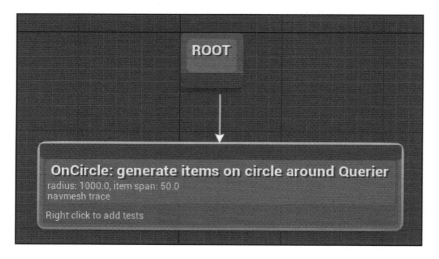

This is a very complex generator, and so there are various settings for this generator. Let's check them out:

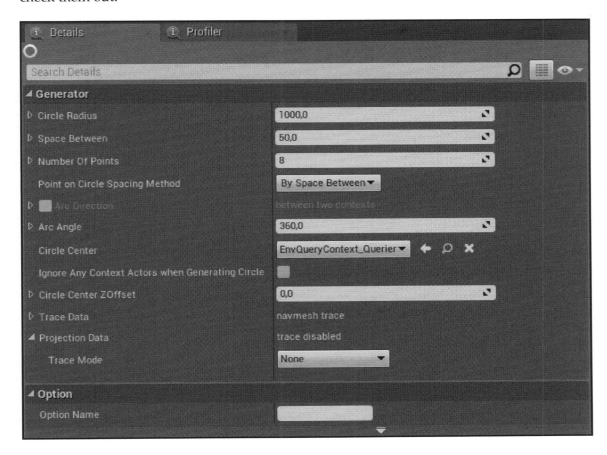

Ideally, it would be great to have a screenshot for each setting so that we can get a better feeling of how each setting affects the generation of the points. Unfortunately, this book already has many screenshots, and dedicating a chapter just to the different settings of these complex generators would take a lot of time and a lot of "*book space*". However, there is a better way for you to get the same feeling: *Experiment yourself!* Yes – once you know how to set up the *EQSTestingPawn*, you can try them out yourself and see how each setting affects the generation process. This is the best way you can learn and really understand all of these settings.

- *Circle Radius*: As the name suggests, it is the radius of the Circle.
- *Space Between*: How much space there should be between each point; if the *Point On Circle Spacing Method* is set to *By Space Between*.
- *Number of Points*: How many points should be generated; if the *Point On Circle Spacing Method* is set to *By Number of Points*.
- *Point On Circle Spacing Method*: Determines if the number of points to be generated should be calculated based on a constant number of points (*By Number of Points*), or by how many points fits the current circle if the space between the points is fixed (*By Space Between*).
- *Arc Direction*: If we are generating only an arc of the circle, this setting determines the direction this should be in. The method to calculate the direction can be either *Two Points* (it takes two *Contexts* and calculate the direction between the two) or *Rotation* (which takes a *Context* and retrieve its rotation, and based on that rotation, decides the direction of the Arc).
- *Arc Angle*: If this is different from *360*, it defines the angle of cut where the points stop being generated, thus creating an *Arc* instead of a circle. The direction (or rotation) of such an *Arc* is controlled by the *Arc Direction* parameter.
- *Circle Center*: As the name suggests, it is the center of the circle, expressed as a *Context*.
- *Ignore Any Context Actor when Generating Circle*: If checked, it will not consider the actors that are used as Contexts for the circle, thus skipping to generate points in those locations.
- *Circle Center Z Offset*: As the name suggests, it is an offset along the z-axis for the *Circle Center*.
- *Trace Data*: When generating the circle, if there is an obstacle, often, we don't want to generate the points behind the obstacle. This parameter determines the rules for doing "*horizontal*" tracing. These options are as follows:
    - *None*: There will be no trace, and all the generated points will be on the circle (or arc).
    - *Navigation*: This is the default option. Where the *NavMesh* ends is where the point is generated, even if the distance from the center is less then the Radius (in some way, the circle assumes the shape of the *NavMesh* if its boarder is encountered).
    - *Geometry*: The same as Navigation, but instead of using the *NavMesh* as a boarder, the tracing will use the Geometry of the level (this might be really useful if you don't have a *NavMesh*).
    - *Navigation Over Ledges*: The same as Navigation, but now the trace is "*over ledges*".

- ***Projection Data***: This works similarly to Trace Data, but does a *"vertical"* trace by projecting the points from above. For the rest, the concept is exactly the same as *Trace Data*. The options are ***None***, ***Navigation***, and ***Geometry***, with the same meaning these assume in *Trace Data*. *"Navigation Over Ledges"* isn't present because it wouldn't make any sense.

By using the same settings that are shown in the preceding screenshot (I'm using *Trace Data* with *Navigation*, and I have a *NavMesh* in the Level), this is what it looks like (I activated the NavMesh with the *P* key so you can see that as well):

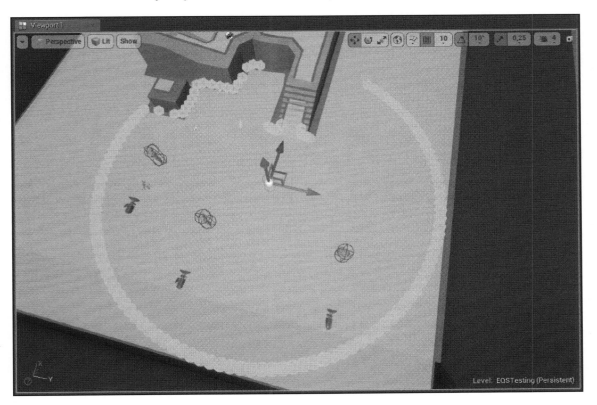

By using *Geometry* for *Trace Data* instead, we obtain a very similar, but slightly different, shape:

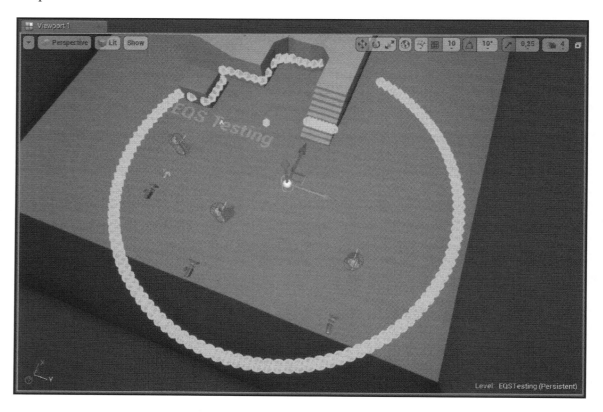

If you have a NavMesh that ends, but not the Geometry of the level, the effect is even clearer.

# Points: Cone

As the name suggests, the ***Cone Generator*** generates the points in a cone of a specific Context (like a spotlight). Moreover, options to interact with the *Navmesh* are available (so that you can project points onto the *Navmesh*).

It is important to understand that its shape is generated from many circles, from which we always take the same arc. So, if we take the whole circle, we are basically generating the points in the area of a single slice.

 This Generator can also be used to generate points to cover the area of an entire circle.

This is what it looks like in the *Environmental Query Editor*:

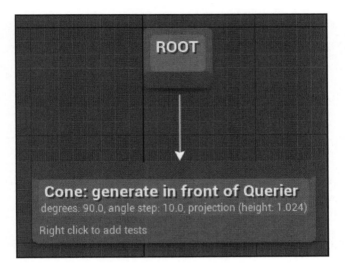

Its settings are mostly related to the shape of the cone, so let's explore them all:

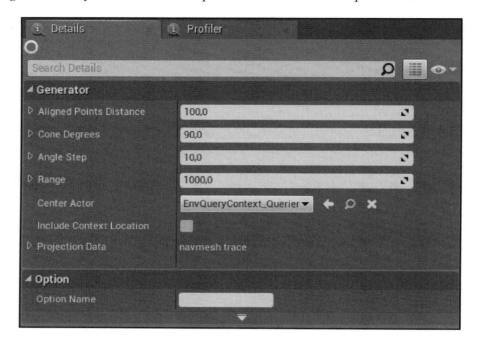

 Once again, it would be ideal to have a screenshot for each combination of settings so that you have a feeling of how each setting affects the generation of points. Because we don't have the space to do so in this book, I encourage you to experiment with an *EQSTestingPawn* so that you get a clearer understanding.

- *Aligned Points Distance*: This is the distance between each arc of the generated points (the distance between points of the same angle from the center). A smaller value generates more points, and the area that's taken into consideration will be more dense.
- *Cone Degrees*: This dictates how big the arc of each circle is (we are taking into consideration how wide the slice is). A value of 360 takes the whole area of the circle into account.
- *Angle Step*: This is the distance, expressed in degrees, between the points of the same arc. Smaller values mean more points, and the area taken into consideration will be more dense.
- *Range*: This determines how far away the cone can be (by using a spotlight as an example, how far it can illuminate).

- *Center Actor*: This is the center of the generated circles and is used to determine the cone. It is the center, and is expressed as a *Context*.
- *Include Context Location*: As the name suggests, if checked, a point will also be generated in the center of the cone/circles.
- *Projection Data*: This performs a *"vertical"* trace, by projecting the points from above by taking into consideration either the Geometry or the *Navigation Mesh*. In fact, the possible options are *None*, *Navigation*, and *Geometry*.

By using the default settings, this is what the cone might look in the level:

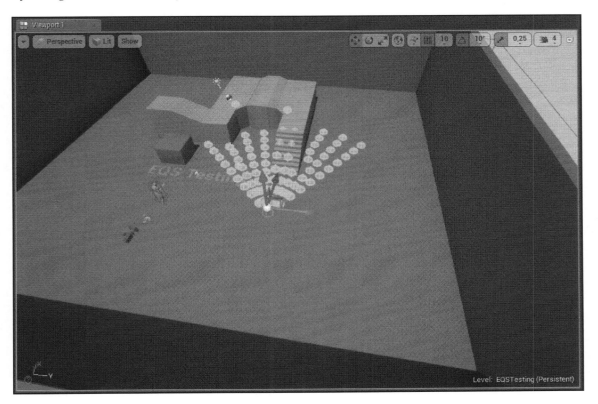

# Points: Donut

As the name suggests, the ***Donut Generator*** generates the points in a donut shape (or "*Annulus*", for those of you who are Math lovers), starting from a specific center that's given as a Context. Moreover, various options so that you can interact with the *Navmesh* are available (so that you can project points onto the *Navmesh*).

This generator can be used to generate spiral shapes as well. Just like the cone shape, this generator can be used to generate points to cover the area of a whole circle. You can do this by setting its *Inner Radius* to zero.

This is what it looks like in the *Environmental Query Editor*:

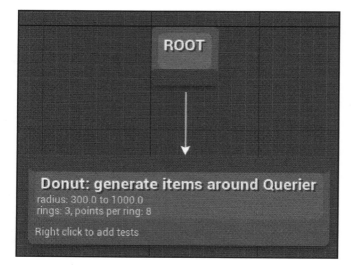

The following settings are available:

- *Inner Radius*: This is the radius of the "*hole*" of the donuts; no points will be generated within this radius (thus it's no closer to this value from the *Center*).
- *Outer Radius*: This is the radius of the whole donut; points will be generated in rings between the *Inner Radius* and the *Outer Radius*. This also means that no points will be generated beyond this radius (thus, it's further to this value from the *Center*).
- *Number of Rings*: How many rings of points should be generated in-between the *Inner Radius* and the *Outer Radius*. These rings are always evenly spaced, which means that their distance is controlled by this variable, along with the *Inner Radius* and the *Outer Radius*.
- *Points per Ring*: This dictates how many points each generated ring should have. The points are evenly spaced along the ring.

- *Arc Direction*: If we are generating only an arc of the donut (to be precise, only an arc of the circles that will generate the donut), this setting determines the direction this should be in. The method to calculate the direction can be either *Two Points* (it takes two *Contexts* and calculates the direction between the two) or *Rotation* (which takes a *Context* and retrieves its rotation, and based on that rotation, decides on the direction of the Arc).

- *Arc Angle*: If this isn't *360*, it defines the angle of cut where the points stop being generated, thus creating an *Arc* instead of a circle. The direction (or rotation) of such an *Arc* is controlled by the *Arc Direction* parameter.

- *Use Spiral Pattern*: If checked, the points in each ring are slightly offset to generate a spiral pattern.

- *Center*: This is the center of the generated rings (as well as the minimum and maximum extensions of the donut specified with *Inner Radius* and *Outer Radius*, respectively). It is expressed as a *Context*.

- *Projection Data*: This performs a *"vertical"* trace by projecting the points from above by taking into consideration either the Geometry or the *Navigation Mesh*. The possible options are *None, Navigation*, and *Geometry*.

To understand these settings, take a look at the following screenshot:

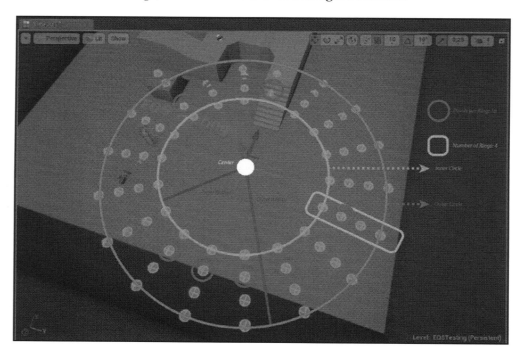

By using these slightly modified settings (please note how I increased the *Inner Radius*, bumped up the *Number of Rings* and *Points per Ring*, and also used *Navigation* for the Projection Data), it is possible to easily visualize the donut. Here are the settings I used:

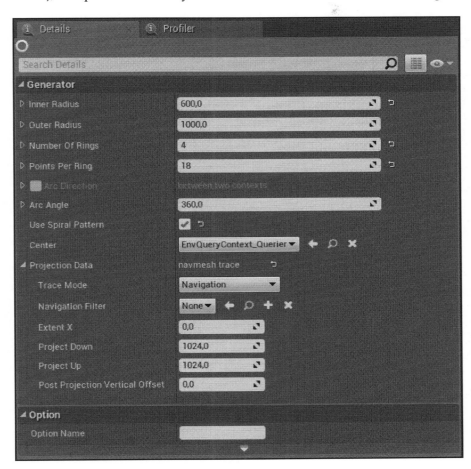

This is the result they produced:

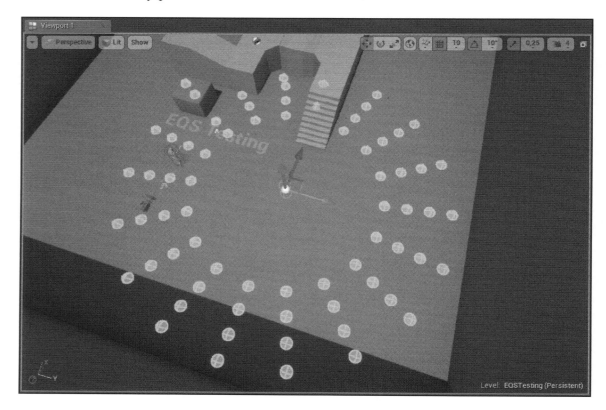

By using the same settings, and checking *Use Spiral Pattern*, you can see how the points in the different rings are slightly offset, creating a spiral pattern:

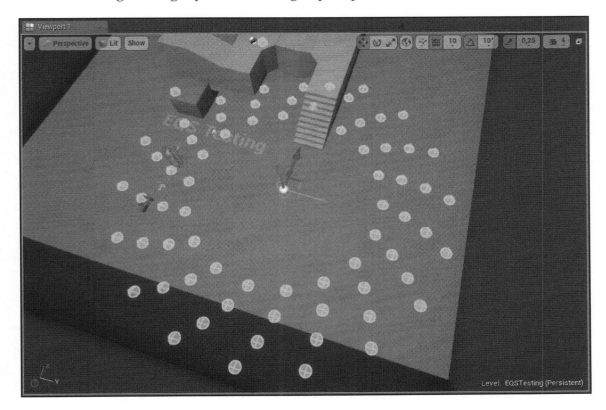

# Points: Grid

As the name suggests, the *Grid Generator* generates the points within a Grid. Moreover, options to interact with the *Navmesh* are available (so that you don't generate points outside the *Navmesh*).

This is what it looks like in the *Environmental Query Editor*:

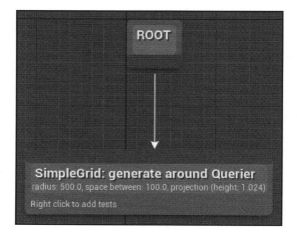

The settings for this generator are quite straightforward:

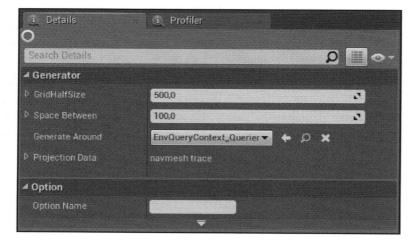

- *GridHalfSize*: How much the grid should extend from its center (which means it is half the size of the full grid). The dimensions of the grid are fully determined by this parameter, along with*Space Between*.
- *Space Between*: How much space there is between each row and column of the grid. The dimensions of the grid are fully determined by this parameter, along with*GridHalfSize*.

- *Generate Around*: This is the center of the grid (where it starts being generated), and it is expressed as a *Context*.
- *Projection Data*: This performs a *"vertical"* trace by projecting the points from above. It does this by taking into consideration either the Geometry or the *Navigation Mesh*. The possible options are *None, Navigation,* and *Geometry*.

By looking at the settings, you can see that this generator is quite simple, yet powerful and very commonly used. With the default settings, this is what it looks like in the level (the projection is enabled at Navmesh, and is present in the map):

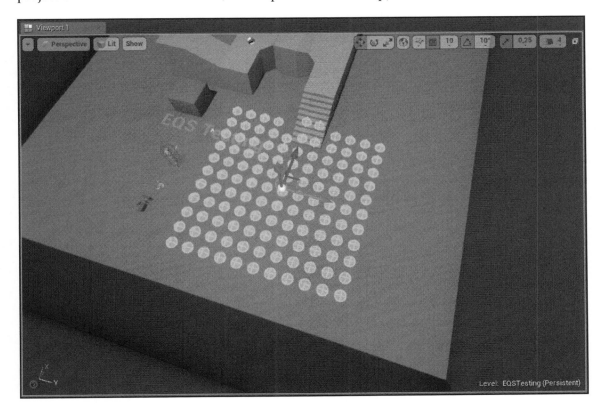

# Points: Pathing Grid

As the name suggests, the *Pathing Grid Generator* generates the points within a Grid, just like the *Grid Generator*. However, the difference in this generator lies in the fact that the *Pathing Grid Generator* check whether the points are reachable by the context specified in the *Generate Around* setting (usually the Querier), within a specified distance.

This is what it looks like in the *Environmental Query Editor*:

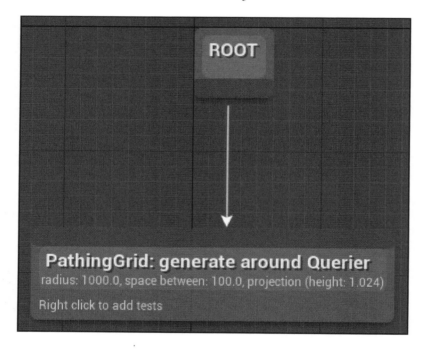

The settings for this generator are almost identical to the *Points: Grid* Generator:

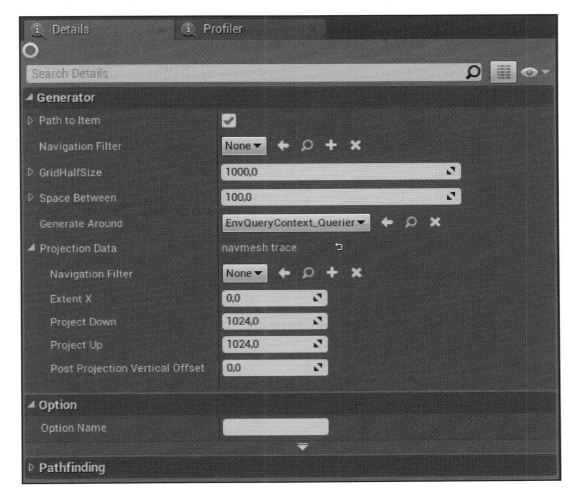

- *Path to Item*: If checked, this excludes all the points that are not reachable from the Context, in the settings of the Querier.
- *Navigation Filter*: As the name suggests, it is the navigation filter that's used to perform pathfinding.

- *GridHalfSize*: This indicates how much the grid should extend from its center (which means it is half of the size of the full grid). The dimensions of the grid are fully determined by this parameter, along with *Space Between*.
- *Space Between*: This indicates how much space there is between each row and column of the grid. The dimensions of the grid are fully determined by this parameter, along with *GridHalfSize*.
- *Generate Around*: This is the center of the grid (where it starts being generated), and is expressed as a *Context*.
- *Projection Data*: This performs a *"vertical"* trace by projecting the points from above. It does this by taking into consideration either the Geometry or the *Navigation Mesh*. The possible options are *None, Navigation,* and *Geometry*.

This is what it looks like in the environment (I changed the level slightly to block the path upstairs. This makes it clear that those points after the stairs that aren't reachable aren't even generated by this Generator):

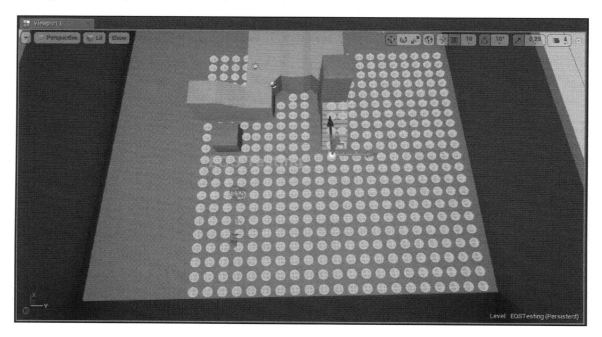

# Built-in Tests

Now that we have explored all the generators, it's time to explore the different *Tests* that are available within the engine. Usually, the return can be either a boolean or a float value.

The Tests that return a float value are most commonly used for *Scoring*, whereas the ones that return a boolean are more commonly used for *Filtering*. However, each Test might have different return values, depending on whether the Test is being used for filtering or scoring.

This is the list of the possible *Built-In Tests*; let's explore them:

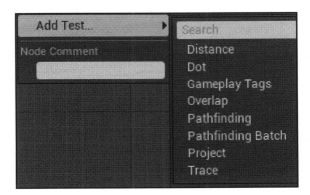

- *Distance*: Calculates the distance between the item (the point generated) and a specific *Context* (e.g. the *Querier*). It can be calculated in *3D, 2D, along z-axis*, or *along z-axis (absolute)*. The return value is a float.
- *Dot*: Calculates the dot product between *Line A* and *Line B*. Both lines can be expressed as either the *line between two Contexts* or as the *rotation of a specific Context* (by taking the forward direction of the rotation). The calculation can be done both in *3D* or *2D*.
- *Gameplay Tags*: Performs a *Query* on the *Gameplay Tags*.
- *Overlap*: Performs an overlapping test with a Box; it is possible to specify some options, such as the offset or the extend, or the overlapping channel.

- **Pathfinding**: Performs a *Pathfind* between the generated point that is being evaluated and a Context. In particular, we can specify whether the return value is a boolean (if the *Path exists*) or a float (*Path Cost* or even *Path Length*). Moreover, it is possible to specify whether the path goes from the *Context* to the *Point* or vice-versa, and it is possible to use a *Navigation Filter*.
- **Pathfinding Batch**: Same as **Pathfinding**, but in a batch.
- **Project**: Performs a *projection*, which is customizable through the different parameters.
- **Trace**: Performs a *Trace Test*, with all the possible options available to perform a Trace elsewhere in the engine. This means that it can trace a *Line*, a *Box*, a *Sphere*, or a *Capsule*; either on the *Visibility* or *Camera Trace Channel*; either complex or simple; either from the Context to the point, or vice-versa.

This concludes our exploration of the built-in nodes.

# Visualizing Environment Queries

As we mentioned previously, there is a simple built-in way to visualize **Environment Queries** within the Game World, directly from the Viewport; the game doesn't even have to be running. In fact, there is a special Pawn that it is able to do this. However, this Pawn cannot be brought directly into the level, because to ensure that it is not misused, it has been declared virtual within the code base. This means that to use it, we need to create our own *Blueprint Pawn* that inherits directly from this special Pawn.

Thankfully, after this step, the Pawn is fully featured, and it doesn't need any more code, just the parameters to work with (i.e. the *Environmental Query* you want to visualize).

To start, create a new Blueprint. The class to inherit from is *EQSTestingPawn*, as shown in the following screenshot:

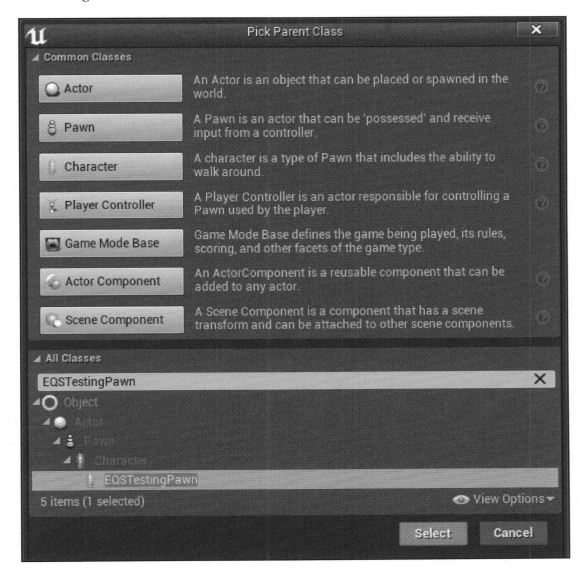

Then, you can rename it *MyEQSTestingPawn*.

If you drag it into the map, from the *Details Panel*, you can change the *EQS* settings, as shown in the following screenshot:

The most important parameter is the **Query Template**, in which you specify the query you want to visualize. If you want an in-depth break down of the parameter, check out Chapter 12, *Debugging methods for AI – Navigation, EQS, and Profiling*.

# Creating components for the Environment Querying System

In this section, we will learn which class we need to expand to create our custom components within the *Environment Querying System*.

# Creating Contexts

Creating custom *Contexts* is key in order to have the right references when you need them during an Environmental Query. In particular, we will create a simple Context to retrieve a single reference to the Player.

Let's explore how to create this *Context*, both in *C++ and Blueprint*.

## Creating the Player Context in Blueprint

To create a context, we need to inherit from the ***EnvQueryContext_BlueprintBase*** class. In the case of Blueprint, at its creation, just select the highlighted class, as shown in the following screenshot:

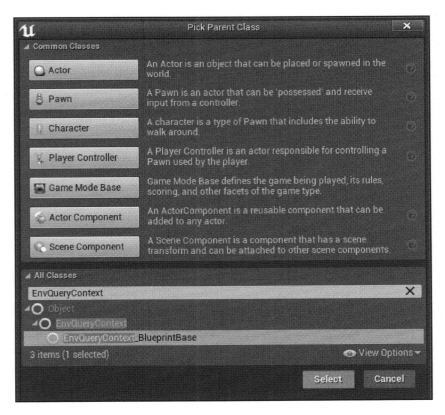

As for the name, the convention is to keep the prefix "*EnvQueryContext_*". We can call our Context something like "***EnvQueryContext_BPPlayer***".

For a Blueprint Context, you can choose to implement one of the following functions:

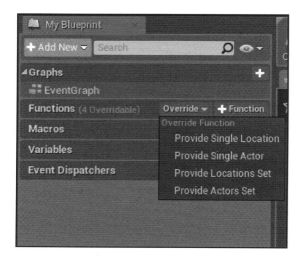

Each will provide a *Context* for the *Environmental Query*.

We can override the ***Provide Single Actor*** function and then return the Player Pawn, simple as that:

As a result, we now have a Context that is able to get a Player reference.

# Creating the Player Context in C++

In the case of creating a C++ Context, inherit from the *EnvQueryContext* class, as shown in the following screenshot:

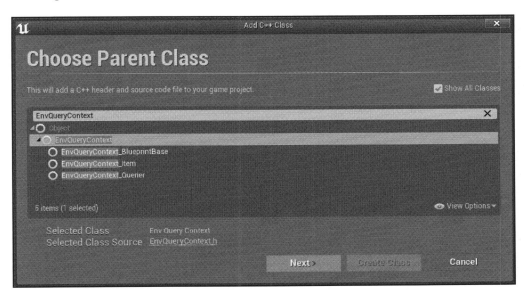

The convention is the same, that is, to prefix the Context with "*EnvQueryContext_*". We will call our class "*EnvQueryContext_Player*":

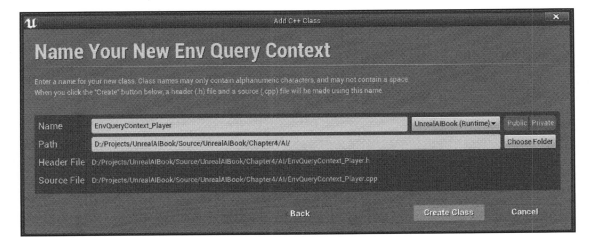

In C++, there is only one function to override: `ProvideContext()`. Hence, we just need to override it in the `.h` file, as follows:

```
#include "CoreMinimal.h"
#include "EnvironmentQuery/EnvQueryContext.h"
#include "EnvQueryContext_Player.generated.h"

/**
 *
 */
UCLASS()
class UNREALAIBOOK_API UEnvQueryContext_Player : public UEnvQueryContext
{
  GENERATED_BODY()
  virtual void ProvideContext(FEnvQueryInstance& QueryInstance,
FEnvQueryContextData& ContextData) const override;
};
```

In the implementation file, we can provide the Context. I'm not going to go into the details of how – you can read the code of the other Contexts to help you understand this. In any case, we can have something like the following for our `.cpp` file (I could have implemented this differently, but I chose this way because I thought it was easy to understand):

```
#include "EnvQueryContext_Player.h"
#include "EnvironmentQuery/EnvQueryTypes.h"
#include "EnvironmentQuery/Items/EnvQueryItemType_Actor.h"
#include "Runtime/Engine/Classes/Kismet/GameplayStatics.h"
#include "Runtime/Engine/Classes/Engine/World.h"

void UEnvQueryContext_Player::ProvideContext(FEnvQueryInstance&
QueryInstance, FEnvQueryContextData& ContextData) const
{
  if (GetWorld()) {
    if (GetWorld()->GetFirstPlayerController()) {
      if (GetWorld()->GetFirstPlayerController()->GetPawn()) {
        UEnvQueryItemType_Actor::SetContextHelper(ContextData,
GetWorld()->GetFirstPlayerController()->GetPawn());
      }
    }
  }
}
```

As a result, we are able to retrieve the Player Context in C++.

# Creating Generators

Similar to how we created Contexts, we can create custom Generators. However, we will not go through this in detail, since they are outside the scope of this book.

In the case of Blueprint, inherit from the *EnvQueryGenerator_BlueprintBase* class, as shown in the following screenshot:

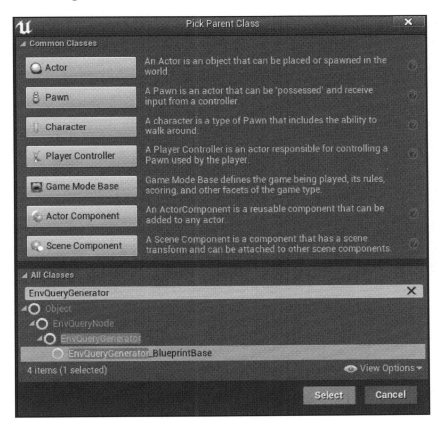

In C++, you need to inherit from *EnvQueryGenerator*:

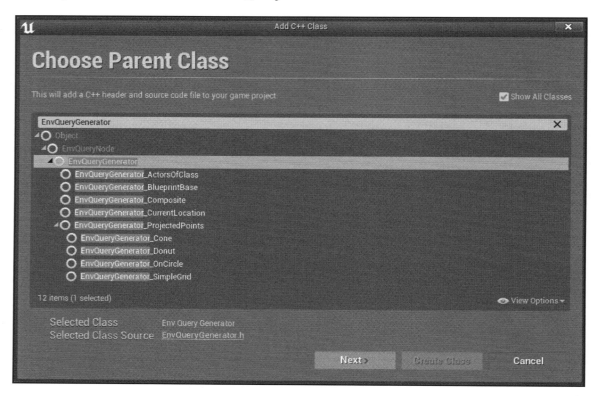

You may want to start directly from
*EnvQueryGenerator_ProjectedPoints* since you already have all the
projections in place. By doing this, you only need to focus on its
generation.

# Creating Tests

In the current version of Unreal Engine, it isn't possible to create a Test in Blueprint – we can only do so with C++. You can do this by extending the *EnvQueryTest* class:

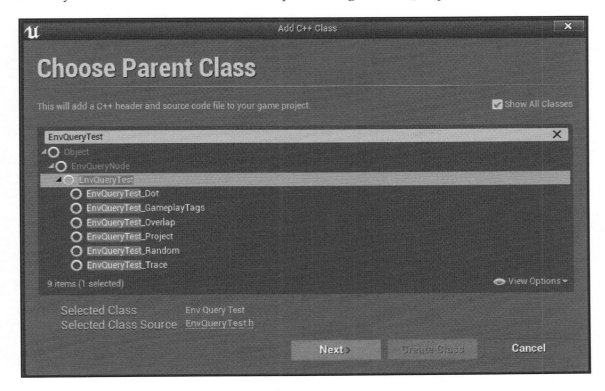

Unfortunately, this is also outside the scope of this book. Exploring the Unreal Engine Source code, however, will give you a great amount of information and an almost infinite source of learning.

# Summary

In this chapter, we explored how the *Environment Querying System* can make spatial reasoning in the Decision-Making domain.

In particular, we have understood how the whole system works in general, and then we went through the built-in nodes of the system. We also saw how it is possible to visualize a Query by using a special Pawn. Finally, we explored how it is possible to extend the system.

In the next chapter, we will explore Agent Awareness, and the built-in Sensing system.

# 5
# Agent Awareness

*You can run, but you can't hide!*

Oh, you're back? That's great, because it means that your eyes are capturing some light information that your brain is perceiving in an act that it is usually called reading. Everything we do, every decision we make, is based on what we perceive, and biologically we make short decision-making processes because time is crucial (e.g. you see a snake and your amygdala processes that information much faster and quicker than your visual cortex!).

With the same very concept, AI needs to base their decisions from facts by gathering information they need to perceive first. This chapter is all about perception, and how AI can get this information from the environment, so that it can be aware of its surroundings. We looked at EQS in the previous chapter, which gathers a lot of information about the surrounding environment and processes. Here, we will just limit ourselves to the simple act of perception. What the AI will do with that information is a topic for other chapters (and some we have already covered).

Here is a quick rundown of the topics we will face in this chapter:

- Perception and awareness in existing video games
- Overview of the Sensing System within Unreal
- Perception Component
- Senses for Sight and Hear
- Perception Stimuli
- Implementing sight in an agent (both in Blueprint and in C++)
- Implementing hearing in an agent (both in Blueprint and C++)

So, let's start by looking at some examples of AI awareness in video games, and then we will see how we can set up a Perceiving system in Unreal.

# Perception of AI in video games

It's all a matter of perception, right? But when it comes to artificial intelligence—and AI in games, in particular—perception can make all the difference between winning and losing. In other words, *how* an AI character is able to perceive a player during gameplay can create a range of different experiences, thus creating environments full of tension and suspense while you turn every corner with slow, tentative footsteps.

## Sound

Have you ever tried to sneak past a guard in a game, trying not to make a noise or get detected? This is one of the most common ways that AI perceive a player and respond accordingly (often not in your favor!). However, one of the benefits of using sounds to influence an AI's perception of a player is that it gives the player the opportunity to initiate surprise attacks (e.g. Hitman, Assassin's Creed). For example, a player can sneak up on an enemy and stun or attack them from behind, therefore providing the player with an advantage. This can be particularly helpful when enemies are challenging to defeat, or a player is low in resources (e.g. ammunition, health packs/potions, etc).

## Footsteps

Just like the preceding example suggests, one of the most common ways that AI can perceive characters via sound is through footsteps. No surprises here about how, but the proximity of detection here can depend on many factors. For example, some characters can walk while crouching to avoid detection, or simply by sneaking (e.g. *Abe's Oddyssey*); other games allow some characters to be undetectable while moving around, unless visually spotted by an enemy (e.g. Natalia in *Resident Evil: Revelations 2*). Another key ingredient in using footsteps as a trigger for an AI's perception is the type of ground material that a player is walking on. For example, a player walking through a forest, crunching on leaves and bark, is going to be a lot more obvious (and loud) than a player who is walking on sand.

# Knocking over objects

While sneaking through a level or walking while crouching, or even in the prone position (e.g. *Battlefield*), will not trigger an enemy, chances are if you knock something over (e.g. a bottle, box, random item) it's going to alert them. In this case, environmental objects play an important role in an AI's ability to perceive a player's location by simply the player themselves fumbling around an environment. In some cases, certain objects are likely to attract more attention than others, depending on how much noise they make. Of course, as game designers, you have the power to determine this!

# Position

Similar to sound, AI have the ability to see you based on your proximity to them. This one is a little more obvious and a bit harder to avoid when you are in plain sight of an enemy. Imagine that you're sneaking past an enemy and as soon as you come close enough to them, that's it, it's all over, you've been spotted! This is the unfortunate peril that many players face, but one that has many pay-offs, especially in terms of satisfaction to having outsmarted the enemy.

Let's examine this concept a little further with some examples. To begin, we have games like *Assassin's Creed*, *Hitman: Absolution*, and *Thief*, where the art of eluding your enemy through manoeuvring is paramount to the player's success in completing a mission. Often, this requires that the play leverages the environmental surroundings such as NPCs, walls, haystacks, plants (trees, bushes), rooftops, and utilizing the element of surprise.

# Zone of proximity

In other cases, there is an explicit zone of proximity that a player can remain out of before they are detected. Often, in games, this is articulated by a light source such as a flashlight, forcing the player to dance between shadow and light to avoid detection. An excellent example of games that have adopted this approach are *Monaco: What's Yours Is Mine* and *Metal Gear Solid*, where certain AI characters have a proximity of visibility via the use of torches or by simply facing you for an extended period of time.

You can see an example of this in the following screenshot:

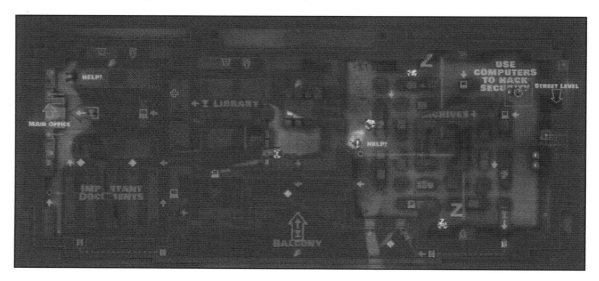

Screenshot from the game *Monaco: What's Yours Is Mine*

Here (in *Monaco: What's Yours Is Mine*), you can see the radius of the flashlights, and as soon as a player enters it, they have a limited amount of time before they grab the attention of the guards.

Since *Monaco: What's Yours Is Mine* is entirely based on this mechanic, let's look at some more screenshots to get a better feeling of how sight perception works in this game.

In the following screenshot, we can see how the perception changes when the player changes room:

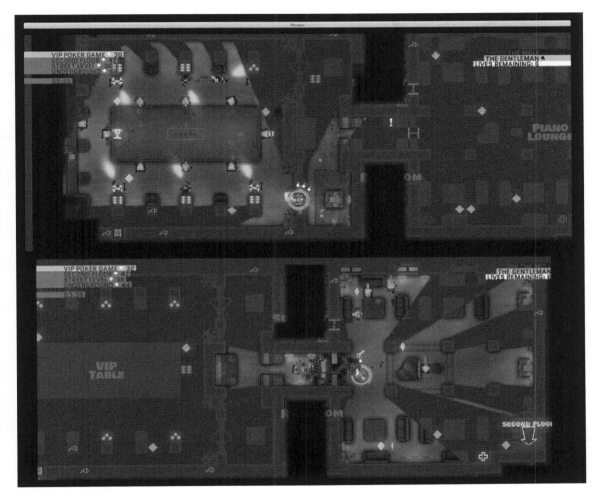

Screenshot from the game *Monaco: What's Yours Is Mine*

In the following screenshot, we have a close-up of the player's perception:

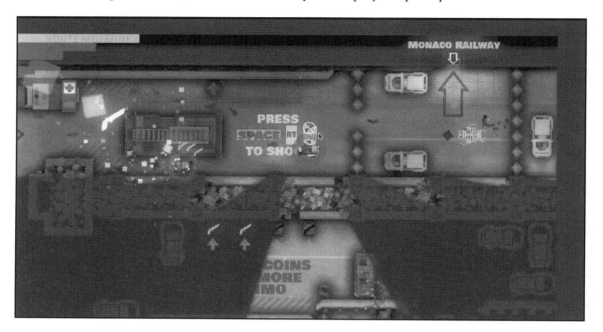

Screenshot from the game *Monaco: What's Yours Is Mine*

Then, we have a close-up of a guard's flashlight:

Screenshot from the game *Monaco: What's Yours Is Mine*

Changing game, In *Metal Gear Solid*, perception is used in a similar way with enemies (red dots) patrolling the environment around the player (white dot). In the following screenshot, you can see a camera (represented as a red dot in the *minimap*) with a yellow cone of view in the *minimap* (guards have a blue cone, instead):

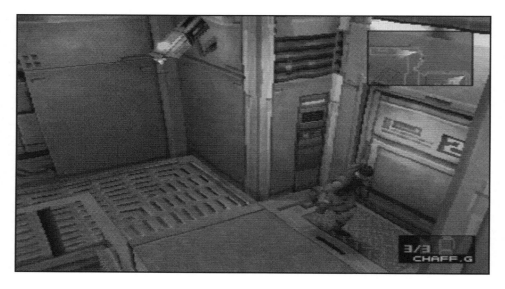

Screenshot from the game *Metal Gear Solid*

The Metal Gear Solid game series is entirely based on perception, and it is worthwhile exploring more and learning about the game if you are interested in developing game AIs with this mechanic.

Wrapping up, if you get too close to NPCs (e.g. within their range of visibility) you will be noticed, and they will try to interact with your character, whether it be good (beggars in *Assassin's Creed*) or bad (enemy attacks you), which unlocks many interesting mechanics based on perception.

# Interacting with other enemies

An AI's perception about your position isn't necessarily related to when you enter their zone of visibility. In other cases (e.g. first-person shooters), this may happen when you start to shoot an enemy. This creates a ripple effect in that many AIs within your initial proximity will then target you (e.g. Metal Gear Solid, Army of Two, Battlefield, etc.).

# It isn't all about the "enemy"

In many sporting games, AI has to be perceptive in order to respond accordingly, e.g. from preventing a goal, hitting a ball, or shooting hoops. AI within sports must be perceptive (and competitive) when it comes to playing *against* you. They need to know your location and the location of the ball (or any other object) so that they can respond (e.g. kicking the ball away from the goal posts).

# Perceptive AI isn't just humanoid or animalistic

Perceptive AI can also include machines, such as cars and other vehicles. Take the games *Grand Theft Auto*, *Driver*, and *The Getaway*, into account, these games require that a player navigates around a 3D world space at some point inside of a car. In some instances, there are NPCs inside, but for the most part, the cars themselves respond to your driving. This is also the case in more sport oriented games such as *Grand Turismo*, *Need for Speed*, and *Ridge Racer* (to name a few).

# Impact of Players

As we have seen, there are many ways in which AI can detect players. But one thing that a game designer must consider among all of this is how this will influence the game's experience; how will it drive gameplay? While the use of perceptive AI is quite a nice addition to any game, it also impacts how a game is played. For example, if you want to have gameplay that is heavily focused on skill, player dexterity, and more environmentally aware, then the perception of AI needs to be quite sensitive, with the player being a lot more vulnerable (e.g. Thief). But if, on the other hand, you want a fast-paced action game, you will need to have perceptive AI with the balance of allowing the player to respond accordingly. For example, they have a level playing field to fight against the AI.

# Overview of the Sensing System

Coming back to Unreal, as you would expect, there is a subsystem of the AI Framework that implements AI Perception. Once again, you are free to implement your own system, especially if you have particular needs...

With *Sensing and Perception*, we are collocating at a lower level than *Decision-Making* (like *Behavior Trees* and *EQS*). In fact, there is no decision to take, no place to select, but just a passage/flow of information.

If the Sensing System perceives something "interesting" (we will define what this means later), then it notifies the AI controller, which will decide what to do about the received stimuli (which is its perception, in Unreal terminology).

Therefore, in this chapter, we will focus on how to properly set up the Sensing System so that our AI can perceive, but we won't deal with what to do once we have received the stimuli (e.g. the player is in sight, so start chasing them). After all, if you already have the behavior ready (e.g. a *Behavior Tree* that chases the player; we will build such a tree later in this book), the logic behind the sensing is simple as "if the player is in sight (the AI controller received a stimuli from the Sensing system), then execute the Chasing Behavior tree".

In practical terms, the built-in sensing system of Unreal is based mainly on the use of two components: **AIPerceptionComponent** and **AIPerceptionStimuliSourceComponent**. The first is able to perceive stimuli, whereas the latter is able to produce one (but it is not the only way we can produce stimuli, as we will soon see).

 As odd as it might seem, the system believes that the AIPerceptionComponent is attached to the AI Controller (and not the Pawn/Character that they control). In fact, it's the AI Controller that will make a decision based on the stimuli received, not the mere Pawn. As a result, the AIPerceptionComponent needs to be attached directly to the AI Controller.

# The AIPerceptionComponent

Let's break down how the **AIPerceptionComponent** works. We are going to do this both in Blueprint and C++.

## AIPerceptionComponent in Blueprint

If we open our Blueprint AI Controller, we are able to add the **AIPerceptionComponent** like we would any other component: from the Components tab, click on **Add Component** and select the **AIPerceptionComponent**, as shown in the following screenshot:

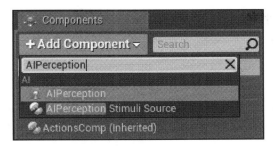

When you select the component, you will see how it appears in the *Details* panel, as shown in the following screenshot:

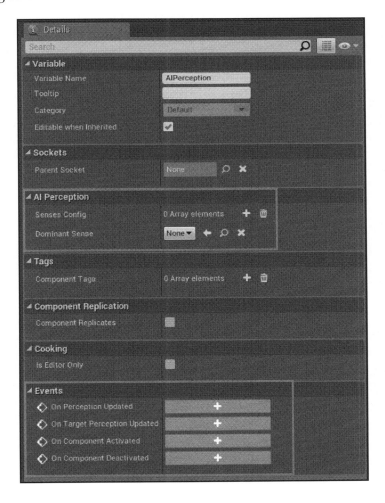

It only has two parameters. One defines the dominant senses. In fact, **AIPerceptionComponent** can have more than one sense, and when it comes to retrieving the location of the target that's been sensed, which one should the AI use? The **Dominant Sense** removes ambiguity by giving one sense priority over the others. The other parameter is an Array of senses. As you fill the Array with the different senses, you will be able to customize each one of them, as shown in the following screenshot:

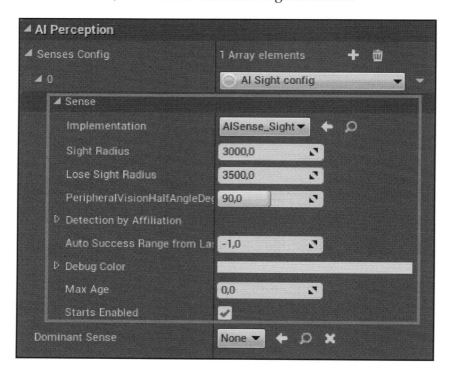

 Keep in mind that you can have more than one sense of each kind. Suppose that your enemy has two heads, facing a different direction: you might want to have two sight senses, one for each head. Of course, in this case, it requires a bit more setup to make them work correctly since you need to modify how the sight component works since, let's say, the AI always watches from its forward vector.

Each sense has its own properties and parameters. Let's go through the two main ones: sight and hearing.

# Sense – Sight

The Sight sense works as you would expect, and it comes pretty ready out of the box (this might not be true for other senses, but sight and hearing are the most common). This is what it looks like:

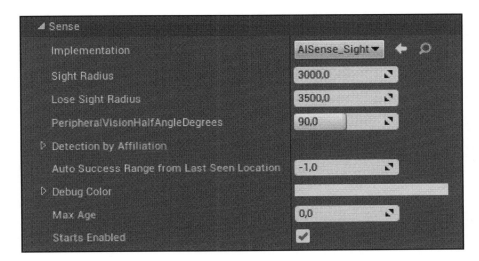

Let's break down the main parameters that control sense of Sight:

- **Sight Radius**: If a target (an object that can be seen) enters within this range, and it is not occluded, then the target is detected. In this sense, it is the "*Maximus sight distance to notice the target*".
- **Lose Sight Radius**: If the target has already been seen, then the target will be still seen within this range, if not occluded. This value is greater than *Sight Radius*, meaning that the AI is able to perceive the target at a greater distance if it is already seen. In this sense, it is the "*Maximus sight distance to notice a target that has already been seen*".
- **PeripheralVisionHalfAngleDegrees**: As the name suggests, it specifies how far (in degrees) the AI can look. A value of 90 means (since this value is just half of the angle) that the AI is able to see everything that is in front of it up to 180 degrees. A value of 180 would mean that the AI can look in any direction; it has 360-degree vision. Also, it is important to note that this half angle is measured from the forward vector.

- The following diagram illustrates this:

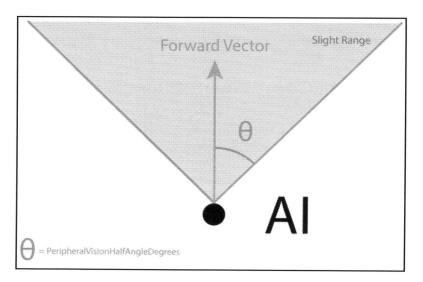

- **Auto Success Range From Last Seen**: By default, this is set to an invalid value (-1.0f), meaning that it isn't used. This specifies a range from the last seen location of a target, and if it is within this range, then the target is always visible.

There are other settings that are more general, and can be applied to many senses (including hearing, so they will not be repeated in the next section):

- **Detection By Affiliation**: *See the Different Teams* section.
- **Debug Color**: As the name suggests, it is the color with which this sense should be displayed in the visual debugger (see `Chapter 11`, *Debugging methods for AI – Logging*, for more information).
- **Max Age**: It indicates the time (expressed in seconds) that a stimulus is recorded for. Imagine that a target exits from the vision of the AI; its last location is still recorded, and it is assigned an age (how old is that data). If the Age gets bigger than the Max Age, then the stimuli are erased. For instance, an AI is chasing the player, who escapes from his/her sight. Now, the AI should first check the last position where the player has been seen to try to bring him/her back into their sight. If it fails, or the position was recorded many minutes ago, that data is not relevant anymore, and it can be erased. In summary, this specifies the age limit after the stimuli that's generated by this sense is forgotten. Moreover, a value of 0 means never.

# Sense – Hearing

The Hearing sense has just one proper parameter, which is the Hearing Range. This sets the distance at which the AI is able to hear. The others are the general ones we already have seen for Sight (e.g. *Max Age*, *Debug Color*, and *Detection By Affiliation*). This is what it looks like:

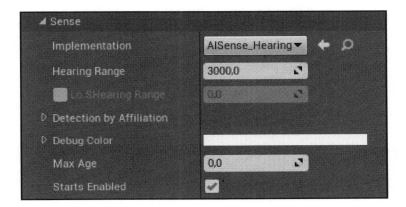

 To make this book complete, it's worth mentioning that there is another option, called *LoSHearing*. To the best of my knowledge, and by looking at the Unreal Source code (version 4.20), this parameter doesn't seem to affect anything (except debugging). As a result, we leave it as not enabled.

In any case, there are other options to control how sound is produced. Actually, the Hearing events need to be manually triggered with a special function/Blueprint node.

# AIPerceptionComponent and Senses in C++

If you skipped the previous sections, please read them first. In fact, all the concepts are the same, and in this section, I'm just going to show the use of the component in C++ without re-explaining all the concepts.

Here are the #include statements for the classes we would like to use (I only included Sight and Hearing):

```
#include "Perception/AIPerceptionComponent.h"
#include "Perception/AISense_Sight.h"
#include "Perception/AISenseConfig_Sight.h"
#include "Perception/AISense_Hearing.h"
#include "Perception/AISenseConfig_Hearing.h"
```

To add the component to a C++ AI Controller, you do so like any other component, with a variable in the `.h` file. So, to keep track of it, you can use the `inerith` variable from the base class, which is declared as follows:

```
UPROPERTY(VisibleDefaultsOnly, Category = AI)
UAIPerceptionComponent* PerceptionComponent;
```

As a result, you are able to use this variable in any *AIController*, without declaring it in the header (`.h`) file.

Then, with the `CreateDefaultSubobject()` function in the constructor in the `.cpp` file, we can create the component:

```
PerceptionComponent =
CreateDefaultSubobject<UAIPerceptionComponent>(TEXT("SightPerceptionCompone
nt"));
```

Moreover, you will need extra variables, one for each of the senses you want to configure. For example, for the Sight and Hearing senses, you will need the following variables:

```
UAISenseConfig_Sight* SightConfig;
UAISenseConfig_Hearing* HearingConfig;
```

To configure a Sense, you need to create it first, and you have access to all its properties and can set what you need:

```
//Create the Senses
SightConfig = CreateDefaultSubobject<UAISenseConfig_Sight>(FName("Sight
Config"));
HearingConfig =
CreateDefaultSubobject<UAISenseConfig_Hearing>(FName("Hearing Config"));

//Configuring the Sight Sense
SightConfig->SightRadius = 600;
SightConfig->LoseSightRadius = 700;

//Configuration of the Hearing Sense
HearingConfig->HearingRange = 900;
```

Finally, you need to bind the senses to the **AIPerceptionComponent**:

```
//Assigning the Sight and Hearing Sense to the AI Perception Component
PerceptionComponent->ConfigureSense(*SightConfig);
PerceptionComponent->ConfigureSense(*HearingConfig);
```

```
PerceptionComponent->SetDominantSense(SightConfig->GetSenseImplementation()
);
```

In case you need to call back for the events, you can do so by bypassing the callback function (it has to have the same signature, not necessarily the same name):

```
//Binding the OnTargetPerceptionUpdate function
PerceptionComponent->OnTargetPerceptionUpdated.AddDynamic(this,
&ASightAIController::OnTargetPerceptionUpdate);
```

This concludes the use of the **AIPerceptionComponent** and **Senses** in C++.

# Different Teams

As the AI perception system that's built into Unreal goes, AIs and anything that can be detected can have a team. Some teams are against each other, whereas some are just neutral. As a result, when an AI comes to perceive something, that something can be Friendly (it is in the same team), Neutral, or an Enemy. For instance, if an AI is patrolling a camp, we can ignore Friendly and Neutral entities, and focus only on Enemies. By the way, the default settings are to perceive only enemies.

The way in which you can change which kind of entities an AI can perceive is through the *Detecting for Affiliation* settings of *Sense*:

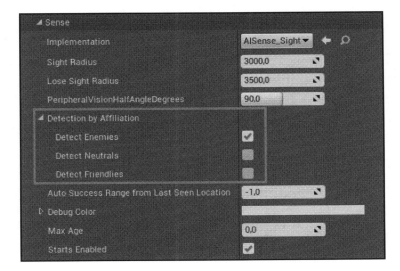

This provides three checkboxes where we can choose what we would like that AI to perceive.

There are 255 teams in total, and by default, every entity is within team 255 (the only special team). Whoever is in team 255 is perceived as Neutral (even if both the entities are in the same team). Otherwise, if two entities are in the same team (different than 255), they "see" each other as Friendly. On the other hand, two entities in two different teams (different than 255) the "see" each other as Enemies.

Now the question is, how can we change teams? Well, at the moment, this is only possible in C++. Moreover, we have talked about entities, but who can actually be in a team? Everything that implements the **IGenericTeamAgentInterface** can be part of a team. *AIControllers* already implements it. As a result, changing teams on an AI Controller is easy, as shown in the following snippet:

```
// Assign to Team 1
SetGenericTeamId(FGenericTeamId(1));
```

For other entities, once they implement the **IGenericTeamAgentInterface**, they can override the `GetGenericTeamId()` function, which provides a way for the AI to check in which team that entity is.

# The AIStimuliSourceComponent

We have seen how an AI can perceive through a Sense, but how are the stimuli generated in the first place?

## All Pawns are automatically detected

In the case of the Sight sense, by default, all the Pawns are already a stimuli source. In fact, later in this chapter, we will use the Player character, who will be detected by the AI without having an **AIStimuliSourceComponent**. In case you are interested in disabling this default behavior, you can do so by going into your project directory, and then going inside the **Config** folder. There, you will find a file named **DefaultGame.ini**, in which you can set a series of configuration variables. If you add the following two lines at the end of the file, Pawns will not produce Sight stimuli by default, and they will need the **AIStimuliSourceComponent** as well as everything else:

```
[/Script/AIModule.AISense_Sight]
bAutoRegisterAllPawnsAsSources=false
```

In our project, we are not going to add these lines, since we want the Pawns to be detected without using having to add more components.

# AIStimuliSourceComponent in Blueprint

Like any other component, it can be added to a Blueprint:

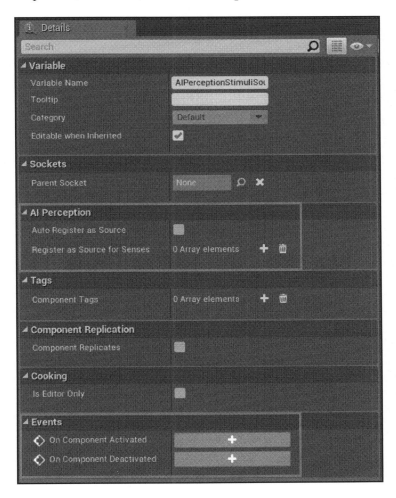

If you select it, you will see in the *Details* panel that it has just two parameters:

- **Auto Register as a Source**: As the name suggests, if checked, the source automatically registers inside the Perception system, and it will start proving stimuli from the start
- **Register as Source for Senses**: This is an array of all the senses that this component provides stimuli for

There is not much more to say about this component. It is very simple to use, but important (your AI might not perceive any stimuli!). Thus, remember to add it to the non-Pawn entities when you want them to generate a stimulus (which can be as simple as being seen from the AI).

# AIStimuliSourceComponent in C++

Using this component in C++ is easy since you just create it, configure it, and it is ready to go.

This is the `#include` statement you need to use so that you have access to the class of the component:

```
#include "Perception/AIPerceptionStimuliSourceComponent.h"
```

Like any other component, you need to add a variable in the `.h` file to keep track of it:

```
UAIPerceptionStimuliSourceComponent* PerceptionStimuliSourceComponent;
```

Next, you need to generate it in the constructor with the `CreateDefaultSubobject()` function:

```
PerceptionStimuliSourceComponent =
CreateDefaultSubobject<UAIPerceptionStimuliSourceComponent>(TEXT("Perceptio
nStimuliComponent"));
```

Then, you need to register a source Sense, as follows (in this case, *Sight*, but you can change `TSubClassOf<UAISense>()` to the Sense you need):

```
PerceptionStimuliSourceComponent->RegisterForSense(TSubclassOf<UAISense_Sig
ht>());
```

The **Auto Register as a Source** bool is protected and true by default.

# Hands-on with the perception system – Sight AI Controller

The best way we to learn about something is by using it. So, let's start by creating a simple perception system in which we print on the screen when something enters or leave the perception field of the AIs, along with the number of currently seen objects (including/excluding the one that just entered/exited).

Once again, we will do this twice, once with Blueprint and another time with C++, so that we can get to know about both methods of creation.

## A Blueprint perception system

First of all, we need to create a new AI controller (unless you want to use the one we've already been using). In this example, I'm going to call it "SightAIController". Open up the Blueprint editor, add the AIPerception component, and feel free to rename it (if you like) to something like "SightPerceptionComponent".

Select this component. In the *Details* panel, we need to add this as a sense to *Sight*, as shown in the following screenshot:

We can set the **Sight Radius** and the **Lose Sight Radius** to something reasonable, such as *600* and *700*, respectively, so that we have something like this:

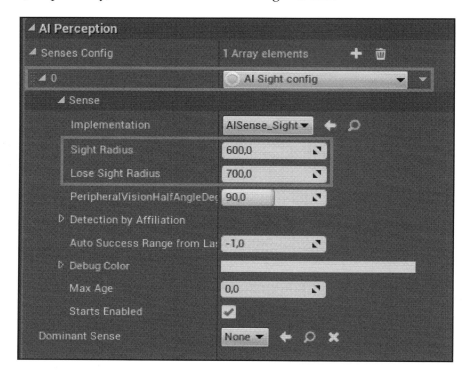

We can leave the angle untouched, but we need to change the **Detection By Affiliation**. In fact, it isn't possible to change the Team from Blueprint, so the player will be in the same 255th team, which is neutral. Since we are just getting our hands dirty on how the system works, we can check all three checkboxes. Now, we should have something like this:

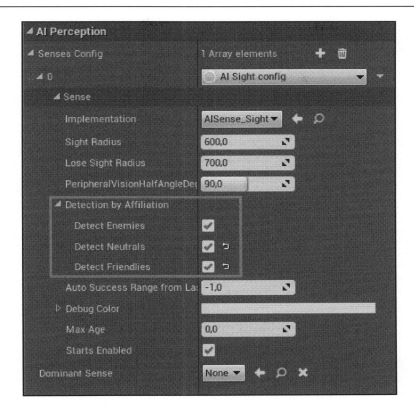

At the bottom of the component, we should have all the different events. In particular, we will need **On Target Perception Updated**, which is called every time a target enters or exits the perception field—exactly what we need:

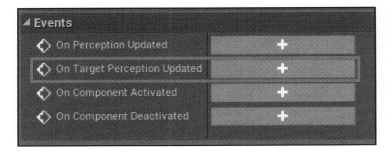

Click on the "+" sign to add the event in the graph:

This event will provide us with the Actor that caused the update and created the stimuli (it's worth remembering that a Perception component might have more than one perception at the time, and this variable tells you which stimuli caused the update). In our case, we have only Sight, so it can't be anything else. The next step is to understand how many targets we have insight and which one left or entered the field of view.

So, drag the **SightPerceptionComponent** into the graph. From there, we can drag a pin to get all the "**Currently Perceived Actors**", which will give us back an array of Actors. Don't forget to set the *Sense Class* to *Sight*:

By measuring the length of this array, we can get the number of currently perceived actors at the moment. Moreover, by checking whether the Actor that was passed from the event is in the currently *"seen Actors"* array, we can determine whether such an actor has left or entered the field of view:

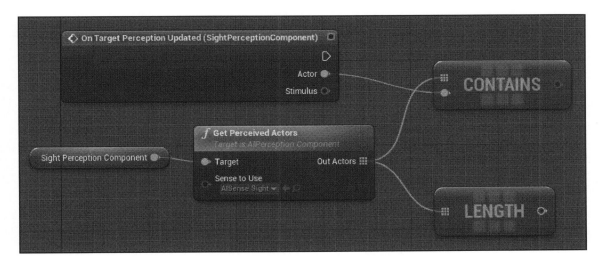

The last step is to format all of this information in a nice formatted string so that it can be shown on-screen. We will use the Append node to build the string, along with a select for the *"entered"* or *"left"* Actor. Finally, we will plug the end result into a *Print String*:

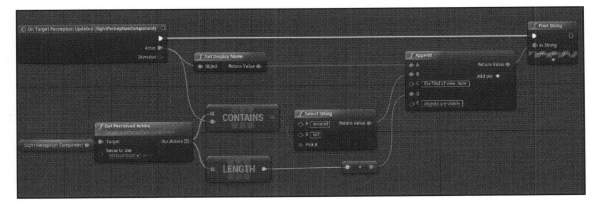

The *Print String* is just for debugging purposes and it is not available when shipping games, but we are just testing and understanding how the perception system works.

Also, I know that when the number of perceived actors is one, the string will produce "*1 objects*", which is incorrect, but correcting plurals (although possible, both with an if statement or in a more complex fashion to take care of language(s) structure(s)) is outside the scope of this book. This is why I am using this expression.

Save the AI controller and go back to the level. If you don't want to do the same in C++, skip the next section, and go directly to "*Test it all*".

# A C++ perception system

Again, if you are more on the C++ side, or want to experiment with how we can build the same AI Controller in C++, this is the section for you. We will follow the exact same steps (more or less), and instead of images, we will have code!

Let's start by creating a new AIController class (if you don't remember how to, have a look at Chapter 2, *Moving the first steps in the AI world*). We will name it SightAIController and place it within the AIControllers folder.

Let's start editing the SightAIController.h file, in which we need to include some other .h files so that our compiler knows where the implementations of the class we need are. In fact, we will need access to the **AIPerception** and **AISense_Config** classes. So, at the top of your code file, you should have the following #include statements:

```
#pragma once
#include "CoreMinimal.h"
#include "AIController.h"
#include "Perception/AIPerceptionComponent.h"
#include "Perception/AISense_Sight.h"
#include "Perception/AISenseConfig_Sight.h"
#include "SightAIController.generated.h"
```

Then, in our class, we need to keep a reference to the AIPerception Component and an extra variable that will hold the configuration for the Sight sense:

```
//Components Variables
UAIPerceptionComponent* PerceptionComponent;
UAISenseConfig_Sight* SightConfig;
```

Moreover, we need to add the `Constructor` function, as well as a callback for the `OnTargetPerceptionUpdate` event. In order to work, this last one has to be a `UFUNCTION()`, and needs to have an **Actor** and a **AIStimulus** as inputs. In this way, the reflection system will work as excepted:

```
//Constructor
ASightAIController();

//Binding function
UFUNCTION()
void OnTargetPerceptionUpdate(AActor* Actor, FAIStimulus Stimulus);
```

Let's move into our `.cpp` file. First, we need to create the `AIPerception` Component, as well as a Sight configuration:

```
ASightAIController::ASightAIController() {
    //Creating the AI Perception Component
    PerceptionComponent =
CreateDefaultSubobject<UAIPerceptionComponent>(TEXT("SightPerceptionCompone
nt"));
    SightConfig = CreateDefaultSubobject<UAISenseConfig_Sight>(FName("Sight
Config"));

}
```

Then, we can configure the *Sight Sense* with the same parameters: **Sight Radius** to *600* and **Lose Sight Radius** to *700*:

```
ASightAIController::ASightAIController() {
    //Creating the AI Perception Component
    PerceptionComponent =
CreateDefaultSubobject<UAIPerceptionComponent>(TEXT("SightPerceptionCompone
nt"));
    SightConfig = CreateDefaultSubobject<UAISenseConfig_Sight>(FName("Sight
Config"));

    //Configuring the Sight Sense
    SightConfig->SightRadius = 600;
    SightConfig->LoseSightRadius = 700;
}
```

Next, we need to check all the flags for the **DetectionByAffiliation** so that we detect our Player (since, at the moment, they both are in the 255th team; look at the *Exercise* section to learn how to improve this):

```
ASightAIController::ASightAIController() {
    //Creating the AI Perception Component
```

```
    PerceptionComponent =
CreateDefaultSubobject<UAIPerceptionComponent>(TEXT("SightPerceptionCompone
nt"));
    SightConfig = CreateDefaultSubobject<UAISenseConfig_Sight>(FName("Sight
Config"));

    //Configuring the Sight Sense
    SightConfig->SightRadius = 600;
    SightConfig->LoseSightRadius = 700;
    SightConfig->DetectionByAffiliation.bDetectEnemies = true;
    SightConfig->DetectionByAffiliation.bDetectNeutrals = true;
    SightConfig->DetectionByAffiliation.bDetectFriendlies = true;
}
```

Finally, we associate the Sight configuration with the `AIPerception` Component, and bind the `OnTargetPerceptionUpdate` function to the homonym event on the `AIPerceptionComponent`:

```
ASightAIController::ASightAIController() {
    //Creating the AI Perception Component
    PerceptionComponent =
CreateDefaultSubobject<UAIPerceptionComponent>(TEXT("SightPerceptionCompone
nt"));
    SightConfig = CreateDefaultSubobject<UAISenseConfig_Sight>(FName("Sight
Config"));

    //Configuring the Sight Sense
    SightConfig->SightRadius = 600;
    SightConfig->LoseSightRadius = 700;
    SightConfig->DetectionByAffiliation.bDetectEnemies = true;
    SightConfig->DetectionByAffiliation.bDetectNeutrals = true;
    SightConfig->DetectionByAffiliation.bDetectFriendlies = true;

    //Assigning the Sight Sense to the AI Perception Component
    PerceptionComponent->ConfigureSense(*SightConfig);
    PerceptionComponent->SetDominantSense(SightConfig->GetSenseImplementation()
);

    //Binding the OnTargetPerceptionUpdate function
    PerceptionComponent->OnTargetPerceptionUpdated.AddDynamic(this,
&ASightAIController::OnTargetPerceptionUpdate);
}
```

This concludes the *Constructor*, but we still need to implement the `OnTargetPerceptionUpdate()` function. First of all, we need to retrieve all the **Currently Perceived Actors**. This function requires an array of actors that it can fill, along with the implementation of the Sense to use.

As a result, we will have our array filled up with the Perceived Actors:

```
void ASightAIController::OnTargetPerceptionUpdate(AActor* Actor,
FAIStimulus Stimulus)
{
    //Retrieving Perceived Actors
    TArray<AActor*> PerceivedActors;
    PerceptionComponent->GetPerceivedActors(TSubclassOf<UAISense_Sight>(),
PerceivedActors);

}
```

By measuring the length of this array, we can get the number of currently perceived actors at the moment. Moreover, by checking if the Actor that was passed from the event (the parameter of the function) is in the currently "*seen Actors*" array, we can determine whether such an actor has left or entered the field of view:

```
void ASightAIController::OnTargetPerceptionUpdate(AActor* Actor,
FAIStimulus Stimulus)
{
    //Retrieving Perceived Actors
    TArray<AActor*> PerceivedActors;
    PerceptionComponent->GetPerceivedActors(TSubclassOf<UAISense_Sight>(),
PerceivedActors);

    //Calculating the Number of Perceived Actors and if the current target
Left or Entered the field of view.
    bool isEntered = PerceivedActors.Contains(Actor);
    int NumberObjectSeen = PerceivedActors.Num();

}
```

Finally, we need to pack this information into a formatted string, and then print it on the screen:

```
void ASightAIController::OnTargetPerceptionUpdate(AActor* Actor,
FAIStimulus Stimulus)
{
    //Retrieving Perceived Actors
    TArray<AActor*> PerceivedActors;
    PerceptionComponent->GetPerceivedActors(TSubclassOf<UAISense_Sight>(),
PerceivedActors);

    //Calculating the Number of Perceived Actors and if the current target
Left or Entered the field of view.
    bool isEntered = PerceivedActors.Contains(Actor);
    int NumberObjectSeen = PerceivedActors.Num();
```

```
    //Formatting the string and printing it
    FString text = FString(Actor->GetName() + " has just " + (isEntered ?
"Entered" : "Left") + " the field of view. Now " +
FString::FromInt(NumberObjectSeen) + " objects are visible.");
    if (GEngine) {
        GEngine->AddOnScreenDebugMessage(-1, 5.0f, FColor::Turquoise, text);
    }
    UE_LOG(LogTemp, Warning, TEXT("%s"), *text);

}
```

Once again, I know that "1 objects" is incorrect, but correcting plurals (although possible) is outside the scope of this book; let's keep it simple.

# Testing it all

Now, you should have an AI controller with the perception system implemented (whether it is in Blueprint or C++ – it doesn't matter, they should behave identically).

Create another `ThirdPersonCharacter` by *Alt + Dragging* the player into the level (if you want to use an AI that we created in the previous chapters, you can do so):

In the *Details* panel, we make it be controlled by our AI controller, and not a player (this should be a process that's easy to you by now):

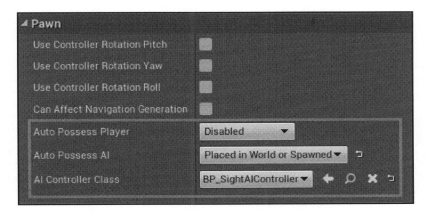

Alternatively, if you are going with a C++ setup, choose the following settings:

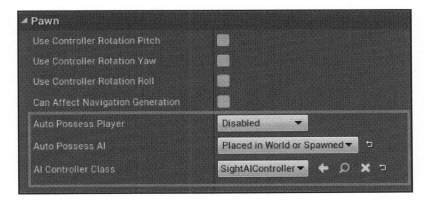

Before pressing play, it would be nice to create some other objects that can be detected. We know that all the Pawns are detected (unless disabled), so let's try something that isn't a Pawn – maybe a moving platform. As a result, if we want to detect it, we need to use the **AIPerceptionStimuliSourceComponent**.

First, let's create the floating platform (which can be easily pushed by our character). If you are in the default level of the *ThirdPersonCharacter Example,* you can duplicate with *Alt + Drag* this big mesh, which is highlighted in the following screenshot (otherwise, if you are using a custom level, a cube that you can squash will work fine):

So far, it's way too big, so let's scale it down to (1, 1, 0.5). Also, to be on the same page, you can move it to (-500, 310, 190). Finally, we need to change the mobility to Movable, since it needs to move:

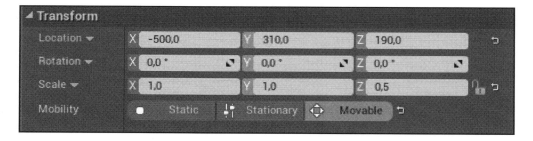

Next, we want to be able to push such a platform, so we need to enable Physics simulation. To keep it pushable by our character, let's give it a mass of *100 Kg* (I know, it seems like a lot, but with little friction and with the fact that the platform floats, it's the right amount). Moreover, we don't want the platform to rotate, so we need to block all the three rotational axes inside **Constraints**. The same goes if we want the platform to float – if we lock the z-axis, the platform can only move along the *XY plane* with no rotation. This will ensure a nice, pushable platform. This is what the Physics part should look like:

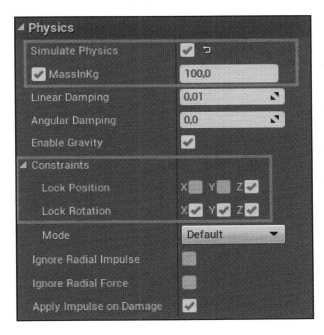

Finally, we need to add a **AIPerceptionStimuliSourceComponent**, from the **Add Component** green button near the name of the Actor:

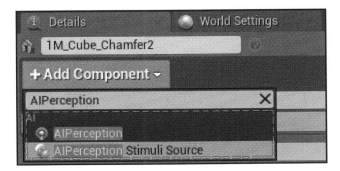

Once the component has been added, we can select it from the preceding menu. As a result, the *Details* panel will allow us to change **AIPerceptionStimuliSourceComponent** settings. In particular, we want to add the *Sight Sense*, and automatically register the component as a source. This is how we should set it up:

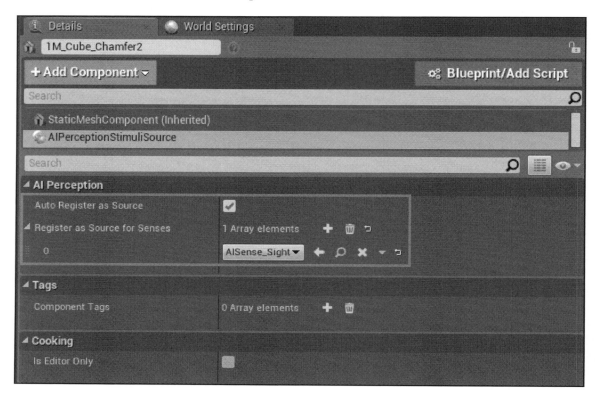

As an optional step, you can convert this into a blueprint so that you can reuse it, and maybe assign a more meaningful name. Also, you can duplicate it a few times if you want to have several objects be tracked by the *Sight Perception System*.

Finally, you can hit play and test what we have achieved so far. If you pass our *AI controlled Character*, you will get a notification on the top of the screen. We get the same output if we push a platform inside or out of the AI's field of view. In the following screenshot, you can see the C++ implementation, but it works very similarly with the Blueprint one (just the color of the print changes):

Also, as anticipation, it is possible to see the AI field of view with the visual debugger, which we will explore in Chapter 13, *Debugging Methods for AI - The Gameplay Debugger*. The following screenshot is a reference of the field of view of the AI Character we have created. For details on how to display it and understand what all this information means, hang on until Chapter 13, *Debugging Methods for AI - The Gameplay Debugger*:

It's time to pat yourself on the back because it might seem like you've only done a little, but actually, you managed to learn about a complex system. Also, if you tried one way (Blueprint or C++), try the other one if you want to be able to master the system both in Blueprint and in C++.

# Summary

And that was a lot of information to perceive, wasn't it?

We started by understanding how the different pieces of the built-in perception system in Unreal works within the AI framework. From there, we explored how we can actually use those components (both in C++ and Blueprint), and learned how to properly configure them as well.

We concluded with a practical example of setting up a *Sight* perception system, and once again did so both in Blueprint and C++.

In the next chapter, we will see how we can simulate large *Crowds*.

# 6
# Extending Behavior Trees

*Empowering a tree with more leaves and branches will make it unstoppable.*

In this chapter, we will understand how to extend *Behavior Trees* by implementing our custom **Tasks**, **Decorators**, and **Services**.

Since in chapters 8, 9, and 10 we are going to create a concrete example of a *Behavior Tree* from scratch and create custom *Tasks*, *Decorators*, and *Services*, you can look at this chapter as a quick theoretical introduction to those chapters in order to give you a ground base for extending *Behavior Trees*. Thus, this chapter might be super fluid and repetitive, but it will teach you about a great tool, which we will refine later in this book in a more playful way.

In this chapter, we will cover the following topics:

- How to create a *Task*, both in *Blueprint and C++*, to make our AI agent capable of executing custom actions.
- How to create a *Decorator*, both in *Blueprint and C++*, to create specific conditions that we can enter in certain sub-branches of the *Behavior Tree*
- How to create a *Service*, both in *Blueprint and C++*, to continuously update the data in our *Blackboard* for the *Behavior Tree*
- How to create *Composite nodes*, *new types of nodes*, or even *new trees*

So, let's dive in!

# A quick recap on Behavior Trees

Here is a quick recap on **Behaviors Trees** to refresh you.

A **Behavior Tree** is a structure for decision-making which uses a *Blackboard* as its memory. In particular, the flow starts from a special node called the **Root**, all the way down to the leaves, which are called Tasks. A **Task** is a single action that the AI can take/perform.

Then, all the nodes that are non-leaves (or the root) are **Composite**. A composite node chooses which one of the children to execute. The two main **Composite** nodes are *Sequence* (which tries to execute all the sequences of its children in order, and if they succeed, it reports a success back, otherwise it reports a fail) and *Selector* (which tries each child until it finds one that succeeds and reports a success or all of them fail and it reports a fail).

Both **Composite** and **Tasks** nodes can use **Decorators** (which impose conditions that must be true so that you can choose that node) or **Services** on top (a continuously running piece of code, e.g. what's used to set Blackboard values).

If you still have some doubts, please revise Chapter 2, *Behavior Trees and Blackboards*.

# Creating a Task

Deep diving into the concepts we looked at earlier, back in Chapter 2, *Behavior Trees and Blackboards*, a *Task* is a single action that our AI Agent can perform. Some examples include walking to a specific location, performing/running an EQS, locating something, chasing the players, etc. All of these actions can either fail or succeed. The final result of a task is then carried back on the *Behavior Tree*, with rules we have seen for Selectors and Sequences.

A task doesn't necessarily have to be executed in a frame, but it can be extended indefinitely. In fact, a Task is not finished until it reports with either a *Failure* or a *Success*. However, they can be interrupted/aborted by external nodes, such as a *Decorator*.

When you create a Task, regardless of whether this is done in Blueprint or C++, you will need to override some functions. Since Blueprint is easier, and share the same concepts that we use in C++, we will first look at how the system works in Blueprint.

# Creating a Blueprint Task

To create a *Blueprint Task*, we have a few options available to us. The easiest one is in the *Behavior Tree Editor*, in which we press the "*New Task*" button in the top bar, as shown in the following screenshot:

However, you will need to manually rename the file and place it in the folder that you wish it to be in.

Another way to create a Task is to create a new Blueprint that inherits from *BTTask_BlueprintBase*, as shown in the following screenshot:

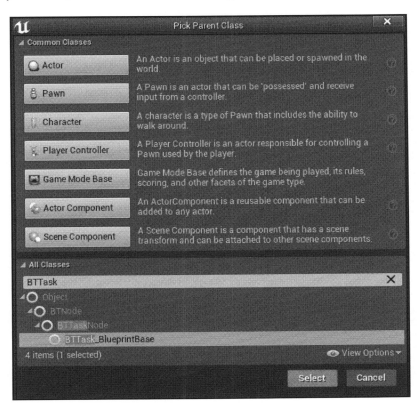

The convention is to prefix the Tasks with "*BBTask_*" (which stands for *Behavior Tree Task*). For instance, we could call our Task something like *BTTask_BPMyFirstTask*:

Once a *Blueprint Task* has been created, there are three type functions that we can override:

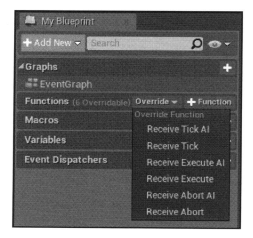

- **Receive Execute**: This is called when the *Task* starts, and here you should implement all the initialization for your task.
- **Receive Tick**: This is called every time the Task ticks, and so you can use it to continuously do something. However, since there might be many agents executing many *Behaviors Trees*, it would be advisable to keep this Tick function as short as possible or not implement it at all (for performance reasons), and use either timers or delegates to handle the task.
- **Receive Abort**: This is called every time that the Task is executing, but the *Behavior Tree* requested to abort it. You need to use this function to clean up your tasks (e.g. restore some Blackboard values).

In Blueprint, these three functions exist in two forms, **AI** and **non-AI**, and are also known as being *generic* (e.g. *Receive Execute* and *Receive Execute AI*). There is not much difference between them. If only one is implemented (as a suggestion, implement the AI version to keep your project consistent), that is the function that is called. Otherwise, the most convenient will be called, which means that the AI version is called when the Pawn is possessed by an *AI Controller*, and the *non-AI* version is called in all the other cases. Of course, most of your cases would be that the *Behavior Tree* is running on top of an *AI Controller*, so the *non-AI* version is for very specific and rarer cases.

So far, the system has no way of understanding when a *Task* has finished its execution or has finished to clean up after an abort. For this reason, there are two functions you will need to call:

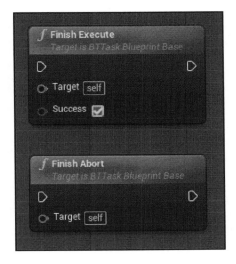

- **Finish Execute**: This will indicate that the *Task* has finished its execution. It has a Boolean parameter to indicate whether the *Task* has **succeeded** (**true** value) or *failed* (*false* value).
- **Finish Abort**: This will indicate that the *Task* has finished to abort. It has no parameters.

Please note that if you don't call these two functions, the task will hang there forever, which is not a desired behavior. Although it would be advisable to call the Finish Abort function at the end of the *Receive Abort* event, there are cases in which you will need more than one frame to clean up. In this case, you can call the *Finish Abort* somewhere else (e.g. in a delegate).

There are also other ways to finish executing a Task, for example, by using AI Messages, but we will not cover them in this book.

This is all you need to know to create a *Task*. You just create the graph that you want, and remember to call the *Finish Execute* node when you are done (either with a *Success* or a *Fail*). We will look at a concrete example of creating a new Task in the following three chapters.

## Creating a Task in C++

The concept of creating a *Task in C++* share the same concepts as its Blueprint counterpart.

First all of, to create a new C++ Task, we need to create a C++ class that inherits from *BTTaskNode*, as shown in the following screenshot:

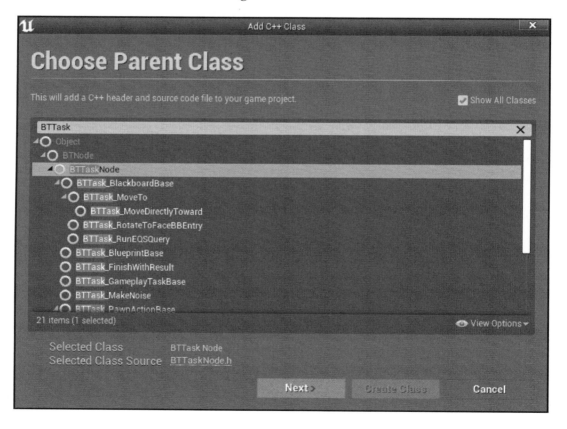

Just like for a Blueprint Task, the convention is to prefix the *Task* with "***BTTask_***" (*Behavior Tree Task*). Therefore, we could name our Task something like "*BTTask_MyFirstTask*":

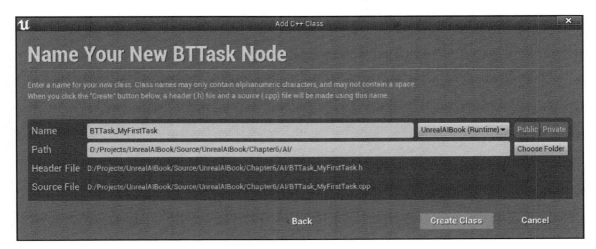

Once you have created the *Task*, you need to override some functions, which have very similar functionalities to the ones in Blueprint. However, there are some differences.

One of the main differences is how to report that the Task has finished its execution (or has finished to abort). For these cases, there is a special enum structure called `EBTNodeResult`. It needs to be returned by a function so that the *Behavior Tree* "*knows*" if it needs to keep calling the Task or not. This structure can have four values:

- **Succeeded**: The Tasks finishes with a success
- **Failed**: The Tasks finishes with a failure
- **Aborted**: The Task has aborted
- **InProgress**: The Task hasn't finished yet

Another difference lies in the fact that the twin of the Blueprint *Receive Execute* has to finish and thus it needs to return a `EBTNodeResult` structure to communicate and state whether the task has finished or whether it needs more than one frame. If so, other functions are then called, as we will see.

Moreover, in C++, there are other special concepts and structures that you can use that in Blueprint you cannot. For example, you have access to NodeMemory, which holds a specific memory for the Task that has been executed. For the correct use of this structure, watch the engine source code, and in particular, the file that's suggested at the end of this section.

The last difference is that there are not the *AI* and the *non-AI* (*Generic*) versions of the functions. You will have to determine by yourself if you have an AI controller and what to do (if you do anything).

The functions to are as follows (this has been taken directly from the source code of the engine, with the two most important functions in bold):

```
/** starts this task, should return Succeeded, Failed or InProgress
 * (use FinishLatentTask() when returning InProgress)
 * this function should be considered as const (don't modify state of
object) if node is not instanced! */
  virtual EBTNodeResult::Type ExecuteTask(UBehaviorTreeComponent&
OwnerComp, uint8* NodeMemory);

protected:
  /** aborts this task, should return Aborted or InProgress
   * (use FinishLatentAbort() when returning InProgress)
   * this function should be considered as const (don't modify state of
object) if node is not instanced! */
  virtual EBTNodeResult::Type AbortTask(UBehaviorTreeComponent& OwnerComp,
uint8* NodeMemory);

public:
#if WITH_EDITOR
  virtual FName GetNodeIconName() const override;
#endif // WITH_EDITOR
  virtual void OnGameplayTaskDeactivated(UGameplayTask& Task) override;

  /** message observer's hook */
  void ReceivedMessage(UBrainComponent* BrainComp, const FAIMessage&
Message);

  /** wrapper for node instancing: ExecuteTask */
  EBTNodeResult::Type WrappedExecuteTask(UBehaviorTreeComponent& OwnerComp,
uint8* NodeMemory) const;

  /** wrapper for node instancing: AbortTask */
  EBTNodeResult::Type WrappedAbortTask(UBehaviorTreeComponent& OwnerComp,
uint8* NodeMemory) const;

  /** wrapper for node instancing: TickTask */
  void WrappedTickTask(UBehaviorTreeComponent& OwnerComp, uint8*
```

```
NodeMemory, float DeltaSeconds) const;

    /** wrapper for node instancing: OnTaskFinished */
    void WrappedOnTaskFinished(UBehaviorTreeComponent& OwnerComp, uint8*
NodeMemory, EBTNodeResult::Type TaskResult) const;

    /** helper function: finish latent executing */
    void FinishLatentTask(UBehaviorTreeComponent& OwnerComp,
EBTNodeResult::Type TaskResult) const;

    /** helper function: finishes latent aborting */
    void FinishLatentAbort(UBehaviorTreeComponent& OwnerComp) const;

    /** @return true if task search should be discarded when this task is
selected to execute but is already running */
    bool ShouldIgnoreRestartSelf() const;

    /** service nodes */
    UPROPERTY()
    TArray<UBTService*> Services;

protected:

    /** if set, task search will be discarded when this task is selected to
execute but is already running */
    UPROPERTY(EditAnywhere, Category=Task)
    uint32 bIgnoreRestartSelf : 1;

    /** if set, TickTask will be called */
    uint32 bNotifyTick : 1;

    /** if set, OnTaskFinished will be called */
    uint32 bNotifyTaskFinished : 1;
    /** ticks this task
     * this function should be considered as const (don't modify state of
object) if node is not instanced! */
    virtual void TickTask(UBehaviorTreeComponent& OwnerComp, uint8*
NodeMemory, float DeltaSeconds);

    /** message handler, default implementation will finish latent
execution/abortion
     * this function should be considered as const (don't modify state of
object) if node is not instanced! */
    virtual void OnMessage(UBehaviorTreeComponent& OwnerComp, uint8*
NodeMemory, FName Message, int32 RequestID, bool bSuccess);

    /** called when task execution is finished
     * this function should be considered as const (don't modify state of
```

```
object) if node is not instanced! */
    virtual void OnTaskFinished(UBehaviorTreeComponent& OwnerComp, uint8*
NodeMemory, EBTNodeResult::Type TaskResult);

    /** register message observer */
    void WaitForMessage(UBehaviorTreeComponent& OwnerComp, FName MessageType)
const;
    void WaitForMessage(UBehaviorTreeComponent& OwnerComp, FName MessageType,
int32 RequestID) const;
    /** unregister message observers */
    void StopWaitingForMessages(UBehaviorTreeComponent& OwnerComp) const;
```

As you can see, there's quite a lot of code, and it might be a bit confusing at first. However, if you have understood Blueprint well, making the jump to understand the C++ functions should be much easier. For instance, the ExecuteTask() function starts the execution of the task, but it doesn't complete it if it returns that the Task is still in progress.

Here is a comment from the Engine Source code, which might help clarify this a bit:

```
/**
 * Task are leaf nodes of behavior tree, which perform actual actions
 *
 * Because some of them can be instanced for specific AI, following virtual
functions are not marked as const:
 * - ExecuteTask
 * - AbortTask
 * - TickTask
 * - OnMessage
 *
 * If your node is not being instanced (default behavior), DO NOT change
any properties of object within those functions!
 * Template nodes are shared across all behavior tree components using the
same tree asset and must store
 * their runtime properties in provided NodeMemory block (allocation size
determined by GetInstanceMemorySize() )
 *
 */
```

The two best ways that I know of to get a better feeling of how to create a C++ Task is to either create one yourself, or read the source code of other Tasks. For instance, you can read the code in the `BTTask_MoveTo.cpp` file within the engine source for a complete example on how to create a C++ Task. Don't be discouraged, because using C++ is awesome!

In any case, we will go through the process of creating a C++ Task from scratch in the following three chapters.

# Creating a Decorator

Recalling from `Chapter 2`, *Behavior Trees and Blackboards*, a ***Decorator*** is a conditional node (which can also be seen as a gate) that controls the execution flow of the sub-branch that it is attached to (if the execution would enter in the sub-branch in the first place).

In a similar fashion on how we *extended/created* a *Task*, we can *extend/create* a ***Decorator***. Once again, we will first dive into how to do it in Blueprint, and then move on to how to extend it in C++.

# Creating a Decorator in Blueprint

To create a ***Blueprint Decorator***, like we did for *Tasks*, you can press the *"**New Decorator**"* button in the top bar of the *Behavior Tree Editor*, as shown in the following screenshot:

Alternatively, you can generate the *Blueprint* class that inherits from **BTDecorator_BlueprintBase**, as shown in the following screenshot:

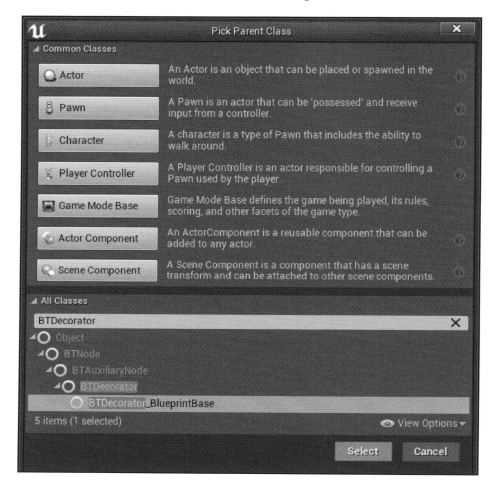

In any case, the naming convention is to prefix the *Decorator* with "***BTDecorator_***" (which stands for *Behavior Tree Decorator*). For instance, we can call our class something like *BTDecorator_BPMyFirstDecorator*:

As for Tasks, all the *overridable* functions come in two flavors: *AI* and *non-AI*. The concept is exactly the same. If only one of them is implemented (to keep your project consistent, it is advisable to override the AI version), then that function is called. If both are implemented, the *AI* is called when the Pawn is possessed by the AI Controller, and the *non-AI* function instead in all the other cases.

Here are the six functions that a *Decorator* can extend:

- **Perform Condition Check**: This is the most important function and the only one you might need to override (if you don't have dynamic things to handle). It has a return value of a bool, which indicates whether the conditional check has succeeded or not.
- **Receive Execution Start**: This is called when the execution of the underlying node (either a Composite or a Task) starts. Use this to initialize the decorator.
- **Receive Execution Finish**: This is called when the execution of the underlying node (either a Composite or a Task) is finished. Use this to clean up the decorator.
- **Receive Tick**: This is the Tick function, in case you need to continuously update something. Performance-wise, is not advisable to use it for heavy operation, but it's even better if it's not used at all (e.g. use timers or delegates).
- **Receive Observer Activated**: As the name suggests, it is called when the Observer is activated.
- **Receive Observer Deactivated**: As the name suggests, it is called when the Observer is deactivated.

As you can see, *Decorators* are pretty easy (at least in Blueprint); mainly, you only need to *override/implement* the *Perform Condition Check* function, which returns a boolean value:

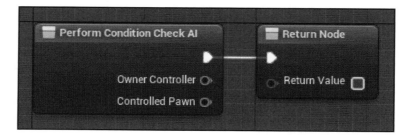

In any case, we will look at a concrete example of creating a *Blueprint Decorator* from scratch in the following three chapters.

# Creating a Decorator in C++

In a very similar fashion to how we extended a *Task* in C++, you can extend a *Decorator in C++* as well. The base class to inherit from is **BTDecorator**, as shown in the following screenshot:

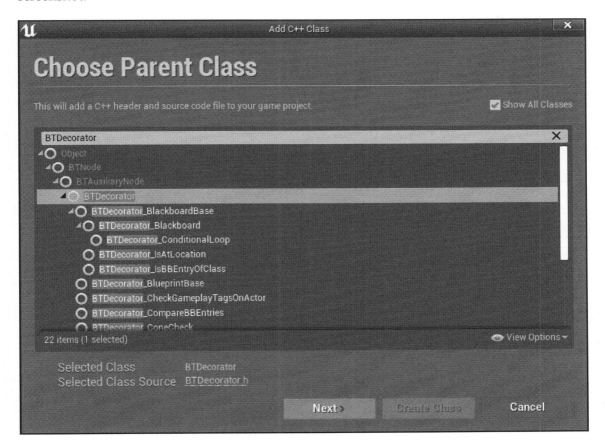

The convention, as usual, is to prefix the *Decorator* with "***BTDecorator_***" (*Behavior Tree Decorator*). A possible name for our *Decorator* could be "*BTDecorator_MyFirstDecorator*":

Diving directly into C++, these are the overridable functions, as taken from the Engine Source code (there are quite a lot):

```
    /** wrapper for node instancing: CalculateRawConditionValue */
    bool WrappedCanExecute(UBehaviorTreeComponent& OwnerComp, uint8*
NodeMemory) const;

    /** wrapper for node instancing: OnNodeActivation */
    void WrappedOnNodeActivation(FBehaviorTreeSearchData& SearchData) const;
    /** wrapper for node instancing: OnNodeDeactivation */
    void WrappedOnNodeDeactivation(FBehaviorTreeSearchData& SearchData,
EBTNodeResult::Type NodeResult) const;

    /** wrapper for node instancing: OnNodeProcessed */
    void WrappedOnNodeProcessed(FBehaviorTreeSearchData& SearchData,
EBTNodeResult::Type& NodeResult) const;

    /** @return flow controller's abort mode */
    EBTFlowAbortMode::Type GetFlowAbortMode() const;

    /** @return true if condition should be inversed */
    bool IsInversed() const;

    virtual FString GetStaticDescription() const override;

    /** modify current flow abort mode, so it can be used with parent
composite */
```

```
   void UpdateFlowAbortMode();

 /** @return true if current abort mode can be used with parent composite
*/
   bool IsFlowAbortModeValid() const;

protected:

   /** if set, FlowAbortMode can be set to None */
   uint32 bAllowAbortNone : 1;

   /** if set, FlowAbortMode can be set to LowerPriority and Both */
   uint32 bAllowAbortLowerPri : 1;

   /** if set, FlowAbortMode can be set to Self and Both */
   uint32 bAllowAbortChildNodes : 1;

   /** if set, OnNodeActivation will be used */
   uint32 bNotifyActivation : 1;

   /** if set, OnNodeDeactivation will be used */
   uint32 bNotifyDeactivation : 1;

   /** if set, OnNodeProcessed will be used */
   uint32 bNotifyProcessed : 1;

   /** if set, static description will include default description of
inversed condition */
   uint32 bShowInverseConditionDesc : 1;

private:
   /** if set, condition check result will be inversed */
   UPROPERTY(Category = Condition, EditAnywhere)
   uint32 bInverseCondition : 1;

protected:
   /** flow controller settings */
   UPROPERTY(Category=FlowControl, EditAnywhere)
   TEnumAsByte<EBTFlowAbortMode::Type> FlowAbortMode;

   void SetIsInversed(bool bShouldBeInversed);

   /** called when underlying node is activated
    * this function should be considered as const (don't modify state of
object) if node is not instanced! */
   virtual void OnNodeActivation(FBehaviorTreeSearchData& SearchData);

   /** called when underlying node has finished
```

```
   * this function should be considered as const (don't modify state of
object) if node is not instanced! */
   virtual void OnNodeDeactivation(FBehaviorTreeSearchData& SearchData,
EBTNodeResult::Type NodeResult);

   /** called when underlying node was processed (deactivated or failed to
activate)
   * this function should be considered as const (don't modify state of
object) if node is not instanced! */
   virtual void OnNodeProcessed(FBehaviorTreeSearchData& SearchData,
EBTNodeResult::Type& NodeResult);

   /** calculates raw, core value of decorator's condition. Should not
include calling IsInversed */
   virtual bool CalculateRawConditionValue(UBehaviorTreeComponent&
OwnerComp, uint8* NodeMemory) const;

   /** more "flow aware" version of calling RequestExecution(this) on owning
behavior tree component
   * should be used in external events that may change result of
CalculateRawConditionValue */
   void ConditionalFlowAbort(UBehaviorTreeComponent& OwnerComp,
EBTDecoratorAbortRequest RequestMode) const;
```

Moreover, in the Engine Source code, we can find the following comment, which explains a couple of implementation choices:

```
/**
 * Decorators are supporting nodes placed on parent-child connection, that
receive notification about execution flow and can be ticked
 *
 * Because some of them can be instanced for specific AI, following virtual
functions are not marked as const:
 *   - OnNodeActivation
 *   - OnNodeDeactivation
 *   - OnNodeProcessed
 *   - OnBecomeRelevant (from UBTAuxiliaryNode)
 *   - OnCeaseRelevant (from UBTAuxiliaryNode)
 *   - TickNode (from UBTAuxiliaryNode)
 *
 * If your node is not being instanced (default behavior), DO NOT change
any properties of object within those functions!
 * Template nodes are shared across all behavior tree components using the
same tree asset and must store
 * their runtime properties in provided NodeMemory block (allocation size
determined by GetInstanceMemorySize() )
 *
 */
```

Unfortunately, we don't have the time to go through all of them in detail, but most of them are very intuitive, and so it shouldn't be hard for you to understand their meaning. In any case, we will look at a concrete example of how to create a *C++ Decorator* from scratch (and we will be using many of these functions) in the next three chapters.

# Creating a Service

Recalling from `Chapter 2`, *Behavior Trees and Blackboards*, a *Service* is a node that runs constantly if attached to one of the parents of the sub-branch. The main use of this node is to update the data in the *Blackboard* for the *Behavior Tree*, and it is among the nodes that you will need to create since they are very specific to your Gameplay.

In a similar fashion to how we extended both Tasks and *Decorators*, we can also *extend/create* **Services** as well. We will go through how to implement the extension in Blueprint first, and then understand how to do it in C++ as well.

## Creating a Service in Blueprint

Just like you did for *Tasks* and *Decorators*, you can create a new **Blueprint Service** by pressing the **New Service** button on the top bar of the *Behavior Tree Editor*, as shown in the following screenshot:

Alternatively, you can generate the *Blueprint* class that inherits from ***BTService_BlueprintBase***, as shown in the following screenshot:

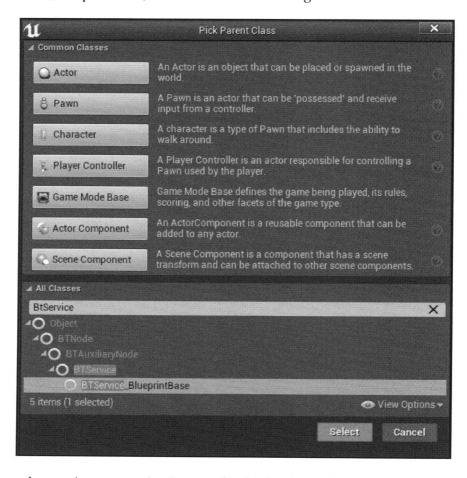

In any case, the naming convention is to prefix the *Service* with "***BTService_***" (which stands for *Behavior Tree Service*). For instance, we can call our class something like *BTService_BPMyFirstService*:

Just like the *Tasks* and *Decorators*, all the *overridable* functions come in two different versions: AI and *non-AI* (*Generic*). The concept is exactly the same: if only one of them is implemented (to keep your project consistent, it is advisable to override the AI version), then that function is called. If both are implemented, the AI is called when the Pawn is possessed by the AI Controller, otherwise the generic function is called instead.

Here there are the four *overridable* functions:

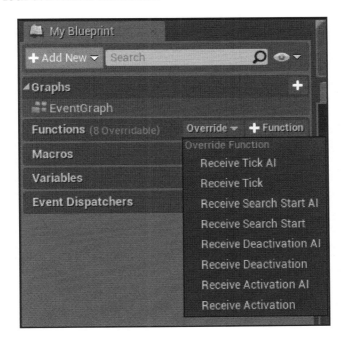

- **Receive Activation**: This is called when the *Service* becomes active. Use it to initialize the *Service*.
- **Receive Tick**: This is called when the Service ticks. Mainly, a *Service* does something continuously (e.g. update a *Blackboard* variables), and so this is the most important function for the service. Performance-wise, it would be advisable to keep it as short as possible. Moreover, back to the *Behavior Tree*, it is possible to adjust how often a Service ticks (with a random value between min and max). However, the implementation, in theory, should not be aware of how often the Service ticks; it just needs to offer a "*service*". Then, the user of the service, the *Behavior Tree*, will decide how often it wants this service.
- **Receive Search Start**: This is a special case in which the service is active (so you should have initialized the service, but in theory, the service should not have performed anything yet). This function is called before a *Task/Node* is searched. In fact, a *Behavior Tree* needs to evaluate which *Task* or *Node* to pick next to execute. In doing so, the *Behavior Tree* checks the conditions of the decorators on top of the possible *Tasks* or *Nodes*. As a result, in this function, you can adjust values before the next *Task* or *Node* is searched, and therefore choose something that influences the choice into being the correct one.
- **Receive Deactivation**: This is called when the service becomes inactive. Use it to clean up the Service.

Mainly, you will need to implement your logic in the **Receive Tick** function, so that you can constantly update the information in the Blackboard. A *Service* is a layer between the Behavior Tree and the game world.

We will implement a *Blueprint Service* during the course of the next three chapters, in which we will face a much more practical and concrete example.

# Creating a Service in C++

In a very similar fashion to how we extended *Tasks* and *Decorators* in C++, you can extend *Services in C++* as well. The base class to inherit from is **BTService**, as shown in the following screenshot:

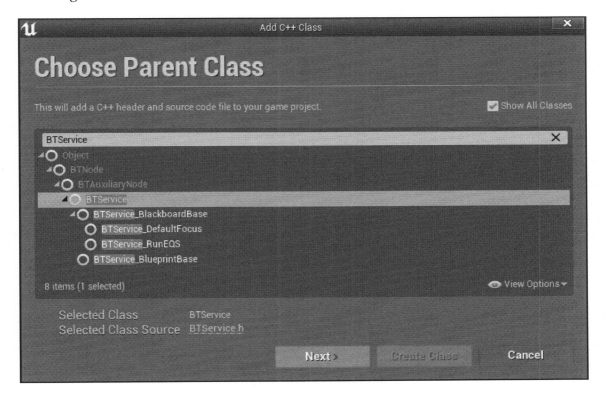

The convention is to prefix the Service class name with "**BTService_**" (*Behavior Tree Service*). A possible name for our class could be *BTService_MyFirstService*:

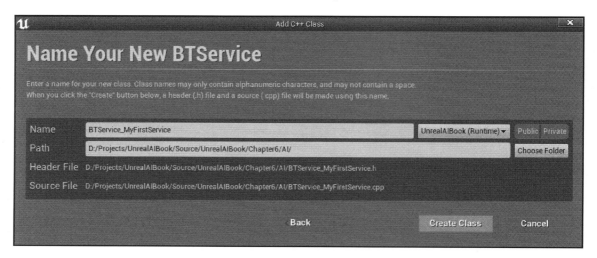

Once we have created the **Service in C++,** the rest is done in a really similar fashion to *extending/creating* a *Decorator* in C++. Here there are the functions to override (taken from the Engine Source Code):

```
virtual FString GetStaticDescription() const override;

    void NotifyParentActivation(FBehaviorTreeSearchData& SearchData);

protected:

    // Gets the description of our tick interval
    FString GetStaticTickIntervalDescription() const;

    // Gets the description for our service
    virtual FString GetStaticServiceDescription() const;

    /** defines time span between subsequent ticks of the service */
    UPROPERTY(Category=Service, EditAnywhere, meta=(ClampMin="0.001"))
    float Interval;

    /** adds random range to service's Interval */
    UPROPERTY(Category=Service, EditAnywhere, meta=(ClampMin="0.0"))
    float RandomDeviation;

    /** call Tick event when task search enters this node (SearchStart will
be called as well) */
```

```
  UPROPERTY(Category = Service, EditAnywhere, AdvancedDisplay)
  uint32 bCallTickOnSearchStart : 1;

  /** if set, next tick time will be always reset to service's interval
when node is activated */
  UPROPERTY(Category = Service, EditAnywhere, AdvancedDisplay)
  uint32 bRestartTimerOnEachActivation : 1;

  /** if set, service will be notified about search entering underlying
branch */
  uint32 bNotifyOnSearch : 1;

  /** update next tick interval
   * this function should be considered as const (don't modify state of
object) if node is not instanced! */
  virtual void TickNode(UBehaviorTreeComponent& OwnerComp, uint8*
NodeMemory, float DeltaSeconds) override;

  /** called when search enters underlying branch
   * this function should be considered as const (don't modify state of
object) if node is not instanced! */
  virtual void OnSearchStart(FBehaviorTreeSearchData& SearchData);

#if WITH_EDITOR
  virtual FName GetNodeIconName() const override;
#endif // WITH_EDITOR

  /** set next tick time */
  void ScheduleNextTick(uint8* NodeMemory);
```

Here there is a comment at the beginning (always taken from the Engine Source Code) that explains some implementation choices:

```
/**
 * Behavior Tree service nodes is designed to perform "background" tasks
that update AI's knowledge.
 *
 * Services are being executed when underlying branch of behavior tree
becomes active,
 * but unlike tasks they don't return any results and can't directly affect
execution flow.
 *
 * Usually they perform periodical checks (see TickNode) and often store
results in blackboard.
 * If any decorator node below requires results of check beforehand, use
OnSearchStart function.
 * Keep in mind that any checks performed there have to be instantaneous!
 *
```

```
   * Other typical use case is creating a marker when specific branch is
being executed
   * (see OnBecomeRelevant, OnCeaseRelevant), by setting a flag in
blackboard.
   *
   * Because some of them can be instanced for specific AI, following virtual
functions are not marked as const:
   * - OnBecomeRelevant (from UBTAuxiliaryNode)
   * - OnCeaseRelevant (from UBTAuxiliaryNode)
   * - TickNode (from UBTAuxiliaryNode)
   * - OnSearchStart
   *
   * If your node is not being instanced (default behavior), DO NOT change
any properties of object within those functions!
   * Template nodes are shared across all behavior tree components using the
same tree asset and must store
   * their runtime properties in provided NodeMemory block (allocation size
determined by GetInstanceMemorySize() )
   */
```

Unfortunately, we cannot go into detail about each function, but they are all quite easy to understand. In any case, we will explore further *Services* in the following three chapters, when we build a *Behavior Tree* from scratch, as well as when we implement a *C++ Service*.

# Creating a Composite Node

In most of these cases, you *will not need to extend a Composite Node*. By *"most of these cases"*, I mean that you can create very complex *AI Behavior Trees* that can perform very complicated tasks, and that you really shouldn't extend or create a Composite Node unless you really need to.

In fact, a Composite Node influences the flow of the *Behavior Tree*, including which node to execute, which *Decorators* to check, and which *Service* to activate. By default, there are only three: *Selector*, *Sequence*, and *Simple Parallel*. These will be more than enough for covering most of our cases.

However, if you really have specific needs, then Unreal Engine is so flexible that it allows you to extend a *Composite Node* as well.

First of all, this is impossible to do in Blueprint, so the only way you can extend a (or create a new) *Composite Node* is through C++.

Let's look at an example of why you would like to create a new *Composite Node*.

**Why**: Because you can implement a flow in the Behavior Tree that might be hard to achieve (or impossible) with the current composite nodes.

**An Example**: You could potentially simulate a Behavior Tree with Simple Parallel nodes, with another one that does not use them. But this would be really complicated and not very clean. Thus, using Simple Parallel nodes simplifies a lot the workflow (originally, in the first versions of the engine, there were no Simple Parallel nodes).

**A Concrete Example**: You want to pick which tasks should execute at random, below this custom Composite node, based on some weights. For instance, the weights can be evaluated by a special type of *Decorators*. Thus, extending a *Composite* might require additional work on other type of nodes.

**Another Concrete example**: You can create a composite node that keeps picking a random child so that it succeeds until either a threshold is reached, or one of the children reports a fail.

Despite this being a very interesting topic, unfortunately, it is outside the scope of this book. Therefore, we will limit our selves to creating new *Tasks*, *Decorators*, and *Services*.

# Creating new type of nodes or new types of Trees

In theory, you can create new types of nodes (for *Behavior Trees*, it's not really needed, because you would create a different kind of structure). Actually, you can create different tree structures that are not *Behavior Trees* anymore (e.g. a *Dialogue Tree*), which are far more useful than creating another node for a Behavior Tree. *Dialogue Trees* are really interesting, because they use a very similar structure to a *Behavior Tree*, and you can use the same *Editor* (or better, a slightly modified version of it) to edit the tree.

As much as I would like to dive into these topics, the main focus of this book is on AI, and so talking about *Dialogue Trees* is outside the scope of this book.

# Summary

In this chapter, we have explored how it is possible to *extend/create* **Tasks**, **Decorators**, and **Services** both in *Blueprint and in C++*. As a result, this gives us the ability to create complex behaviors for our AI agents, especially if combined with what we learned in the previous chapters, such as *navigation, EQS*, and *perception*.

In the next chapter, we will deal with *Crowds*, before jumping into creating a concrete example in Chapter 8, *Designing Behavior Trees – Part I*, Chapter 9, *Designing Behavior Trees – Part II*, and Chapter 10, *Designing Behavior Trees – Part III*.

# 7
# Crowds

In this chapter, we are going to wrap up our talk about what comes built-in in terms of Artificial Intelligence in Unreal. Then, we will embark on a journey in which we will build an interesting AI Behavior Tree from scratch, before checking the huge Debug system (which includes AI Debugging) underneath Unreal.

In this chapter, we will cover the following topics:

- Crowds in Games
- RVO avoidance
- Crowd Manager

These topics may be short, but that doesn't make them less important or easy to implement. So, let's get started!

## Crowds in games

Have you ever been stuck in a busy mall at Christmas or surrounded by a large crowd during a sporting event? Perhaps you were shopping among the bazaars of heavily fragrant spice markets? Now, imagine that all of the people in this environment disappeared. How would this change the mood? Quite significantly, I would imagine. Regardless of how big or how small a crowd of people is within an environment, they definitely add to the overall atmosphere.

Some great examples of crowds in games include the *Assassin's Creed* series:

Crowds in *Assassin's Creed: Syndicate*

Crowds can include both interactive NPCs and those that simply just wander around, minding their own business. In some cases, like in *Assassin's Creed*, members of the crowd will play an important role such as requiring you to protect them, offering you protection, or even requiring your resources (e.g. beggars asking for money). In other situations, crowds will have no impact on your gameplay other than getting in your way!

# Building believable crowds

While crowds are large collections of people, usually with a common purpose when in a given location, they require a bit of thought behind their creation. It's not as simple as dumping a bunch of NPCs, giving them some autonomy (e.g. via artificial intelligence), and pressing play. Building a believable crowd requires us to consider a few things.

The first consideration is the different kinds of people that should be there. Going back to our example of spice markets, you're likely to find shop merchants, buyers, beggars, children, and so on. In the following screenshot from the game *Stacking*, there are no large crowds or groups of people:

A small crowd in *Stacking*

However, in *Dead Rising*, as shown in the following screenshot, there is quite an extensive crowd of people (zombies, in this case), all trying to attack you:

A big crowd of zombies attacking the player in *Dead Rising*

The next consideration is more of an aesthetic one. For instance, depending on its location in both space and time, the type of movement, clothes, ages, etc., will also vary. It is highly unlikely (unless that is the angle you're going for) that you will have characters dressed as if they are going to a 1930s cocktail party, if you're attacking templars during the third crusade.

Then, we have the aural consideration. What does this crowd sound like? Are they loud or are do they speak in soft murmurs? Perhaps there are bikes whizzing past with kids ringing their bells. All of these aspects are important in creating a convincing crowd.

Last, but not least, we have the crowd's movement. How do they move? Do they follow a specific path, are they guided down particular areas, or are they free to roam wherever they choose?

# Animals

Now, not all crowds take on human (or part/like human) form. Crowds can also exist in terms of groups of animals. As we discussed previously, the same considerations also need to be taken into account when developing crowds of animals. You also have to pay attention to how animals interact with each other because it is quite different from the way humans do. For example, wolves are likely to be in different sized crowds, or "packs", than, say, a  flock of vultures or a herd of deer, as in the following image:

(Top): Attacking groups of Vultures in *Assassin's Creed: Origins*
(Bottom): Herd of deer in *Far Cry 4*

# Crowd movement

When it comes to more technical aspects of a crowd's functionality, we must consider the extent of interaction that a crowd has with the player. For example, if a player hits them while running past them, do members of the crowd respond? If so, how?

In games like Pro Evolution Soccer, FIFA, Rocket League, etc., crowds don't interact with the player beyond cheering or booing, depending on the situation. Of course, they also add to the atmosphere with inaudible chanting/conversations/cheering:

Crowd in *FIFA 2018*

Often, this behavior is created by using cleverly animated (vertex) materials to simulate a large crowd that the player sees only over a distance and doesn't interact with.

# Crowd dynamics and creating realistic behavior

Since we have talked about some of the characteristics that help to create realistic crowd behavior, let's talk about the ways that we can implement this from a more technical standpoint.

## Flow-based

These types of approaches focus on the crowd rather than its components. This means that the distinctive behaviors of individuals (within the crowd) occur due to input from their surroundings.

## Entity-based

These types of approaches mean that the characters in these crowds do not have any autonomy. This is because their behavior is based on a set of predefined rules that are meant to simulate social/psychological influences that occur in individuals that are a part of a crowd. In this way, all the movements of characters are determined by these rules.

## Agent-based

This is perhaps the most dynamic and flexible approach to crowds. In agent-based approaches, characters are autonomous and can interact with individuals. This is to say that each character within a crowd of this type has (to a certain extent) a level of intelligence, which allows them to react based on a set of rules that are influenced by their surroundings.

This is the kind of approach that we will be using with our AI systems, and, in this chapter, we will explore the built-in Unreal systems that handle crowds.

# Crowds in Unreal

In Unreal, handling a huge crowd might be challenging, especially if you are going to have a complicated system. In fact, a crowd system needs to run fast and make the crowd behave realistically.

Having a huge crowd that built-in systems don't scale properly means that you are probably basing (almost) your entire gameplay on the crowd. In this case, you should go for implementing your own Crowd system, even by modifying the built-in one. However, for most games, the built-in systems are more than enough.

In Unreal, there are two built-in systems for crowd simulation/management. These are as follows:

- UCharacterMovementComponent's RVO
- Detour Crowd System

Although it is possible to keep them both running, it is not advisable to do so. So, be sure to use the one that suits your needs the best, or create your own.

# Reciprocal Velocity Obstacles (RVO)

**Reciprocal Velocity Obstacles** (**RVO**) is an algorithm that was discovered by the three researchers Jur van den Berg, Ming C. Lin, and Dinesh Manocha in 2008 in their paper *"Reciprocal Velocity Obstacles for Real-Time Multi-Agent Navigation"*.

The RVO algorithm is path agnostic, which means that it is not aware of the path that the agent is following, nor the navmesh where the agent is navigating. Moreover, each agent navigates independently of one another without explicit communication. As a result, RVO is very fast to run, even for a large number of agents, and provides sufficient realistic behavior if the number of incoming collisions is limited.

## RVO in Unreal

The implementation of the RVO algorithm within the Unreal Engine goes way back to the Unreal Development Kit, or UDK (UE3). In UE4, you can find the algorithm that was implemented within the Character Movement Component.

To activate RVO on a specific character, open up its *Character Movement Component* and navigate to the *Character Movement: Avoidance* section. Here, you will be able to turn on the algorithm and set a few settings, as shown in the following screenshot:

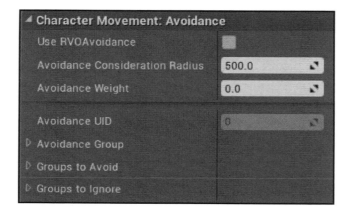

The following settings are available (you need to click on the little arrow at the bottom to expand all the settings):

- **Use RVOAvoidance**: Specifies whether or not the RVO algorithm is used on this character.
- **Avoidance Consideration Radius**: The RVO algorithm will consider only obstacles that fall within this radius. Hence, if nothing is within this radius, RVO will not change the course of the character. On the other hand, if obstacles (e.g. other characters) are present within this radius, RVO will try to avoid them. This parameter is really important, and it needs to be tweaked properly (depending on what kind of obstacles your character will encounter) when RVO is used.
- **Avoidance Weight**: This indicates how heavily RVO needs to intervene on the avoidance of the obstacles. In fact, the algorithm will try to average between the direction the character is heading, and a direction to avoid the obstacles. This is the strength of the RVO algorithms and determines its behavior. The default value is 0.5, which works in the majority of cases.
- **Avoidance UID**: This is an identification number that is automatically generated when RVO is used (you cannot set it). It is important when you want to interact with the Avoidance Manager (see the *RVO in C++* section for more information).
- **Avoidance Group**: This indicates which avoidance group(s) this character belongs to.
- **Groups to Avoid**: This indicates which of the avoidance groups this character needs to avoid.
- **Groups to ignore**: This indicates which of the avoidance groups this character needs to ignore, and thus not take them into consideration when performing RVO avoidance.

 In the case of multiplayer games, the RVO algorithm will only run on the server.

This is enough to use the algorithm and use it in production for your game. However, if you are curious and want to dig a little bit deeper, move on to the following subsection.

# Advanced RVO settings

This section is divided in two sections: what we can do in a blueprint, and what we can do in C++.

# RVO in Blueprint

If you have a reference to the character component, you will notice that you can read all of its variables (all of the Get-functions are here), but that you cannot set them (there are no Set-functions), as shown in the following screenshot:

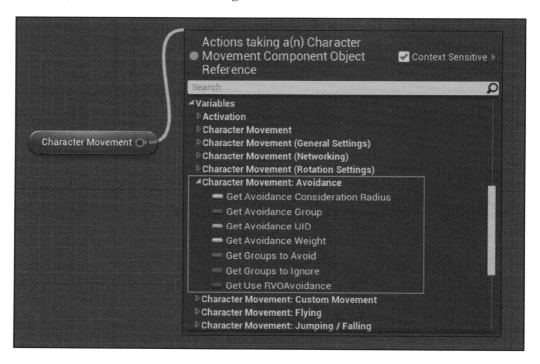

It seems like you cannot turn RVO on and off any time you like during gameplay in Blueprint, but this is not true. In fact, it is still possible to slightly change RVO settings in real-time (at gameplay time). In particular, you can change whether RVO is running or not with the following node:

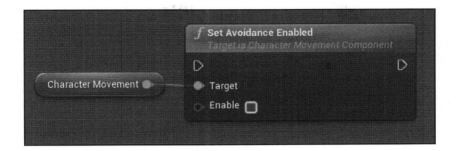

The reason why you cannot edit the bool variable directly is clear if you look at the C++ implementation, in which the character needs to be registered to an RVO manager. In fact, it might be the first time that RVO is turned on, and all the initialization (e.g. registering to the RVO manager) needs to be handled.

Moreover, you can also change in which avoidance group(s) the character belongs and which ones, instead, should be avoided, by using the following two nodes:

Besides these three functions, you are pretty limited in what you can do in real-time with RVO, but C++ unlocks new possibilities.

# RVO in C++

Of course, every time you reach the C++ realm in Unreal, your possibilities gets really wide in terms of what you can do. In this section, we explore some of these possibilities.

First of all, you will have direct access to the *UAvoidanceManager*, which stores data of all the agents that use RVO.

From a reference of the *Character Movement Component*, you can retrieve the ***Avoidance UID***, which can be used to query the Avoidance Manager on getting the *FNavAvoidanceData* structure, which holds the specific avoidance data of the character. Besides having access to the data in the structure, you can use it to further query the *Avoidance Manager* to obtain more grain information.

Let's say you want to do manual velocity planning. You can gain access to the current velocity by using the `GetAvoidanceVelocity()` function.

However, the best way to learn about all of your possibilities is by looking at the source code. In particular, you will need to look at the following file:
`Runtime/Engine/Classes/AI/Navigation/AvoidanceManager.h`.

# RVO observations

The following are some of my observations from using this approach:

- Since it is path and navmesh agnostic, the agent could potentially be pushed away from the Navmesh. This means that you need to take into consideration this possibility (and how often this might happen, e.g. if your maps have wall boundaries, then the character cannot be pushed away from the navmesh).
- If you want RVO working on non-character actors, then you will need to reimplement the RVO algorithm on your own (or adapt your actors to use the Character Movement Component).
- RVO might not work well if there are many characters in a very confined space (e.g. non-realistic behavior, such as lateral sliding).
- If the Avoidance Consideration Radius is high and the character needs to position itself among other characters, the position might be difficult for the character (and thus lead to strange, weird, and unnatural behaviors).
- RVO is very fast, even with many characters running RVO at the same level. In fact, the overhead cost is almost nothing if there are no obstacles, so by using an appropriate Avoidance Consideration Radius, many characters can be handled without any issues.

- You can implement the father of the RVO algorithm, the VO, which is RVO but without weighting. It is even faster if performance is really a concern, but realism will decrease. You can gather more information on this by taking a look at the references in the next section. For instance, by modifying the avoidance manager in the source code of the engine, you will be able to easily implement this algorithm (or anything else of your choice).

## RVO resources

The following are some further RVO resources you can have a look at:

- The original RVO paper is available at the following link: `http://gamma.cs.unc.edu/RVO/icra2008.pdf`
- More information about RVO from the creators: `http://gamma.cs.unc.edu/RVO`
- RVO version 2 (the version that's implemented within Unreal engine): `http://gamma.cs.unc.edu/RVO2/`

## Detour Crowd

Another built-in Unreal system is the *Detour Crowd*. It is based on the *Recats Library*, and in contrast to RVO, it will take into consideration the Navmesh on which the agents are moving. The system works pretty much out of the box already, but, let's dig deep into how it works and how we can use it.

## How the Detour Crowd system works

Within your Game World exists an object called **DetourCrowdManager**. It is responsible for coordinating crowds in your game. In particular, an agent that is registered to the **DetourCrowdManager** will be taken into consideration. The **DetourCrowdManager** accepts anything that implements the **ICrowdAgentInterface**, which provides data to the Manager about the agent.

 Actually, under the hood, the *Detour Crowd Manager* is using the Detour Crowd algorithm that was developed by *Mikko Mononen* in the *Recast Library*, which has been slightly modified by Epic Games for their needs. Therefore, the Detour Crowd Component offers an interface between the *Unreal Framework* and the *Recast Detour*. You can find more information about this by reviewing the resources at the end of this section.

Potentially, you can create an agent by implementing the **ICrowdAgentInterface**. However, Unreal provides you with a special component called **UCrowdFollowingComponent**, which implements the **ICrowdAgentInterface**, along with other functionalities. As a result, anything that has the **UCrowdFollowingComponent** is eligible to be an agent with the Crowd Manager. Actually, the component itself will auto-register itself to the Crowd Manager and will activate the *Detour Behaviour*.

To make things easier, the **ADetourCrowdAIController** is a pre-made controller that will automatically add the **UCrowdFollowingComponent** to the controller itself. Hence, this time, the system is triggered by the AI Controller from the **Character Movement Component** directly.

The following diagram helps explain this:

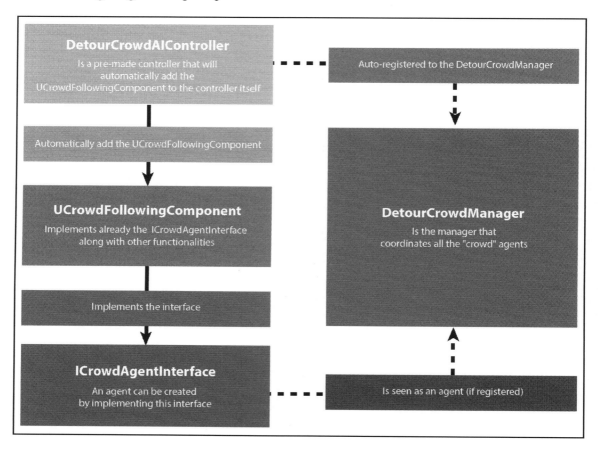

# Using the Detour Crowd system

The easiest way to use the *Detour Crowd* system is by letting your AI controller inheriting from the Detour Crowd AI Controller, as shown in the following screenshot:

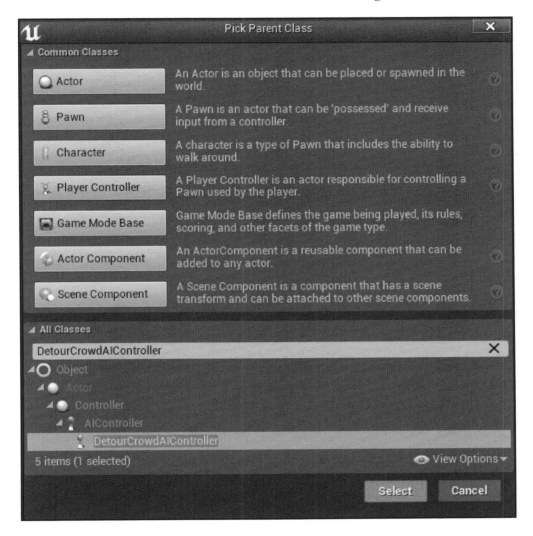

In C++, you will need to inherit from **ADetourCrowdAIController** (or add the *UDetourCrowdFollowingComponent* to your controller).

Once you have done this for all the controllers that you want to use the *Detour Crowd*, the system will pretty much work out of the box.

## Detour Crowd settings

If you are using the **UCrowdFollowingComponent**, this component will implement the **ICrowdAgentInterface** by using the **Avoidance Settings** in the **Character Movement Component** (if one is available).

As a result, all the **Avoidance Settings** we saw in the *RVO* section will be taken into consideration by the *Detour Crowd*. Therefore, all of the settings that are highlighted in the following screenshot will still be valid for our AI Character:

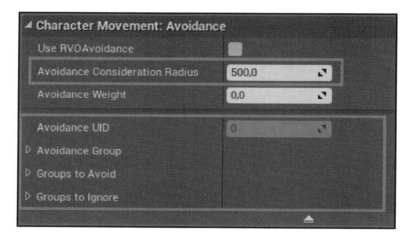

 Please note that the **Avoidance Weight** will not be taken into consideration by the Detour System since it is an *RVO*-specific parameter.

Consequently, all the blueprint functions we have seen (e.g. to change the group mask) are also valid.

These were specific settings on a per-character basis, but it is possible to tweak the overall *Detour Crowd settings*. To do this, navigate into the **Project Settings**, and under the **Engine** section, you will find an entry called **Crowd Manager**, as shown in the following screenshot:

From here, we have access to all the ***Detour Crowd Manager settings***. Most of these settings are from the original *Recast Crowd algorithm*, and the *Unreal Detour Crowd Manager* offers an interface where you can set these variables in the algorithm. Let's start from the easier ones:

- **Max Agents**: This is the maximum number of agents that the Crowd Manager will handle. Of course, the higher the number, the more agents you can place at once, but this will hit performance. You should plan how many agents your game needs carefully. Moreover, if you look at the source code, this number will be used to allocate the memory that's necessary for the Crowd Manager to handle the agents. This is useful to keep in mind in situations in which memory is low.

- **Max Agent Radius**: This is the maximum size that an agent that has detoured from the Crowd Manager can go.
- **Max Avoided Agents**: This is the maximum number of agents that the Detour System takes into consideration, and it also called neighbors. In other words, this specifies how many neighbor agents (maximum) should be taken into account for the avoidance behavior.
- **Max Avoided Walls**: This is the maximum number of walls (in general, obstacle segments) that the Detour System should take into consideration. It works in a similar fashion to Max Avoided Agents, but asks about how many segments of the surrounding obstacles around the system need to be taken into account.
- **Navmesh Check Interval**: This is for implementing how many seconds an agent that has gone off the navmesh should check and recalculate its position (the system will try to push the agent back onto the navmesh).
- **Path Optimization Interval**: This checks, in seconds, how often an agent should try to re-optimize its own path.
- **Separation Dir Clamp**: When another agent is behind, this value indicates the clamp separation force to left/right (dot product between *forward* and *dirToNei*; thus, a value of -1 means that this separation behavior is disabled).
- **Path Offset Radius Multiplier**: When the agent is turning close to a corner, an offset to the path is applied. This variable is a multiplier to this offset (so that you are free to reduce and increase this offset).
- **Resolve Collisions**: Despite the best efforts of the Detour System, agents may still collide. In such an event, the collision should be handled by the Detour System (with a value of true for this variable). In this case, this variable is set to false and the agents will be using a Character Movement Component. This component will take care of resolving the collision.

The **Avoidance Config** parameter, which is shown in the following screenshot, is the heart of how sampling is done within the Detour Crowd Algorithm:

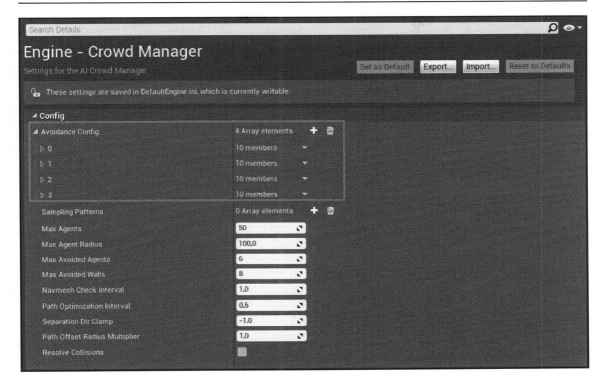

**Avoidance Config** is an array of different sampling configurations, with slightly different parameters set. By default, there are four of them, corresponding to different sampling avoidance quality: low, medium, good, and high, respectively.

The quality level is set in the **UCrowdFollowingComponent** with the **AvoidanceQuality** variable, which uses the **ECrowdAvoidanceQuality** enum. If you have a reference to your **UCrowdFollowingComponent**, you can use the `SetCrowdAvoidanceQuality()` function.

Going back to the setting, if you want to add or remove a configuration, you will need to create your own version of the **UCrowdFollowingComponent** (alternatively, you can inherit from it and override functions), which takes into consideration a different number of configurations.

However, changing the number of configuration means that your game/application is making particular use of the *Detour System*!

Without changing the number of configurations, you can change the settings of these four quality configurations. These parameters are shown in the following screenshot (this is from the first configuration):

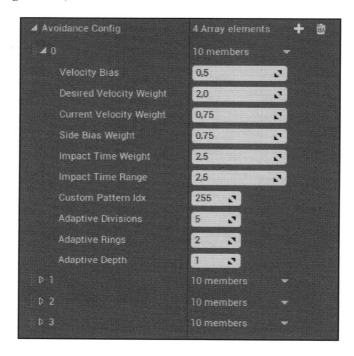

To fully understand these settings, you should get to know how the algorithm works, but let's try and get our head around it without this.

The part of the algorithm that does the sampling starts by creating a set of rings (the number is indicated in the **Adaptive Rings** parameter) around the center point (where the agent is initially, with a bias, due to the **Velocity Bias** parameter, in the direction of the velocity). Each of these rings is sampled (divided) by **Adaptive Division**. Then, the algorithm recursively refines the search by using a smaller set of rings, which are centered on the best sample of the previous iteration. The algorithm repeats this process **Adaptive Depth** times. At each iteration, the best sample is chosen by considering the following, and the different parameters determine the weight (how important the consideration is with respect to the others):

- Does the direction of the agent match the current velocity? The weight is **DesiredVelocityWeight**.
- Does the agent go sideways? The weight is **SideBiasWeight**.

- Does the agent collide with any known obstacle? The weight is **ImpactTimeWeight** (it scans a range by considering the current velocity of the agent if it collides using that velocity within **ImpactTimeRange** seconds).

The following diagram should help you understand the different parameters:

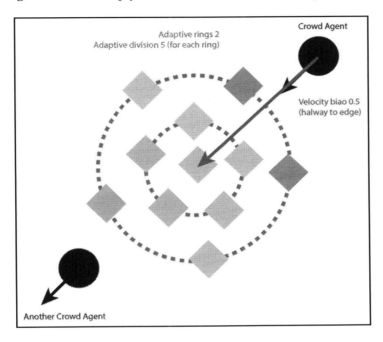

# Debugging the Detour Crowd Manager

The Crowd Manager has an integration with the visual logger, which means that, with some work, we can visually debug the Detour Crowd Manager. We will explore this in more detail in Chapter 13, *Gameplay Debugger*, in which we will learn more about the Visual Logger further.

# More crowd resources

Here some resources if you want to extend your knowledge of the Detour Crowd Algorithm and/or explore other alternatives:

- Mikko Mononen's original Recast Library: `https://github.com/recastnavigation/recastnavigation`
- A collection of many interesting research algorithms for handling crowds: `http://gamma.cs.unc.edu/research/crowds`

Of course, you are welcome to keep exploring on your own!

# Summary

In this chapter, we have seen how the Unreal Engine handles crowds. In particular, we have seen two built-in systems. The first one is called *Reciprocal Velocity Obstacles (RVO)*, which is very fast, but not very precise. The second is the **Detour Crowd**, which is a bit more expensive, but more precise and realistic.

In the next chapter, we will move on and learn how to implement our own *Behavior Tree* from scratch.

# Section 2: Designing and Implementing Behavior Trees

This section, composed of three chapters, will take you on a little journey on the whole process of creating a Behavior Tree, from Design to Implementation. In particular, a concrete example is shown (crafted in such way that we will need to use almost all the skills learnt in the previous chapters), thus giving you the possibility to get some practice.

The following chapters will be covered in this section:

- Chapter 8, Designing Behavior Trees - Part I
- Chapter 9, Designing Behavior Trees - Part II
- Chapter 10, Designing Behavior Trees - Part III

# Designing Behavior Trees - Part I

**8**

This chapter (and the two that follow) will take you through a more practical approach of what we have learned so far. In particular, we will be focusing on how to implement a *Behavior Tree* so that we can chase our character in the game.

In fact, we will use all the content from `Chapter 2`, *Behavior Trees and Blackboards*, along with a *blackboard*, to execute these actions, a *NavMesh* to move around the environment, and the *Perception System* to sense the Player.

In this chapter, we will cover the following topics:

- How to design a **Behavior Tree**, starting from the **Expected Behavior**
- Analyzing the nodes that we might need on a **Behavior Tree**
- Implementing a **Custom Decorator** (both in Blueprint and C++) to check boolean variables
- Implementing a **Custom Task** (both in Blueprint and C++) to find a random location around the character
- Using the **Navigation System** to query the **NavMesh** to find the random location
- Implementing a **Custom AI Controller** (both in Blueprint and C++) to use the **Perception System**
- Using the **Perception System** to sense the Player

We will cover more in the two chapters that follow.

We will be implementing everything in both Blueprint and C++ to give you a broader idea of what you can use. Alternatively, if you already know what you want to use, you can just follow one of the two implementations.

If you want to follow along, I'm creating this example by starting a clean project (in my case, I'm doing this in C++, but if you want to follow just the Blueprint part of this chapter, you can use the Blueprint Template), as shown in the following screenshot:

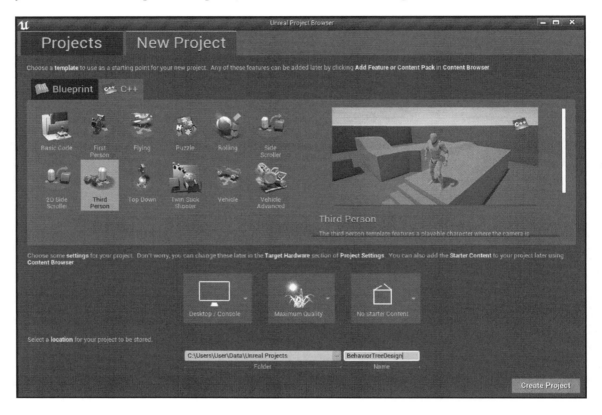

Unreal Project Browser

The project is called `BehaviorTreeDesign` and I am using the `Third Person` template.

With all this said and done, let's dive in!

# The Expected Behavior

The first step in **Designing a Behavior Tree** is to pin down the **Expected Behavior** we would like to see in our character. This seems like a simple phase, but trying to take all the cases into consideration isn't trivial. However, it will avoid many headaches later on.

While writing down the **Expected Behavior**, try to be as specific as possible. If something is unclear, try to rephrase it. The sentences that you use should be short and always add information. Don't be scared if you have sentences starting with "In this case…" or "If…", because it will just mean that you are taking all the different possibilities into consideration. Once you have written it, read it out loud, maybe to a friend, and ask him/her if he/she clearly understands its meaning.

This is my attempt of describing the behavior we are going to implement in this chapter: *"The agent checks whether it has the player in sight. If it is true, then it chases the player until he/she is no longer in sight. If the player is not in sight, then the agent goes to the last location where it saw the player (if the location is known). Otherwise, the agent chooses a random location around it and goes to that location"*

# Building the Nodes

After you've written the **Expected Behavior**, the next step is to analyze it so that you understand which kind of Behavior Tree nodes we will need. Of course, we can always add them at a later stage, but it is better to try and anticipate as much as possible so that you can proceed smoothly during the creation of the **Behavior Tree**. Let's break down the expected behavior so that we can try and understand which node we need to implement.

# Nodes that already exist

We need to check which part of our behavior already exists in our project, and whether it is either a built-in functionality or whether we have already created the node for that functionality (maybe for another *AI Behavior Tree*).

"The agent checks whether it has the player in sight. If it is true, **then it chases the player** until he/she is no longer in sight. If the player is not in sight, **then the agent goes** to the last location where it saw the player (if the location is known). Otherwise, the agent chooses a random location around it **and goes to that location**."

In particular, it's worth noting that we already have a *Behavior Tree Task* already built in that allows the agent to chase after an object or reach a location. Therefore, all the highlighted parts of the **Expected Behavior** are covered.

# Decorator – check variable

"***The agent checks whether it has the player in sight.*** *If it is true, then it chases the player until he/she is no longer in sight. If the player is not in sight, then the agent goes to the last location where it saw the player (if the location is known). Otherwise, the agent chooses a random location around it and goes to that location.*"

To perform this check, we need to decide how the agent is going to "*perceive*" the player. In chapter 5, we saw how the built-in perception system works, and for such a trivial task, the system is more than perfect. Therefore, it is worth using it. However, we need to transfer this information into the *Behavior Tree*. Therefore, we need to start making assumptions on how we will implement the whole AI Behavior. For now, let's assume that this information regarding whether the player is in sight or not is stored within a boolean *Blackboard* variable. As a result, we need to implement a decorator that it is able to check this boolean variable.

 You could also use the ***Blackboard*** decorator (which is displayed for "*Blackboard Based Conditions*") to check whether a variable is assigned or not and use that to determine whether the player is on-sight or not. However, since the main goal of this chapter is to learn how to build a *Behavior Tree* from scratch from a practical point of view, it is more useful for you to create an extra Decorator node so that you are more familiar with the process of creating Decorators as well.

Also, while designing nodes, we need to try and be as general as possible, so that if we have a similar need in another *Behavior Tree*, we can reuse the node we have created. Therefore, we can create a check, by using a *Decorator* node, for boolean variables in general, and we will use this to check if a variable in our Blackboard tells us whether the player is in sight.

Once we have established this, we need to think about how we are going to implement the node. In this specific case, it is quite straightforward, but to keep things as general as possible, let's think of other possible use of this node.

For instance, what if we want to check if the variable is false instead? Actually, we will need this functionality (you will understand why later in this chapter). Thankfully, Unreal has us covered. In fact, there is a handy checkbox in the details panel of a decorator named **Inverse Condition**, which (as the name suggests) inverts the result of the condition, allowing us somehow check for the opposite:

As an exercise, ignore this checkbox and try to implement your own version of inverting the condition. Even though it has no practical application, and *it is actually bad practice* doing something like that, it is still a useful exercise so that you can understand how inputs are given to a Decorator. In this exercise, there are two inputs for this node: the Blackboard key value (which is assumed to be a boolean type) to check, and another boolean variable to establish if the check is on the "true" or "false" value of the variable.

Without further ado, let's move on to the actual implementation of this node. As usual, I will do this both in Blueprint and C++.

## Check Variable Blueprint implementation

First of all, let's create a new *Decorator* (recall that you can either create it from the Behavior Tree editor or from the content browser; the first one is easier, but you need to have a Behavior Tree open). Either way, name it BTDecorator_CheckBooleanVariableBP (the ending "BP" is only used to distinguish it from the C++ version of it, since you might be doing both. In a real project, you usually have only one version).

In case you close the Editor without adding anything to your Decorator (for instance, to rename it), when you open it, you might see a screen like the following:

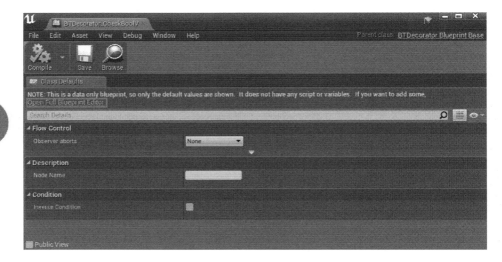

In this case, just click on **Open Full Blueprint Editor** to go to the Blueprint Editor.

As we stated previously, we just need a single variable of type *Blackboard Key Selector* as input, which we will name BoolVariableToCheckKey. This holds a reference to the blackboard boolean variable we would like to check. Moreover, it needs to be public (open the eye next to the variable name) so that it can be seen within the Behavior Tree Editor. This is what it should look like:

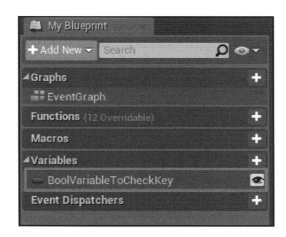

Next, we need to implement/override the Perform Condition Check AI function, which can be found in the override dropdown menu, as shown in the following screenshot:

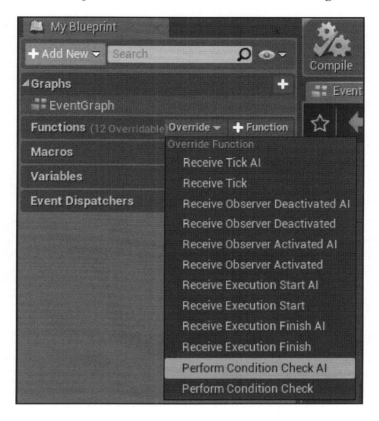

Once the function has been created, this is what it looks like by default:

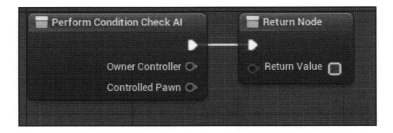

First, we need to retrieve the boolean value of our Blackboard Key, which can be done by using the **Get Blackboard Value as Bool** node. Then, we can plug the **Return Value** pin of this node into the **Return Value** pin of the **Return Node**. This is what the final graph should look like:

Save the Blueprint, and the Decorator will be ready. If you wish, you can place it somewhere in a Behavior Tree to see if the inputs show up properly. In particular, this is what it looks like when placed in a Behavior Tree:

Finally, the *Details Panel* of the *Decorator* (within the Behavior Tree Editor) should look as follows:

# Check Variable C++ implementation

For details on how to extend a Decorator, you can have a look at Chapter 6, *Extending Behavior Trees*.

First of all, let's create a new C++ class that inherits from **UBTDecorator**. You need to search for all the classes and select **BTDecorator**, as shown in the following screenshot:

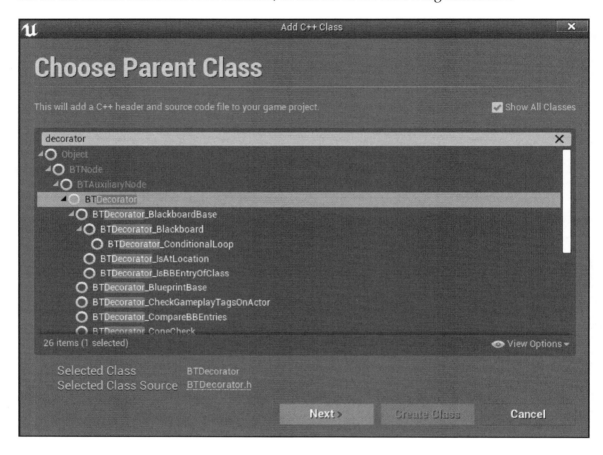

Then, you can rename your class BTDecorator_CheckBoolVariable. Also, if you wish, you can place the file in a sub-folder, such as AI. As example of this is shown in the following screenshot:

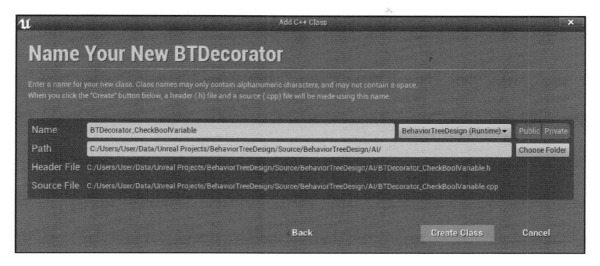

Press **Create Class**, and your *Decorator* class will be created.

After you have created the Class, Unreal will try to compile your code. If you haven't set up your Public Dependencies in your project properly (as we learned back in Chapter 1 and Chapter 2; and especially in Chapter 6, *Extending Behavior Trees*), you should have a message similar to the following:

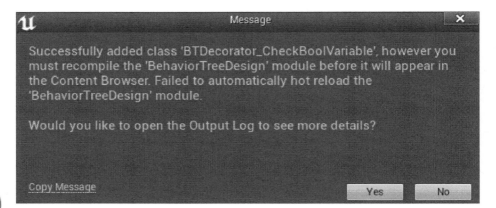

However, when you try to compile from Visual Studio, this is what the error will look like:

Therefore, you need to change your .cs file (in our case, *BehaviorTreeDesign.cs*), and add "**GameplayTasks**" and "**AIModule**" as public dependencies, as shown in the following code:

```
PublicDependencyModuleNames.AddRange(new string[] {
"Core", "CoreUObject", "Engine", "InputCore",
"HeadMountedDisplay", "GameplayTasks", "AIModule" });
```

Now, you should be able compile without any issues.

In the header file, we need to add an input variable, the *Blackboard Key Selector* that references a Boolean, named `BoolVariableToCheck`. We also need to expose this variable to the Behavior Tree editor by using the `UPROPERTY()` macro, as shown in the following code:

```
protected:
  UPROPERTY(EditAnywhere, Category = Blackboard)
  FBlackboardKeySelector BoolVariableToCheck;
```

Then, we need to override the `CalculateRawConditionValue()` method, which is public, and so its override needs to be public as well. Insert (always in the header file) the following lines of code:

```
public:
  virtual bool CalculateRawConditionValue(UBehaviorTreeComponent&
OwnerComp, uint8* NodeMemory) const override;
```

Next, we need to implement this function.

First, we need to retrieve `BlackboardComponent`, which allows us to resolve and get the values from the Blackboard Key Selectors. Thankfully, we can retrieve it from `BeheviorTreeComponent` (on which this decorator is running), which is passed to the node as a variable named `OwnerComp`. However, to use `BlackboardComponent`, we need to include its definition in our `.cpp` file, with the following statement:

```
#include "BehaviorTree/BlackboardComponent.h"
```

If, for some reason, this `BlackboardComponent` is invalid (this might happen if you create a Behavior Tree in your Project but you have no Blackboards; otherwise this is difficult to do, since the Behavior Tree editor automatically picks a Blackboard), we can just `return false`:

```
  //Get BlackboardComponent
  const UBlackboardComponent* BlackboardComp =
OwnerComp.GetBlackboardComponent();
  if (BlackboardComp == NULL)
  {
    return false;
  }
```

Then, we need to retrieve and return the value, as a Boolean, from our *Blackboard Key Selector* variable. This is how we can do this:

```
//Perform Boolean Variable Check
return
BlackboardComp->GetValueAsBool(BoolVariableToCheck.SelectedKeyName);
```

This is what the whole function should look like:

```
#include "BTDecorator_CheckBoolVariable.h"
#include "BehaviorTree/BlackboardComponent.h"

bool
UBTDecorator_CheckBoolVariable::CalculateRawConditionValue(UBehaviorTreeCom
ponent & OwnerComp, uint8 * NodeMemory) const
{
  //Get BlackboardComponent
  const UBlackboardComponent* BlackboardComp =
OwnerComp.GetBlackboardComponent();
  if (BlackboardComp == NULL)
  {
    return false;
  }

  //Perform Boolean Variable Check
  return
BlackboardComp->GetValueAsBool(BoolVariableToCheck.SelectedKeyName);
}
```

Save your code and the *Decorator* will be ready. If you wish, you can place it somewhere in a Behavior Tree to see if the inputs show up properly. This is how it appears on the tree:

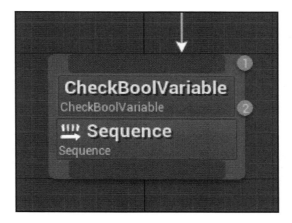

The *Details Panel* of the *Decorator* (within the *Behavior Tree Editor*) should look as follows:

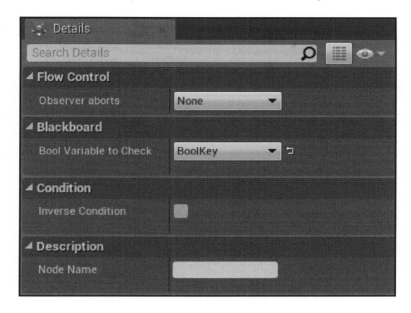

As you may have noticed, the description of our Decorator doesn't change based on which variable we put into it, nor does it have an icon. If you are working on a large project, paying attention to these details might help you and your team greatly. In this small example, I will leave this as an exercise. You can consult Chapter 5, *Agent Awareness*, for more information on how to do it. You can also consult the source code, in particular, BTDecorator_TimeLimit, which implements functions such as GetStaticDescription(), DescribeRuntimeValues(), and GetNodeIconName(). In this section, we are going to implement the **GetStaticDescription()** function so that you can get used to implementing these kinds of functions as well.

If you haven't read the preceding tip box, do so. Now, we are going to implement the GetStaticDescription() function for our Decorator so that we can see which Blackboard key has been selected for the BoolVariableToCheck variable.

To start, we need to add the following override to the header file:

```
virtual FString GetStaticDescription() const override;
```

Then, we can implement it by returning an `FString` that has been formatted with the `Printf()` function. By using a `?` statement, we can determine whether the Key has been set or not and show the right string value:

```
FString UBTDecorator_CheckBoolVariable::GetStaticDescription() const
{
   return FString::Printf(TEXT("%s: '%s'"), TEXT("Bool Variable to Check"),
BoolVariableToCheck.IsSet() ?
*BoolVariableToCheck.SelectedKeyName.ToString() : TEXT(""));
}
```

If you compile and add the decorator to the *Behavior Tree*, this is what it should look like now:

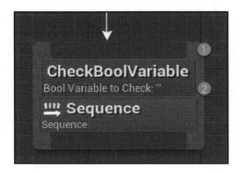

Much better! Now, it's time to implement a *Behavior Tree Task*.

# Task – Find Random Location

*"The agent checks whether it has the player in sight. If it is true, then it chases the player until he/she is no longer in sight. If the player is not in sight, then the agent goes to the last location where it saw the player (if the location is known). Otherwise, **the agent chooses a random location around it and goes to that location**."*

During our Behavior, the agent selects a random location around it. This means that we need to create a Task that, starting from the current location of the agent, picks a random location that it will go to. Moreover, we should add that this location needs to be reachable by the agent. Thankfully, we have some pre-made functions to query the *Navigation Mesh* and select a *Random Location* for us.

This also means that we need to assume that we have a *Navigation Mesh* available for our agent. Since this is the case, we can use this node. However, we still need to create a Task that can be executed in the Behavior Tree, and that stores this value properly somewhere in the *Blackboard*.

Thinking like a general node, we would like to add some additional options so that we can customize the behavior. For instance, how far away would we like this Random Location could be?

We have two input variables. The first is a Blackboard Key Selector that holds the Random Location we want to go to (since we need to save it in the Blackboard). The second will be just a float indicating the maximum Radius of where this Random Location can be taken.

Once again, we will do this process both in Blueprint and C++ (so you can choose the implementation you are the most comfortable with).

# Find Random Location Blueprint implementation

Create a *Blueprint Behavior Tree Task* (read the previous chapter to learn how to do this) and name it BTT_FindRandomLocation.

Create the two variables we need, one of the Blackboard Key Selector type named **"RandomDestination"** and the other one of the *float* type named **"Radius"**. For the float, set a *default value different from zero*, for example, **3,000**. Finally, make them both *public*:

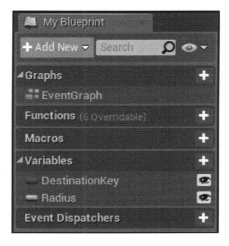

Let's implement/override the **Receive Execute AI** event, as shown in the following screenshot:

From the event, we can retrieve the *Controller Pawn* actor (the agent) from which we can get its location, as shown in the following screenshot:

Then, we can use the **GetRandomReachablePointInRadius** node to generate a random reachable location within the *NavMesh*. We need to use as *Location* as the *Origin* from the **Controlled Pawn** (the agent), and *Radius* as our *Radius variable*:

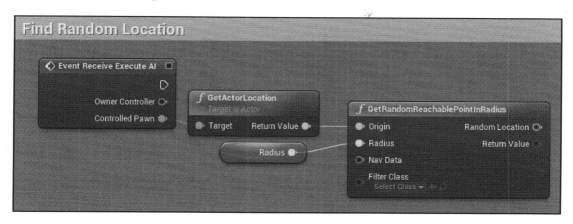

Find Random Location Blueprint

From the return value of the **GetRandomReachablePointInRadius** node, we create a **Branch** node. However, the call to generate the random location can fail. If it does, we need to terminate the task with an *insuccess (not Success)*. From the **Branch True** pin, we can set the **Random Location** in our **Destination Key** variable, as shown in the following screenshot:

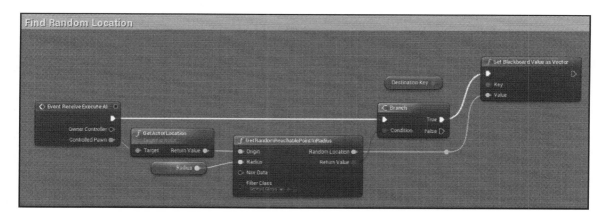

Find Random Location Blueprint

Then, regardless of the **Branch** (from both the end of the **Set Blackboard Value as Vector** node and from the **False** pin of the **Branch**), we need to **Finish Execute** the task. To do this, we can plug the return value of the *GetRandomReachablePointInRadius* node into the **Success** pin of the **Finish Execute**:

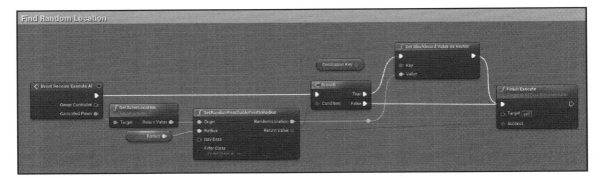

This concludes our task, which we can now save.

If we place this node in a *Behavior Tree*, this is what it will look like:

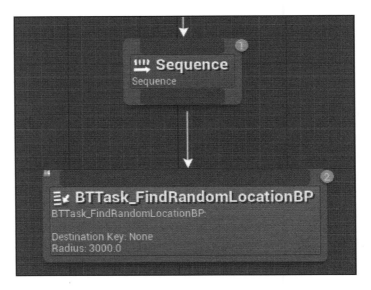

The *Details Panel* will look as follows:

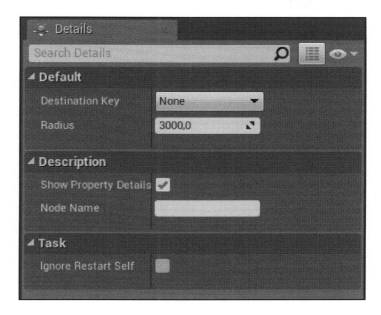

If you want, you can read the next section to learn how to implement this task in C++, otherwise, you are free to skip the next section.

# Find Random Location C++ implementation

Creating the Find Random Location task in C++ will be a bit more complicated than creating the Decorator, since we need to retrieve many components and check if they are valid.

First of all, create a C++ **Behavior Tree Task** that inherits from **UBTTaskNode** by selecting **BTTaskNode** as the class you want to extend, as shown in the following screenshot:

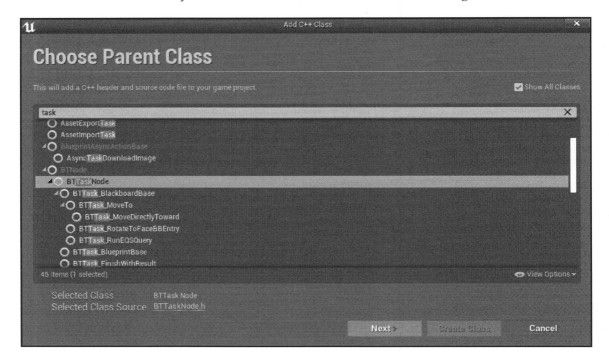

Then, we can name it `BTTaskNode_FindRandomLocation` and place it (as we did for the Decorator) inside a folder, such as `AI`:

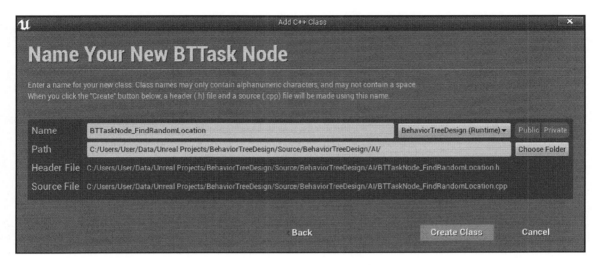

First of all, in the header file, we need to add our two variables. The first one is the *Blackboard Key Selector* named `DestinationVector`, which will hold the reference to the newly calculated Destination. The second is a *float* containing a parametrization of the **Radius** (in which we will select a Random Reachable Point). Moreover, both of them need to be accessible to the *Behavior Tree Editor*; hence we need to expose them by using the `UPROPERTY()` macro. We need to use the following lines of code for these two variables:

```
UPROPERTY(EditAnywhere, Category = Blackboard)
    FBlackboardKeySelector DestinationVector;

UPROPERTY(EditAnywhere, Category = Parameters)
    float Radius = 300.f;
```

As always, in the header file, we need to override the `ExecuteTask()` method, which will be called when this task needs to be executed:

```
virtual EBTNodeResult::Type ExecuteTask(UBehaviorTreeComponent& OwnerComp,
uint8* NodeMemory) override;
```

This is what the whole header file should look like:

```
#pragma once

#include "CoreMinimal.h"
#include "BehaviorTree/BTTaskNode.h"
#include "BTTaskNode_FindRandomLocation.generated.h"

/**
 *
 */
UCLASS()
class BEHAVIORTREEDESIGN_API UBTTaskNode_FindRandomLocation : public
UBTTaskNode
{
  GENERATED_BODY()

  UPROPERTY(EditAnywhere, Category = Blackboard)
  FBlackboardKeySelector DestinationVector;

  UPROPERTY(EditAnywhere, Category = Parameters)
  float Radius = 300.f;

  virtual EBTNodeResult::Type ExecuteTask(UBehaviorTreeComponent&
OwnerComp, uint8* NodeMemory) override;
};
```

Now, that we are getting to our `.cpp` file, we need to do some preparation, especially in the `include` statements. In fact, we are going to use the **Blackboard Component** (like we did for the Decorator), the **Navigation System**, and the **AI Controller** classes. Thus, we need to include all of them, which we can do by using the following code:

```
#include "BTTaskNode_FindRandomLocation.h"
#include "BehaviorTree/BlackboardComponent.h"
#include "NavigationSystem.h"
#include "AIController.h"
```

So, let's define the `ExecuteTask()` function:

```
EBTNodeResult::Type
UBTTaskNode_FindRandomLocation::ExecuteTask(UBehaviorTreeComponent &
OwnerComp, uint8 * NodeMemory)
{
  //[REST OF THE CODE]
}
```

Then, we need to start filling up the `ExecuteTask()` function. The first thing we need to do is get the **Blackboard Component**. In case this component is not available (as explained in the *Decorator* section, this seldom happens, but it still might), we need to return that the Task has failed, as shown in the following code:

```
EBTNodeResult::Type
UBTTaskNode_FindRandomLocation::ExecuteTask(UBehaviorTreeComponent &
OwnerComp, uint8 * NodeMemory)
{
  //Get Blackboard Component
  UBlackboardComponent* BlackboardComp =
OwnerComp.GetBlackboardComponent();
  if (BlackboardComp == NULL)
  {
    return EBTNodeResult::Failed;
  }

  //[REST OF THE CODE]

}
```

From the Blackboard Component, we can retrieve the *Controlled Pawn* of the AI Controller that is running this instance of the *Behavior Tree*. This can be done by using a couple of GET functions. However, once again, the *Pawn* needs to be checked for its validity, and in case it isn't valid, then the tasks need to return a failure:

```
EBTNodeResult::Type
UBTTaskNode_FindRandomLocation::ExecuteTask(UBehaviorTreeComponent &
OwnerComp, uint8 * NodeMemory)
{
  //[PREVIOUS CODE]

  //Get Controlled Pawn
  APawn* ControlledPawn = OwnerComp.GetAIOwner()->GetPawn();
  if (!ControlledPawn) {
    return EBTNodeResult::Failed;
  }

  //[REST OF THE CODE]

}
```

Next, we need to get our Navigation System. As per Unreal 4.21, we will use the
`UNavigationSystemV1` class to do so.

 Starting from Unreal 4.20, the Navigation System has been refactored.
Therefore, many functions and classes became deprecated. If the version
of your Engine is below 4.20, this code will not work. In this case, you will
need to use the `UNavigationSystem` class. This isn't covered in this book
since it may only be of interest to a few readers with specific needs of
using an old version of the engine.

To get the **Current Navigation System**, we need to specify the **World** from which we want
to retrieve this data by using a specific function named `GetCurrent()` (referring to the
Navigation System). Once we have obtained the Navigation System, we want to check its
validity, and in case it isn't valid, then we make the Task fail:

```
EBTNodeResult::Type
UBTTaskNode_FindRandomLocation::ExecuteTask(UBehaviorTreeComponent &
OwnerComp, uint8 * NodeMemory)
{
  //[PREVIOUS CODE]

  //Get Navigation System
  UNavigationSystemV1* NavSys =
UNavigationSystemV1::GetCurrent(GetWorld());
  if (!NavSys)
  {
    return EBTNodeResult::Failed;
  }

  //[REST OF THE CODE]

}
```

There's one more step to go before we can perform the query on the Navigation System. We
need to create a variable of the `FNavLocation` type named `Result`, which is a structure
that our **Navigation System** will fill with the result of our query. In our case, we are only
interested in the Location. As a result, the **Navigation System** is able to perform the query:

```
EBTNodeResult::Type
UBTTaskNode_FindRandomLocation::ExecuteTask(UBehaviorTreeComponent &
OwnerComp, uint8 * NodeMemory)
{
  //[PREVIOUS CODE]

  //Prepare variables for Query
  FNavLocation Result;
```

```
    FVector Origin = ControlledPawn->GetActorLocation();

  //[REST OF THE CODE]

}
```

The request to the Query can be done by using
the `GetRandomReachablePointInRadius()` function. It has three mandatory parameters,
which are the ***Origin*** from where this query needs to be performed, the **Radius**, and the
Structure to return the result. In fact, its pure return value is a *boolean* that indicates if the
query has succeeded or not, which we can use to check whether the task has failed or not:

```
EBTNodeResult::Type
UBTTaskNode_FindRandomLocation::ExecuteTask(UBehaviorTreeComponent &
OwnerComp, uint8 * NodeMemory)
{
  //[PREVIOUS CODE]

  //Perform Query
  bool bSuccess = NavSys->GetRandomReachablePointInRadius(Origin, Radius,
Result);
  if (!bSuccess) {
    return EBTNodeResult::Failed;
  }

  //[REST OF THE CODE]

}
```

In case we were able to get a random point, we need to assign it within the blackboard and
return that the task has succeeded:

```
EBTNodeResult::Type
UBTTaskNode_FindRandomLocation::ExecuteTask(UBehaviorTreeComponent &
OwnerComp, uint8 * NodeMemory)
{
  //[PREVIOUS CODE]

  //Save Result and return success
  BlackboardComp->SetValueAsVector(DestinationVector.SelectedKeyName,
Result.Location);
  return EBTNodeResult::Succeeded;
}
```

If you try to compile this right now, you will get an error. The reason for this is that we have been using the **Navigation System**, but it was not included in the public dependencies of our module. Also, if you didn't include `AIModule` and `GameplayTasks`, this is the right moment to add them so that you can compile the code without any errors.

Open the `BehaviourTreeDesign.Build.cs` file and add the `NavigationSystem` module to the public dependencies, as shown in the following code:

```
PublicDependencyModuleNames.AddRange(new string[] { "Core", "CoreUObject",
"Engine", "InputCore", "HeadMountedDisplay", "GameplayTasks", "AIModule",
"NavigationSystem" });
```

Now, we can compile without any problems.

If we add this *Task* node to our *Behavior Tree*, this is what it will look like:

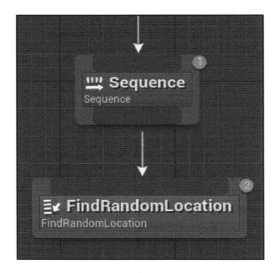

The *Details Panel* looks as follows:

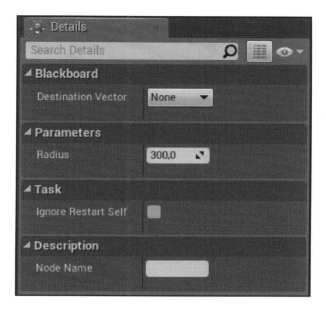

As we discussed earlier for the Decorator, it is always good practice to implement the functions that describe the node so that we can use it easier. I understand that we might not have an icon ready, but at least we can change the description to show which variables we have assigned.

To do this, we need to implement/override the GetStaticDescription() function. Declare it in the header file by adding the following line:

```
virtual FString GetStaticDescription() const override;
```

Then, in the .cpp file, we need to return a FString that has been formatted to show the variables of the Task. In particular, we want to show the DestinationKey and how big the *Radius* is. We can easily format the string with the Printf() function, as shown in the following code:

```
FString UBTTaskNode_FindRandomLocation::GetStaticDescription() const
{
   return FString::Printf(TEXT("%s: '%s'"), TEXT("DestinationKey"),
DestinationVector.IsSet() ? *DestinationVector.SelectedKeyName.ToString() :
TEXT(""))
       .Append(FString::Printf(TEXT("\n%s: '%s'"), TEXT("Radius"),
*FString::SanitizeFloat(Radius)));
}
```

If we compile and add this *Task* again to a *Behavior Tree,* this is how it should appear now:

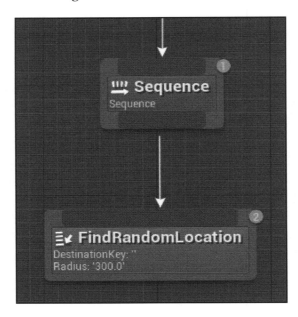

This concludes the implementation of our Task in C++.

# AI Controller

From the *Expected Behavior,* we have concluded that we need a *Perception System* to check whether the agent is able to see the *Player*.

Once again, we can create our AI Controller both in Blueprint or C++.

# Implementing the AI Controller in Blueprint

First of all, create a new AI Controller and name it BP_ChasingAIController by selecting
the AIController *Class*:

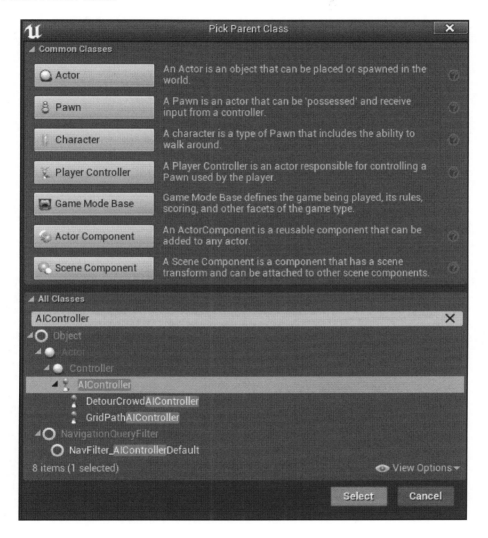

In the editor, we need to add two variables (so that the Service we build in the next chapter will be able to retrieve the values within them). The first variable is `LastKnownPlayerPosition` of type *Vector*, and the second is `CanSeePlayer` of type *boolean*, as shown in the following screenshot:

Now, we need to add the perception component. So, from the **Components** tab, add the **AIPerception** system, as shown in the following screenshot:

Then, in the **Details** panel, we need to select the options for it. In particular, we need to set the *Sense of Sight*:

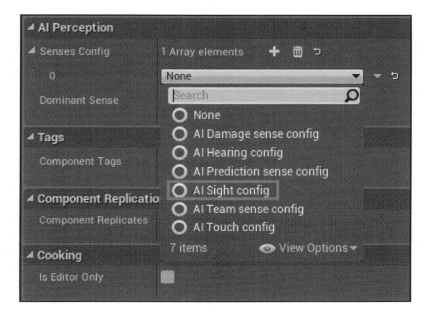

Next, in the **Sense Of Sight Config** settings, check all the detection flags (as we explained in Chapter 5, *Agent Awareness*, we need to detect the player, which by default is neutral). In the end, this is what the settings should look like:

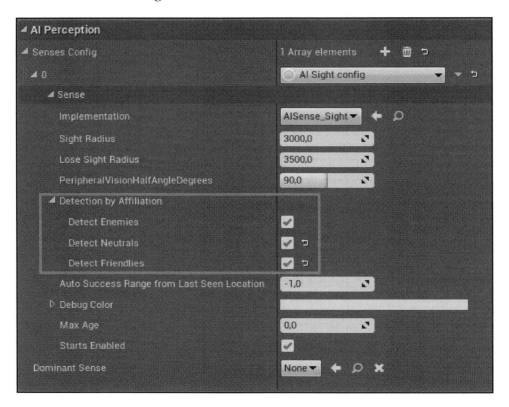

From the **Details** panel, we need to generate the **On Target Perception Updated** event by clicking on the **+** symbol next to it:

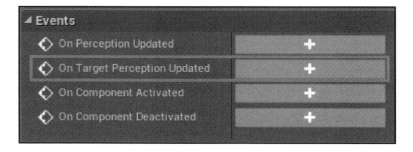

Now, we cast the **Actor** pin from the event into our player (for
example, `FirstPersonCharacter` or `ThirdPersonCharacter`, depending which
template you choose, or your *Player class* if you are using this in your project), to check if
the object of the perception is actually the player:

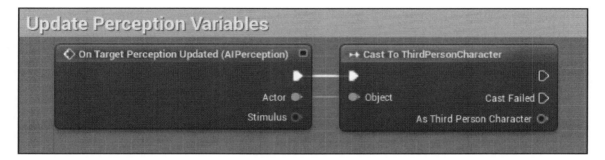

Then, we break the **Stimulus** pin to get the **Stimulus Location,** which we store inside the
**LastKnownPlayerPosition** variable, and **Successfully Sensed,** which we store inside the
*CanSeePlayer* variable. Of course, these Set functions need to be placed after the cast. This
is the final code:

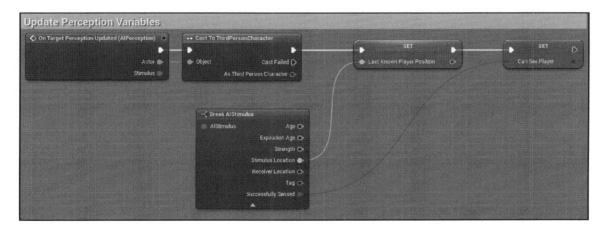

The *AI Controller* is now ready to be used.

# Implementing the AI Controller in C++

First of all, create a new class that inherits from AIController:

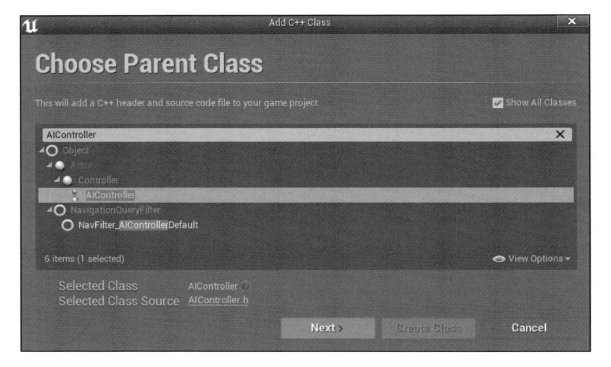

Then, name it `ChasingAIController` and place it in our `AI` folder, as shown in the following screenshot:

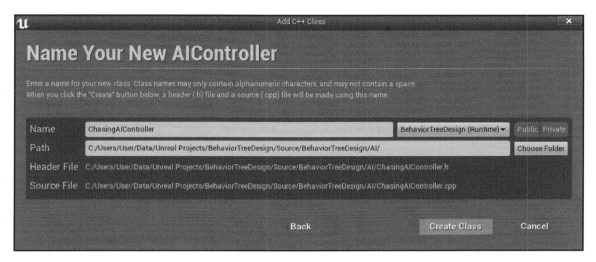

As we explained in the Chapter about the *Perception*, we first need to include the classes that concern the perception to be able to use them. Add the following `#include` statements in the header file:

```
#include "Perception/AIPerceptionComponent.h"
#include "Perception/AISense_Sight.h"
#include "Perception/AISenseConfig_Sight.h"
```

Next, we need to add the declaration of our *Class Constructor,* since we will be using one to set up our controller. Just below the `GENERATE_BODY()` macro, add the following code:

```
GENERATED_BODY()

AChasingAIController();
```

We need to keep track of the `PerceptionComponent` that we will add to the controller. However, the AI Controller base class, has already a reference to a Perception Component, so we don't need to declare it. You will find this very signature in the base class:

```
UPROPERTY(VisibleDefaultsOnly, Category = AI)
UAIPerceptionComponent* PerceptionComponent;
```

However, we need to have a reference to the *Sight Configuration* that we will create, so we need this variable:

```
UAISenseConfig_Sight* SightConfig;
```

Since in the next chapter we will create a service that will gather some variables from this controller, we need to make two public variables. The first variable is the `LastKnownPlayerPosition` of type Vector, and the second is `CanSeePlayer` of type boolean. You can add them in the header with the following snippet of code:

```
public:
  FVector LastKnownPlayerPosition;
  bool bCanSeePlayer;
```

Finally, in our header file, we need to **add a delegate** for our Perception System that will update our variables. We can call this delegate `OnTargetPerceptionUpdated()` and make it protected. It has `AActor*` and `FAIStimuli` as inputs, as shown in the following code:

```
protected:
  UFUNCTION()
  void OnTargetPerceptionUpdate(AActor* Actor, FAIStimulus Stimulus);
```

Now, we need to create the **Perception Component** in the **Constructor** of the class. Add the following code:

```
AChasingAIController::AChasingAIController() {

  //Creating the AI Perception Component
  PerceptionComponent =
CreateDefaultSubobject<UAIPerceptionComponent>(TEXT("SightPerceptionCompone
nt"));

  //[REST OF THE CODE]

}
```

Then, we need to create the *Sight Sense*, and configure it to set all the `DetectionByAffiliation` to true, as shown in the following code:

```
AChasingAIController::AChasingAIController() {

  //[PREVIOUS CODE]

  //Create the Sight Sense and Configure it
  SightConfig = CreateDefaultSubobject<UAISenseConfig_Sight>(FName("Sight
Config"));
  SightConfig->DetectionByAffiliation.bDetectEnemies = true;
  SightConfig->DetectionByAffiliation.bDetectNeutrals = true;
  SightConfig->DetectionByAffiliation.bDetectFriendlies = true;

  //[REST OF THE CODE]

}
```

Now that we have `PerceptionComponent` and `SightConfig`, we need to assign the latter to the first:

```
AChasingAIController::AChasingAIController() {

  //[PREVIOUS CODE]

  //Assigning the Sight Sense to the AI Perception Component
  PerceptionComponent->ConfigureSense(*SightConfig);
PerceptionComponent->SetDominantSense(SightConfig->GetSenseImplementation()
);

  //[REST OF THE CODE]

}
```

The last step is to **bind our delegate** function to the **Perception System**, as shown in the following code:

```
AChasingAIController::AChasingAIController() {

  //[PREVIOUS CODE]

  //Binding the OnTargetPerceptionUpdate function
  PerceptionComponent->OnTargetPerceptionUpdated.AddDynamic(this,
&AChasingAIController::OnTargetPerceptionUpdate);

}
```

Now, we need to implement our `OnTargetPerceptionUpdate()` Delegate. First of all, we need to include the header file of our Player class. In this example case, we have a C++ class named `BehaviorTreeDesignCharacter` (the Blueprint `ThirdPersonCharacter` inherits from this class). In my case, I added the following `#include` statement (you can include the one of your Player class):

```
#include "BehaviorTreeDesignCharacter.h"
```

In particular, we need to check if the Actor (passed as input) is really the *Player* class, which we can do with a cast (to the Player class we have included):

```
void AChasingAIController::OnTargetPerceptionUpdate(AActor * Actor,
FAIStimulus Stimulus)
{
   if(Cast<ABehaviorTreeDesignCharacter>(Actor)){

   }
}
```

If this is the case, we can use the *Stimulus* input to retrieve the `StimulusLocation` if it `WasSuccessfullySensed` and assign it to our `LastKnownPlayerPosition` and `CanSeePlayer` variables, as shown in the following code:

```
void AChasingAIController::OnTargetPerceptionUpdate(AActor * Actor,
FAIStimulus Stimulus)
{
   if(Cast<ABehaviorTreeDesignCharacter>(Actor)){
      LastKnownPlayerPosition = Stimulus.StimulusLocation;
      bCanSeePlayer = Stimulus.WasSuccessfullySensed();
   }
}
```

The AI Controller is now ready to be used!

# Using the AI Controller

Regardless of whether you used a Blueprint or C++ implementation, you need to assign the controller to your Chasing Agent. Whether you do so directly in the blueprint, or directly in the instanced version of the game, under the Pawn settings, you need to change the AI Controller so that it's the one we just created. We also need to ensure that the AI is able to auto-posses this pawn.

As a result, you should have something like this:

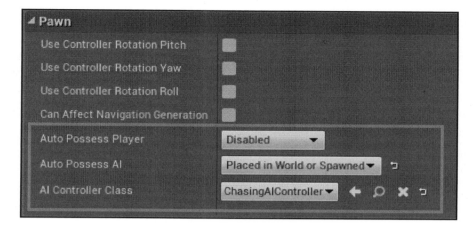

Now, we have (almost) all the pieces to build our Chasing agent.

# Summary

In this chapter, we started to look at our in-depth example of how to create a *Behavior Tree*, and have used all of the systems we have encountered so far.

In particular, we have seen how we can write down the *Expected Behavior* and work from there to gather all the different pieces that we need to build our AI. We have seen how we can do this in both C++ and Blueprint. The pieces we have created were a *Custom Decorator*, to check *boolean* variables in our **Behavior Tree**, a **Custom Task**, to find a random location by using the **Navigation System**, and a **Custom AI Controller** so that we can use the **Perception System** to sense the **Player**.

In the next chapter, we will continue with this example and build the last piece we need so that we can update the variables for the Chasing Behavior. At the end of the next chapter, you will be ready to build the Behavior Tree. So, let's move on!

# Designing Behavior Trees - Part II

# 9

This chapter is a continuation of the previous one. In particular, we will build the last missing piece of the puzzle before we build the final Behavior Tree in the next chapter.

In particular, we will be covering the following topics:

- Creating the *Player Character*, along with the *Chasing Agent*
- Setting up the *Navigation System* within the Level
- Implementing a *Custom Service* (both in Blueprint and C++) to update the variables that are needed in the Chasing Behavior

Once again, we will be implementing everything in both Blueprint and C++ to give you a broader idea of what you can use. Alternatively, if you already know what you want to use, you can just follow one of the two implementations.

Making the Custom Service is the part that will take the most time since we will be going through it step by step.

Let's get to it!

# Setting up the environment for testing the Behavior Tree

Before we move on, let's take a break from coding and create the environment that we need to test our Behavior Tree. Preparing a good test environment allows you to easily spot bugs and fix them.

In this section, we are not going to do anything fancy, but we will look at what is required for testing our AI, step by step.

# Creating the Player

First of all, we need to have a Player on the level, since our AI agent will chase the Player. Moreover, in the code we are going to write in this chapter, we will need to reference a Player class.

In this case, we already have the **ThirdPersonCharacter** in our project (if you created the project from the *Third Person Template*). Right-click on it and select **Create Child Blueprint Class**, as shown in the following screenshot:

Then, we can rename it *Player*:

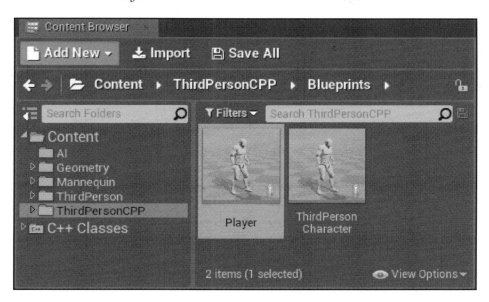

Double-click on the Player open it in the *Blueprint Editor*. In the **Details** Panel, under the **Pawn** tab, we need to change the **Auto Possess Player** to **Player 0** and the **Auto Possess AI** to **Disabled**, as shown in the following screenshot:

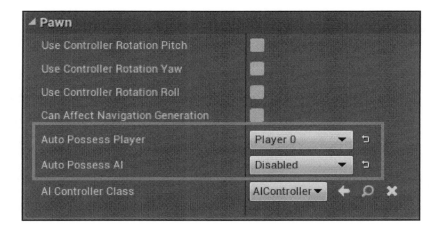

As a result, we will have a class just for the *Player Actor* (and it is a Blueprint class, which is important). Once that has been placed in the map, it will be possessed by the *Player* (to be precise, by the *Player Controller 0*).

# Creating the Chasing Agent

The next step is to set up the Chasing Agent.

We created a controller for this in the previous chapter, both in Blueprint and C++. However, we need to create the actual Pawn that will be possessed. We can achieve this in a very similar manner to how we created the player.

Create another child blueprint of the **ThirdPersonCharacter**, but this time rename it **AI_ChasingAgent**:

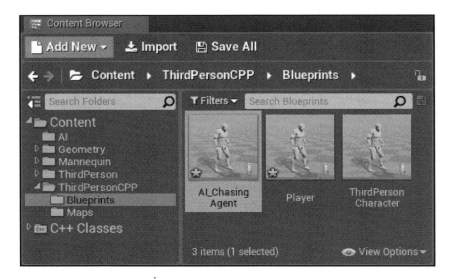

Double-click on this to open the **Blueprint Editor**. As we anticipated in the previous chapter, in the *Using the AI Controller* section, in the **Details** *Panel*, under the **Pawn** tab, we need to set **Auto Possess Player** to **Disabled**, **Auto Possess AI** to **Placed in World or Spawned** and **AI Controller Class** to **ChasingAIController** (or BP_ChasingAIController, if you prefer the Blueprint version of it), as shown in the following screenshot:

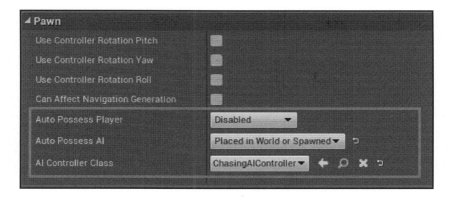

Since we are going to have many agents trying to chase the Player they would probably get stuck if they were to use the current settings that we have. However, in Chapter 7, *Crowds*, we looked at many techniques that we can use to handle these kinds of situations. In particular, if we have just a few agents, it might be sufficient to activate *RVO Avoidance*. Hence, select the *CharacterMovementComponent* from the **Components** panel:

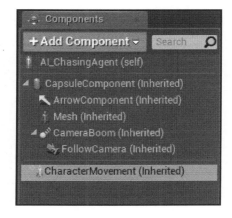

Then, in the **Character Movement: Avoidance** tab, we just need to check **Use RVOAvoidance**. The default settings should be fine, but feel free to adapt them as per your needs (check out Chapter 7, *Crowds*, again if you need more assistance):

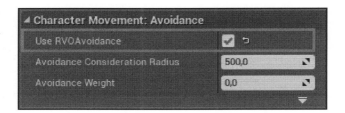

Save the `AI_ChasingAgent`. As a result, our Chasing Agent is ready to be placed in the map, and once we have implemented the Behavior Tree and started it, it will start chasing the Player.

# Preparing the Level

We have our *Player* and the *Chasing Agent*. However, we need to set up a Level where we can test our Behavior. Therefore, we can duplicate (or directly use it, if you prefer) the `ThirdPersonExampleMap` and rename it to something more familiar (for example, `TestingChasingBehavior`).

Here, I leave you to your imagination so that you can build a nice test map for our character. Once you are done, come back here and continue reading. For simplicity's sake, I will not modify the map, but just describe the next steps that should be taken.

The first step is to erase all the characters that might be in the map (for example, the `ThirdPersonCharacter`) since we will replace them with ours. Then, we will place (by dragging from the *Content Browser* into the *Viewport*) one, and only one, Player:

Then, we can place a couple of Chasing agents, in the same way as we did for the Player:

We are almost done. The last step is setting up the navigation for the level. In fact, our ***Find Random Location Task*** relies on the fact that the Navigation Mesh is set for the level. We went into detail about the Navigation System in Chapter XX, so revise that chapter if you need further assistance on the navigation. This section will just describe how to very quickly set up the navigation for our level.

To build the Navigation System, we just need to select the *Nav Mesh Bounds Volume* from the **Modes** panel (by selecting the *All Class Tab*) and drag it into the map:

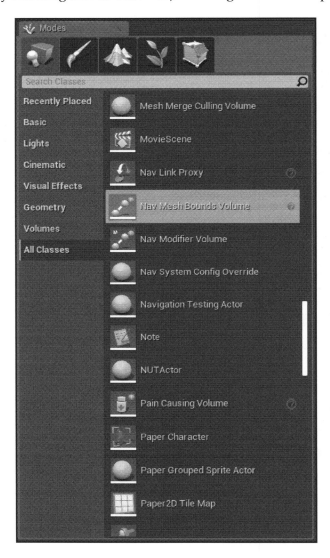

Then, you need to extend it to cover the whole map. If you press the *P* key, you will be able to preview your *NavMesh*, as shown in the following screenshot:

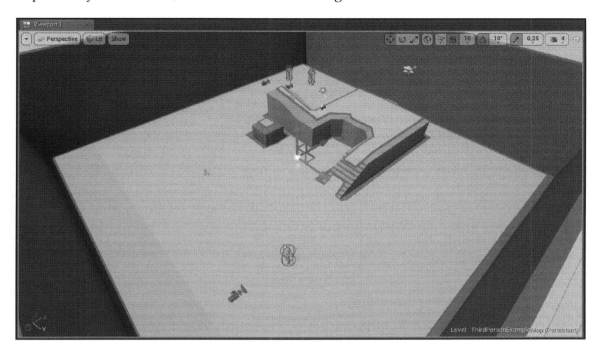

Now, we are set to go. Let's continue with the coding part.

# Service – Update Chasing Behavior

We didn't describe anything like a service in our *Expected Behaviour*, and that's fine – it means that we don't need anything like a service for our Behavior, per-se. However, each Behavior Tree has to update the relevant values somehow. One way to do this is by using a service.

The kinds of services that update specific values are often specific (in the implementation) and less likely reusable, but sometimes they are needed to run the Behavior Tree. Moreover, since we already looked at a practical example on how to create a *Task* and a *Decorator*, this is the occasion to learn a bit more about *Services*.

We need to think about the variables contained in the *Blackboard*, and which one needs to be updated.

The first variable that we need to assign is the **Player**. In fact, we need to have a reference to the Player Pawn so that they can chase when the agent is in sight. However, we don't need to update this value every time the Service is updated, just when the service starts up.

 It is worth noting that this service will be placed at the beginning of the tree. Every time the Behavior Tree restarts, the Service is "*rebooted*" again, updating the Player reference. This is intended because if the Player dies, and another Pawn spawns, this service will update the reference to the new Pawn as well.

Then, we have to update the boolean variable if the *Player* is currently *in Sight* or not. Since this variable will determine which part of the Behavior Tree to execute (decorators will cut the tree if the condition is not met in our case, as we will see later in this chapter), we must update it at every tick of the Service.

The last variable to update is the ***Destination*** (in the case, the Player is not in sight). In fact, this variable will contain the ***Last Known Player Position*** in the case that the Player has just left the view. Otherwise, the variable will contain the random location we assign in our *Task*. Therefore, we need to check whether to update this variable or not at every tick of the service (since we want the last seen position of the player to be updated only when the player leaves the field of view of our agent). At the moment, the Player is no longer in sight, and so we update this value once, since the ***Last Known Player*** position will not change until the *Player* is in sight again, and the Behavior Tree will keep it until it isn't required and overrides it with a *Random Location*. We can achieve this behavior by using a local variable within the service that keeps track of the last value of the boolean variable (if the player is in sight), and if it differs from the current cycle (tick) of the service, then we update the ***Destination*** variable with the ***Last Known Player Position***.

Moreover, it is worth noting that we are going to take the values of this variable from the agent controller, making this Service dependent on this specific controller (which is why I stated previously that these kinds of services aren't as reusable).

Now that we have a clear overview of what our service should do, let's jump into how to implement it (both in Blueprint and C++, so that you can choose the method that you prefer).

# Update Chasing Behavior Blueprint implementation

First, we need to create the service and name it `BTService_UpdateChasingBehavior`. Then, we need to add some variables. We will call the first ***CanSeePlayerKey***, of type *Blackboard Key Selector*, which will hold the reference to the boolean variable in the Blackboard that determines if the AI can currently see the player or not. Of course, this variable needs to be public so that it can be set from the Behavior Tree. The second variable, which always of type *Blackboard Key Selector*, named ***PlayerKey***, is a reference to the Player Pawn in the Blackboard; this has to be public as well. The third is another public *Blackboard Key Selector* named ***LastKnownPositionKey***, but it will be fed with the *Destination* vector in the Blackboard, as we discussed in the previous section. The last variable is a local private variable of type boolean named ***LastCanSeePlayer***, which stores the previous state (during the last tick) of the ***CanSeePlayer*** boolean. In this way, it is possible to know whether the state has changed and if an update of the Destination is required or not. In the end, this is how our variables should appear in the editor:

The next step is to *override/create* the ***Receive Activation AI*** event, as shown in the following screenshot:

This event is fired only when the service is activated, which in our case will be every time the Behavior Tree restarts. Here, we need to get the reference to the *Player*. We can easily achieve this by using a ***Get All Actor of Class*** node. We need to provide the class player so that we can just insert the *Player* class we choose. In this case, we will be using the Player class we created at the beginning of this chapter:

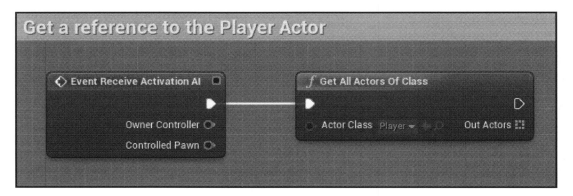

 If you want to make your service a bit more modular, you can pass the Player class as a variable so that you can change it depending on the Behavior Tree. In the C++ implementation, we will do this, mainly because it is easier to reference Blueprint classes as well.

Then, we assume that there is just one Player in the game (otherwise, you should have the logic to find the right Player to chase; maybe the closest one?) and we get it from the array. Finally, we save it in the **Player Key** *Object Reference* in the Blackboard by using the **Set Blackboard Value as Object** node. This is the final graph of the event:

Now, we need to *override/create* the **Receive Tick AI** event, as shown in the following screenshot:

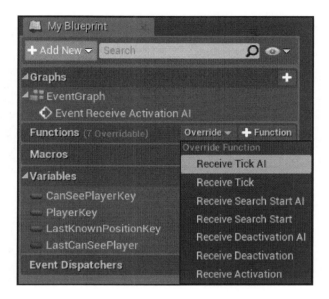

The first thing we can do is cast the Owner Controller into the Controller class we created earlier:

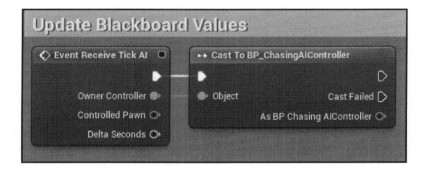

You can use also the `ChasingAIController` (the non-blueprint version written in C++). However, if you do, you will not be able to have access to its variables. Even if they are declared public, they are invisible to Blueprint if they don't have the ***UPROPERTY ()*** macro before them. So, if you want to use the C++ version of the controller, be sure to add the `UPROPERTY ()` macro (with the proper parameters) before each variable to make them visible to the blueprint as well.

Now, if the cast succeeds, we can gather the reference to the **CanSeePlayer** variable from the BP_ChasingAIController. Then, by using the **CanSeePlayerKey** variable, we can set its value within the Blackboard by using the **Set Blackboard Value as Bool**. This is the graph we have so far:

Next, we need to compare this value (the current **CanSeePlayer** boolean) with the one stored in the **LastCanSeePlayer** variable (which stores the value of the last Tick). We can achieve this by using an **Equal** node along with a **Branch**, as shown in the following screenshot:

If these two values are different, then we need to retrieve the **LastKnownPlayerPosition** from BP_ChasingAIController and set it in the Blackboard through the **LastKnownPlayerPositionKey** variable:

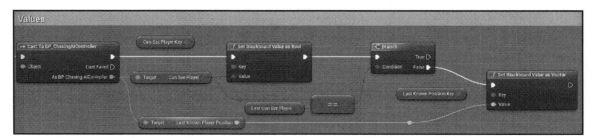

Finally, regardless of whether we have updated this vector or not (in both the *True* and *False* branches), we need to update the **LastCanSeePlayer** variable with the current value. This is the final part of the graph:

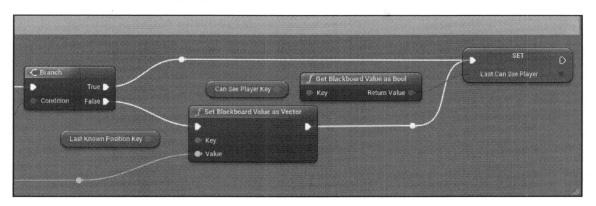

Save the *Service*, and we are finally ready to build our *Behavior Tree*!

If you drop this service within a *Behavior Tree*, this is what it will look like:

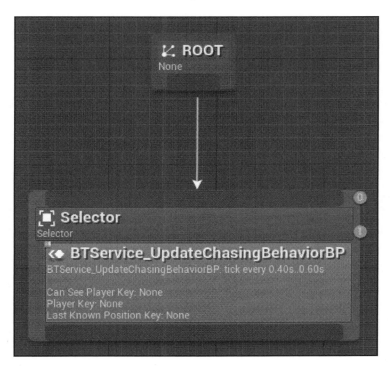

The *Details Panel* of the *Service* (within the Behavior Tree Editor) should look as follows:

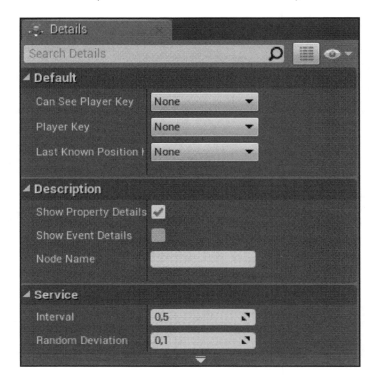

In the next section, we are going to implement this *Service in C++*, and there will be many things to take into consideration. Of course, you are welcome to repeat this process in C++ as well to improve your skills; otherwise, you can skip to the next section, in which we will build our Behavior Tree.

# Update Chasing Behavior C++ implementation

In this section, we are going to recreate the *Update Chasing Behavior Service in C++*.

Let's start by creating a new class that inherits from **BTService:**

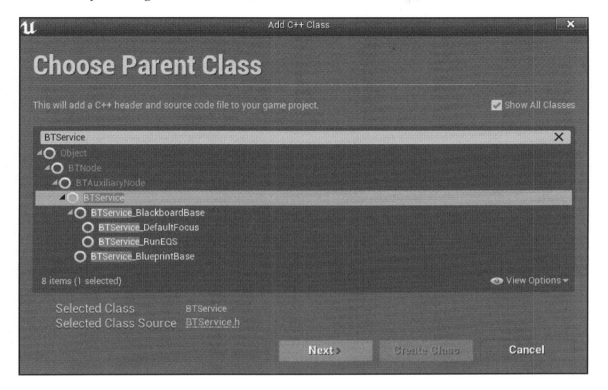

We will rename our class BTService_UpdateChasing and place it in the AI folder, like we did for the other AI classes in the previous chapter:

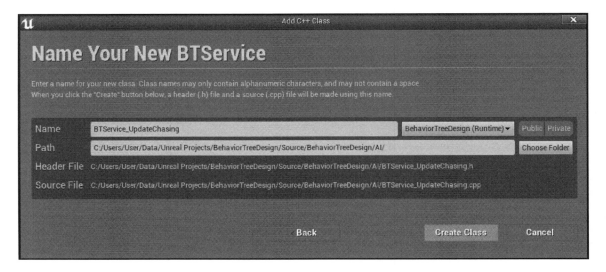

If, after the creation the code, it doesn't compile, ensure that you followed the previous chapter. In fact, we added both **GameplayTasks** and **AIModule** to the Public Dependencies of our Project. For your convenience, here is what we did in the previous chapter:

You need to change your .cs file (in our case, *BehaviorTreeDesign.cs*) and add **GameplayTasks** and **AIModule** as public dependencies, as shown in the following code:

```
PublicDependencyModuleNames.AddRange(new string[] {
"Core", "CoreUObject", "Engine", "InputCore",
"HeadMountedDisplay", "GameplayTasks", "AIModule" });
```

Now, you should be able compile without any problems.

The next step is to add some variables to our Service in the header file. We can call the first **CanSeePlayerKey** of type Blackboard Key Selector, which will hold the reference to the boolean variable in the Blackboard that determines whether the AI can currently see the player or not. Of course, this variable needs to have the UPROPERTY() set so that it can be set from the Behavior Tree. The second variable, which is always of type Blackboard Key Selector, named **PlayerKey**, is a reference to the Player Pawn in the Blackboard; this needs to have the UPROPERTY() macro as well. The third is another Blackboard Key Selector named **LastKnownPositionKey**, always with the UPROPERTY() macro, but it will be fed with the Destination vector in the Blackboard, as we discussed previously. The last variable is a local private variable of type boolean named "*Last***CanSeePlayer**, which stores the previous state (during the last Tick) of the **CanSeePlayer** boolean. In this way, it is possible to know whether the state has changed and if an update of the Destination is required or not.

The following code needs to be inserted in the header file:

```
UPROPERTY(EditAnywhere, Category = Blackboard)
FBlackboardKeySelector CanSeePlayerKey;

UPROPERTY(EditAnywhere, Category = Blackboard)
FBlackboardKeySelector PlayerKey;

UPROPERTY(EditAnywhere, Category = Blackboard)
FBlackboardKeySelector LastKnownPositionKey;

private:
    bool bLastCanSeePlayer;
```

Now, we need another variable – not for the logic of the service, like in the previous cases, but one to select the Player class from the Behavior Tree. We will name the variable **PlayerClass** of type **TSubclassOf<AActor>** so that we can select any class that derives from AActor. Of course, this variable needs to have the UPROPERTY() macro as well so that it can be sent directly from the Behavior Tree:

 We are going to mirror the blueprint version of the service, in which we find all the actors of that class, and assume that there is only one. At the end of this chapter, a different approach is proposed.

```
UPROPERTY(EditAnywhere, Category = PlayerClass)
TSubclassOf<AActor> PlayerClass;
```

The next step is to declare some functions so that we can override/create both the C++ versions of the Blueprint **Receive Activation AI** and **Receive Tick AI** events. These are called `OnBecomingRelevant()` and `TickNode()`, respectively, and the signature to override them is as follows:

```
protected:

    virtual void OnBecomeRelevant(UBehaviorTreeComponent& OwnerComp, uint8*
NodeMemory) override;

    virtual void TickNode(UBehaviorTreeComponent& OwnerComp, uint8*
NodeMemory, float DeltaSeconds) override;
```

Finally, we need to declare a constructor for our Service. You will understand why shortly:

```
    UBTService_UpdateChasing(const FObjectInitializer& ObjectInitializer =
FObjectInitializer::Get());
```

Now, in the `.cpp` file, we need to implement these functions.

Let's start with the constructor. In this function, we need to initialize some values for our service; in particular, we want to notify (by setting the respective variable to true) that we want to use the `OnBecomeRelevant()` function. Even if this is not necessary, because the variable is set to *true* by default, it's very good practice to explicitly set the values of these kinds of variables in the constructor. Since we are here, it's worth turning off the call to the `OnCeaseRelevant()` function (the inverse of the `OnBecomeRelevant()`). The following code shows the constructor with the names of the boolean variables we need to set:

```
    UBTService_UpdateChasing::UBTService_UpdateChasing(const
    FObjectInitializer& ObjectInitializer)
        : Super(ObjectInitializer)
    {
      bNotifyBecomeRelevant = true;
      bNotifyCeaseRelevant = false;
    }
```

The next event to implement is `OnBecomRelevant()`, and it is only fired when the service becomes relevant (it gets activated), which in our case will be every time the Behavior Tree restarts. Here, we need to get the reference to the Player so that we can store it in Blackboard. First of all, we need to retrieve the Blackboard Component:

```
    void UBTService_UpdateChasing::OnBecomeRelevant(UBehaviorTreeComponent &
    OwnerComp, uint8 * NodeMemory)
    {
```

```
  //Get Blackboard Component
  UBlackboardComponent* BlackboardComp =
OwnerComp.GetBlackboardComponent();
  if (BlackboardComp == NULL)
  {
    return;
  }

  //[REST OF THE CODE]

}
```

Then, we need to retrieve the Player by using something very similar to the Blueprint node called GetAllActorsOfClass. In particular, we will create an empty TArray<AActor*> and use the UGameplayStatics::GetAllActorsOfClass() function to bypass the world, the Player class, and the empty array. Now, this function will fill up our array:

```
void UBTService_UpdateChasing::OnBecomeRelevant(UBehaviorTreeComponent &
OwnerComp, uint8 * NodeMemory)
{
  //Get Blackboard Component
  UBlackboardComponent* BlackboardComp =
OwnerComp.GetBlackboardComponent();
  if (BlackboardComp == NULL)
  {
    return;
  }

  //Retrieve Player and Update the Blackboard
  TArray<AActor*> FoundActors;
  UGameplayStatics::GetAllActorsOfClass(GetWorld(), PlayerClass,
FoundActors);

  //[REST OF THE CODE]

}
```

Next, we assume that there is just one Player in the game (otherwise, you need to find the right player to chase; maybe the closest one?) and check if the first element of the Array is valid, and if so, we use the **PlayerKey** variable to save it in the Blackboard component.

Here's the code for doing so:

```
void UBTService_UpdateChasing::OnBecomeRelevant(UBehaviorTreeComponent &
OwnerComp, uint8 * NodeMemory)
{
  //Get Blackboard Component
  UBlackboardComponent* BlackboardComp =
OwnerComp.GetBlackboardComponent();
  if (BlackboardComp == NULL)
  {
    return;
  }

  //Retrieve Player and Update the Blackboard
  TArray<AActor*> FoundActors;
  UGameplayStatics::GetAllActorsOfClass(GetWorld(), PlayerClass,
FoundActors);
  if (FoundActors[0]) {
    BlackboardComp->SetValueAsObject(PlayerKey.SelectedKeyName,
FoundActors[0]);
  }
}
```

 Once again, we have mirrored the blueprint service.

Furthermore, in C++ we can do an extra step and avoid to Set the *Player* again if the *Key* is already *set* (something we couldn't do in Blueprint). So we can add this *if-statement*:

```
void UBTService_UpdateChasing::OnBecomeRelevant(UBehaviorTreeComponent &
OwnerComp, uint8 * NodeMemory)
{

  //Get Blackboard Component
  UBlackboardComponent* BlackboardComp =
OwnerComp.GetBlackboardComponent();
  if (BlackboardComp == NULL)
  {
    return;
  }

  if (!PlayerKey.IsSet()) {
    //Retrieve Player and Update the Blackboard
    TArray<AActor*> FoundActors;
    UGameplayStatics::GetAllActorsOfClass(GetWorld(), PlayerClass,
FoundActors);
```

```
    if (FoundActors[0]) {
      UE_LOG(LogTemp, Warning, TEXT("Found Player"));
      BlackboardComp->SetValueAsObject(PlayerKey.SelectedKeyName,
FoundActors[0]);
    }
  }

}
```

Now, in regards to the implementation of the `TickNode()` function, we first retrieve the
*Blackboard Component*:

```
void UBTService_UpdateChasing::TickNode(UBehaviorTreeComponent & OwnerComp,
uint8 * NodeMemory, float DeltaSeconds)
{

  //Get Blackboard Component
  UBlackboardComponent* BlackboardComp =
OwnerComp.GetBlackboardComponent();
  if (BlackboardComp == NULL)
  {
    return;
  }

  //[REST OF THE CODE]
}
```

Then, we need to retrieve the AI Controller from the `OwnerComp` and check whether it is
valid:

```
void UBTService_UpdateChasing::TickNode(UBehaviorTreeComponent & OwnerComp,
uint8 * NodeMemory, float DeltaSeconds)
{

  //[PREVIOUS CODE]

  //Get AI Controller
  AAIController* AIController = OwnerComp.GetAIOwner();
  if (!AIController) {
    return;
  }

  //[REST OF THE CODE]
}
```

Once we have the AI Controller, we need to **Cast** it into our `AChasingAIController` (the one we created in the previous chapter) and check its validity. As a result, this service will work only if the AI agent is controlled by a `ChasingAIController`:

```
void UBTService_UpdateChasing::TickNode(UBehaviorTreeComponent & OwnerComp,
uint8 * NodeMemory, float DeltaSeconds)
{

  //[PREVIOUS CODE]

  //Get ChasingAIController (the controller we have created in the previous
chapter)
  AChasingAIController* ChasingController =
Cast<AChasingAIController>(AIController);
  if (!ChasingController) {
    return;
  }

  //[REST OF THE CODE]

}
```

From `ChasingAIController`, we can retrieve the (current) **CanSeePlayer** and save it within the Blackboard by using the `CanSeePlayerKey` variable:

```
void UBTService_UpdateChasing::TickNode(UBehaviorTreeComponent & OwnerComp,
uint8 * NodeMemory, float DeltaSeconds)
{

  //[PREVIOUS CODE]

  //Update the Blackboard with the current value of CanSeePlayer from the
Chasing Controller
  BlackboardComp->SetValueAsBool(CanSeePlayerKey.SelectedKeyName,
ChasingController->bCanSeePlayer);

  //[REST OF THE CODE]

}
```

If the private `LastCanSeePlayer` variable (which contains the value of the `CanSeePlayer` of the last Tick) is different from the current `CanSeePlayer` (which means that the Player is either entered or exited from the Sight of our Agent), then retrieve the `LastKnownPlayerPosition` from the `ChasingAIController` and save it within the Blackboard by using the `LastKnonwPositionKey` variable:

```
void UBTService_UpdateChasing::TickNode(UBehaviorTreeComponent & OwnerComp,
uint8 * NodeMemory, float DeltaSeconds)
{

    //[PREVIOUS CODE]

    //If the LastCanSeePlayer is different from the current one, then update
    the LastKnownPlayerPosition
    if (ChasingController->bCanSeePlayer != bLastCanSeePlayer) {
        BlackboardComp->SetValueAsVector(LastKnownPositionKey.SelectedKeyName,
    ChasingController->LastKnownPlayerPosition);
    }
    //[REST OF THE CODE]

}
```

After the previous check, we need to update the `LastCanSeePlayer` with the current value of it so that in the next Tick we will have the right value:

```
void UBTService_UpdateChasing::TickNode(UBehaviorTreeComponent & OwnerComp,
uint8 * NodeMemory, float DeltaSeconds)
{

    //[PREVIOUS CODE]

    //Update the LastCanSeePlayer with the current CanSeePlayer
    bLastCanSeePlayer = ChasingController->bCanSeePlayer;

    //[REST OF THE CODE]
}
```

Finally, we can make a call to the parent `TickNode()` (as per good practice):

```
void UBTService_UpdateChasing::TickNode(UBehaviorTreeComponent & OwnerComp,
uint8 * NodeMemory, float DeltaSeconds)
{

  //[PREVIOUS CODE]

  //Call to the parent TickNode
  Super::TickNode(OwnerComp, NodeMemory, DeltaSeconds);
}
```

The code for our service is now complete. For your convenience, here is the code of the `TickNode()` function:

```
void UBTService_UpdateChasing::TickNode(UBehaviorTreeComponent & OwnerComp,
uint8 * NodeMemory, float DeltaSeconds)
{

  //Get Blackboard Component
  UBlackboardComponent* BlackboardComp =
OwnerComp.GetBlackboardComponent();
  if (BlackboardComp == NULL)
  {
    return;
  }

  //Get AI Controller
  AAIController* AIController = OwnerComp.GetAIOwner();
  if (!AIController) {
    return;
  }

  //Get ChasingAIController (the controller we have created in the previous
chapter)
  AChasingAIController* ChasingController =
Cast<AChasingAIController>(AIController);
  if (!ChasingController) {
    return;
  }

  //Update the Blackboard with the current value of CanSeePlayer from the
Chasing Controller
  BlackboardComp->SetValueAsBool(CanSeePlayerKey.SelectedKeyName,
ChasingController->bCanSeePlayer);

  //If the LastCanSeePlayer is different from the current one, then update
the LastKnownPlayerPosition
```

```
   if (ChasingController->bCanSeePlayer != bLastCanSeePlayer) {
      BlackboardComp->SetValueAsVector(LastKnownPositionKey.SelectedKeyName,
ChasingController->LastKnownPlayerPosition);
   }

   //Update the LastCanSeePlayer with the current CanSeePlayer
   bLastCanSeePlayer = ChasingController->bCanSeePlayer;

   //Call to the parent TickNode
   Super::TickNode(OwnerComp, NodeMemory, DeltaSeconds);
}
```

Save and compile the Service. Now, you will be able to use it in the Behavior Tree.

This is what the Service looks like once placed in the Behavior Tree:

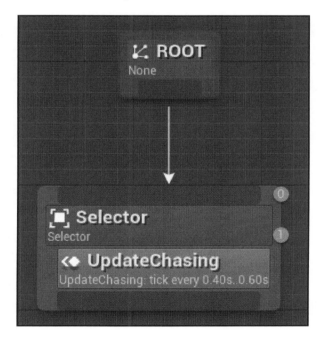

The *Details Panel* of the Service (within the *Behavior Tree Editor*) should look as follows:

Before we move on, as we did for the *Decorator* and the *Task*, it is good practice to add a static description to the *Service* so that we can visualize which Keys (*Blackboard Key Selector* variables) we assigned, along with the *Player* class. Here, we need to add the signature of the function in the header file, as shown in the following:

```
protected:

    virtual FString GetStaticDescription() const override;
```

As for the implementation (in the .cpp file), we can just return a formatted *FString* with all the information we need to show. We can easily format the string with the Printf() function. I'm using the Append() function here to increase the clarity of each line. In particular, we need to show which line is for the PlayerClass, and which values we have assigned to each *Blackboard Key Selector* variable:

```
FString UBTService_UpdateChasing::GetStaticDescription() const
{
    return FString::Printf(TEXT("%s: '%s'"), TEXT("Player Class"),
PlayerClass ? *PlayerClass->GetName() : TEXT(""))
        .Append(FString::Printf(TEXT("\n%s: '%s'"), TEXT("PlayerKey"),
```

```
PlayerKey.IsSet() ? *PlayerKey.SelectedKeyName.ToString() : TEXT("")))
    .Append(FString::Printf(TEXT("\n%s: '%s'"),
TEXT("LastKnownPositionKey"), LastKnownPositionKey.IsSet() ?
*LastKnownPositionKey.SelectedKeyName.ToString() : TEXT("")))
    .Append(FString::Printf(TEXT("\n%s: '%s'"), TEXT("CanSeePlayerKey"),
CanSeePlayerKey.IsSet() ? *CanSeePlayerKey.SelectedKeyName.ToString() :
TEXT("")));
}
```

Now, the Service will look as follows in the Behavior Tree:

Now that our *Service* has been implemented, we are ready to build our *Behavior Tree* in the next chapter!

# Summary

In this chapter, we continued our in-depth example of how to create a *Behavior Tree* and used all of the systems we have encountered so far.

In particular, we have seen how we can set up the *Testing Environment* and create both the *Player Character* and the Chasing Agent. This latter needed to have the right controller, and also needed to have *RVO Avoidance* activated.

Then, we implemented our *Update Chasing Behavior Service*, and looked at how to do so in both C++ and Blueprint.

In the next chapter, we will continue with this example and build the final Behavior Tree. By the end of this next chapter, we will have completed this project and we will have our *Chasing Behavior*. So, let's keep going!

# 10
# Designing Behavior Trees - Part III

This chapter is a continuation of the previous one, and is the final part of *Designing Behavior Trees*. We will finish what we started. In particular, we will build the final *Behavior Tree* and make it run.

In particular, we will cover the following topics:

- Generating the **Blackboard** and the **Behavior Tree** assets
- Setting up the **Blackboard** so that it can be used with the *Behavior Tree*
- Implementing the **Behavior Tree** (using either the Blueprint or C++ nodes) to make a Chasing Behavior
- *Making the Behavior Tree running* (both in a Blueprint or C++)
- *Improving the C++ nodes* of the Behavior Tree to better align with *best practices*

Once again, we will be implementing everything in both Blueprint and C++ to give you a broader idea of what you can use. Alternatively, if you already know what you want to use, you can just follow one of the two implementations.

This will conclude our journey of *Designing a Behavior Tree* from scratch, and at the end, we will have our Chasing Behavior complete.

So, without further ado, let's dive into building the *Behavior Tree*!

# Building the Behavior Tree

The last step in creating the Chasing Behavior is to build the Behavior Tree.

At this stage, if you feel like you have missed something, just revise the ***Expected Behavior*** (the one we have described in Chapter 8) and *do a checklist* of what you will need to build this *Behavior Tree*. However, even if you did miss something, don't worry – you can create it at a later stage.

 Many developers start developing the *Behavior Tree* and then build the nodes when they need them. Unless you are really good or the tree is particularly simple, it is always advisable to plan a little bit ahead, like we have did in the last two chapters. By doing this, you will avoid many headaches later on, and by having a little work overhead at the beginning, you avoid a large, bug-fixing time cost. Of course, you will still need to do bug fixing, but planning should reduce the chance of introducing bugs, or achieving a different behavior from the one that was originally planned.

From this point onward, you can use the Blueprint and C++ implementations (in case you have been using both), or just stick to the one you have been using so far. I will use the names from the Blueprint implementation, but the concepts for using our C++ nodes are exactly the same. In the end, I'll show a screenshot of the *Behavior Tree* build with CPP nodes instead.

 It's worth noting that we can also create a Mix tree. In fact, we can use both the C++ and the Blueprint nodes in the same tree. Since, in our case, we have a replica of each node in both Blueprint and C++, we should be free to use any as we like. However, this is not true, because we have made some nodes depending on the C++ AI controller, which was specific for that implementation. Thankfully in a project, you will not have replicas of everything, so if you have a specific AI Controller, both Blueprint and C++ node should refer to the same one.
During the development of your project, keep in mind that you can create some *Behavior Tree* nodes in C++ and some in Blueprint. Some developers prototype their nodes in Blueprint and then move the development to C++. Try to find the formula and the right balance between C++ and Blueprint that works best for you or your team.

To start, if you haven't already, create the *Behavior Tree Asset*, along with the *Blackboard*. In my case, I'm going to call the *Behavior Tree* **BT_ChasingBehavior** and the Blackboard **BB_ChasingBlackboard**. Both are placed in the AI folder (where we created our Blueprint nodes), as shown in the following screenshot:

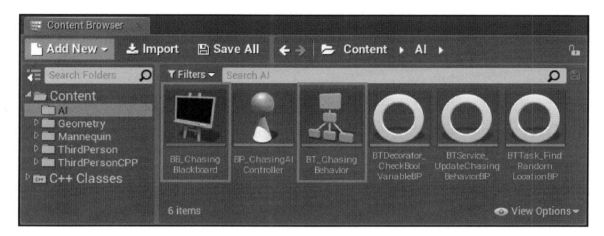

 You can reorder the AI folder a bit by creating sub-folders. For instance, you can create a sub-folder for your Decorators, another for your Tasks, and a third for your Services. Either way, this is a relatively small example, so we will leave the folder as it is.

# Setting up the Blackboard

Let's start by opening the *Blackboard Editor* (double-click on the asset). As you may recall, we need to have a Player reference.

Thus, create a *New Key* of type *Object*:

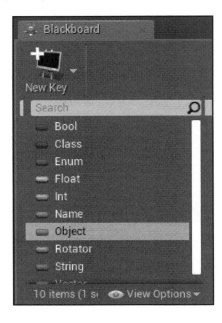

Rename it *Player*, and in the *Details Panel*, under the *Key Type* (you might need to expand this), set the *Base Class* to be the Player Pawn of our choice (e.g. *Player*, the class we created at the beginning of this chapter), as shown in the following screenshot:

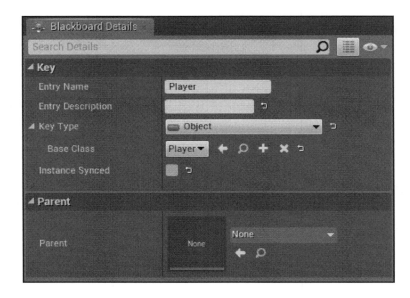

The next *Key* to add is the **Destination**, which is of type Vector. This will be useful for determining a goal when the player is not in sight. Speaking of which, we need a third Key of type *boolean* named **CanSeePlayer**, which is used to check if the Player is currently in sight or not. This is what the values of the *Blackboard* should look like:

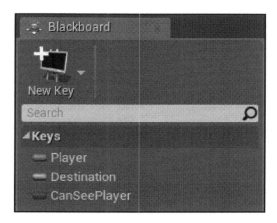

# Building the Tree

Double-click on the **BT_ChasingBehavior** asset to open the *Behavior Tree Editor*. Make sure that you have **BB_ChasingBlackboard** selected for the tree, as shown in the following screenshot:

From the **Root** node, we need to start with a **Selector**. This *Selector* will be where the tree will split into two branches: the one that will chase the Player when in sight, and the other when he/she isn't. On this very *Selector*, we need to attach our **BTService_UpdateChasingBehavior** Service (or if you wish, its C++ version, named **UpdatedChasing**). Don't forget to assign all the variables in the *Details Panel* (the *three Blackboard variables*), as shown in the following screenshot:

In the C++ version, we also need to assign the Player Class, along with the Blackboard Variables (since this is the way we designed our Service in C++). Hence, you will have something similar to this:

Once we have assigned all the variables, then this is what our Service will look like in the *Behavior Tree* when attached to the *Selector* node:

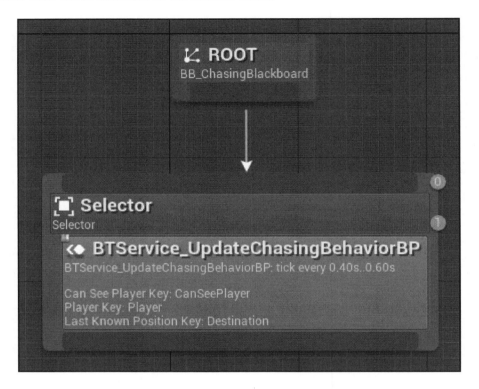

From the *Selector*, add two **Sequence** nodes (each representing the two branches of the tree). Which one the *Selector* chooses will depend on the decorators we are going to place on these two nodes.

Add both the **Sequence** nodes to **BTDecorator_CheckBoolVariableBP** (or the **CheckBoolVariable** C++ version of it). In the details panel, the *Bool Variable To Check* variable needs to be fed with the **CanSeePlayer** *Blackboard Key*, as shown in the following screenshot:

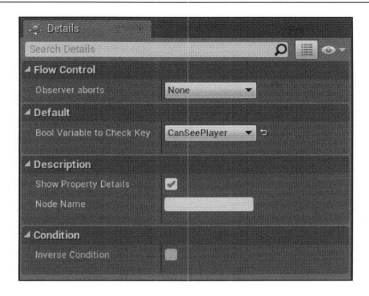

However, for the sequence on the right, you should set the *Inverse Condition* checkbox to *true*. By doing this, we can check whether *CanSeePlayer* is set to *false*. This is a bit wordy, but here are the final results in the **Details** panel:

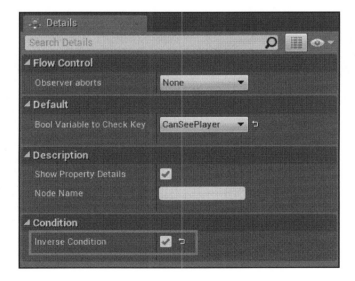

So far, our tree looks as follows:

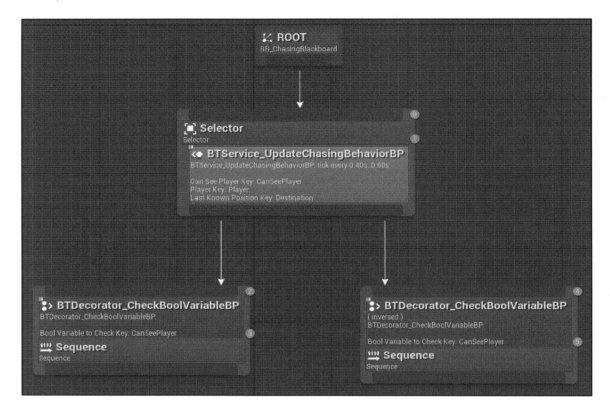

From the sequence node on the left, we just need to chase the player by using the *Move To* task. You need to select the *Player* blackboard variable as the *Blackboard Key*, as shown in the following screenshot:

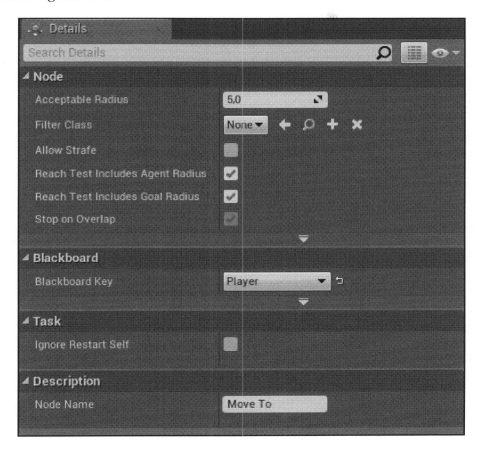

This is the current stage of the tree:

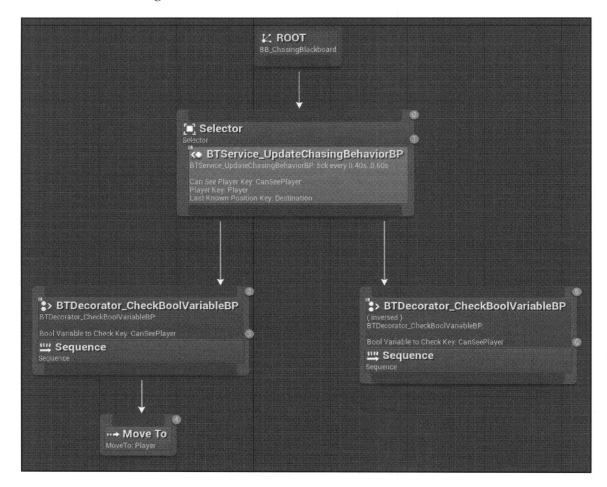

From the *Sequence* node on the right, we need to have two tasks. The first one is *Move To* again, but this time select the *Destination* variable as the *Blackboard Key*, as shown in the following screenshot:

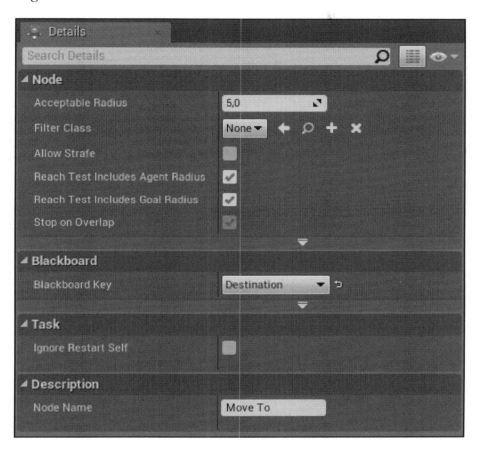

This is what the tree looks like so far:

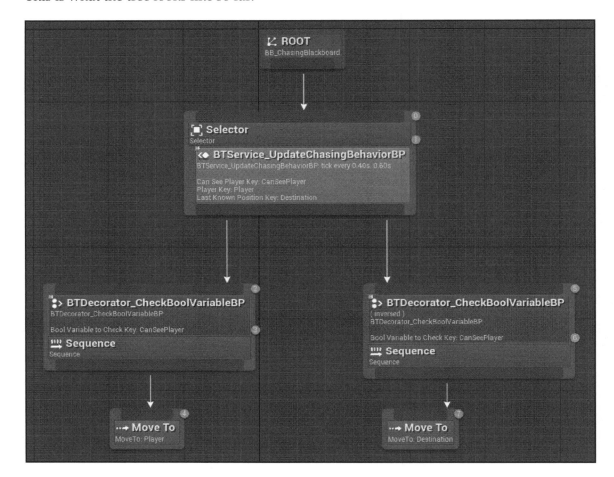

The second *Task* is the one we have already created, **BTTask_FindRandomLocationBP** (or the **Find Random Location** C++ version). We need to set the **DestinationKey** with the **Destination** *Blackboard variable*, and as for the **Radius**, we can choose a value (e.g. 30000, ten times more the default value). This is what the *Details* panel looks like:

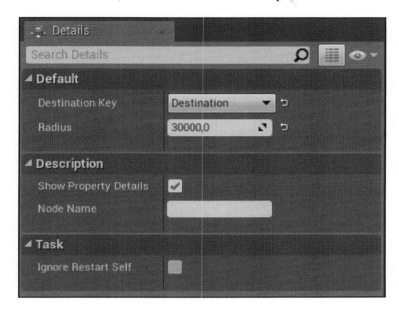

This is what the complete tree should look like:

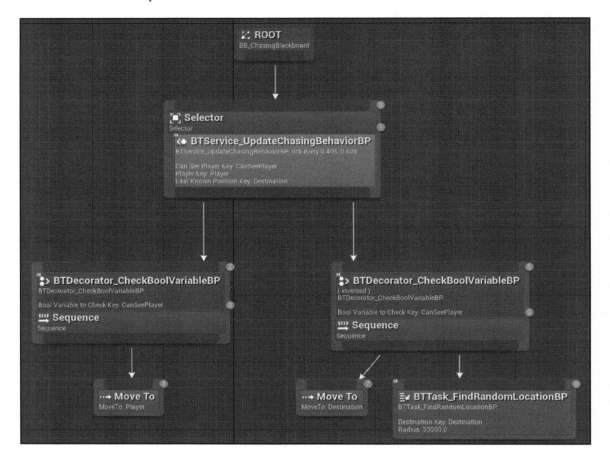

It seems like we have finished, but we have one more thing to do. In fact, at the moment, the Decorators don't control the flow of the Sub-Tree once the AI is executing it. In fact, we would like to abort the Task of moving to the Player if he/she is not in sight anymore; on the other hand, if the agent is going to a random location, we want the agent to chase the Player if he/she is in sight again.

To achieve this, we need to select our *Decorators* (one at the time) and set *Observer Abort* to *Self*, as shown in the following screenshot:

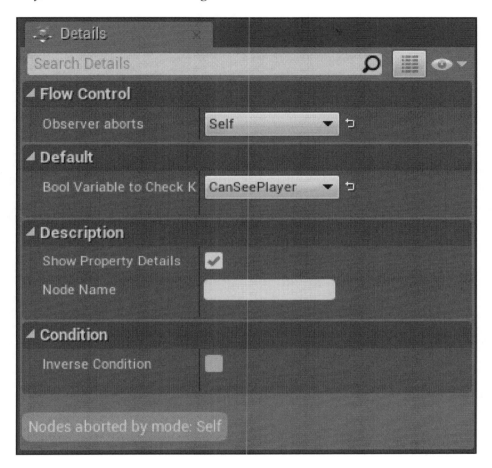

If the Decorator is still selected, the nodes that will be aborted are highlighted in the Tree:

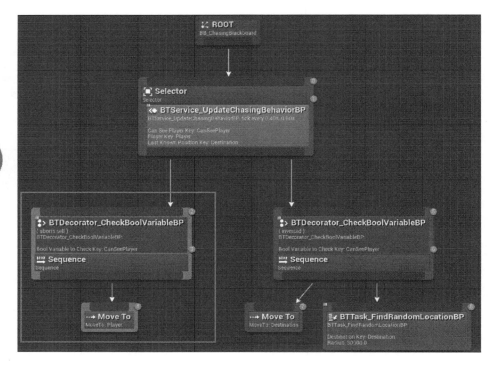

The tree slightly changes to reflect this behavior (under the *Decorators*, the abort conditions are shown):

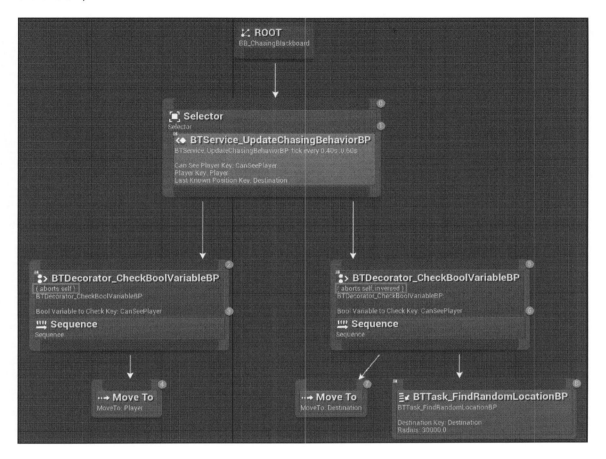

If you have built the tree using C++ nodes, you will have something similar to this instead:

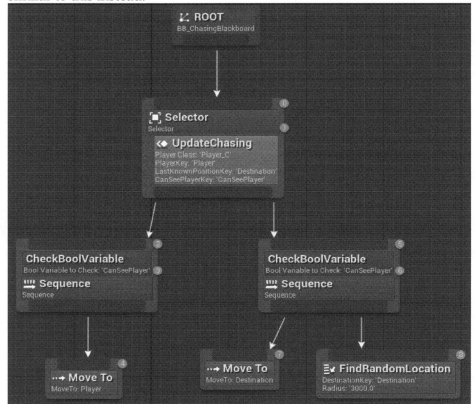

Moreover, you should notice that, just down below the Node name, not all information are displayed (e.g. in the *Decorators*, it doesn't say if its condition is inverted and what the abort conditions are). Later in the chapter, we will tackle this issue as well.

As you can see, the structure is very simple (and I have seen the same behavior being implemented in different trees), but it contains all the main concepts for *Designing a Behavior Tree* (including creating a node of each type: *Decorator, Service,* and *Task*). The fact that the structure is simple doesn't mean that the behavior that represents it is simple too. In fact, what we have built is a very nice *Chasing Behavior*!

We haven't touched upon Simple Parallel nodes, but those are used in more complicated trees for particular kind of behaviors with sub-trees. You don't have to worry – once you start mastering the art of creating *Behaviors Trees*, the use of Simple Parallel nodes will become natural.

The last thing that's left to do is make this *Behavior Tree* run and then to test it in the game!

# Running the Behavior Tree

We have already created the whole setup, including actors, controllers, perception, and navigation. However, we don't have any code that makes this Behavior Tree run on our agent. Of course, we will cover both the Blueprint case and the C++ one.

## Running the Behavior Tree using the Blueprint controller

If we have a Blueprint controller set up, we can easily modify it to get the Behavior Tree running immediately.

In fact, once we open the Editor, we can add the *Run Behavior Tree* node after overriding the *Event OnPossess* and choose the right *Behavior Tree*, as shown in the following screenshot:

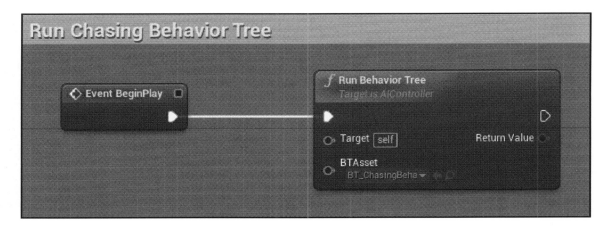

Save it, and you are good to go! Run the game and see if it works (of course, the AI controller needs to be set to **BP_ChasingAIController**).

# Running the Behavior Tree using the C++ controller

Unluckily for C+,+ this is not as straightforward (as we already saw in `Chapter 2`, *Behavior Trees and Blackboards*). In particular, we have two choices: we hardcode the value or we get a reference to the tree using blueprints.

The first option is not very practical for this kind of stuff and it is not a best practice.

For the second option, we have a variety of choices. In particular, I suggest that you create a *Behavior Tree* variable in the controller and use it so that it can be run on the `OnPossess()` function. Then, we can create a child of this class in the blueprint, where we can easily assign this variable. Finally, we can change the reference to the controller for our *AIChasingAgent*.

 Alternatively, you can place the *Behavior Tree* on the *Character/Pawn* that the AI will control, like we did in *Chapter 2*. That would be the best approach; however, in this moment it is good to see different alternatives in case you are in a situation in which you will need the *Behavior Tree* directly on the controller.

Let's start by opening the header file of our C++ controller and adding the following public variable (with the `UPROPERTY()` macro, since it needs to be editable in Blueprint):

```
UPROPERTY(EditAnywhere)
UBehaviorTree* BehaviorTree;
```

Then, we need to override the `OnPossess()` function:

```
virtual void OnPossess(class APawn* InPawn) override;
```

Next, in the `.cpp` file, we need to include the *Behavior Tree class*, so we need to add the following statement:

```
#include "BehaviorTree/BehaviorTree.h"
```

Finally, in the `OnPossess()` implementation, we just run the Behavior Tree:

```
void AChasingAIController::OnPossess(APawn * InPawn)
{
  Super::OnPossess(InPawn);
  if (BehaviorTree != nullptr) {
    RunBehaviorTree(BehaviorTree);
  }
}
```

After compiling the code, we can right-click on the C++ controller and select *Create Blueprint class based on ChasingAIController*, as shown in the following screenshot:

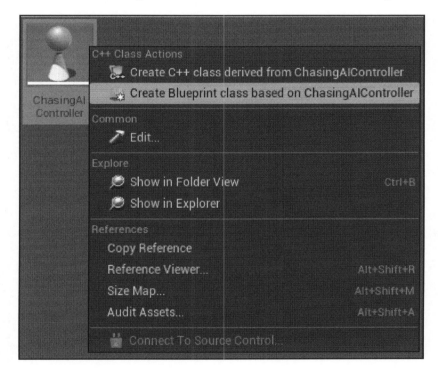

Then, we can place this Blueprint inside the AI folder and name it *CPP_ChasingAIController* (to distinguish it from *BP_ChasingAIController*):

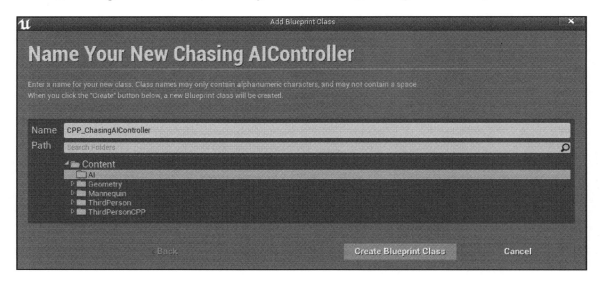

Its *Blueprint Editor* should open automatically (if not, just double-click on the asset to open it). Set the *Behavior Tree* variable in the *Details Panel*, as shown in the following screenshot (of course, we will need to set the *C++ version* of the *Behavior Tree*):

Compile and save the *Blueprint*.

Finally, in the ***AI_ChasingAgent*** blueprint, let's change its settings (from the *Details* panel in the ***Pawn*** tab) so that it will use the new controller:

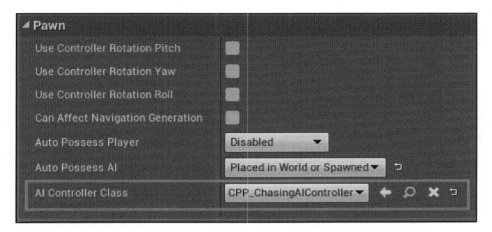

This concludes how to run the *Behavior Tree* on a *C++ controller*.

# Bug Correction

If you have though to have finished, well, that's not it. In fact, when designing a Behavior Tree, there must always be a phase of debugging and check if everything works as it should. Actually, on purpose I built the tree with something that doesn't work. Can you figure it out? Give it a try before keep reading.

The first problem is that, the Destination Key in the Blackboard, until the Player is not on sight, it will never get initialized. Moreover, there is another problem, when the AI enemy is seeking the Last Known Position of the player, but it is not reachable, it will fail the task. As a result, the sequence will not allow to go in the next Task to select a *Random Destination*. How can we fix this? Let's give it a try before we keep reading.

There are many approaches to this. For instance, you might have though to use the "*Force Success*" Decorator. It is not a bad idea at all, actually, this are the kind of cases in which you would use this Decorator (to add an optional Branch to the Sequence, so regardless if the Move To fails, we can still pick a Random Destination). Unfortunately, it doesn't work well with the setup we have with the other two decorators.

Thus, another solution is to modify the tree in the following way. We need to substitute the second Sequence with a Selector, with two Sequences as children. In the first Sequence, we place our Move To Task followed by the Find Random Destination one. In the other Sequence they are inverted. As result, in case the Task to follow the Last Known Player Position fails, the tree can revert back to Find a Random Location. If you wish, you could also remove the last Move To in the second Sequence, but I'm leaving it there for clarity; especially for those who struggle to grasp how *Behavior Tree* works. At the end, this is how it should look like the Behavior Tree (Blueprint version):

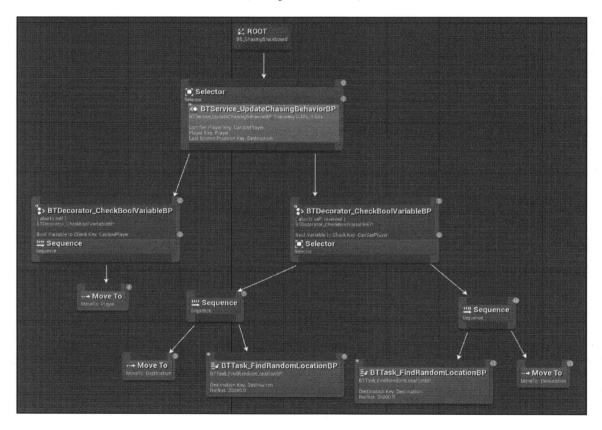

And this is how the C++ version should change (the changes of the next section have already been implemented in this picture):

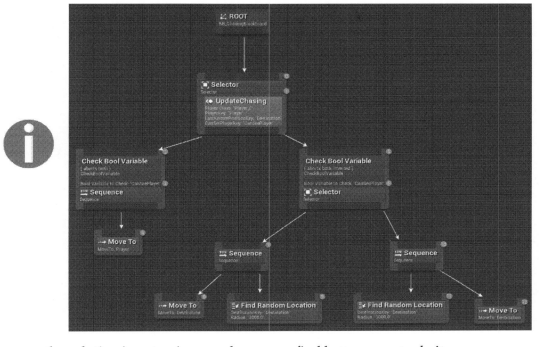

Of course the solution is not unique, and you may find better ways to do it.

What about our first problem of the *Destination* never be initialized? Well, we don't have this problem anymore with the proposed solution, since if the first *Sequence* (in the right-branch) fails, then the second one will set the *Destination* to a *Random Location*. In fact, when debugging Behavior Trees, you always need to be careful to each modification and how this affects the whole tree. Imagine this for a complex Behavior, and you can get an idea of the time required for such Task.

Once we have fixed this, we can always check for other bugs and/or try to improve the set up. Here a couple of other issues, which I leave you to fix, in order to practice with *Behavior Trees*:

- When the *Behavior Tree* starts its execution, the *Destination* is set to the zero vector. This means, that the AI, if doesn't see the Player, will go straight to the *World Origin*. Can you try to avoid it? Try to think, which are the different alternatives we have? The best would be to have a Random Destination In range. How can we achieve that?

- At the moment, when we do the Cast in the Perception System, we just select a broader class of *BehaviorTreeDesignCharacter*. However, this causes problems if you have more than one AI in the level. How can you fix that? For sure, you can change the Cast into something more specific, so to reduce it only to the Player. But what if you cannot do that, because both Players and friendly AI must share the same class? You could try to use the different Teams to distinguish enemies, allies and neutral; recall from Chapter 5.

Of course, this was just a very small example of *Behavior Tree*, yet it took three solid chapters to go through it in details. I will leave you exploring Behavior Trees for your games, but before that, the next section will talk about some suggestions on how to improve the C++ code.

# Improving further (C++ only)

We have made a very nice Behavior Tree by programming the different nodes we have used. However, when you work on a big project or with other team members, you should ensure that your nodes are as solid as possible. In fact, in the C++ implementation, we added a static description to our nodes to show which variables were set, and that was fantastic. But we can do more!

This section will guide you through improving the C++ nodes even further.

## Node Name

Unreal does a good job in C++ Behavior Tree nodes by cutting out the prefix (e.g. "*BTTask_*") and directly showing the name of the Task (or Decorator or Service). In the blueprint, it keeps the whole prefix instead, as you see in the following screenshot:

As we saw in the previous chapters, you can modify the name that will be displayed by changing the **Node Name** property in the *Details* panel:

This is reflected in the Behavior Tree:

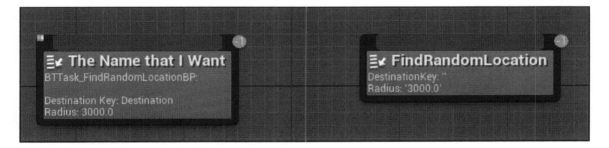

Thus, when you write a C++ node, it's good practice to give a default **Node Name**. You can do this by simply assigning it in the constructor. So, let's do this for all three C++ nodes we have created.

In the *Decorator* header file, we need to add the declaration of the constructor:

```
UBTDecorator_CheckBoolVariable(const FObjectInitializer& ObjectInitializer
= FObjectInitializer::Get());
```

Its implementation in the `.cpp` file is straightforward, since we just need to add the following:

```
UBTDecorator_CheckBoolVariable::UBTDecorator_CheckBoolVariable(const
FObjectInitializer & ObjectInitializer)
  : Super(ObjectInitializer)
{
  NodeName = "Check Bool Variable";
}
```

This is the final result:

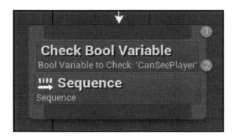

We need to do this with our Task, too. So, let's declare the constructor in the header file:

```
UBTTaskNode_FindRandomLocation(const FObjectInitializer& ObjectInitializer
= FObjectInitializer::Get());
```

Its implementation in the `.cpp` file is as follows:

```
UBTTaskNode_FindRandomLocation::UBTTaskNode_FindRandomLocation(const
FObjectInitializer & ObjectInitializer)
  : Super(ObjectInitializer)
{
  NodeName = "Find Random Location";
}
```

This is how it looks in the Behavior Tree Editor:

Finally, we already have a constructor for our Service, so we just need to add a line to its constructor in the `.cpp` file:

```
UBTService_UpdateChasing::UBTService_UpdateChasing(const
FObjectInitializer& ObjectInitializer)
   : Super(ObjectInitializer)
{
  NodeName = "Update Chasing Behavior";

  bNotifyBecomeRelevant = false;
  bNotifyCeaseRelevant = true;
}
```

The service will appear with a nice name in the Behavior Tree Editor:

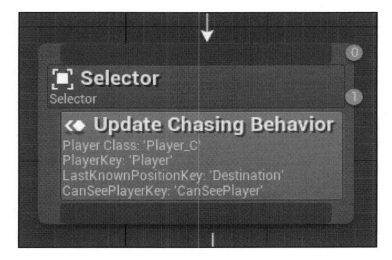

# A better description for the Decorator

As we mentioned previously, when we use the C++ version of the Decorator, we are unable to see whether the condition is reversed, or the aborts settings.

To add them into our static description, we need to change the code slightly. Fortunately, the header describing all of these properties is given in the parent class of our Decorator, and so we don't need to write the code from scratch. We need to store the return value of the parent function (by using the `Super::GetStaticDescription()` function) in a local FString Variable.

Then, we can add a couple of new lines and append the original Static Description we made. Finally, we return the new variable:

```
FString UBTDecorator_CheckBoolVariable::GetStaticDescription() const
{
  FString ReturnDesc = Super::GetStaticDescription();
  ReturnDesc += "\n\n";
  ReturnDesc += FString::Printf(TEXT("%s: '%s'"), TEXT("Bool Variable to
Check"), BoolVariableToCheck.IsSet() ?
*BoolVariableToCheck.SelectedKeyName.ToString() : TEXT(""));
  return ReturnDesc;
}
```

This is the final effect:

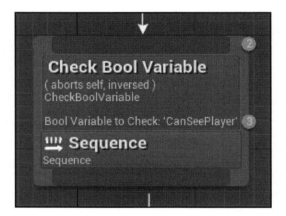

 Of course, you can use the `Super::GetStaticDescription()` function for Tasks and Services as well.

# Filtering Blackboard Keys

When we insert *Blackboard Keys* in the *Details Panel*, we can insert any key that's present in the *Blackboard*. However, when we use our **CheckBoolVariable** Decorator, we only want boolean keys in the **BoolVariableToCheck**.

We can achieve this by adding some filters in the constructor, as we learned back in Chapter 6, *Extending the Behavior Tree*. Let's do this for all three nodes.

In the implementation of the *Constructor* of our **Check Bool Variable Decorator** (.cpp file), we need to add the following filter so that it can only select boolean keys:

```
UBTDecorator_CheckBoolVariable::UBTDecorator_CheckBoolVariable(const
FObjectInitializer & ObjectInitializer)
  : Super(ObjectInitializer)
{
  NodeName = "Check Bool Variable";

  BoolVariableToCheck.AddBoolFilter(this,
GET_MEMBER_NAME_CHECKED(UBTDecorator_CheckBoolVariable,
BoolVariableToCheck));
}
```

Now, our *Decorator* will only be able to accept Boolean keys:

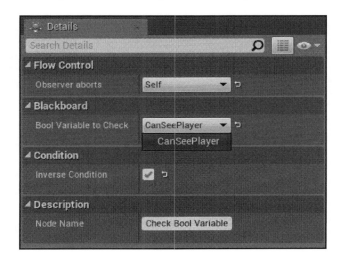

Likewise, we can do the same for our *Task* for the Destination Vector, which is of type Vector. In its *Constructor* (.cpp file), add the following:

```
UBTTaskNode_FindRandomLocation::UBTTaskNode_FindRandomLocation(const
FObjectInitializer & ObjectInitializer)
  : Super(ObjectInitializer)
{
  NodeName = "Find Random Location";

  DestinationVector.AddVectorFilter(this,
GET_MEMBER_NAME_CHECKED(UBTTaskNode_FindRandomLocation,
DestinationVector));
}
```

Now, our *Find Random Location Task* can only accept Vector Keys:

Finally, in our *Update Chasing Behavior Service*, we need to do the same, but for each of the three variables. In particular, in the *Object* filter, we need to specify a class. In this example, we can just filter based on AActor. So, in the .cpp file, add the following lines:

```
UBTService_UpdateChasing::UBTService_UpdateChasing(const
FObjectInitializer& ObjectInitializer)
  : Super(ObjectInitializer)
{
  NodeName = "Update Chasing Behavior";

  bNotifyBecomeRelevant = true;
  bNotifyCeaseRelevant = false;

  // Filter the Blackboard Key Selectors
  PlayerKey.AddObjectFilter(this,
GET_MEMBER_NAME_CHECKED(UBTService_UpdateChasing, PlayerKey),
AActor::StaticClass());
  LastKnownPositionKey.AddVectorFilter(this,
GET_MEMBER_NAME_CHECKED(UBTService_UpdateChasing, LastKnownPositionKey));
  CanSeePlayerKey.AddBoolFilter(this,
GET_MEMBER_NAME_CHECKED(UBTService_UpdateChasing, CanSeePlayerKey));
}
```

This is how it appears when we try to select a key for our *Service*:

This concludes this section and our journey of creating a *Behavior Tree* from scratch.

# Summary

In this chapter, we have completed what we started in the previous two chapters. In fact, we have built a Behavior Tree from scratch, starting from the design phase, and implementing all the components we needed along the way (both in Blueprint and C++!).

In particular, in this chapter we have seen how to build the Behavior Tree, along with the Blackboard; make the Behavior Tree run (both in a Blueprint and C++ setup); and improved the C++ implementation of the nodes by assigning node names, placing a header in the Decorator, and filtering the *Blackboard Key* selectors based on their type.

This chapter concludes the main features of the Unreal Engine AI Framework. However, this doesn't mean that we are finished with this Framework just yet. In fact, we can now perform an extensive debugging of the AI, which is the topic we are going to face in the next chapters.

# Section 3: Debugging Methods 3

In this last section, we will explore Debugging Methods. In fact, this is a topic to not underestimate, since it is of vital importance for becoming a professional AI Game Developer. Being able to analyze, profile and visualize the AI you program it is key to achieve the intended behavior and hitting the right performance for your project.

The last chapter concludes with some suggestions on how to explore the concepts presented (and others) beyond this book and some thoughts regarding AI systems.

The following chapters will be covered in this section:

- Chapter 11, Debugging Methods for AI - Logging
- Chapter 12, Debugging Methods for AI - Navigation, EQS, and Profiling
- Chapter 13, Debugging Methods for AI - The Gameplay Debugger
- Chapter 14, Going Beyond

# Debugging Methods for AI - Logging

# 11

In this chapter, we will look at a series of methods that we can use to debug our AI systems. Of course, they can be used in general, and not only for AI. However, since AI can be tricky sometimes, mastering how to do proper logging in Unreal can be a time-saver when you need to find and fix a bug related to AI. In fact, often, due to variables that haven't been properly set, maybe with wrong values, we end up not executing a portion of code, or make a miscalculation.

In this chapter, we will cover the following topics:

- Console Logging and on-screen messages in Blueprint
- On-screen messages in C++
- Console Logging in C++
- Creating a Custom Logging Category (C++)

By mastering the art of logging, you will be able to easily keep track of your values and which part of the code you are executing. Moreover, creating a Custom Logging Category allows you to define different levels of logging, and change the quantity of logging you want to see (even at runtime) based on what you are debugging. Furthermore, it is possible to easily strip away all the debugging code (at compilation time) by changing a variable, so that your shipped game can run as smoothly as possible.

With this being said, let's get started!

# Basic Logging

In the previous chapters we already looked at how to make logs. For example, in `Chapter 5`, *Agent Awareness*, we saw how to print the information we needed both on the Console and on-screen. However, in this section, we will explore those concepts in more detail, and learn how to master logging within Unreal.

- **On-Screen messages**: Often, during the Debugging phase, you and your team will need to be aware of certain variable values while playing the game. Thus, the easiest way to continuously test the value of the variable is by printing its value on the screen. We can achieve this in different ways, both in Blueprint and C++.

- **Console Messages**: These are printed on the Console (actually, there is more than one) and into Log files (so that even when the game is not running, you can analyze the log files to understand what happened (or what went wrong)).

 While in Blueprint we have a unique function to print both on-screen and into the Console, in C++, we have separate functions. In fact, the Logging System in Unreal is very powerful, and C++ unlocks its full power.

# Console Logging and on-screen messages in Blueprint

When it comes to Blueprint, we have simple and easy debug nodes that we can use. The most common one is **Print String**, but its counterpart, **Print Text**, also exists. The following is a screenshot showing **Print String** and **Print Text**:

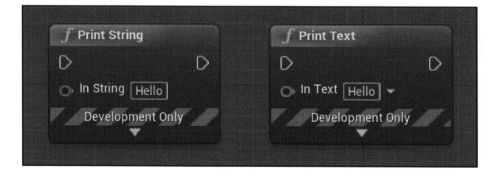

Both of them are marked as *Development Only*, which means that they will not working in shipping builds.

Their simple usage is straightforward. You just need to plug a *String* (or *Text*) into the homonym variable.

However, if we expand them and look at their more advanced options, we can find a full list of parameters, as shown in the following screenshot:

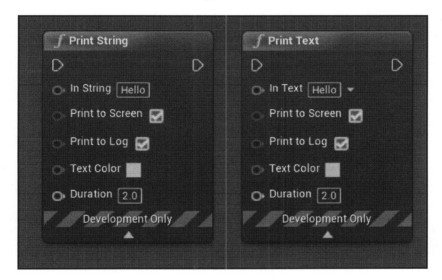

Let's look at them in detail:

- **String / Text**: This is the String or Text that will be displayed on-screen. Thus, any information that needs to be displayed has to be within this String or Text.
- **Print to Screen**: If true, the node will actually print the message on-screen (by default, it is true).
- **Print to Console**: If true, the node will print the message in the Console as well (by default, it is true).
- **Text Color**: This is the color in which the String/Text will be displayed (by default, it is a light blue). This is useful when you need to visually distinguish different information. Colors help a lot in these kinds of situations.
- **Duration**: This is how long the message will be displayed on the screen. Make sure that you have enough time to read/assimilate the information. Of course, longer messages need a longer duration to be read.

This is how they should appear in-game:

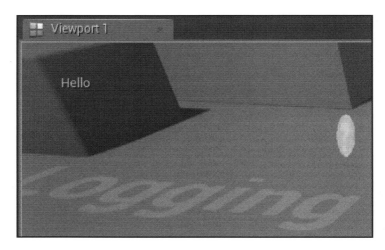

The same log also appears in the console if "***Print to Console***" is set to true, and looks as follows:

# On-screen messages in C++

In C++, we have an handy function to print messages on-screen. We do this within the UEngine class. The easiest way to have access to it is by using the **GEngine** variable, which is a global variable that's available everywhere and contains the instance of the *UEngine* class. Keep in mind that this variable might be empty (e.g. the game is running on a shipping build). Thus, it is very good practice to check the variable before you use it, like in the following code snippet:

```
if (GEngine) {
    //Do stuff with GEngine
}
```

Within the if statement, we can use the **GEngine** variable to call the AddOnScreenDebugMessage() function. As you would have guessed from the name, it prints a message on-screen. This is its full declaration:

```
void AddOnScreenDebugMessage(uint64 Key,float TimeToDisplay,FColor
DisplayColor,const FString& DebugMessage, bool bNewerOnTop = true, const
FVector2D& TextScale = FVector2D::UnitVector);
```

Let's go through the different parameters:

- **Key**: This is a unique key that's given to a "slot" on the screen. When a new message needs to be written, but there is already one with the same key displayed, then the new one will replace the old one. This is particularly useful when you have a variable that updates often and you don't want to flood the screen with a lot of debug messages, especially when only the last one is relevant. Remember to use the same key when you print the same information, just updated.

 In the definition, the Key parameter is a **uint64**. However, there is wrapper that works with **int32**. Don't worry if you define your keys as **int32**, as they will work anyway.

- **TimeToDisplay**: This is the duration, expressed in seconds, of how long the message needs to remain displayed on-screen. Make sure that you have enough time to read/assimilate the information. Of course, longer messages need longer durations to be read.

- **DisplayColor**: This is the color in which the debug message will be displayed. This is useful when you need to visually distinguish different information. Colors help a lot in these kinds of situations.
- **DebugMessage**: This is the string that will be displayed on-screen. Thus, any information that needs to be displayed has to be packed into an *FString*.
- **bNewerOnTop**: iThis s a boolean that it is used only when the key is equal to **INDEX_NONE** (which means a value of -1). If true, every new message will be displayed on top of the others. Otherwise, every new message will be placed below the others (like in a normal console). This is an option parameter, which is set to true by default. In fact, unlike a normal console, the text doesn't scroll down, so placing the most recent information on top guarantees that it is always available to developers.
- **TextScale**: This is the scale of the text, expressed as an *FVector2D*. This is useful when the text needs to be bigger or smaller than others for visualization reasons. This is an optional parameter, which is set to be the unitary vector (no scaling) by default.

Now that we've covered these parameters, its usage is pretty straightforward. You can use the following snippet to quickly print some text:

```
if (GEngine) {
    GEngine->AddOnScreenDebugMessage(-1, 5.0f, FColor::Turquoise,
TEXT("Some text to Display"));
}
```

In case you want to check if a **Key** already exists before printing your message (to avoid overriding already displayed information), you can use the `OnScreenDebugMessageExists()` function, which takes the Key as a parameter (only *uint64*, since there's no wrapper for *int32*) and returns a bool. It will be true if already it exists. Here is an example:

```
if (GEngine) {
    bool bExistMessageInSlot2 = GEngine->OnScreenDebugMessageExists(2);
    // ... continue
}
```

If you wish to completely clear the screen of any displayed message, you can do so by using the `ClearOnScreenDebugMessages()` function – no parameters, no return value. Here is an example:

```
if (GEngine) {
    GEngine->ClearOnScreenDebugMessages();
}
```

In case you want to temporarily suppress any on-screen messages, you can do so by changing the bEnableOnScreenDebugMessages boolean. The advantage of this variable is that changing its value in real-time allows you to suspend debugging on-screen *on-the-fly*. Its usage is very simple:

```
if (GEngine) {
    //Disable On-Screen Messages
    GEngine->bEnableOnScreenDebugMessages = false;
}
```

To test this code, we can create a new C++ class of type Actor, as shown in the following screenshot:

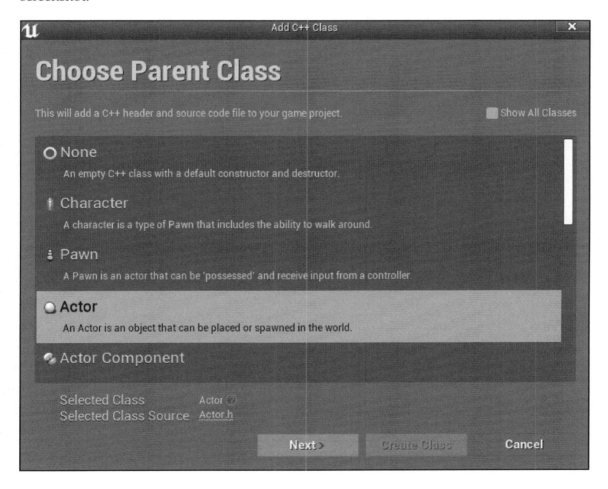

Then, we can rename it as *LoggingActor*, and place it within a folder named "*Chapter11*":

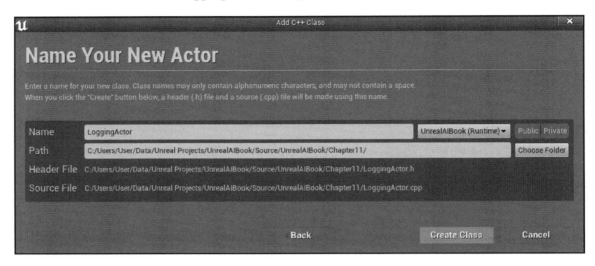

Next, we need to add the `BeginPlay()` function override in the header (.h) file if it is not already present (depending on which version of the Engine you are using, or if you have created the class in Visual Studio). In case you don't have it, this is the code:

```
protected:
  // Called when the game starts or when spawned
  virtual void BeginPlay() override;
```

Then, in the implementation (.cpp) file, we can write the function to log the message on the screen within the `BeginPlay()` function:

```
// Called when the game starts or when spawned
void ALoggingActor::BeginPlay()
{
  Super::BeginPlay();

  if (GEngine) {
    GEngine->AddOnScreenDebugMessage(-1, 8.0f, FColor::Turquoise,
TEXT("Some text to Display"));
  }
}
```

Compile this code and place the actor in the level (remove the blueprint one, in case you already have that, or keep it, if you prefer).

 Keep in mind that we didn't create a Scene Component for this Actor, since we were focusing on the logic. As a result, you are able to place it in the level, but not in a specific location. For our purposes, this is fine, but remember that when you create a C++ Actor, you might want a Scene Component (at least), or some other component.

Once you hit play, you will be able to see the following message:

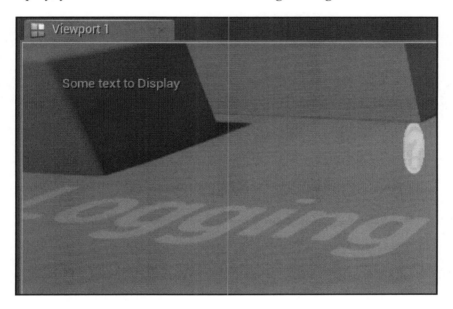

# Console Logging in C++

When it comes to print on the console using C++, the possibilities are much vaster than Blueprint. In fact, logging in Unreal is a complex beast that does many things.

If you are searching just for a quick shortcut to print something into the console using C++, you can just use the following line of code:

```
UE_LOG(LogTemp, Warning, TEXT("Message to Display"));
```

This is how it appears in the **Output Log** (I have place this line of code in the
`LoggingActor`):

However, if you want to learn about the potential of the *Unreal Logging system*, than keep
reading.

A good logging system doesn't just display information – it needs to display the right
information.

So, to get started and look at serious logging in Unreal, we need to understand two
concepts: *Log Category* and *Log Verbosity*:

- **Log Category**: Log Categories are like labels that are given to the debug
  messages: they classify the kind of information that these messages convey into a
  category. For instance, you can have a category for AI, another for UI, and a third
  for Gameplay. As a result, when a message appears on the console, it is possible
  to know which category the message belongs to.
  However, the usefulness of category doesn't stop here. Imagine that you are
  debugging your AI, but when you play the game, you are flooded with
  Gameplay debugging messages that your teammate (or you, in another time-
  slice) is using for testing. In this case, it would be nice to have only your debug
  messages. If all the messages are in different Log Categories, it is possible to filter
  them. As a result, you can completely suppress debug messages that are coming
  from a specific Log Category.
  It is possible to go a step further with *Log Verbosity*.

- **Log Verbosity**: Log Verbosity is another label that's given to the debug message that indicates how *"verbose"* the message is. In other words, how detailed the debug message is.

  For example, a message saying *"Error occurred in the AI Controller"* and another saying *"Error occurred in the AI controller when executing the AttackPlayer Task in the Behavior Tree"* convey the same error, but the second is more detailed. A Gameplay programmer might need to be aware that there is an error in the AI controller, so if the game doesn't behave as it should, it might not due to his/her code, but rather because of an error in the AI programming. The AI programmer, instead, while trying to fix what might have caused the error, needs to know more details regarding the error.

  There are seven ordered verbosity levels for logging. Once a verbosity level is selected, then every verbosity level equal or less than the selected one will be displayed/logged into files.

These are the different verbosity levels that are available in Unreal. They are ordered from least verbose to the most:

- **Fatal**: This verbosity level is always printed both to the console and into log files, and it always crashes the system, even if logging is disabled. This means that every time you use this level of logging, it will crash your game/application. You may want to use this in very rare and special cases in which if the runtime execution reaches a "fatal" no-returning point, then it crashes the game by giving some useful information on how to avoid it in the future.

- **Error**: This verbosity level is printed both into the console and into log files. They appear in red by default.

- **Warning**: This verbosity level is printed both into the console and into log files. They appear in yellow by default.

- **Display**: This verbosity level is printed both into the console and into log files.

- **Log**: This verbosity level is printed only into log files, not into the console. However, they can still be viewed in the Editor inside the Output Log Window. This is also the most common level to use, since it doesn't spam the console, and you receive all the information in the Output Log Window.

- **Verbose**: This verbosity level is printed only into log files, not in the console. This is usually used for detailed logging, especially when you print the values of many variables..
- **VeryVerbose**: This verbosity level is printed only into log files, not in the console. This is the most detailed log level, and it is usually used for very detailed messages, giving the full view of the situation (e.g. every single value of each variable involved in the process). These kind of logs are so detailed that they are almost spam in the output log, and so they are used when such a level of detail is really needed.

With the power of the Unreal Logging system, it is possible to decide on the level of verbosity for each logging category. In this way, if you are an AI programmer, you can set your AI logging to *VeryVerbose*, whereas the other categories (e.g. Gameplay-related stuff) is just set to a *Log* level.

# Creating a Custom Logging Category (C++)

So far, we have seen how a log category that's been set to a certain verbosity level is able to log the right amount of information regarding a system. However, the true power comes when you are able to create your own Logging Category. The process is quite straightforward, since it relies on the use of a couple of macros.

The best spot to define your category is in the *YOUR_PROJECT_NAME.h* and *YOUR_PROJECT_NAME.cpp* files, which in my case is in the UnrealAIBook.h and UnrealAIBook.cpp files.

In the header (.h) file, we need to declare the following macro:

```
DECLARE_LOG_CATEGORY_EXTERN(CategoryName, DefaultVerbosity,
CompileTimeVerbosity);
```

These are the parameters we need to insert:

- **CategoryName**: This is the name of the new category that you want to define. Try to provide a meaningful name, which is not too long, but descriptive enough. The choice depends on your game/application as well. In fact, if you have just a simple AI system, you can log everything into the same *LogAI* category. However, if you have a very large and complex AI system that it is composed of many subsystems, then dividing into different log categories might be a winning choice.

- **DefaultVerbosity**: This is the default verbosity level that's used if another part of it is not specified (either in a configuration file, or directly from the command line). Everything that it is above this level will not be displayed. For example, if you set this level to be just "*Log*", then neither Verbose or *VeryVerbose* will be logged.

- **CompileTimeVerbosity**: This is the maximum verbosity level at which the compiler will include the log instruction. Anything that is defined more verbose than this level will not be compiled, which means that it will not be available, not even if the verbosity level is changed. For example, once you have finished working on a system, you probably don't want to keep many log instructions that are *VeryVerbose* inside a *Tick* function in your code base. By stripping them away from the compiled code, you can ensure that those instructions will never impact your performance, especially if the system is consolidated and those are logs that will never be read. Another use might be in shipping games, in which you don't want a certain level of verbosity for specific log categories to be present in the game.

For example's sake, we can add this to our project:

```
DECLARE_LOG_CATEGORY_EXTERN(MyAwesomeAILogCategory, Log, All);
```

In the .cpp file, we need to have the following macro instead:

```
DEFINE_LOG_CATEGORY(CategoryName);
```

The only parameter that you need to insert is the name of the category, and it must match the name you inserted in the header file.

So, in our case, we can use the following:

```
DEFINE_LOG_CATEGORY(MyAwesomeAILogCategory);
```

Once you have done this, you are ready to use your brand new logging category so that you can add your C++ code in the following way:

```
UE_LOG(MyAwesomeAILogCategory, Log, TEXT("I'm logged from a custom
Category!"));
```

 If you get a compile error, it might be due to the fact that the C++ code in which you place the log doesn't have access to the definition of the category. For instance, in my case, I had to include my general project(/module) header file for it to work; I added `#include "UnrealAIBook.h"`.

This is how it appears in the *Output Log*:

```
Output Log

Filters ▾   Search Log                                                                    🔍

PIE: New page: PIE session: LoggingExampleMap (27/mar/2019 04:42:11)
LogPlayLevel: Creating play world package: /Game/Chapter11/UEDPIE_0_LoggingExampleMap
LogPlayLevel: PIE: StaticDuplicateObject took: (0.038595s)
LogAIModule: Creating AISystem for world LoggingExampleMap
LogPlayLevel: PIE: World Init took: (0.003546s)
LogPlayLevel: PIE: Created PIE world by copying editor world from /Game/Chapter11/LoggingExampl
LogInit: XAudio2 using 'Altoparlanti (Realtek High Definition Audio)' : 2 channels at 48 kHz us
LogInit: FAudioDevice initialized.
LogLoad: Game class is 'UnrealAIBookGameMode'
LogWorld: Bringing World /Game/Chapter11/UEDPIE_0_LoggingExampleMap.LoggingExampleMap up for pl
LogWorld: Bringing up level for play took: 0.006359
MyAwesomeAILogCategory: I am logged from a custom Category!
PIE: Play in editor start time for /Game/Chapter11/UEDPIE_0_LoggingExampleMap 0.722
LogBlueprintUserMessages: Late PlayInEditor Detection: Level '/Game/Chapter11/LoggingExampleMap
oggingExampleMap.LoggingExampleMap:PersistentLevel.LoggingExampleMap'

Cmd ▾   Enter Console Command
```

# Summary

In this chapter, we explored how to log both in C++ and Blueprint. This allows us to easily spot portions of our code that are wrong, or variables that contain wrong values.

It was particularly useful to learn about Custom Categories, since this is a very powerful part of the logging system within Unreal. In fact, it allows us to create a specific category for each part of our game, and increase or decrease the quantity of messages (based on importance) for each category, potentially even at runtime. Furthermore, it allows us to easily strip away debugging code once we need to ship the game, which we can do by simply changing the values of the `DECLARE_LOG_CATEGORY_EXTERN()` macro.

In the next chapter, we will explore more specific tools for performing debugging on the AI tools we have encountered during this book, from the *Navigation System* to *EQS*. Mastering these is important when it comes to becoming an AI Programmer in Unreal, and they will be very useful when you create complex AI systems.

# 12
# Debugging Methods for AI - Navigation, EQS, and Profiling

Welcome to Chapter 12, *Debugging Methods for AI – Navigation, EQS, and Profiling*.

Here, we are going to explore some more specific tools for the AI systems that are built-in within Unreal Engine. We will focus on **Navigation** and **EQS**, covering what we have left out (because it was debugging and/or visualization related) respectively from Chapter 3, *Navigation* and Chapter 4, *Environment Querying System*.

At the end of the chapter, we will see some more tools for analyzing performance related to AI code. In the next chapter, we will complete the discussion by exploring the **Gameplay Debugger** as a way to have a quick real-time feedback for our AI.

In this chapter, we will cover the following topics:

- Checking the execution of a behavior tree
- Visualizing environmental queries with the EQS testing pawn and exploring how its settings can help to better understand the query
- How to use the EQS profiler to spot queries that have performance issues and how to dive deeper to understand what causes the bad performance
- Visualizing the navigation mesh and how it works under the hood
- Using the navigation test actor to check the path between two points of the navigation mesh
- Profiling by using **AI Stat Groups** to gather useful information regarding the performance of the AI systems
- Creating a **Custom Stat Group**, to be able to analyze performance of your customized AI systems

So, let's get started!

# Debugging behavior trees

Before jumping into the rest of the chapter, we should learn how to debug behavior trees. Actually, there are many methods, and some we will explore later in this chapter (with stats) and in the next one (such as the gameplay debugger).

However, I wanted to point out that it is possible to see the execution of a behavior tree. If you leave the behavior tree editor open while you play the game, you will see highlighted the current branch being executed on the behavior tree, and which decorators are blocked. Also, in the blackboard panel, it is possible to check the current values for each of the blackboard values. Here is an example from the designing behavior trees project:

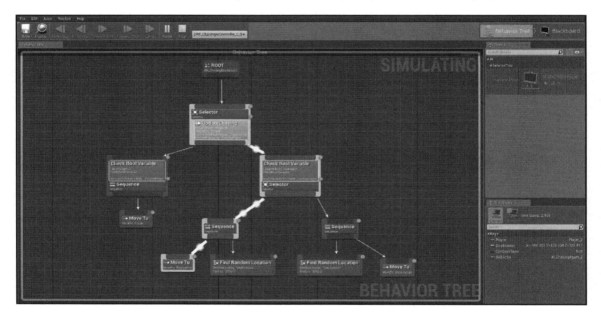

Also, if you have more than one **enemy** running a behavior tree, you can change which one to view from the top menu, as shown:

In the same way, it is possible to see the execution of blueprints as well. This is not strictly related to AI, but it was worthwhile mentioning it in an infobox.

# Profiling and visualizing environmental queries

In this section, we will explore how to visualize and profile **Environmental Queries**. In fact, we will gain a better understanding of how the EQS testing pawn can visualize an **Environment Query**, and we will explore the **Profiler** tool, which allows us to check the performance for each query.

## Visualizing environmental queries with the EQS testing pawn

As anticipated back in Chapter 4, *Environment Querying System*, there is a simple built-in way to visualize environment queries within the game world, directly from the viewport; the game doesn't even have to be running. In fact, there is a special pawn that it is able to do that. However, this pawn cannot be brought directly into the level, because, to ensure that it is not misused, it has been declared virtual within the code base. This means that in order to use it, we need to create our own blueprint pawn that inherits directly from this special pawn.

Thankfully, after this step, the pawn is fully featured, and it doesn't need any more code, just the parameters to work with (for example, the environmental query you want to visualize).

You will need the environment-querying system to be enabled, check Chapter 4, Environment Querying System, to see how to do this.

If you already have created the EQS testing pawn back in Chapter 4, *Environment Querying System*, feel free to skip the next section.

# Creating the EQS testing pawn

To start, create a new blueprint; the class to inherit from is **EQSTestingPawn**, as shown in this screenshot:

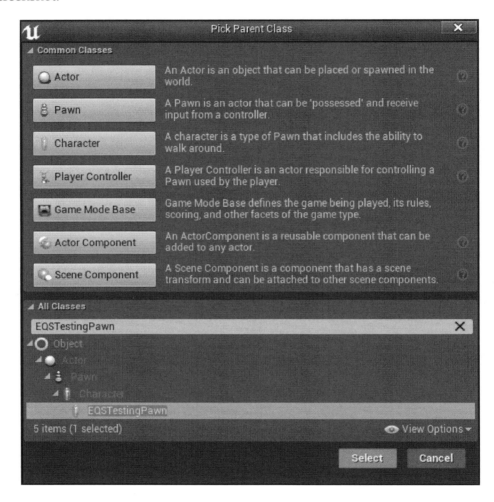

Then, you can rename it **MyEQSTestingPawn**, or if you already have done this in Chapter 4, *Environment Querying System*, you can either skip this part, or give it another name.

If you just drag it into the map from the **Details** panel, you can change the EQS settings, as shown in the next screenshot:

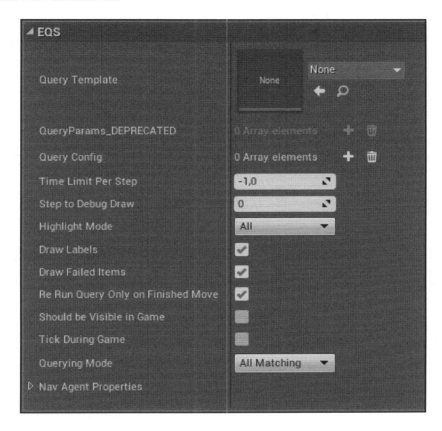

In Chapter 4, *Environment Querying System*, we got this far, but now that we have some more time for debugging, let's dive in deeper.

# Creating a test environmental query

We need an **Environmental Query** to perform, in order to visualize what's going on with the different settings. As such, we need to prepare a simple query that generates points in a grid, and then score them based on the distance from the **Querier**. So, let's build the environmental query, as shown in the following screenshot (within the EQS editor):

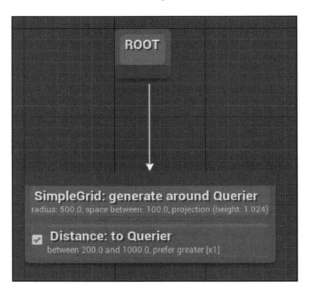

We are going to leave the default settings, but for your convenience, this is how a simple grid generator looks in the **Details** panel:

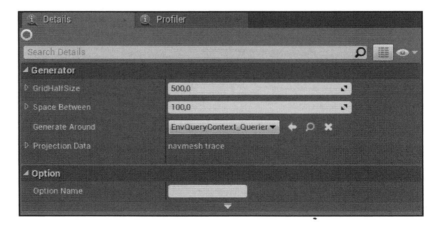

For the **Distance Test**, instead, we are going to leave mainly the default values, but for showcase purposes, we can change the **Filter** settings, so that **Float Value Min** and **Float Value Max** are respectively 200 and 1,000. As a result, we will be able to filter out the points that are too close to the querier, and see how the EQS testing pawn visualizes these points:

# Settings of the EQS testing pawn to visualize environmental queries

Now let's explore the settings we have seen in the **Details** panel of our **MyEQSTestingPawn**. For your convenience, here is the screenshot of the settings:

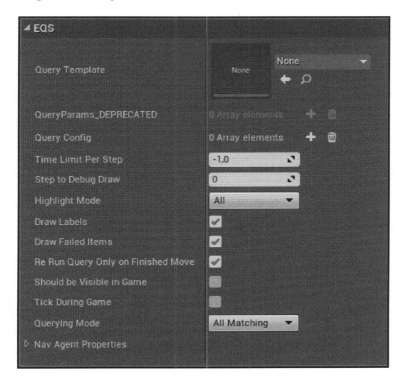

 Remember that you need to select the testing pawn in the level in order to visualize the query (and also a query template must be set).

- **Query Template**: As the name suggests, it is the **Environmental Query** that we want to visualize.
- **QueryParams_DEPRECATED**: (*don't use this*) This was the old way to set parameters for the environmental query; now please use **Query Config**.
- **Query Config**: It is an array that allows you to quickly change the settings of the **Environmental Query** for rapidly testing and debugging.
- **Highlight Mode**: It determines which locations (or items) should have a visual representation that is highlighted, which means having a big sphere, instead of a small one. The possible values that can assume are the following:
  - **All**: This means that all the locations or items are highlighted, and it is the default option; so it appears exactly as shown in the following screenshot, which is also how it appears by default once we set the **Query Template**:

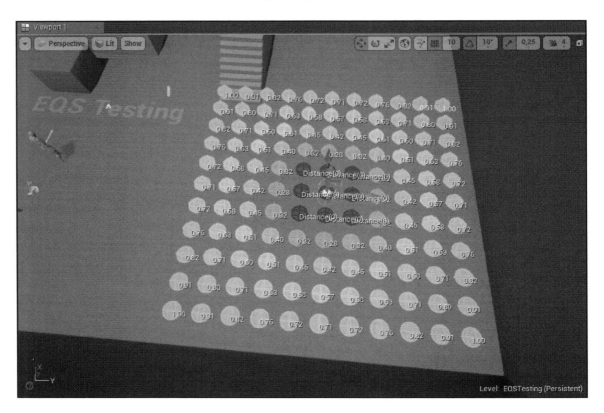

Viewport. This is an image of the viewport. The other (overlapped) information is not important here

- **Best 5%**: As the name suggests, it shows just the points that have a score so that it is within the best 5% score of all the points. All the other points will have a smaller sphere:

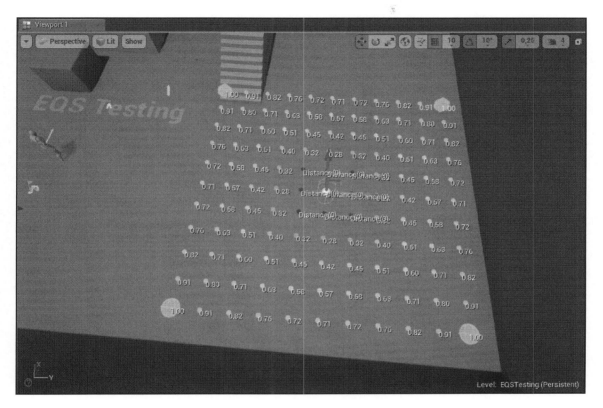

Viewport. This is an image of the viewport. The other (overlapped) information is not important here

- **Best 25%**: As the previous option does, it shows just the points that have a score so that it is within the best 25% scores of all the points. All the other points will have a smaller sphere:

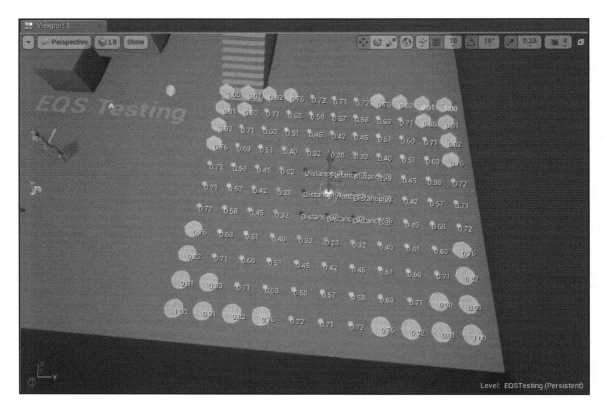

Viewport. This is an image of the viewport. The other (overlapped) information is not important here

- **Draw Labels**: If checked, it shows next to the point its score. If a point has been filtered out instead, it shows which test has filtered that point out. In our example, the points closer to the querier have been filtered out by the **Distance Test**. This option is enabled by default; if we turn it off.

- **Draw Failed Items**: If checked, it shows also the points that have been filtered out. It is enabled by default, and if we turn it off, in our example, we would see the following:

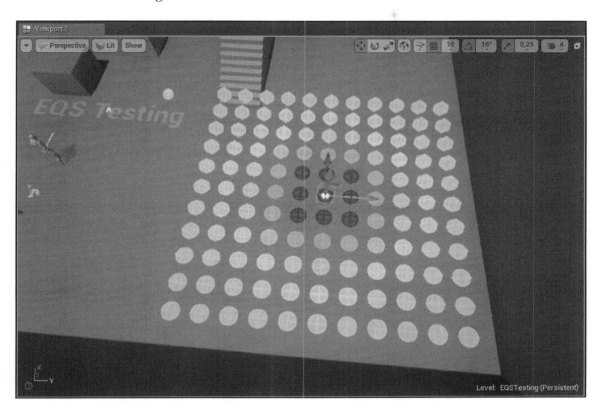

- **Rerun Query Only on Finished Move**: If checked, it will perform the query only when this testing pawn stops moving, and not all the time. It is enabled by default, and for performance reasons, you should keep this on, unless you need to visualize the query also when the testing pawn moves:

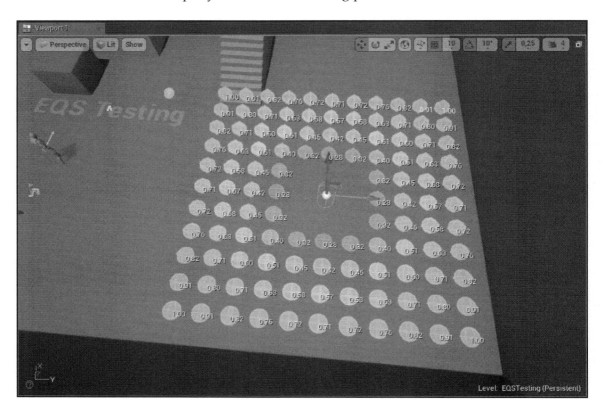

- **Should Be Visible In Game**: if checked, it will show the testing pawn as a small icon in the game, as in this screenshot; it is disabled by default:

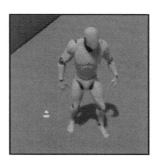

- **Tick During Game**: As the name suggests, if it is checked, it allows ticking during the execution of the game.
- **Querying Mode**: Determines which is the final result of the query, and it has many possible options:
    - **All Matching**: This is the default option; it shows all the points that match the query (the ones in blue have been filtered out). Moreover, the points are color-coded from orange to green based on the score, with green being the highest score of 1:

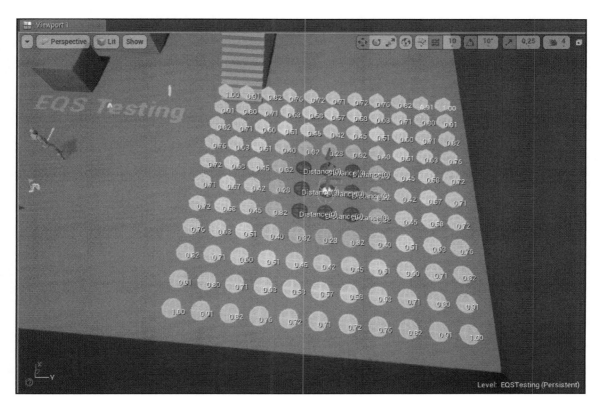

Viewport. This is an image of the viewport. The other (overlapped) information is not important here

- **Single Best Item**: Shows the point that has the highest score (hence the best one) in green, and all the others in a darker shade of green (the ones that have been filtered out are still in blue):

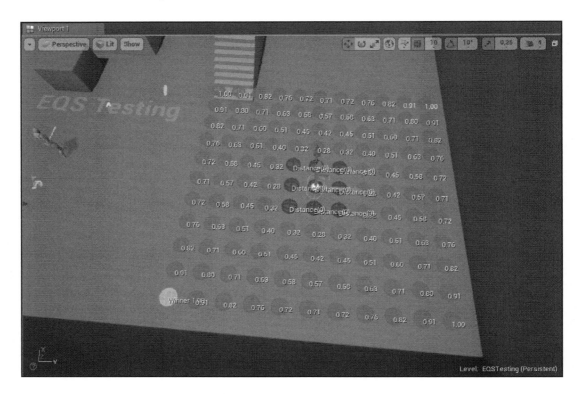

Viewport. This is an image of the viewport. The other (overlapped) information is not important here

- **Single Random Item from Best 5%**: It shows (or returns) a random point among the best 5% of the points that have scored the highest. In the next example, a random one has been picked:

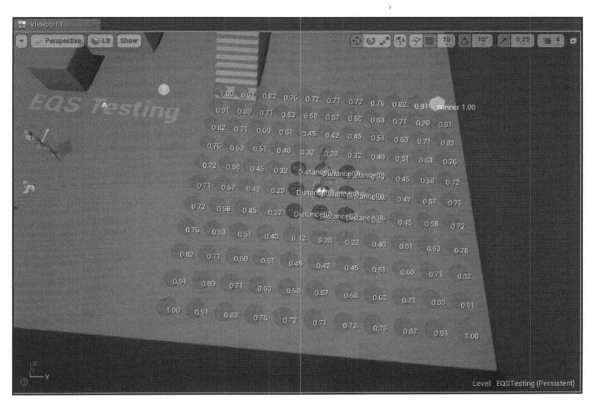

Viewport. This is an image of the viewport. The other (overlapped) information is not important here

- **Single Random Item from Best 25%**: It shows (or returns) a random point among the best 25% of the points that have scored the highest. In the next example, a random one has been picked:

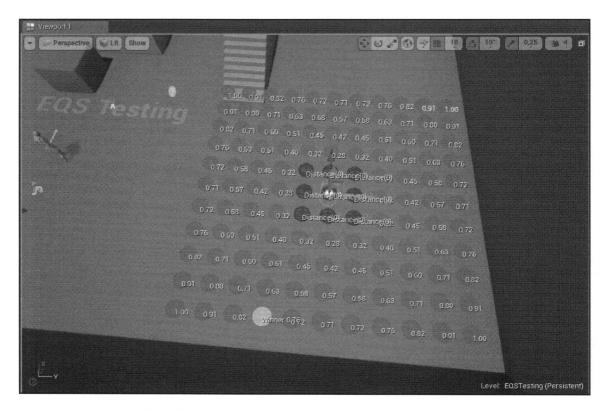

Viewport. This is an image of the viewport. The other (overlapped) information is not important here

- **Nav Agent Properties**: Since some **Environmental Queries** depend on the navigation system, as we have seen, then this set of options let you tweak how the agent that performs the query appears to the navigation system. We are not going into detail regarding those, but here are the possible options:

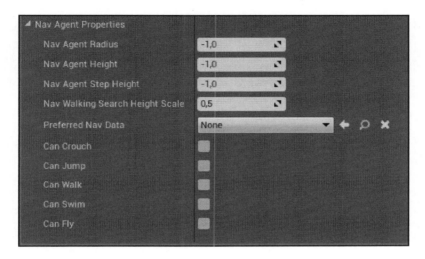

And that concludes our discussion about visualizing environmental queries with the testing pawn. However, there is more about EQS in the next section, where we will see how we can profile an environmental query to check its performance, and in the next chapter, we will see how to visualize an environmental query at run time with the gameplay debugger.

# Profiling environmental queries

In this section, we will learn how we can quickly profile environmental queries.

You may have noticed that in the EQS editor, next to the **Details** panel, there is a **Profile** tab, as shown in the following screenshot:

If we click on it, we will have a whole new section in which we will be able to quickly profile environmental queries. At the moment, it is empty, because the game is not running, and no environmental query is performed:

If we have already have some queries running in the game, we could just press **Play** and come back to this menu with all the queries that are currently running. However, if you don't have any in your game, we could quickly create a behavior tree to run some queries, making this behavior tree run on an AI controller and finally assign this AI controller to some AI agent in the game. Since we have done this many times in the book, I'm not going to guide you step by step. However, the next section will provide an overview of the process, if you want to follow along. Otherwise, feel free to skip the next section, and go directly to the *Environmental query profiler* section.

## Setting up the test assets for EQS profiling

First, we need to create the environmental queries; you should already have these in the game since you would have been using them, but if you just want to test this profiling tool, create a couple of queries, for instance, **EnvQueryA** and **EnvQueryB**. I made the first query heavier than usual (many points generated) so that it stood out in the Profiler later on:

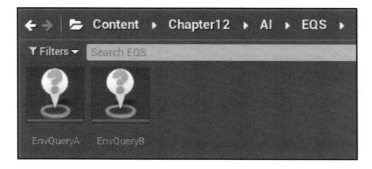

Then, we need to create a blackboard asset for the behavior tree; we can name it **BB_EQSTesting** and we just need a vector key inside it:

Next, we can create the behavior tree that runs the queries. Name it BT_EQSTesting, and assign within it the blackboard. Then, we can run the two queries one after another with a sequence node (along with a little delay). Remember to assign the query to the Run Query node, and use the vector key from the blackboard (so the query doesn't fail). The run mode should be by default set to Single Best Item; be sure that it is the option you have. Here is the behavior tree:

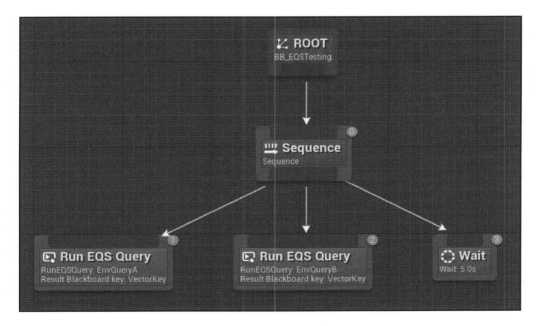

Now we need an AI controller; for simplicity, we can create it in Blueprint and name it **BP_EQSTestingAIController**. Override the **On Possess** function, and run the *behavior tree*:

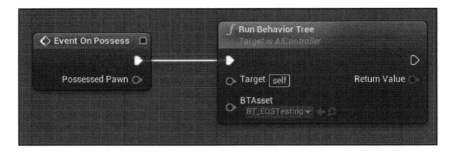

Finally, create an AI agent in the level (you can duplicate the player if you start form the **Third-Person Example Map**) and assign the freshly created AI controller:

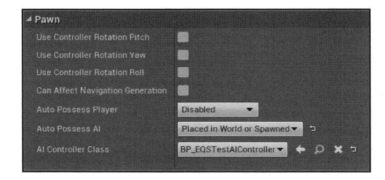

Now we are ready to see the profiler in action!

# The environmental query profiler

If you reach this far, you should press Play and have an environmental query running in your game. If so, when the game is running, the Profiler tab of the EQS editor will get filled with all the environmental query  running, and it shows stats for them:

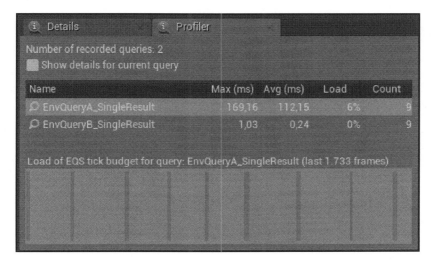

For each query type, the profiler shows the number of times it got executed, the maximum time taken from the worst of these queries, and their average time.

As you can see, **EnvQueryA** is very heavy (because I designed it so), and the profiler helps you understand which one needs to be changed/improved or even removed. Also, we will see red because it's run time is very bad. For **EnvQueryB**, we would see any of these things.

Moreover, the profiler divides the queries based also on the run mode. In the following screenshot, **EnvQueryB** has two entries, based on whether the run mode was **Single Result** or **All Matching**:

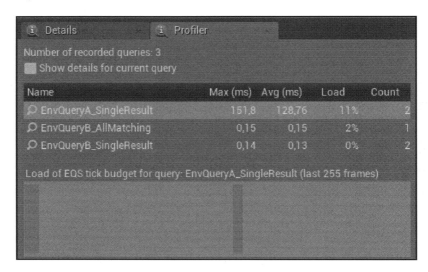

Of course, when you see the Profiler tab, you have the EQS editor opened on a specific query. Thus, at the bottom of the profiler, there is some more information about the query whose EQS editor is currently opened. In fact, we can see a graph showing the **Load of EQS tick budget** (how heavy was its tick) for the query.

Finally, at the top, there is the number of how many types of queries have been recorded so far and a checkbox named **Show details for current query**. If we check this box, we will be able to see directly on the environmental query tree the worst and the average time for each generator (and its pick rate), and for each test, we have the following:

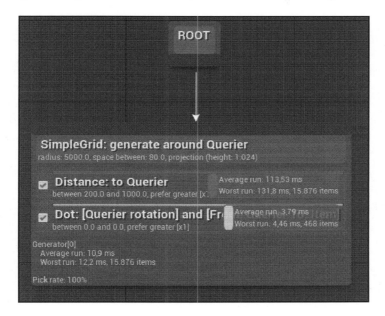

It is color-coded here as well:

- **Red** means a very bad performance.
- **Yellow** means an intermediate performance.
- **Green** means that the performance is good.

Again, the **EnvQueryA** has been designed to perform badly to showcase the profiler. If we pick **EnvQueryB**, we see that it performs much better:

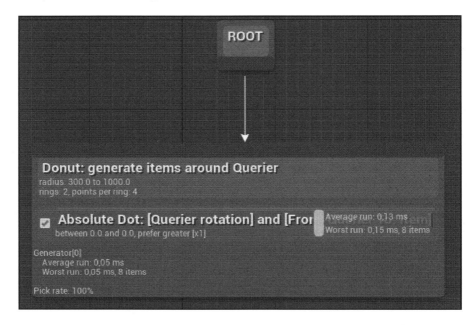

As a result, this peak into each single generator and each test allows you to dive deeper into which part of your environmental query is actually performing badly. So, you can use the profiler to identify which queries have problems, and then dive deeper into those that need to be optimized.

## Saving and loading EQS stats

Another cool feature of profiling environmental queries is that you can save your stats and load them again. This gives you powerful and flexible tools to share your findings with the rest of your team.

In order to save an EQS stat, you just need to press the **Save Stats** button in the top menu, as shown in the following screenshot:

You will be prompted to choose a location to save the file containing your stats.

Loading is easy as well. Just press the **Load Stats** button in the top menu, as shown in the next screenshot:

You will be prompted to choose a file containing your EQS stats, and after that, all your stats will be loaded.

# Testing and visualizing the navigation mesh

In this section, we will explore some built-in tools to test and visualize the **Navigation Mesh**.

In particular, we will see how it is possible to visualize the navigation mesh under the hood and how the navigation test actor can quickly show us "the way" (the path generated by the pathfinding algorithm).

# Visualizing the navigation mesh

As we mentioned back in Chapter 3, *Navigation*, when we generated a **Navigation Mesh**, for instance, by bringing into the map the **Nav Mesh Bounds Volume**, we also created a **RecastNavMesh-Default** actor in the level. If we select it, we can see many options there are to generate the navigation mesh, and some of them we already explored. However, we have a whole section about **Display Settings** that back in Chapter 3, *Navigation*, we didn't have the time to explore properly. Thus, let's quickly go through these settings; here, for your convenience, is a screenshot of the display settings in the **Details** panel:

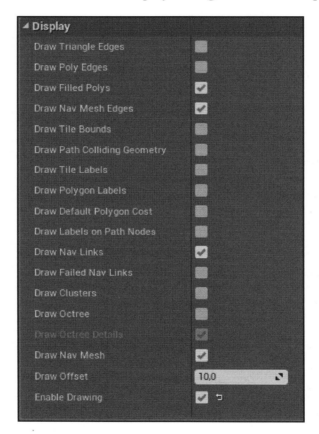

With the default settings, this is how it looks like (in our example map):

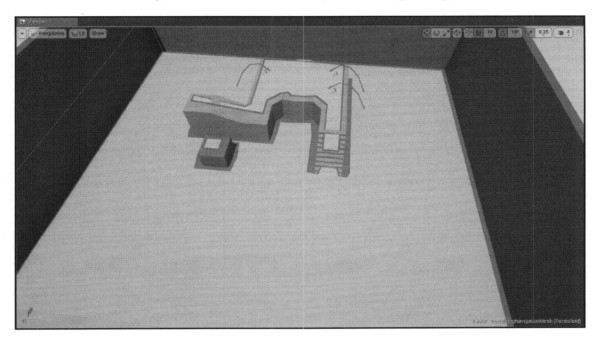

We have a lot of them, so without going too much into the details, let's dive in:

 To fully understand all of the options, you should be familiar with how the navigation mesh is generated. However, covering this is outside the scope of this book. In any case, you can still play with the settings and learn some more about the navigation system.

- **Draw Triangle Edge**: Shows the triangles of which the nav mesh is made. Ultimately, the connections of these triangles will generate a graph on which **Pathfinding** algorithms will run (actually, it is more complicated than that, since the system needs to scale for bigger worlds, and a hierarchical pathfinding is used on different graphs at different levels). By enabling this option, you can actually see the nodes of this graph:

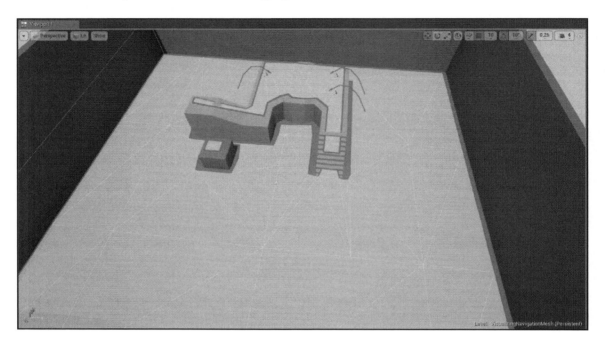

- **Draw Poly Edges**: Shows the edges of the polygons. In fact, the nav mesh is generated starting from sectioning the level in polygons, and if a polygon contains complex geometry (for example, there are static meshes), the algorithm subdivides the polygon into smaller polygons based on the geometry. Then, these polygons get divided into triangles (the one we have seen before). With this option enabled, you are able to see which are the polygons for this static mesh, and if you leave the previous option on, you can see clearly see how all of these polygons have been divided into triangles:

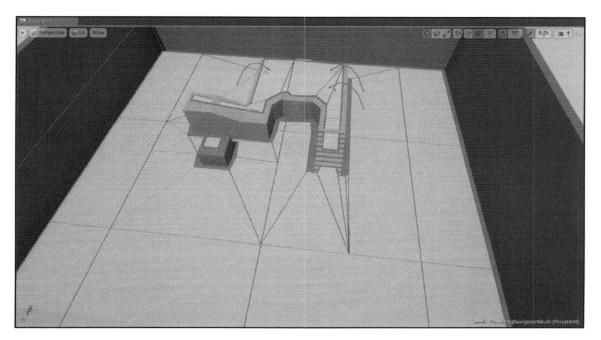

- **Draw Filled Polys**: If checked, it shows the polygon filled with the usual green we have already seen; in fact, this option is on by default. However, if we disable it, we can have a clearer look at the *bare bones* of the nav mesh:

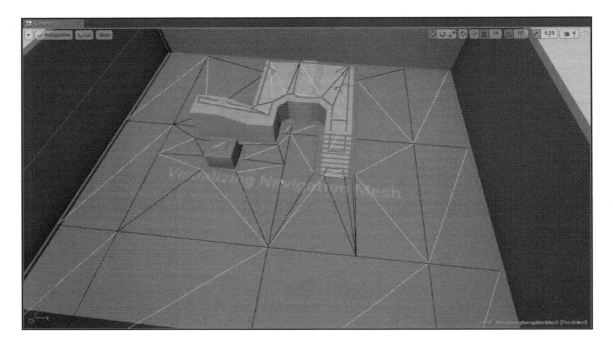

- **Draw Nav Mesh Edges**: If checked (and it is by default), it shows the edge of the nav mesh. In the following screenshot, this is how it looks with this option turned off:

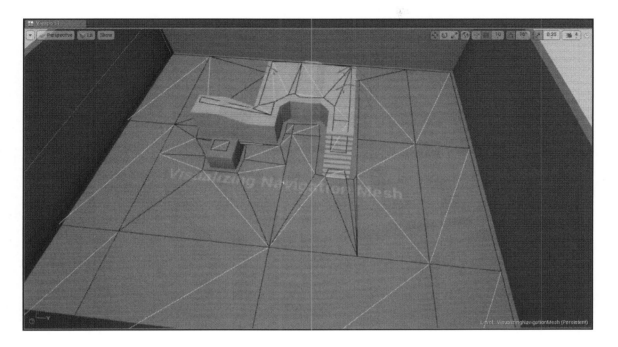

- **Draw Tile Bound**: If enabled, it shows the bounds of the tiles of the navigation mesh:

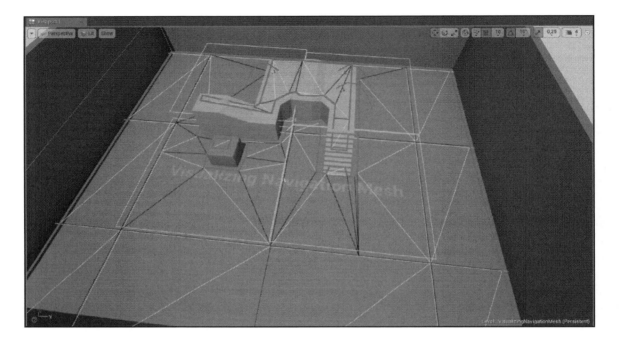

- **Draw Path-Colliding Geometry**: By enabling this option, it is possible to visualize the geometry that has been passed as input to the **Navigation Mesh Generator**, so it is basically all the geometry that the navigation system "is aware of." This is useful to check whether something is considered by the navigation system, so you can include or exclude what you don't want (remember that there is an option for actors and objects to influence the navigation mesh, and this option allows you to spot the one that is currently being considered by the navigation system). By checking this option, this is what it is possible to see:

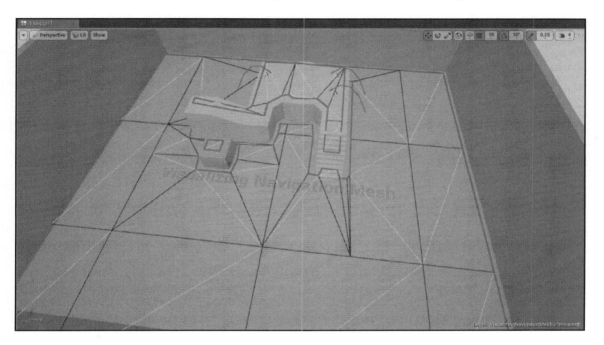

- However, keep in mind that Unreal renders this geometry independently from the rest. So, you can also use other views in the engine to isolate this geometry to better check what it is like. For instance, you can turn on the Wireframe View, and it is still possible to see the geometry passed to the navigation mesh generator, and this is how it looks:

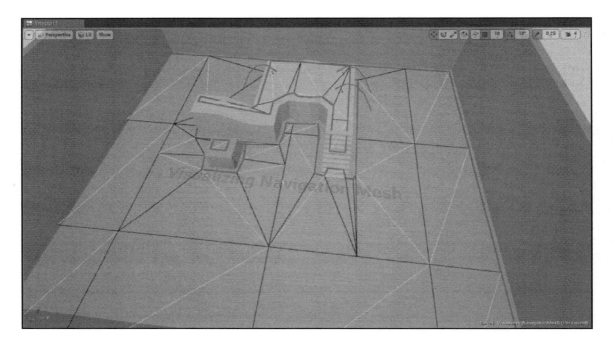

- **Draw Tile Labels**: If enabled, these options show the label (expressed as a coordinate) of each tile of the navigation mesh:

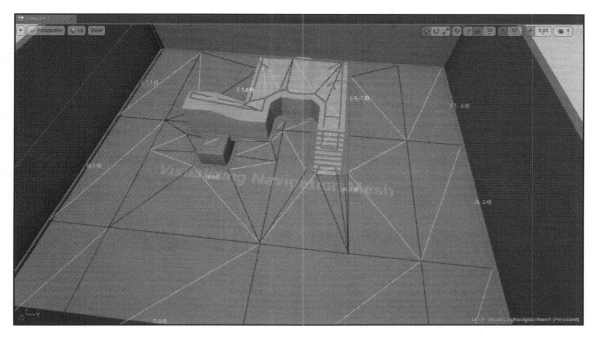

Viewport. This is a screenshot of the viewport. The other (blurred out) information is not important here

- **Draw Polygon Labels**: If enabled, this option shows a label (that also express how many iterations that polygon went through before being generated) for each polygon generated in the navigation mesh:

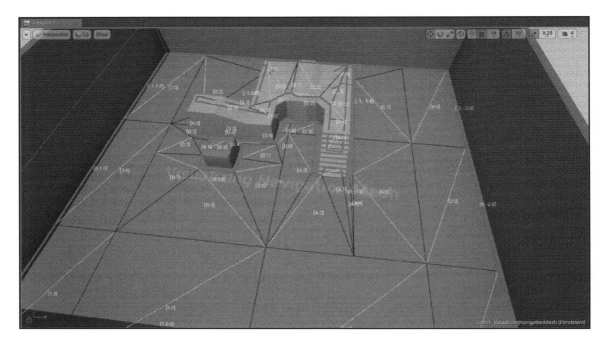

Viewport. This is a screenshot of the viewport. The other (blurred out) information is not important here

- **Draw Default Polygon Cost**: If this option is enabled, it shows all the costs for the different parts of the navigation mesh. This is very useful for checking which parts are more expensive to traverse. By enabling it in our example, this is how it looks:

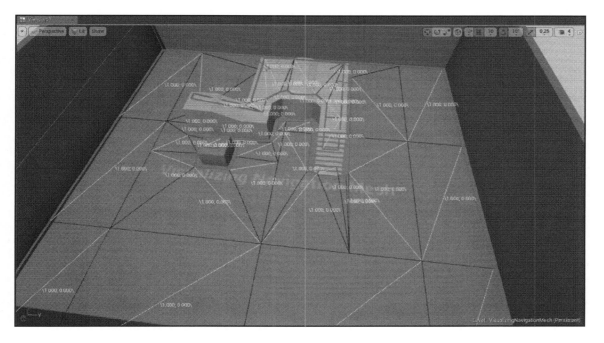

Viewport. This is a screenshot of the viewport. The other (blurred out) information is not important here

- As you can see, all the costs are just 1, and this is because we don't have any other type of nav areas than the default ones. If we bring a nav modifier and we set a custom nav area (different than null), for instance, the **Desert** (or **Jungle**) **Area**, as we did back in Chapter 3, *Navigation*, this would be the result (you will notice a change in how the navigation mesh is generated, and how in the desert area the cost is higher):

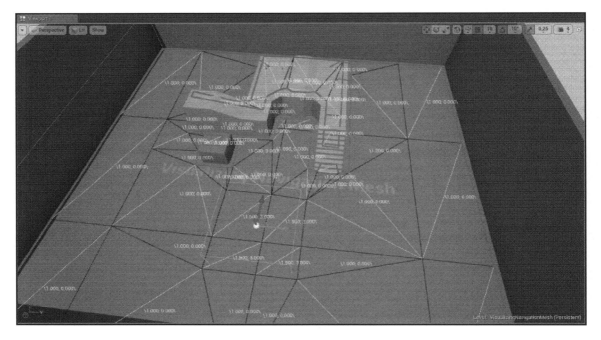

Viewport. This is a screenshot of the viewport. The other (blurred out) information is not important here

- **Draw Labels on Path Nodes**: If this option is on, it will draw labels on the path nodes.

- **Draw Nav Links**: As the name suggests, if the option is on, it will draw nav links. It is enabled by default, since usually, you want to be able to see the nav links. If we disable it, this is how it would look in our example:

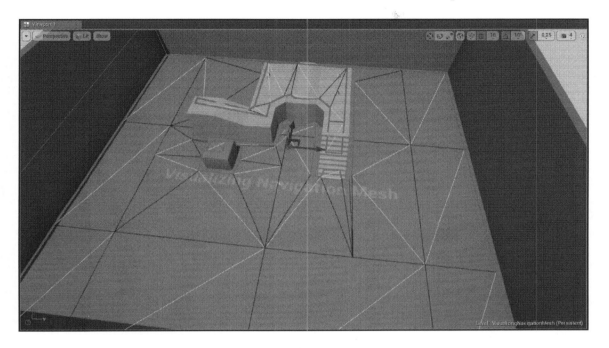

- **Draw Failed Nav Links**: This is the same as the previous option, but on **Failed Nav Links**, it is disabled by default.

- **Draw Clusters**: If enabled, it allows you to see the clusters. I'm not going into detail, but as we mentioned earlier, the pathfinding needs to be optimized to scale on large worlds (for example, **Hierarchical Pathfinding**); thus, with this option, you can see which regions of the navigation mesh are connected (meaning that it is guaranteed that between those two regions a path exists in some way), and so the pathfinding can first find the connected region, before refining the search of the path. If this option is enabled, here is how it looks:

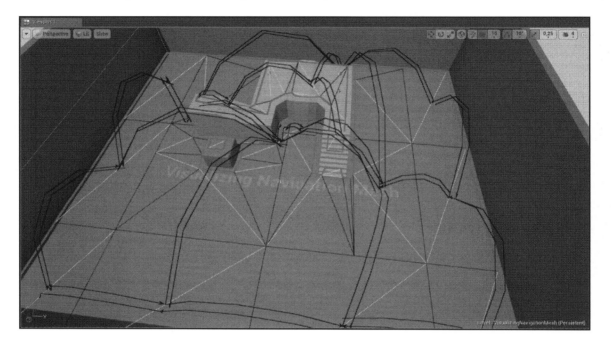

- **Draw Octree and Draw Octree Details**: If enabled, it allows you to see the **Octrees**. Octrees are mathematical structures (trees with eight children) used to partition a 3D space. In fact, the navigation mesh is only on the same surface, but it lives in (and needs to work with) a 3D space. Just as in our example map, we have some stairs and some regions of the navigation mesh that are not at the same level; and also **Nav Links** connects regions from above the stairs to down below. If we enable it, here is how it should look (you will be able to notice that the octrees are mainly in the parts of the navigation mesh that needs to develop in height):

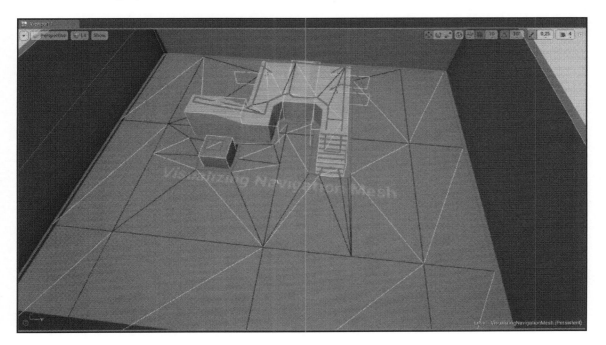

- **Draw Offset**: As you may have already noticed, the navigation mesh is not drawn at the same level of the geometry of the level, but there is a small offset. The **Draw Offset** parameter controls this offset from the ground where the navigation mesh is drawn. The default value is 10 (which means 10 centimeters if we keep the convention with the Unreal units). If we change this value (I also enabled **Draw Filled Polys** to better see the offset), for example, to a higher value, this is what we would end up with:

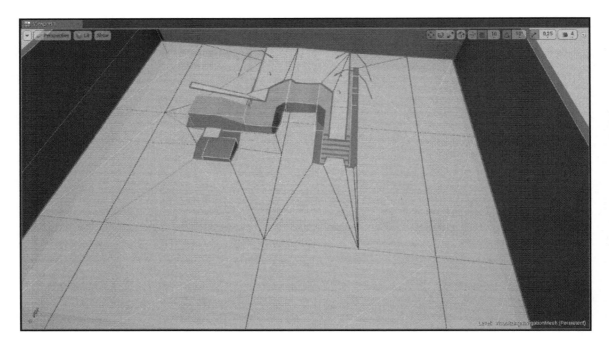

- **Enabling Drawing**: As the name suggests, if this is enabled, it is possible to see the navigation mesh along with all the previous settings.

 Of course, all of these options are better combined when we start playing with the other settings that determine how the navigation mesh is generated. In fact, by tweaking the display settings, you can better understand how the generation settings work, and actually "see" how they affect the generation of the navigation mesh.

# Navigation test actor

As we have seen for the **EQS Testing Pawn**, there is a built-in **Navigation Test Actor** that we can use.

This actor is not declared virtual (as the EQS counterpart is), so it can be directly placed in the map. Actually, we can access it from the **Modes** panel, as shown:

Once placed in the level, this is how it looks:

If we place another one in the level, then in the **Details** panel, we can assign under the Pathfind section the as shown:

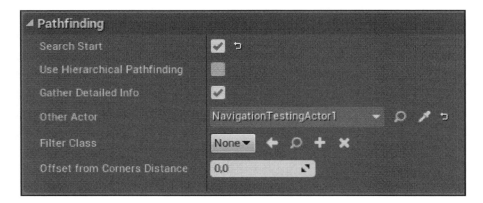

This will result in a preview of the path between the two navigation test actors:

Here is a different example from a different viewpoint:

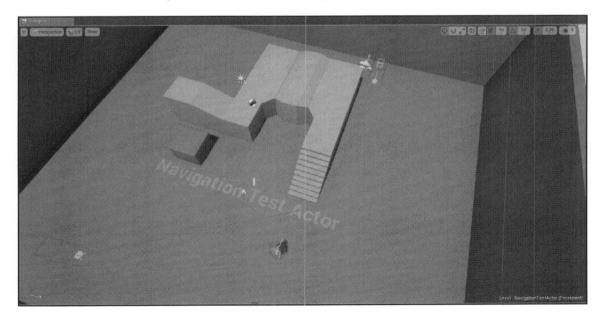

Also, you can "smooth" the edges of the path if we modify the **Offset From Corner Distance**, always in the pathfinding section of the navigation test actor. For instance, a value of 150 will produce this path:

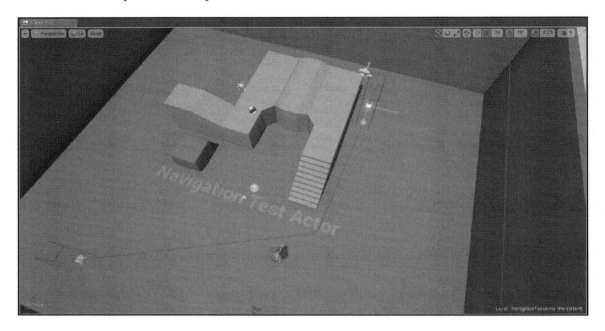

Of course, this pathfinding test can be used with **Nav Areas** as well. If we drop a **Desert Area** (created back in `Chapter 3`, *Navigation*) in the level, the pathfinder will try to avoid it, since it has a higher cost. In the following example (the highlighted volume is the desert area), the desert area is small, and passing through it is still the shortest path:

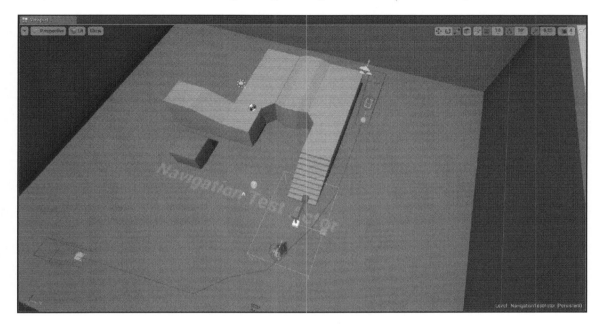

However, if we expand the area, then going from the other side has a cheaper cost:

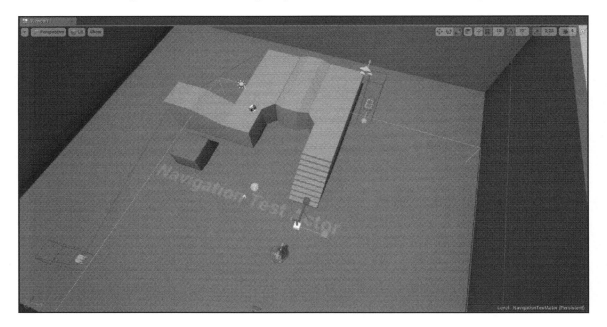

Finally, it's worthwhile mentioning that we can also use nav filters within the navigation test actor, always in the pathfinding section in its **Details** panel. For instance, we can place the **NavFilter_DesertAnimal** (that we created in Chapter 3, *Navigation,*), then the desert area is even preferred, producing this other path:

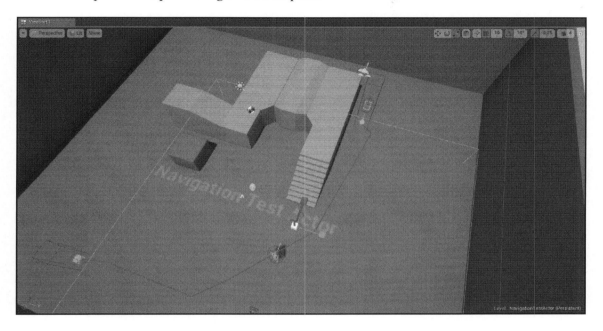

This navigation test actor has more functionalities, as you can see from its **Details** panel, but, unfortunately, they are outside the scope of this book. However, we have seen its basic use.

# Profiling AI

When it comes to profiling, Unreal offers many solutions and tools. This section explores some that are related to AI.

In particular, we will see how it is possible to visualize stats directly from the console and how to create a custom stat group. At the end of this section, we will mention the **Session Frontend** tool.

# Profiling with the console

The most used profiling tool is activating stats through the console, because it is very quick and you can track performance in real time. In fact, just typing `stats game` into the console makes a whole page of stats appear on the screen:

Here are all the stats that appear:

As you can see, there's a lot of information, but it is quite general, since it tracks the general performance of your game. This is a perfect starting point to start optimizing your game; however, as an AI Developer, you will need more specific tools.

If we start typing just `Stat`, a series of options (as a suggestion) appears on the screen (86!):

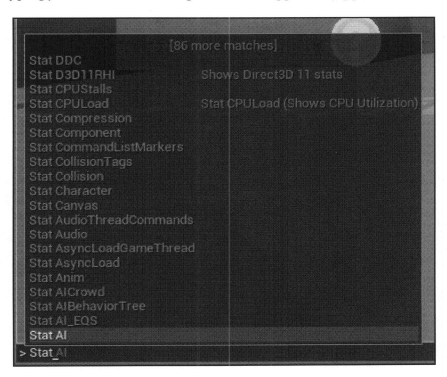

But we can refine our search even more by typing `Stat AI`, and we can have the AI-related stats (after all, these options were the first ones on the list, since they are in alphabetical order):

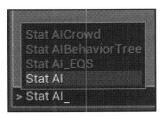

These are very useful when it comes down to quickly tracking the performance of your AI.

 In order to close the stats, just retype the same command as you did when closing those specific stats.

If we type `Stat AI`, we get a generic AI performance track (it depends also on which AI systems you have active). On the right, you are also able to check how many AIs there are in the level, and how many are currently rendered:

Typing `Stat AI_EQS` gives us more information about EQS. Of course, by using a level that has five AIs performing the `EnvQueryA` and `EnvQueryB` that we have created before, this has a huge impact on how EQS performs in this specific example:

Typing `Stat AIBehaviorTree` gives us informational about the behavior trees that are running. Currently, in our example, we have very simple behavior trees, so performance- and memory-wise they are very easy:

Finally, typing `Stat AICrowd` gives us information about the crowd that is handled at the current stage. Since we are not using a crowd in this example, the category is empty:

Of course, if you need to keep track of more than one category at the time, you can do it, just by inserting console commands, and they will stack up together, as shown in this screenshot:

# Creating a custom stat group

If you are programming a complex AI, you might want to keep track of more specific functions and how they perform. Of course, this can be useful not only for AI programming, but for any part of your game. Unreal offers some simple Macros to add to your C++ code to quickly start outputting stats for those functions to check their performance.

To create a **Custom Stat Group**, you need to declare this within a header file (or if your system uses inheritance, you can declare it at the highest level of the headers file, so the same stat group is available for all the classes that inherit from this):

```
DECLARE_STATS_GROUP(TEXT("CustomStatGroupName"),
STATGROUP_CustomStatGroupName, STATCAT_Advanced);
```

Then, inside the header (.h) file of the class that contains the function you want to track, we need to add this macro (one for each function we need to track):

```
DECLARE_CYCLE_STAT(TEXT("Name of how you want to display this function"),
STAT_NameOfTheFunction, STATGROUP_CustomStatGroupName);
```

Finally, in the implementation (.cpp) file, you need to add this macro at the beginning of the function we want to track:

```
SCOPE_CYCLE_COUNTER(STAT_NameOfTheFunction);
```

Let's start with a practical example, so that you can have a better idea of how it works. I'm going to create a simple actor, create the stat group within this actor, and start tracking the performance of its tick function.

Let's create a new C++ class that inherits from **Actor**:

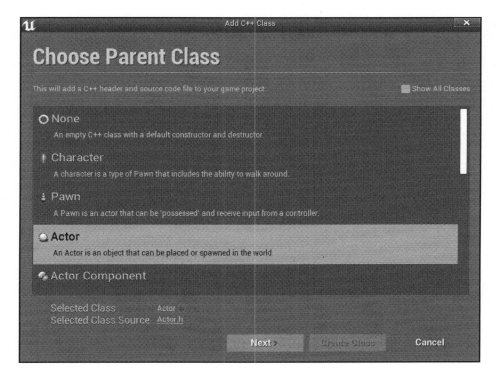

We can rename it *TestingStatActor* and place it within the `Chapter12` folder:

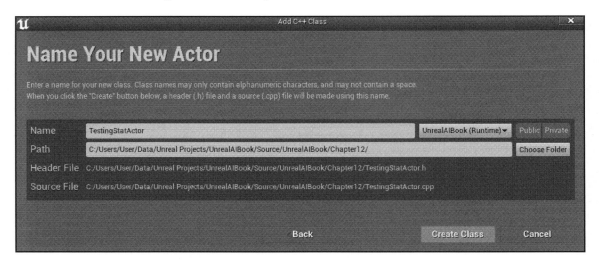

Next, in its header (`.h`) file, we need to declare the stat group (just below the include statements):

```
#include "CoreMinimal.h"
#include "GameFramework/Actor.h"
#include "TestingStatActor.generated.h"

DECLARE_STATS_GROUP(TEXT("AI_MyCustomGroup"), STATGROUP_AI_MyCustomGroup,
STATCAT_Advanced);
```

Then, since we want to track a function in this very class, we can declare the intention to track a function just below the previous line:

```
#include "CoreMinimal.h"
#include "GameFramework/Actor.h"
#include "TestingStatActor.generated.h"

DECLARE_STATS_GROUP(TEXT("AI_MyCustomGroup"), STATGROUP_AI_MyCustomGroup,
STATCAT_Advanced);
DECLARE_CYCLE_STAT(TEXT("StatTestActor ~ PerformTick"), STAT_PerformTick,
STATGROUP_AI_MyCustomGroup);
```

Finally, in the C++ file, we can add the following macro at the beginning of the `Tick` function (even before `Super::Tick()` if you want to track that part as well), and maybe we can add a log (which is a heavy task, especially for a `Tick` function, so we can better see its spike in performance):

```
void ATestingStatActor::Tick(float DeltaTime)
{
    SCOPE_CYCLE_COUNTER(STAT_PerformTick);
    Super::Tick(DeltaTime);

    UE_LOG(LogTemp, Warning, TEXT("Test Message on Tick"));
}
```

Now you can compile your code, and when it is finished, you can drag the **TestingStatActor** directly into the level (remember that it doesn't have a scene component, so it exists in the level, but it cannot be positioned).

If we type in the console, we are now able to access our **AI_MyCustomGroup**:

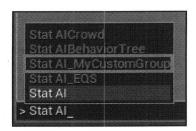

If we enable it, we are able to check on screen the performance of our `Tick` function for each TestingStatActor in the game (in this case, just one):

This concludes how to create a custom stat group. This is indeed a very powerful tool that allows you to quickly start profiling your C++ functions.

# Session frontend

**Session frontend** is a very powerful profiling tool within Unreal. It allows you to check the performance of specific parts of the game, record and save profiling sessions, and much, much more (including automatic tests! We will not touch those in this book).

You can activate it by navigating from the top menu **Window | Developer Tools | Session Frontend**, as shown in the following screenshot:

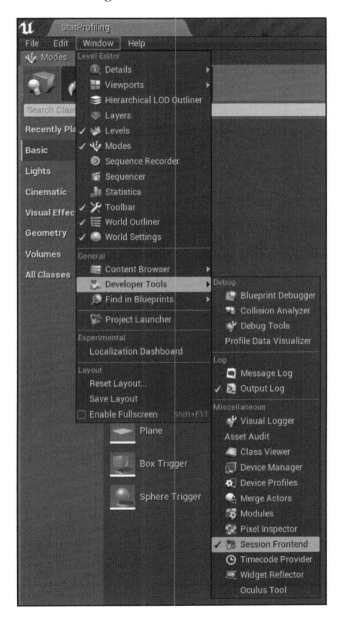

Once opened, this is how it looks (it should be in the **Console** tab):

Console tab. This is an image of Console tab. The other (blurred out) information is not important here

In the **Profiler** tab, you will find all of what you need to dive deeper into profiling.

When you start profiling, here, you will find even more information about AI performance (actually, you can find the performance of every part of your game). For instance, in the next screenshot, you can see that I'm profiling some AI systems:

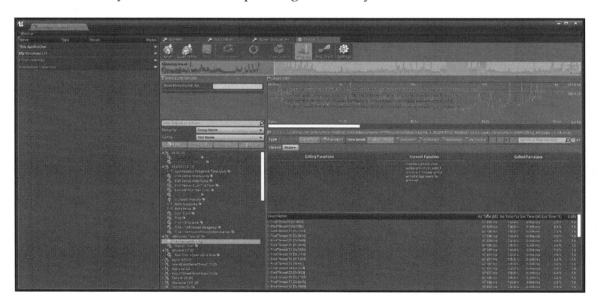

Profiler tab. This is an image of Profiler tab. The other (blurred out) information is not important here

If you have created a custom stat group before, you will be able to profile that as well in the session frontend! So, keep in mind that creating a stat group is very important, as later on, you will need to check the performance of your system.

Unfortunately, we don't have the time to explore the **Session Frontend** tool, since it would require a whole chapter and it is outside the scope of this book (since it would require digging really deeply into performance profiling). However, I mentioned this tool not just because it is very important, but because you should definitely be aware of its existence, and it is worthwhile exploring it more on your own. In fact, you can find more information about this tool in the official documentation here: `https://docs.unrealengine.com/en-us/Engine/Performance/Profiler`, which provides a good starting point for learning more about this tool.

# Summary

In this chapter, we have explored some debugging tools for our AI. Of course, this was not comprehensive, and there is much more that we haven't covered. However, we learned about the most important ones and how to use them.

In particular, we have further explored the options available to an EQS testing pawn, and how they can help us visualize an environmental query running. We also learned about using EQS Profiler as a way to identify how our environmental queries perform, and we dived deeper into those that need optimization.

We also looked at the display settings for the navigation system in more detail, to have a better idea of how our navigation mesh is generated. Also, we discussed the navigation-testing actor, which is really useful to visually query the navigation system and quickly receive feedback regarding how the Pathfinder performs; but we didn't have the time to go into detail about the available options.

Finally, we learned more about profiling our game AI, especially with the use of `stat` commands in the console. In fact, we have explored what the built-in stat groups are and how to create a customized one. We also mentioned the session frontend, a powerful tool for profiling our game.

In the next chapter, we will cover the gameplay debugger, which is another important tool for debugging AI.

# 13
# Debugging Methods for AI - The Gameplay Debugger

In this chapter, we are going to face a powerful debugging tool. It is so powerful that it was worth having a separate chapter for it, and it is the best friend of any AI developer within Unreal. Actually, it's the best friend of any developer in Unreal, since it can have different uses, especially when it comes to covering *Gameplay* (although it has been mainly used for AI so far).

We are going to explore the *Gameplay Debugger* (as it is referred to in the official documentation), but sometimes people or books use *Visual Debugger* to refer to it. I presume that the reason it is called *Gameplay Debugger* is due to the fact that the tool has a **great level of abstraction to debug any gameplay aspects (including AI)**. However, the built-in categories of the *Gameplay Debugger* are AI-related, and this is the reason why it is included in this book.

 Do not confuse the Visual Logger with the Visual Debugger, which is the *Gameplay Debugger*!!

In particular, we are going to cover the following topics:

- Explore the *anatomy of the Gameplay Debugger*
- Learn about the *Extensions and Categories* of the Gameplay Debugger
- Understand what kind of *information each Category displays*
- Create a custom module by *creating a new plugin* (we need this to extend the *Gameplay Debugger*)
- *Extend the Gameplay Debugger* by adding a new *Category*
- *Extend the Gameplay Debugger* by adding a new *Extension*

This is the last technical part of this book before the last chapter, in which we will explore *Game AI* in broader terms. Thus, without further ado, let's dive in!

# The anatomy of the Gameplay Debugger

While the game is running, you can open the *Gameplay Debugger* (or *Visual Debugger*) by pressing the " ' " (apostrophe) key.

 All the key bindings of the visual debugger can be changed/customized. We will see how we can change them in the *Project Settings* section, later in this chapter.

The *Gameplay Debugger* is divided into two: *Extensions* and *Categories*:

- *Extensions* are specific key bindings (toggles) that trigger a specific function.
- *Categories* are *toggleable* pieces of information that appear on the screen (and also in 3D spaces) in regards to a specific system

On-screen, the *Gameplay Debugger* is visually divided into two sections:

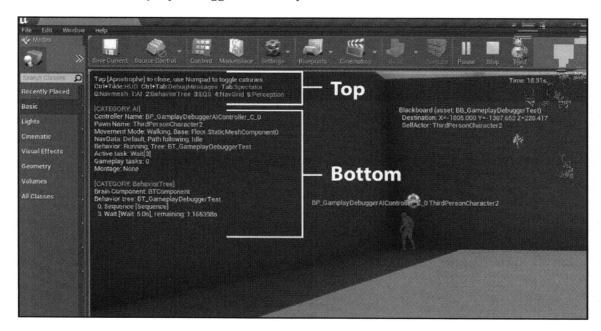

The top section is the control section and shows which options are available. In particular, it displays which *Extensions* are available and highlights the active *Categories* that are displayed in the bottom part:

```
Tap [Apostrophe] to close, use Numpad to toggle catories.
Ctrl+Tilde:HUD  Ctrl+Tab:DebugMessages  Tab:Spectator
0:Navmesh  1:AI  2:BehaviorTree  3:EQS  4:NavGrid  5:Perception
```

The bottom section, instead, displays different information for each of the selected *Categories*. Here is an example with some Categories showing:

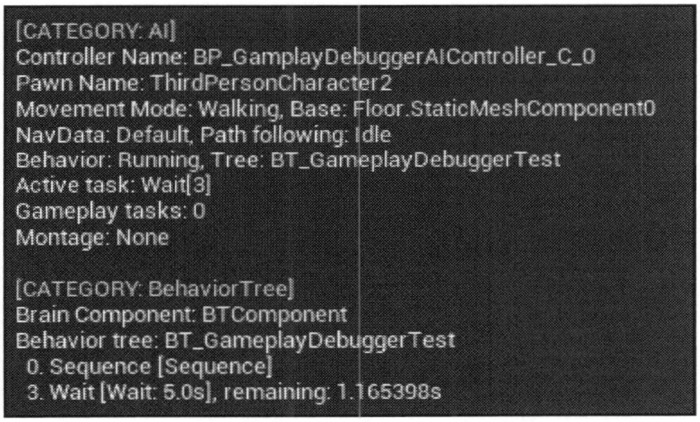

```
[CATEGORY: AI]
Controller Name: BP_GamplayDebuggerAIController_C_0
Pawn Name: ThirdPersonCharacter2
Movement Mode: Walking, Base: Floor.StaticMeshComponent0
NavData: Default, Path following: Idle
Behavior: Running, Tree: BT_GameplayDebuggerTest
Active task: Wait[3]
Gameplay tasks: 0
Montage: None

[CATEGORY: BehaviorTree]
Brain Component: BTComponent
Behavior tree: BT_GameplayDebuggerTest
  0. Sequence [Sequence]
  3. Wait [Wait: 5.0s], remaining: 1.165398s
```

# Gameplay Debugger Extensions

The *Gameplay Debugger* has only two default *Extensions* and a built-in one, as you can see in the following screenshot:

```
Tap [Apostrophe] to close, use Numpad to toggle catories.
Ctrl+Tilde:HUD  Ctrl+Tab:DebugMessages  Tab:Spectator
0:Navmesh  1:AI  2:BehaviorTree  3:EQS  4:NavGrid  5:Perception
```

The two default Extensions and a built-in one are as follows:

- The ***Spectator Extension*** allows you (at runtime, while the game is playing) to detach the control from the *Player Character* and control a *Spectator Pawn* so that you are free to fly over the level and have an external point of view. At any time, you can gain back control of the *Player Character* by toggling the *Spectator Extension* or by closing the *Gameplay Debugger*. The default key to toggle the *Spectator Extension* is the *Tab* key.
- The ***HUD Extensions*** allows you to toggle the *HUD* on and off (in particular, the *HUD* class contained in the *Game Mode* instance). The default key to toggle the *HUD Extension* is *Ctrl + Tilde*.
- ***DebugMessages*** is the *built-in Extension*, and as its name suggests, it toggles the debug messages. The default key is *Ctrl + Tab*.

# Gameplay Debugger categories

The *Gameplay Debugger* is divided into different categories, which can be enabled and disabled (with the use of the *Keypad (or Numpad)*, not just the numbers of your keyboard).

If you don't have a *Keypad/Numpad* (e.g. you are using a small laptop), later in this chapter, you will find the settings of the *Gameplay Debugger* in which you can change the key binding to something that your keyboard has.

The number next to the ***Category*** indicates its default position (and the number to press on the *Keypad* to activate it). However, this can be changed in the settings later.

To explore the *Categories*, I have created a simple test map, in which there should be a bit of everything so that we can see all the *Gameplay Debugger* categories in action. This test map is available in the project files associated with this book.

## Category 0 – Navmesh

The first category is ***Navmesh***, which is assigned to the *"0"* key by default.

Once you toggle it, you will be able to see the *Navmesh* directly on the map – simple as that. This is very useful when you need to check the *Nav Mesh* in real time, especially if you have dynamic obstacles so that the *Nav Mesh* is rebuilt at runtime.

This is how it appears when this category is enabled:

This is a screenshot of the output. The other (blurred out) information is not important here

# Category 1 – AI

This category, once enabled, shows a lot of information about the selected AI. By default, it is assign to the "*1*" key.

 If no actor is selected, no information will be shown in this category. However, it will highlight the available AIs with their affiliation (in a 3D space).

When the category is toggled (and a *Debug Actor* is selected), it looks as follows:

This is a screenshot of the output. The other (blurred out) information is not important here

In this category, all of the AIs on the map are displayed with their affiliation (in a 3D space), and the selected *Debug Actor* also has the name of the controller (always in a 3D space). However, the information that's displayed directly on the screen is of the single *Debug Actor*.

The following is the kind of information that this category displays (with a close-up of *Categories Information*):

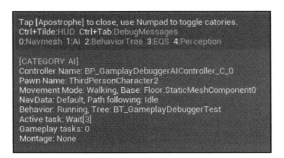

- **Controller Name**: This displays the name of the *AI Controller* that possesses this *Pawn*.

- **Pawn Name**: This displays the name of the *Pawn* that is currently possessed by the *AI*.
- **Movement Mode**: If there is a *Character Movement Component* attached to the Pawn, then this displays the current movement mode (e.g. walking, running, swimming, flying, falling, etc...)
- **Base**: If there is a *Character Movement Component* attached to the Pawn, this displays on the base that the character is grounded on. In the case of walking or running, this is the mesh of the piece of floor where the AI is currently walking or running. In the case of falling, this is "*none*".
- **NavData**: This displays that *NavData* that the AI is currently using. Most likely, the value will be "*Default*", unless you gave a specific *NavData* to the AI character by using C++.
- **Path following**: This displays the state of the Path to follow when the AI character is moving. Information such as the *Dot-Product*, the *2D-Distance*, and the *Z-Distance* are displayed as well. Here is an example when the character is moving:

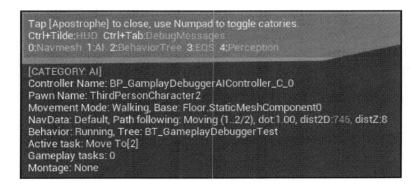

```
Tap [Apostrophe] to close, use Numpad to toggle catories.
Ctrl+Tilde:HUD  Ctrl+Tab:DebugMessages
0:Navmesh  1:AI  2:BehaviorTree  3:EQS  4:Perception

[CATEGORY: AI]
Controller Name: BP_GamplayDebuggerAIController_C_0
Pawn Name: ThirdPersonCharacter2
Movement Mode: Walking, Base: Floor.StaticMeshComponent0
NavData: Default, Path following: Moving (1..2/2), dot:1.00, dist2D:745, distZ:8
Behavior: Running, Tree: BT_GameplayDebuggerTest
Active task: Move To[2]
Gameplay tasks: 0
Montage: None
```

- **Behavior**: This indicates whether there is a behavior running or not (e.g. is a *Behavior Tree* running on this *AI Controller*?).
- **Tree**: This indicates which *Behavior Tree* the AI is currently running (if a *Behavior* is running).
- **Active Task**: This indicates which *Behavior Tree Task* is currently executing, along with the *Task number* (the number that that Task is ordered in the Tree).

 For more information aregarding the current task in the *Behavior Tree Category*, see the next section.

- **Gameplay Tasks**: This displays how many *Gameplay Tasks* are currently assigned to this AI.
- **Montage**: This displays the current montage that the Character is playing (if any).

 Although we didn't touch on this topic in this book, syncing AI actions with Animations is an in-between land for AI programmers and Animators.

It is worth mentioning that if the AI is moving, even if the *Navmesh* category is not toggling, it will show the piece of the *Nav Mesh* that the AI is currently using to navigate, as shown in the following screenshot:

This is a screenshot of the output. The other (blurred out) information is not important here

# Category 2 – Behavior Tree

This category displays information about the **Behavior Tree** that's currently running on the AI. By default, it is assigned to the "2" key.

 If no *Behavior Tree* is running, this section will not display anything.

When activated, the ***Behavior Tree Category*** looks as follows:

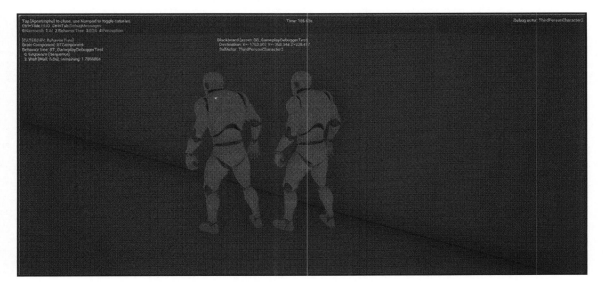

This is a screenshot of the output. The other (blurred out) information is not important here

This category only displays information on the screen (so nothing in the 3D space). In particular, it shows the following information on the left-hand side:

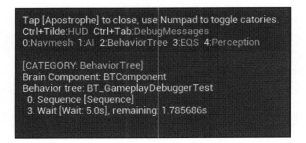

- **Brain Component**: This shows which kind of *Brain Component* the *AI Controller* is currently using, which will be of the *BTComponent* type.

 Since Unreal is developed with *modularity* in mind, a *Brain Component* is anything that can hold AI logic. At the time of writing, the only built-in *Brain Component* is the *Behavior Tree* (*BTComponent*).

- **Behavior Tree**: This is the name of the *Behavior Tree* that the AI is using.
- **Task Tree**: After the *Behavior Tree* property, there is the all branch of the task that is currently being executed. This is the path from the root (with all the node names and their respective numbers) to the *Task* the AI is executing.

This is very useful when you need to understand why a determined tasks has been chosen, rather than another, by following the path along the tree.

On the right, instead, the name of the *Blackboard* asset that's being used by the *Behavior Tree* is displayed. Below this, there's the keys of the *Blackboard* that's being used, along with their current value:

Blackboard (asset: BB_GameplayDebuggerTest)
Destination: X=-1763.001 Y=-368.344 Z=228.417
SelfActor: ThirdPersonCharacter2

The following example shows just two *Blackboard keys*, *Destination* and *Self Actor*. Try to test the *Gameplay Debugger* in the *Designing Behavior Tree Project* to see more and get a better feeling of what it is going on, since you have been building these structures from scratch. Here is a sneak peek of what you will see:

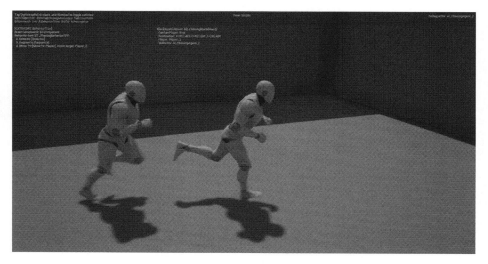

This is a screenshot of the output. The other (blurred out) information is not important here

Of course, this is very useful when you want to test that the right values in the *Blackboard* are set.

Here is one more example, showing the character moving:

This is a screenshot of the output. The other (blurred out) information is not important here

# Category 3 – EQS

This category displays the ***Environmental Queries*** that the AI is currently performing. By default, it is assigned to the "**3**" key.

If the AI is not performing any *Environment Query*, than this category will just show that the number of queries is zero.

When the *EQS Category* is activated, we get the following output on-screen:

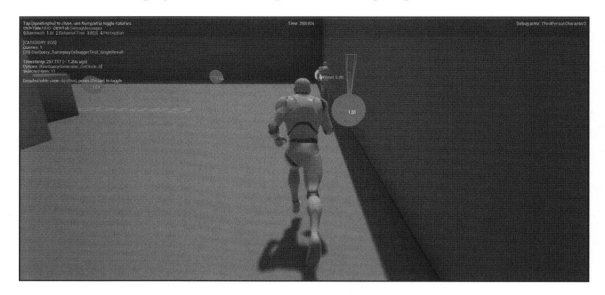

This is a screenshot of the output. The other (blurred out) information is not important here

From the preceding screenshot, we can see that this *Category* highlights the different points that are generated by the query, along with their score. Depending on the *Run Mode* of the query, it is possible to see which of these points is the winner (it has the highest score and its color is a brighter green than the other colors).

Furthermore, a red arrow on top of a point means that it has been selected (which means that it is the closest that you are looking at). This is useful because, in the information displayed on the side, it is possible to check at which place of the scoreboard that specific point has been ranked.

On the side, you will find some extra information about the query:

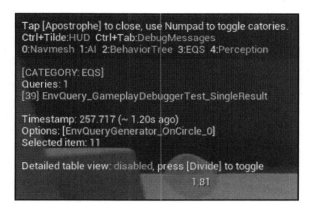

In particular, the following information is shown:

- **Queries**: This is the number of queries that the *Debug Actor* is running.
- **Query Name(s) and Run Mode**: This displays which *Query* has been (or currently is being) executed. Then, after an underscore, it displays the *Run Mode* (in the preceding screenshot, it is *Single Result*).
- **Time Stamp**: This is the timestamp of when the *Query* was executed, along with how long ago this occurred.
- **Options**: This displays which the *Generator* for the Query.
- **Selected Item**: This displays the *position/rank* of the selected item in the scoreboard. In the preceding screenshot, the item we have selected is 11th on the scoreboard (from the full-screen screenshot, you can see that it has a score of *1.31*, against the winner point, which has a score of *2.00*). This is very useful for checking how the point you are looking at is ranked, since it gives you a quick idea of the relative score among the points.

 Keep in mind that when a point is ranked, ***the rank starts from zero***, and so the ***Winner Point is ranked 0th***. So, in the preceding screenshot, "*Selected Item: 11*" means that it is 11th on the scoreboard, but it is the 12th point in the list.

For your convenience, here is another example, in which the Selected Point is the Winner Point (notice that its rank is 0):

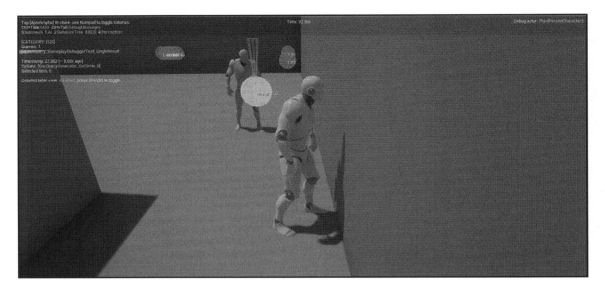

This is a screenshot of the output. The other (blurred out) information is not important here

# Category 4 – Perception

This category displays information regarding the *Perception* of the *AI agent* that has been selected. By default, it is assigned to the "**4**" key, that is, unless the "*NavGrid*" *Category* is enabled; in that case, the default key is "**5**".

 This category doesn't show anything if no Actor has been selected.

When activated, the *Perception Category* appears as follows:

This is a screenshot of the output. The other (blurred out) information is not important here

On-screen, this category displays all the senses that have been implemented, along with their debug colors. Then, each sense can show additional information, depending on the implementation of their `DescribeSelfToGameplayDebugger()` function. For instance, in the case of Sight, there is the debug colors for **RangeIn** and **RangeOut**, as shown in the following screenshot:

In the level, you will be able to see the stimuli of a given sense as a sphere (along with the name of the sense, the stimulus strength, and the age of the stimulus, which is zero when on sight). Then, there is a line connecting the AI Pawn to each of the *stimuli*, and a line connecting the single *stimulus* to the target (e.g. the *Player*) if the target is not on sight. This is how it appears in the case of Sight:

This is a screenshot of the output. The other (blurred out) information is not important here

To show off how it appears when the target (e.g. the *Player*) is not in sight, and thus the *stimulus* has an age greater than zero and it is possible to see the black line connecting the *stimulus* to the target, here is another screenshot:

This is a screenshot of the output. The other (blurred out) information is not important here

If we were to add the sense of *Hearing* as well, this is what it would look like:

This is a screenshot of the output. The other (blurred out) information is not important here

Please note that the *Hearing Sense* (in yellow) is displayed on a different level (z-axis) of the *Sight Sense*. As a result, even if we have the same value, like in the preceding screenshot where both have a range of 1500, they stack up nicely.

Of course, the information on the side gives you more information about the debug colors that are being displayed in the game world:

```
Tap [Apostrophe] to close, use Numpad to toggle catories.
Ctrl+Tilde:HUD  Ctrl+Tab:DebugMessages
0:Navmesh 1:AI 2:BehaviorTree 3:EQS 4:Perception

[CATEGORY: Perception]
Sight: green rangeIN:green rangeOUT:neonpink
Hearing: yellow range:yellow rangeLoS:cyan
```

# The Nav Grid Category

Depending on your settings, you might have enabled the **Nav Grid** Category, which is different from the *NavMesh Category*.

This *Category* should deal with grid movement, which we haven't covered in this book. However, if you activate this *Category* in our example map, it will just show that the number of sources is equal to zero:

```
Tap [Apostrophe] to close, use Numpad to toggle catories.
Ctrl+Tilde:HUD  Ctrl+Tab:DebugMessages
0:Navmesh  1:AI  2:BehaviorTree  3:EQS  4:NavGrid  5:Perception

[CATEGORY: NavGrid]
Num sources: 0
```

## Multiple Categories on-screen

We have seen how each of the categories behave individually. However, just to be clear, it is possible to have as many categories as you like on display. This means that you can have multiple categories showing up at the same time. Actually, often, you will need to see more that one system at the same time:

This is a screenshot of the output. The other (blurred out) information is not important here

One thing that I personally like about the *Gameplay Debugger* is that once you get the hang of it, even with so many *Categories* open, the information is not overwhelming the screen, and is nicely displayed.

# More Categories

Although it seems that we went through all the different *Categories*, we haven't. In fact, there are some extra *Gameplay Debugger Categories* built into the Engine, for instance, the ones related to *HTN Planner* or the *Ability System*.

Unfortunately, they are outside the scope of this book, but you can search for them in C++. You can start your research by searching for ***GameplayDebuggerCategory*** in the *Engine Source* to find out more about them.

# Gameplay Debugger settings

As we mentioned previously, it is possible to configure the *Gameplay Debugger* by changing its settings.

If you navigate to the ***Project Settings***, it is possible to find a whole section dedicated to the *Gameplay Debugger*, as shown in the following screenshot:

The *Input* tab allows you to override the default keys for opening and closing the *Gameplay Debugger* (the default is the " ' " apostrophe key) and for triggering the different categories (by default, the numbers from 0 to 9 on the *keypad/numpad*):

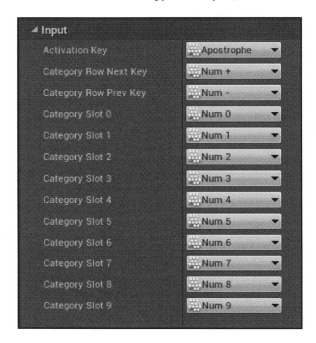

The *Display* tab allows you to define some padding on so that you can show information about the *Gameplay Debugger*. By doing this, you don't have it attached to the screen. The default values are all *10*:

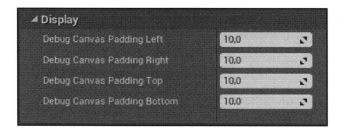

The *Add-Ons tab*, allows you to configure the single settings for both *Categories* (when a category is enabled by default, and which key/number it is associated with) and *Extension* (to override their input key):

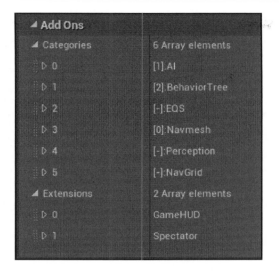

A value of "-1" for a *Category* means that the *number/position/key* of the *Category* has been assigned by the Editor, since this *Category* doesn't have a *"preference"* of its position on the screen.

# Extending the Gameplay Debugger

So far, we have seen how all the different categories of the *Gameplay Debugger* can help us understand how our *AI Character* is behaving. However, wouldn't it be awesome if we could have our own category so that we can visualize the data of a custom (sub-)system we have developed for our game?

The answer is yes, and this section explains how to do it.

Keep in mind that the tool is called *Gameplay Debugger*, so you can extend it not only for AI, but for anything in your game, especially related to *Gameplay* (since it is a real-time tool to visualize information). So far, it has been extensively used for AI, but it has the potential to be used for anything else!

As we already have seen, the *Gameplay Debugger* is divided into *Categories* and *Extensions*.

First, we will explore how to create a ***Custom Category*** in more detail, starting from creating a separate module for it, along with all the dependencies and compiler directives that we need. We will see how we can create the class that controls the ***Category***, and how we can register it to the *Gameplay Debugger*. As a result, we will have a fully functioning ***Gameplay Debugger Category*** that will print the location of our *Debug Actor* on-screen:

```
[CATEGORY: Locator]
If a DebugActor is selected, this is its position:
Location: X=908.544 Y=515.342 Z=228.417
```

Lastly, we will look at how to create a ***Custom Extension*** for the ***Gameplay Debugger***, which will be able to print the Player's location when a specific key is pressed.

With this being said, let's get into creating a new *plugin*!

# Creating a module with the use of a new plugin

To extend the *Gameplay Debugger* with a new ***Category***, you will need a new module in your game. In fact, the engine is a collection of different modules, and your game is as well (usually, the game is just one module, especially if the game is small; it is created with only one module when you start a fresh project in C++, so you will need to add more if need be).

There are different ways in which we can create a module, and I'm not going to go into the details of how module works, and how to create one for your project. Rather, I will guide you on how to set up a custom module for running a new ***Gameplay Debugger Category***.

The easiest way to create another module is to create a plugin. As a result, the code is separated from the rest of our game, which has good and bad implications. However, we aren't going to discuss this in this section. Instead, I will show you how to create a custom ***Gameplay Debugger Category*** that you will then adapt to your specific needs.

Let's start by opening the **Plugins** menu, from the **Settings** menu button on top of the *Viewport*, as shown in the following screenshot:

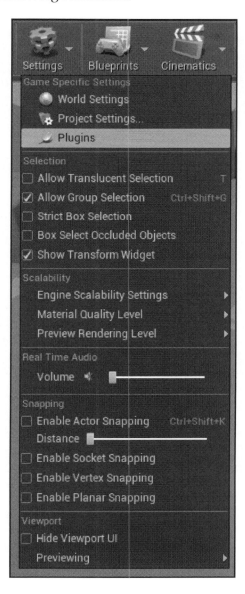

Once the *Plugins* windows is open, you will need to click on the **New Plugin** button in the bottom right-corner:

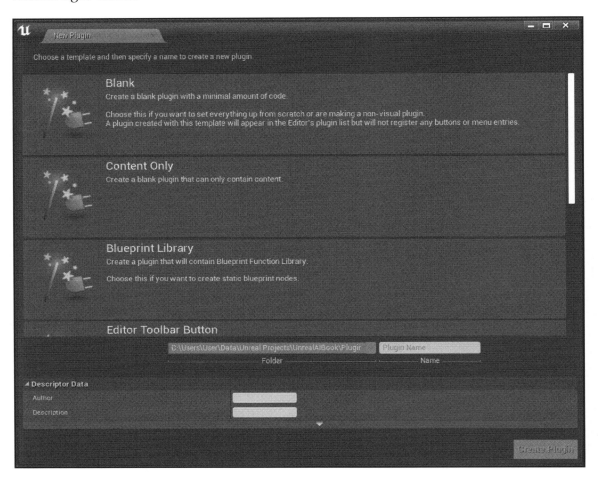

 It is not the only way to create a *Plugin*, but this is the fastest, since Unreal contains a simple Wizard to create different templates of *Plugins*.

As a result, we will open the *New Plugin* windows, which is a wizard for creating new plugins:

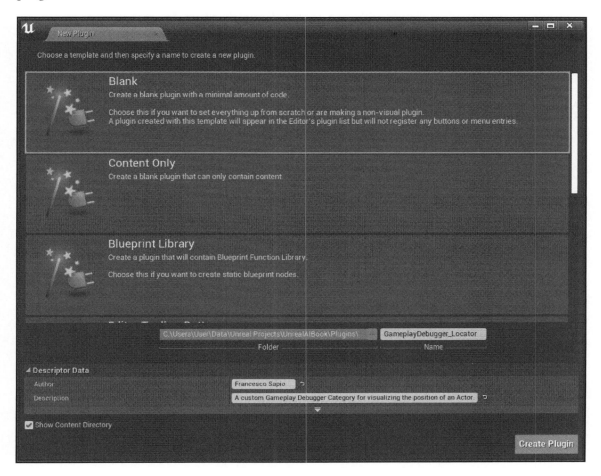

We need to select the Blank template (since we just want a bare-bones a module to load).
Then, we can fill in the *Name*, which in our case is ***GameplayDebugger_Locator***. Next, there
are input fields to fill for your plugin: *Author* and *Description*. I put myself as *Author*, and for
the description, I inserted "*A custom Gameplay Debugger Category for visualizing the position of
an Actor*". This is what the screen should look like now:

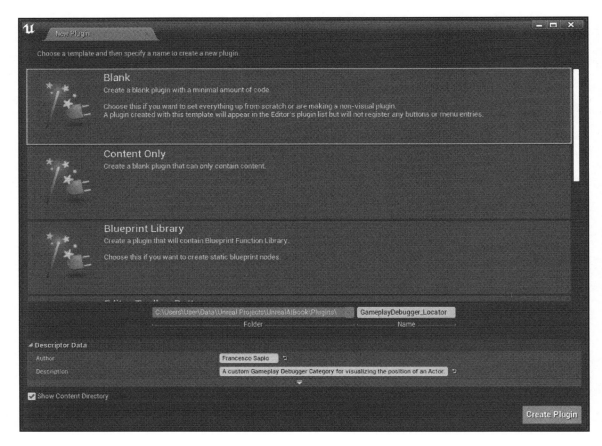

Press **Create Plugin** and our plugin will be created. It might take some time to process, so be patient:

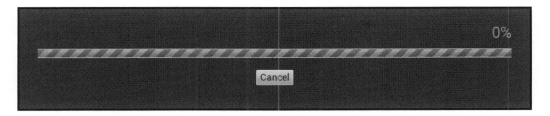

Once it has compiled, you will have the basic structure and code of the *Plugin* as a single module. You can check it out in *Visual Studio*. Under the *Plugins* folder, you should have the following structure:

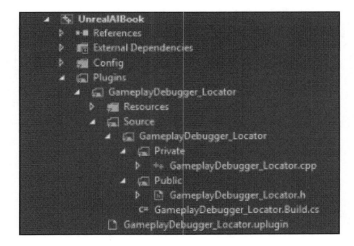

Also, if you go back to the *Plugin* window, you will be able to see our *Plugin* (and ensure that it is enabled):

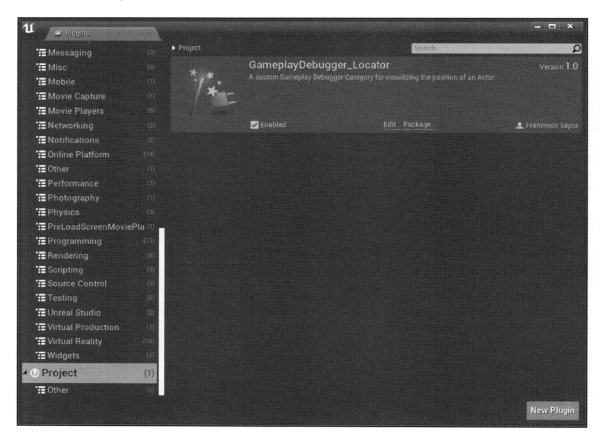

Of course, you are free to "*edit*" the *Plugin*, for instance, to change its icon or the category.

# Setting up the module to work with the Gameplay Debugger

Before we add the code for a new category of our *Gameplay Debugger*, there are some considerations to make.

First of all, the *Gameplay Debugger* is, as its name suggests, a Debug tool. This means that it shouldn't be shipped with the game. As such, we need a way to strip away all the code related to the *Gameplay Debugger* if we are compiling a shipping version of the game. Of course, the *Plugin* we are creating only includes code for the *Gameplay Debugger*, but in your game, it is more likely that it lives in a broader context.

To strip away the code, you need to defy a compilation variable that can be used with compilation macros; however, we only want to define this variable as true (value equal to one) if the game is not being shipped. To achieve this, we need to navigate to our Plugin *.build.cs* file. In our case, it is called ***GameplayDebugger_Locator.build.cs***, and you can find it within the hierarchy of files of our *Plugin* in *Visual Studio* (or the code editor of your choice). In fact, Unreal runs some tools before compiling (e.g. to generate reflection code and replace the macro in the C++ code), and these tools are written in C#. Therefore, we can modify their behavior with a piece of C# code.

Once you open the file, you will find one function, which defines the different dependencies of the module. At the end of this function, add the following code:

```
//Code added for a Custom Category of Gameplay Debugger
if (Target.bBuildDeveloperTools || (Target.Configuration !=
UnrealTargetConfiguration.Shipping && Target.Configuration !=
UnrealTargetConfiguration.Test)) {
    PrivateDependencyModuleNames.Add("GameplayDebugger");
    Definitions.Add("WITH_GAMEPLAY_DEBUGGER=1");
} else {
    Definitions.Add("WITH_GAMEPLAY_DEBUGGER=0");
}
```

It is an if statement that checks whether ***BuildDeveloperTools*** is true OR the Target Configuration (the configuration we are going to compile the C++ code with) is different from ***Shipping*** or ***Test***. If this condition is verified, then we add a ***Private Dependency*** for this module, that is, the ***GameplayDebugger*** module, and define the WITH_GAMEPLAY_DEBUGGER variable as true (for compiling C++ code). Otherwise, we just declare the WITH_GAMEPLAY_DEBUGGER variable false.

As a result, we are able to use the WITH_GAMEPLAY_DEBUGGER variable in our compiler directives to include of exclude (depending which kind of configuration we are building) specific code related to the *Gameplay Debugger*. So, from now on, when we write code for our *Gameplay Debugger* category, let's not forget to wrap it in the following compile directives:

```
#if WITH_GAMEPLAY_DEBUGGER
    //[CODE]
#endif
```

# Creating a new Gameplay Debugger Category

The next step is to create a new class for our *Gameplay Debugger Category*.

As usual, we can create a new C++ class, but this time, we will select *None* as the Parent class (we will write the class on our own and manually make the inheritance):

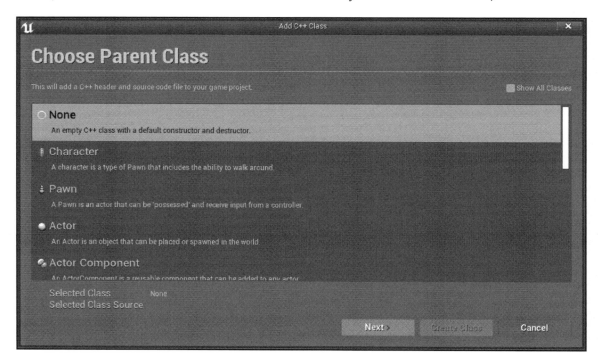

Then, we can rename it *GameplayDebuggerCategory_Locator* (which follows the convention of starting the class name with *GameplayDebuggerCategory_*, followed by the *Category Name*). Now, be careful and select the right module; next to the module's name, you can choose the module that the class belongs to. So far, we have always worked with one module, so we didn't have this problem. You need to select the *GameplayDebugger_Locator (Runtime)* module, as shown in the following screenshot:

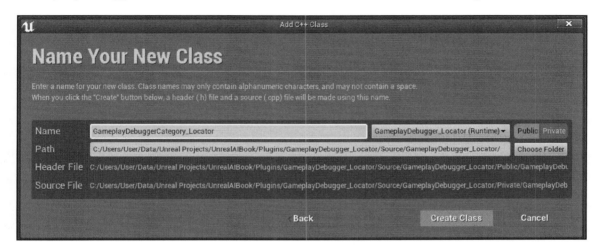

Create the class, and wait until it is added to our *Plugin*.

Now, it's time to actively start creating our class. Go into the header (.h) file of our newly created class and remove everything. We will start by including the engine minimal core, and then within the `#if WITH_GAMEPLAY_DEBUGGER` compiler directive, we will also include the `GameplayDebuggerCategory.h` file, since it will be our Parent class:

```
#pragma once

#include "CoreMinimal.h"

#if WITH_GAMEPLAY_DEBUGGER

#include "GameplayDebuggerCategory.h"

//[REST OF THE CODE]

#endif
```

Then, we need to create the class itself. By following conventions, we can rename the class so it has the same name as the file, *FGameplayDebuggerCategory_Locator*, and make it inherit from *FGameplayDebuggerCategory*:

```
class FGameplayDebuggerCategory_Locator : public FGameplayDebuggerCategory
{
    //[REST OF THE CODE]
};
```

The *Gameplay Debugger* is a powerful tool, and as such it as many functionalities. One of those is its ability to support replication. As a result, we need to set up a structure that supports that. If you open the source files (from the Engine) of the other *Gameplay Debugger Categories*, you will see that they follow the convention of declaring a protected structure named *FRepData*. Within this structure, we declare all the variables that we need in order to visualize the category. In our case, we just need a string, which we will call *ActorLocationString*. It is also important that this structure has a way to be serialized, so we need to add the `void Serialize(FArchive& Ar)` function, or at least its declaration. Finally, we can create (always under "*protected*") a variable of the *FRepData* type named *DataPack*, as shown in the following code:

```
protected:
    struct FRepData
    {
        FString ActorLocationString;

        void Serialize(FArchive& Ar);
    };

    FRepData DataPack;
```

Next, we will need to override some public functions to make our category to work. These functions are as follows:

- *Constructor*: This sets the initial parameter of the class, and will set the data replication for the *DataPack*.
- *MakeInstance()*: This creates an instance of this category (using a shared reference). This is required from the *Gameplay Debugger* when we register our category at a later date (meaning that we will add it to the editor).

- ***CollectData()***: This collects and stores the data that we would like to show, which we then store in the *DataPack* (which can be replicated). It is given in input (so that we can use it), the *Player Controller*, and the ***DebugActor*** (if available), which is the Actor we have set the focus on in the *Gameplay Debugger* (remember that we selected a specific Character when we were analyzing its behavior; here, under the hood, it is passed as a parameter to the `CollectData()` function).

- ***DrawData()***: This displays the data on-screen; we will use the *DataPack* variable to retrieve the data that was collected in the `CollectData()` function. It is given in input (so that we can use it), the *Player Controller*, and the ***CanvasContext***, which is what we will use to actually display the data on-screen.

Now, we can declare them in our header (`.h`) file:

```
public:

    FGameplayDebuggerCategory_Locator();

    static TSharedRef<FGameplayDebuggerCategory> MakeInstance();

    virtual void CollectData(APlayerController* OwnerPC, AActor* DebugActor)
override;

    virtual void DrawData(APlayerController* OwnerPC,
FGameplayDebuggerCanvasContext& CanvasContext) override;
```

This concludes what we need in the header (`.h`) file. For your convenience, here is the whole code for the header (`.h`) file:

```
#pragma once
#include "CoreMinimal.h"
#if WITH_GAMEPLAY_DEBUGGER
#include "GameplayDebuggerCategory.h"
class FGameplayDebuggerCategory_Locator : public FGameplayDebuggerCategory
{
protected:
  struct FRepData
  {
    FString ActorLocationString;
    void Serialize(FArchive& Ar);
  };
  FRepData DataPack;
public:
  FGameplayDebuggerCategory_Locator();
  static TSharedRef<FGameplayDebuggerCategory> MakeInstance();
  virtual void CollectData(APlayerController* OwnerPC, AActor* DebugActor)
```

```
override;
    virtual void DrawData(APlayerController* OwnerPC,
FGameplayDebuggerCanvasContext& CanvasContext) override;
};
#endif
```

The next step is to write the implementation. So, open the `.cpp` file and wipe everything off (if you haven't already) so that you can start clean.

Once again, we need to include some headers. Of course, we need to include the header file of our class itself (the header file we just edited). Then, under the `#if` `WITH_GAMEPLAY_DEBUGGER` compiler directive, we need to include the *Actor* class, since we will need to retrieve the position of an *Actor*:

```
#include "GameplayDebuggerCategory_Locator.h"

#if WITH_GAMEPLAY_DEBUGGER
#include "GameFramework/Actor.h"

//[REST OF THE CODE]

#endif
```

Now, we can start implementing all of our functions. We will start from our **Constructor** of the main class. Here, we can set the default parameters of the *Gameplay Debugger Category*.

For instance, we can set **bShowOnlyWithDebugActor** to *false*, which, as its name suggests, allows this category to be displayed, even if we haven't selected a *Debug Actor*. In fact, even if our *Category* will need the *DebugActor* to show its location, we can still print other information (in our case, we will do a simple print). Of course, when you create your category, you can decide whether this bool will be true or not.

However, it is more important to set our **DataPack** variable for replication through the `SetDataPackReplication<FRepData>(&DataPack)` function:

```
FGameplayDebuggerCategory_Locator::FGameplayDebuggerCategory_Locator()
{
    bShowOnlyWithDebugActor = false;
    SetDataPackReplication<FRepData>(&DataPack);
}
```

Next, we need to implement our `Serialize()` function for our ***RepData*** structure. Since we just have a String, its implementation is quite straightforward; we just need to insert the *String* in the *Archive*:

```
void FGameplayDebuggerCategory_Locator::FRepData::Serialize(FArchive& Ar) {
    Ar << ActorLocationString;
}
```

To register this *Category* to the *Gameplay Debugger*, we have to implement the `MakeInstance()` function, which will return a shared reference to an instance of this *Category*. Hence, here, the code is quite straightforward as well; just create a new instance of this class as a shared reference and return the value:

```
TSharedRef<FGameplayDebuggerCategory>
FGameplayDebuggerCategory_Locator::MakeInstance()
{
    return MakeShareable(new FGameplayDebuggerCategory_Locator());
}
```

We have two more functions to implement. The former collects the data, while the latter displays it.

The `CollectData()` function already has the *DebugActor* passed as a parameter. Thus, after we have verified that the reference is valid, we can retrieve the *DebugActor's* position and assign it within the ***ActorLocationString*** variable inside the *FRepData* structure that's contained in the ***DataPack*** variable. It's easier to show this than explain it:

```
void FGameplayDebuggerCategory_Locator::CollectData(APlayerController *
OwnerPC, AActor * DebugActor)
{
    if (DebugActor) {
        DataPack.ActorLocationString =
DebugActor->GetActorLocation().ToString();
    }
}
```

 Of course, within the `CollectData()` function, you can run any logic to retrieve your own data. Just remember to store it within the ***DataPack*** variable, which is the pointer to the ***FRepData*** structure, which can be as complex as you like (and remember to serialize that as well).

Finally, the `DrawData()` function is responsible for actually displaying the information we have collected. In particular, we have a reference to the ***Canvas Context***, which we will use to "*print*" the information. We even have some formatting options, such as coloring the text by prefixing it with "*{color}*".

First, we will print some text, and then print the location of the *DebugActor* (if available). We will use colors too, so let's learn about how to use them:

```
void FGameplayDebuggerCategory_Locator::DrawData(APlayerController *
OwnerPC, FGameplayDebuggerCanvasContext & CanvasContext)
{
  CanvasContext.Printf(TEXT("If a DebugActor is selected, here below is its
location:"));
  CanvasContext.Printf(TEXT("{cyan}Location: {yellow}%s"),
*DataPack.ActorLocationString);
}
```

This was the last function for our implementation (.cpp) file. For your convenience, here is the whole file:

```
#include "GameplayDebuggerCategory_Locator.h"

#if WITH_GAMEPLAY_DEBUGGER
#include "GameFramework/Actor.h"

FGameplayDebuggerCategory_Locator::FGameplayDebuggerCategory_Locator()
{
  bShowOnlyWithDebugActor = false;
  SetDataPackReplication<FRepData>(&DataPack);
}

void FGameplayDebuggerCategory_Locator::FRepData::Serialize(FArchive& Ar) {
  Ar << ActorLocationString;
}

TSharedRef<FGameplayDebuggerCategory>
FGameplayDebuggerCategory_Locator::MakeInstance()
{
  return MakeShareable(new FGameplayDebuggerCategory_Locator());
}

void FGameplayDebuggerCategory_Locator::CollectData(APlayerController *
OwnerPC, AActor * DebugActor)
{
  if (DebugActor) {
    DataPack.ActorLocationString =
DebugActor->GetActorLocation().ToString();
  }
}

void FGameplayDebuggerCategory_Locator::DrawData(APlayerController *
OwnerPC, FGameplayDebuggerCanvasContext & CanvasContext)
{
```

```
    CanvasContext.Printf(TEXT("If a DebugActor is selected, here below is its
location:"));
    CanvasContext.Printf(TEXT("{cyan}Location: {yellow}%s"),
*DataPack.ActorLocationString);
}

#endif
```

Now, we have our *Gameplay Debugger Category*, but we need to "*register*" it to make it appear in the *Gameplay Debugger*. So, without further ado, let's jump into the next section.

# Registering the Gameplay Debugger Category

In the previous section, we created a *Gameplay Debugger Category*, but now we need to "*register*" it to the *Gameplay Debugger*.

The easiest way to do this is by registering the category inside the `StartupModule()` function of our module, so let's open the `GameplayDebugger_Locator.cpp` file.

The first thing we need to do is include the *Gameplay Debugger Module*, along with the *Gameplay Debugger Category* we have created. We need to surround the `#include` statements with the `#if WITH_GAMEPLAY_DEBUGGER` compiler directive, as shown in the following piece of code:

```
#if WITH_GAMEPLAY_DEBUGGER
#include "GameplayDebugger.h"
#include "GameplayDebuggerCategory_Locator.h"
#endif
```

Inside the `StartupModule()` function, we need to check whether the *Gameplay Debugger Module* is available, and if so, retrieve a reference to it. Then, we can use this reference to register our category with the `RegisterCategory()` function, which takes three parameters (the name of the *Category*, a reference to the function to create an instance of the category, and some options as enum). Finally, we need to notify the changes. Of course, once again, this code is wrapped up by the `#if WITH_GAMEPLAY_DEBUGGER` compiler directive:

```
void FGameplayDebugger_LocatorModule::StartupModule()
{

#if WITH_GAMEPLAY_DEBUGGER

    if (IGameplayDebugger::IsAvailable())
    {
```

```
        IGameplayDebugger& GameplayDebugger = IGameplayDebugger::Get();

        GameplayDebugger.RegisterCategory("Locator",
    IGameplayDebugger::FOnGetCategory::CreateStatic(&FGameplayDebuggerCategory_
    Locator::MakeInstance),
    EGameplayDebuggerCategoryState::EnabledInGameAndSimulate);

        GameplayDebugger.NotifyCategoriesChanged();
    }

#endif
}
```

So far, so good, but when we register something in a module, we also need to "*unregister*" when the module shuts down. Thus, in the `ShutdownModule()` function, we need to follow the same steps as before, but this time *unregister* the category. First, we need to check the validity of the *Gameplay Debugger Module*, and then we retrieve it, *unregister* the category, and notify the changes. Once again, the code is wrapped up by the `#if WITH_GAMEPLAY_DEBUGGER` compiler directive:

```
    void FGameplayDebugger_LocatorModule::ShutdownModule()
    {

#if WITH_GAMEPLAY_DEBUGGER

      if (IGameplayDebugger::IsAvailable())
      {
        IGameplayDebugger& GameplayDebugger = IGameplayDebugger::Get();

        GameplayDebugger.UnregisterCategory("Locator");

        GameplayDebugger.NotifyCategoriesChanged();
      }
#endif
    }
```

For your convenience, here is the full code of the file:

```
    #include "GameplayDebugger_Locator.h"

    #if WITH_GAMEPLAY_DEBUGGER
    #include "GameplayDebugger.h"
    #include "GameplayDebuggerCategory_Locator.h"
    #endif

    #define LOCTEXT_NAMESPACE "FGameplayDebugger_LocatorModule"
```

```cpp
void FGameplayDebugger_LocatorModule::StartupModule()
{

#if WITH_GAMEPLAY_DEBUGGER

  if (IGameplayDebugger::IsAvailable())
  {
    IGameplayDebugger& GameplayDebugger = IGameplayDebugger::Get();

    GameplayDebugger.RegisterCategory("Locator",
IGameplayDebugger::FOnGetCategory::CreateStatic(&FGameplayDebuggerCategory_
Locator::MakeInstance),
EGameplayDebuggerCategoryState::EnabledInGameAndSimulate);

    GameplayDebugger.NotifyCategoriesChanged();
  }

#endif
}

void FGameplayDebugger_LocatorModule::ShutdownModule()
{

#if WITH_GAMEPLAY_DEBUGGER

  if (IGameplayDebugger::IsAvailable())
  {
    IGameplayDebugger& GameplayDebugger = IGameplayDebugger::Get();

    GameplayDebugger.UnregisterCategory("Locator");

    GameplayDebugger.NotifyCategoriesChanged();
  }
#endif
}

#undef LOCTEXT_NAMESPACE
IMPLEMENT_MODULE(FGameplayDebugger_LocatorModule, GameplayDebugger_Locator)
```

Compile, and our code is ready to go. Also, ensure that the *Plugin* is activated, and then close and reopen the editor (sothat we are sure that our module has been loaded properly).

Let's explore how what we have created works in Unreal.

# Visualizing the custom Gameplay Debugger Category

Once we have restarted the editor, our *Plugin* will be loaded as well, which means that our *Gameplay Debugger Category* has been loaded as well. To check this, we can navigate to the *Project Settings*, under the *Gameplay Debugger Section*. Here, we have all the options to configure the *Gameplay Debugger*, including the categories that have been loaded. Thus, if we scroll down, we should be able to find our *Locator Category*, as shown in the following screenshot:

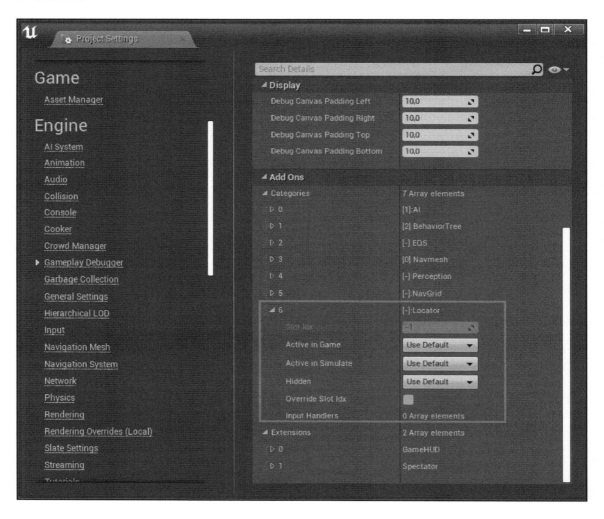

As you can see, all the options are set to "*Use Default*", which we set when we passed the third parameter for registering the category. However, you can also override them here (for instance, by ensuring that it is always enabled). Optionally, you can change the key that this category is triggered on, or just leave the default settings as is if you don't have any preference. The *Editor* will assign one for you:

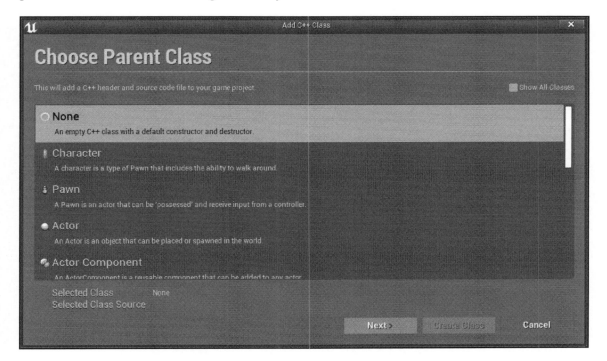

If you are having trouble making the plugin load with the Gameplay Debugger available, you should navigate from the top menu of Unreal to *Window | Developer Tools | Modules*. From here, search for our Locator Module, and then press on Reload, as shown in the following screenshot:

You may need to do this every time you load the editor in order to use your Categories and/or Extension.

Now, if we press play and activate the *Gameplay Debugger*, we will see our category listed (it may be active or not by default, depending on the settings you set previously):

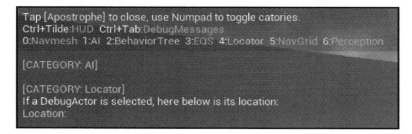

If we select another Actor, we will be able to see that the ***Locator Category*** will display its position:

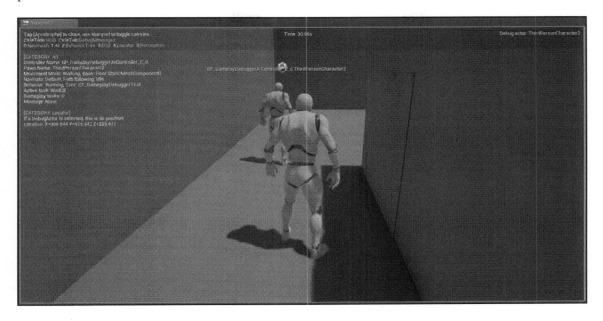

This is a screenshot of the output. The other (blurred out) information is not important here

Here is a close-up:

[CATEGORY: Locator]
If a DebugActor is selected, this is its position:
Location: X=908.544 Y=515.342 Z=228.417

This concludes our discussion on creating a ***Custom Gameplay Debugger Category***. Of course, it was a very simple example, but you can easily imagine the potential of such a tool and how this can be used in your project workflow.

Before we conclude this chapter, as we mentioned previously, let's have a look at how we could extend the *Gameplay Debugger* by adding an *Extension*.

# Creating an Extension for the Gameplay Debugger

As we mentioned previously, the *Gameplay Debugger* is composed of *Categories* (we have already seen how to create a custom one) and *Extensions*. Once again, creating an *Extension* is only available in C++.

Like the *Gameplay Debugger Category*, an *Extension* needs to live on a *Custom Module*, but it can be the same one as the *Category* (or *Categories*). Thus, I'm going to use the same plugin we just developed.

In particular, we are going to create a simple extension that, when we press a specific key, prints the position of the Player in the output log.

## The structure of the Extension

We need to create a new C++ class and inherit from *GameplayDebuggerExtension* (by starting from an empty class, like we did when extending the Categories, and then build on that). The naming convention that we'll be using here is "*GameplayDebuggerExtension_Name*" (however, keep in mind that there might be a limit of 32 characters for the file name). In our case, we will go for *GameplayDebuggerExtension_Player*:

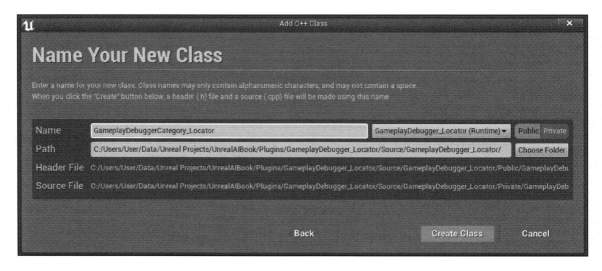

The structure of a *Gameplay Debugger Extension* is quite straightforward, since we will need to implement and/or override the following functions:

- **Constructor**: This sets the default value for the extensions, including settings. More importantly, it sets the key binding for the extension (and passes a reference to the function you wish to bind).
- **MakeInstance()**: This creates an instance of the *Gameplay Debugger Extension* as a shared reference. This function is required when the *Extension* is registered.
- **OnActivated()**: This performs initialization when the *Extension* is activated (e.g. the *Gameplay Debugger* opens).
- **OnDeactivated()**: This cleans up when the *Extension* is deactivated (e.g. the *Gameplay Debugger* closes). For instance, the Spectator extension uses this function to destroy the spectator controller (if it exists) and return control to the *Player Controller* that was there before.
- **GetDescription()**: This describes the *Extension* to the *Gameplay Debugger*. This means that this function returns a *String* that's used to display the text in the Gameplay Debugger; the usual format with the color is allowed. Moreover, you are able to use `FGameplayDebuggerCanvasStrings::ColorNameEnabled` and `FGameplayDebuggerCanvasStrings::ColorNameDisabled` for the String that describes the colors of enabled or disabled for the extension, respectively. This is very useful if your *Extension* uses a toggle.
- **Action Function**: This performs the action that you want your *Extension* to do, so here, it can be whatever you want. This function will be passed to the Input Binding in the *Constructor*.

# Creating the Extension class

Of course, we don't need all the functions we just looked at. In our case, we can start by declaring the `Constructor`, `GetDescription()`, and `MakeInstance()` functions in the header (`.h`) file:

```
public:
  GameplayDebuggerExtension_Player();

  //virtual void OnDeactivated() override;
  virtual FString GetDescription() const override;

  static TSharedRef<FGameplayDebuggerExtension> MakeInstance();
```

Next, we will need a protected function, which we will bind to a specific input:

```
protected:

    void PrintPlayerLocation();
```

Then, we will need some protected variables: a boolean variable to check if an input has been binded, another boolean variable to see if the description has been cached, and a third variable that contains the cached description itself:

```
protected:
    uint32 bHasInputBinding : 1;
    mutable uint32 bIsCachedDescriptionValid : 1;
    mutable FString CachedDescription;
```

 For performance reasons, it is always good practice to cache the description of a *Gameplay Debugger Extension*.

Of course, don't forget to enclose the whole class within the conditional compiler directive and the *WITH_GAMEPLAY_DEBUGGER* macro. This is what the header (.h) file should look like:

```
#include "CoreMinimal.h"

#if WITH_GAMEPLAY_DEBUGGER
#include "GameplayDebuggerExtension.h"

/**
 *
 */
class GAMEPLAYDEBUGGER_LOCATOR_API GameplayDebuggerExtension_Player :
public FGameplayDebuggerExtension
{
public:
    GameplayDebuggerExtension_Player();

    //virtual void OnDeactivated() override;
    virtual FString GetDescription() const override;

    static TSharedRef<FGameplayDebuggerExtension> MakeInstance();

protected:

    void PrintPlayerLocation();
```

```
    uint32 bHasInputBinding : 1;
    mutable uint32 bIsCachedDescriptionValid : 1;
    mutable FString CachedDescription;

};

#endif
```

For the implementation, we can start by adding the following `#include` statements, since we will need to have access to the Player Controller and its Pawn to retrieve the Player's location. Also, we will need to bind inputs, so we need to include the *Input Core Types* as well:

```
#include "InputCoreTypes.h"
#include "GameFramework/PlayerController.h"
#include "GameFramework/Pawn.h"
```

Next, we will implement our Constructor. Here is where we bind the input to a specific key. In our case, we can bind it to the *P* key. Of course, we will need a delegate, and we can pass our `PrintPlayerLocation()` function to do so:

```
GameplayDebuggerExtension_Player::GameplayDebuggerExtension_Player()
{
   const FGameplayDebuggerInputHandlerConfig KeyConfig(TEXT("PrintPlayer"),
EKeys::NumLock.GetFName());
   bHasInputBinding = BindKeyPress(KeyConfig, this,
&GameplayDebuggerExtension_Player::PrintPlayerLocation);
}
```

As we mentioned previously, if you can, cache your description so that your *Extension* gains some performance. Here is the code structure for caching our description:

```
FString GameplayDebuggerExtension_Player::GetDescription() const
{
  if (!bIsCachedDescriptionValid)
  {
    CachedDescription = [SOME CODE HERE TO RETRIEVE THE DESCRIPTION]

    bIsCachedDescriptionValid = true;
  }

  return CachedDescription;
}
```

Now, we need to get the Description. In this case, it can just be the Input Handler (so that we remember which key this Extension is bound to, and the word "Player" to remember that this is the Extension that retrieves the Player's location. As for the colors, the Gameplay Debugger Extension provides some shortcuts for accessing specific colors (for instance, for toggling different kinds of Extensions, the color can changed based on whether it is toggled or not). We won't pay much attention to colors at the moment, and we will use the default ones, assuming that everything is always enabled. As a result, this is the `GetDescription()` function:

```
FString GameplayDebuggerExtension_Player::GetDescription() const
{
  if (!bIsCachedDescriptionValid)
  {
    CachedDescription = !bHasInputBinding ? FString() :
      FString::Printf(TEXT("{%s}%s:{%s}Player"),
        *FGameplayDebuggerCanvasStrings::ColorNameInput,
        *GetInputHandlerDescription(0),
        *FGameplayDebuggerCanvasStrings::ColorNameEnabled);

    bIsCachedDescriptionValid = true;
  }

  return CachedDescription;
}
```

The `MakeInstance()` function, on the other hand, is pretty straightforward and very similar to the one we used for the *Gameplay Debugger Categories*; it just needs to return a shared reference to this Extension:

```
TSharedRef<FGameplayDebuggerExtension>
GameplayDebuggerExtension_Player::MakeInstance()
{
  return MakeShareable(new GameplayDebuggerExtension_Player());
}
```

Finally, in our `PrintPlayerPosition()` function, we can just use a *UE_LOG* to print the Player's location. However, in a *Gameplay Debugger Extension*, its in these kind of functions (which are bound to the input) that the real magic happens:

```
void GameplayDebuggerExtension_Player::PrintPlayerLocation()
{
  UE_LOG(LogTemp, Warning, TEXT("Player's Location: %s"),
  *GetPlayerController()->GetPawn()->GetActorLocation().ToString());
}
```

Once again, don't forget to wrap your C++ class with the compiler directive.

As a result, this is the `.cpp` file of our class:

```cpp
#include "GameplayDebuggerExtension_Player.h"

#if WITH_GAMEPLAY_DEBUGGER
#include "InputCoreTypes.h"
#include "GameFramework/PlayerController.h"
#include "GameFramework/Pawn.h"
//#include "GameplayDebuggerPlayerManager.h"
//#include "Engine/Engine.h"

GameplayDebuggerExtension_Player::GameplayDebuggerExtension_Player()
{
  const FGameplayDebuggerInputHandlerConfig KeyConfig(TEXT("PrintPlayer"),
EKeys::NumLock.GetFName());
  bHasInputBinding = BindKeyPress(KeyConfig, this,
&GameplayDebuggerExtension_Player::PrintPlayerLocation);
}

FString GameplayDebuggerExtension_Player::GetDescription() const
{
  if (!bIsCachedDescriptionValid)
  {
    CachedDescription = !bHasInputBinding ? FString() :
      FString::Printf(TEXT("{%s}%s:{%s}Player"),
        *FGameplayDebuggerCanvasStrings::ColorNameInput,
        *GetInputHandlerDescription(0),
        *FGameplayDebuggerCanvasStrings::ColorNameEnabled);

    bIsCachedDescriptionValid = true;
  }

  return CachedDescription;
}

TSharedRef<FGameplayDebuggerExtension>
GameplayDebuggerExtension_Player::MakeInstance()
{
  return MakeShareable(new GameplayDebuggerExtension_Player());
}

void GameplayDebuggerExtension_Player::PrintPlayerLocation()
{
  UE_LOG(LogTemp, Warning, TEXT("Player's Location: %s"),
*GetPlayerController()->GetPawn()->GetActorLocation().ToString());
}

#endif
```

# Registering the Extension

Just like we did for *Gameplay Debugger Categories*, we need to register the *Extensions* as well.

However, before we do that, if we try to compile, we will get an error. In fact, since we handle inputs for the *Extension*, the module in which the *Extension* lives requires the **Public Dependency** to the "*InputCore*". Add the following line to your .build.cs file:

```
PrivateDependencyModuleNames.Add("InputCore");
```

Specifically, for our Locator Module, this is how you should insert this dependency in the GameplayDebugger_Locator.build.cs file:

```
        if (Target.bBuildDeveloperTools || (Target.Configuration !=
UnrealTargetConfiguration.Shipping && Target.Configuration !=
UnrealTargetConfiguration.Test)) {
        PrivateDependencyModuleNames.Add("GameplayDebugger");
        PrivateDependencyModuleNames.Add("InputCore");
        Definitions.Add("WITH_GAMEPLAY_DEBUGGER=1");
    } else {
        Definitions.Add("WITH_GAMEPLAY_DEBUGGER=0");
    }
```

If you compile after this modification, you shouldn't get any errors.

Now, it's time to register the Extension and notify the *Gameplay Debugger* of this change. We need to use specific functions to do so. Thus, in our StartupModule() function (in the GameplayDebugger_Locatot.cpp file), we need to add the following bold lines of code so that we can register and notify the *Gameplay Debugger* accordingly (note that we need to do this for both *Extensions* and *Categories*, since they are two different functions):

```
    void FGameplayDebugger_LocatorModule::StartupModule()
    {

#if WITH_GAMEPLAY_DEBUGGER

    UE_LOG(LogTemp, Warning, TEXT("Locator Module Loaded"));

    if (IGameplayDebugger::IsAvailable())
    {
        IGameplayDebugger& GameplayDebugger = IGameplayDebugger::Get();

        GameplayDebugger.RegisterExtension("Player",
IGameplayDebugger::FOnGetExtension::CreateStatic(&GameplayDebuggerExtension
_Player::MakeInstance));

        GameplayDebugger.NotifyExtensionsChanged();
```

```
    GameplayDebugger.RegisterCategory("Locator",
IGameplayDebugger::FOnGetCategory::CreateStatic(&FGameplayDebuggerCategory_
Locator::MakeInstance),
EGameplayDebuggerCategoryState::EnabledInGameAndSimulate);

    GameplayDebugger.NotifyCategoriesChanged();

    UE_LOG(LogTemp, Warning, TEXT("GameplayDebugger Registered"));
    }

#endif
}
```

The same goes for unregistering the *Extension* when the module shuts down. Here is the code we need to add in the ShutdownModule() function:

```
void FGameplayDebugger_LocatorModule::ShutdownModule()
{

#if WITH_GAMEPLAY_DEBUGGER

    if (IGameplayDebugger::IsAvailable())
    {
        IGameplayDebugger& GameplayDebugger = IGameplayDebugger::Get();

        GameplayDebugger.UnregisterExtension("Player");

        GameplayDebugger.NotifyExtensionsChanged();

        GameplayDebugger.UnregisterCategory("Locator");

        GameplayDebugger.NotifyCategoriesChanged();

    }
#endif
}
```

Compile the code, and your plugin will be ready. You might need to restart the editor for the effects to take place.

If you are still having trouble making the plugin load with the Gameplay Debugger available, navigate from the top menu of Unreal to **Window -> Developer Tools | Modules**. From here, search for our Locator Module and then press on Reload, as shown in the following screenshot:

You may need to do this every time you load the editor in order to use your Categories and/or Extension.

If you go into the *Gameplay Debugger Settings*, you will find our *Extension* listed (and you will be able to change the key bind if you wish):

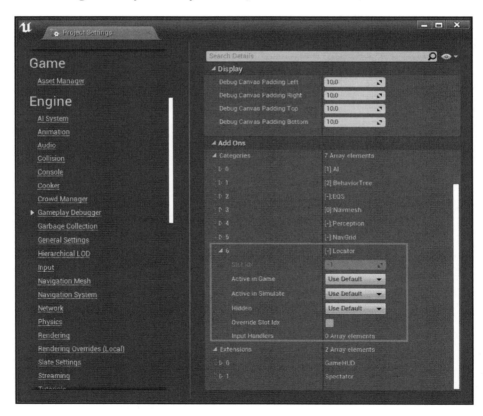

## This is how it will appear in-game:

This is a screenshot of the output. The other (blurred out) information is not important here

## Here is a close-up:

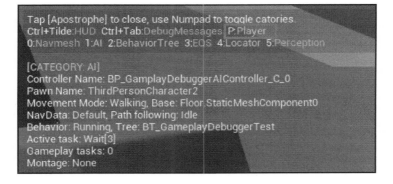

If you press *P*, then the Extension will produce the following result in the *Output Log*:

For more information about *Gameplay Debugger Extensions*, you should have a look at the classes contained in `GameplayDebuggerExtension.h` (the vase class to create an *Extension* of the *Gameplay Debugger*) and `GameplayDebuggerExtension_Spectator.h` (an implementation of an *Extension*, with an example of *Input Binding* and *Cached Description* as well).

This concludes our adventure into extending the *Gameplay Debugger*.

# Summary

In this chapter, we look at how to take advantage of the **Gameplay Debugger** for testing our AI systems. In particular, we looked at the default **Categories and Extensions** of the *Gameplay Debugger*, how they work, and which kind of information they display.

Then, we saw how it is possible to *extend the Gameplay Debugger* by *creating a new Category* and a *new Extension* within a *Plugin*. As a result, we unlocked great potential for debugging our own systems.

In the next chapter, we will explore *AI in Games* further, and see what's beyond.

# 14
# Going Beyond

In this final chapter, we are going to discuss what we have been covered in this book, and what has been left out. There will be some general thoughts on AI and Psychology that every Game AI Developer should be aware of. Therefore, this chapter will conclude with some suggestions on how to explore the concepts that were presented (and others) in this book and some thoughts about AI.

It is not possible to imagine a future where **artificial intelligence (AI)** will not be omnipresent. It will be integrated into everything in ways that we haven't even imagined. Therefore, for AI to be designed in a way that can truly connect with human beings, psychology will need to remain at the center of the design of such experiences. Year by year, we can observe the world becoming increasingly reliant on technology, and in some cases, technology fills the void of human interaction. This allows us to interact with highly personalized and customized experiences that make up feel among a sea of individuals truly unique.

Often, AI programmers forget who they are implementing the system for: the players. As such, psychology plays an important role: how an AI system is perceived by the player is more important than the performance of the system itself. This chapter explores this link between the psychology of the player and AI in games.

In this chapter, we will learn about the following topics:

- Why is psychology an important consideration for AI?
- What we haven't covered in this book
- Some useful resources
- AI and philosophy

# Why is psychology an important consideration for AI?

By now, you may have begun to suspect why psychology is an integral part of the development of artificial intelligence. Psychology is important because it teaches us about the fundamental reasoning behind how humans think and behave. Therefore, it makes sense for us to find ways to incorporate this into our designs when it comes to personalizing, customizing, and automating experiences for users. When considering the autonomous role of AI within an interactive experience, it must, in some way, align with how we, as players, interact and engage with the virtual world; how we interact with objects, **non-roleplaying characters** (NPCs), and other players. One way to think of this is via cause and effect. For example, we perform a particular action such as stealing from different characters or behaving badly, and that, in turn, will have an effect on how other NPCs respond to you. An excellent example of this is in the game Overlord, where the more that you go out of your way to terrorize villages, the less likely and willing they are to help you or even interact with you. While it can be humorous, it can be quite frustrating too, especially when you need to achieve certain objectives and are forced to do it the hard way because now everyone hates you! Therefore, remember that to create AI within games, you need to define a metric to evaluate the progress of the player and tweak it accordingly as you begin to playtest your game.

There are many ways that psychology is used in conjunction with AI. For example, many websites use Recommendation Systems that either pay attention to what you purchase or look at and make suggestions based on that. This can either be done while you're browsing catalogs, adding items to your cart, or even via email to lure you back in with "personalized promotions".

# Psychology and AI in games

More specifically in games, AI is used quite extensively. Unlike AI, machine learning has the possibility to be implemented within a game, but given the brevity of most gaming experiences, there is often not enough data to go on for the machine to really "learn" anything, let alone apply it to gameplay. Therefore, it is not really an economically nor resource viable option. In this instance, the saying "just because you can, doesn't mean you should" would be the most sensible approach to this situation.

More specifically talking, the use of psychology in AI can target many other areas, such as playing on a character's (and player's) emotions. In an era of emerging technologies and ways to use them, we find that some games set out to make the game feel "real" for the player. The developers try to find ways to cross the threshold of reality and game and really encourage the player to make morally questionable choices (e.g. Spec Ops: The Line, Heavy Rain), ones of which really tug on the heartstrings and make us even reflect on our own behavior.

Some games aim to "psychologically" profile you while you are playing. For example, Silent Hill: Shattered Memories, uses psychological profiling to get to know you and then uses this information to change the game while you are playing it, to, as they put it, create your own personal nightmare.

This is very intuitively done via a part within the game where a psychologist where Dr. Michael Kaufmann—or Dr. K—asks you a range of different questions to begin the profiling process. But this is only the basis of the profiling—the profiling itself is modified as you play, how you interact with different objects, what things you do frequently, or not (e.g. checking your map).

In a game, when it comes to player interactions, emotions are one of the most useful indicators to a player. A character's emotions can convey anger, happiness, sadness, and frustration, and many games communicate this via complex and detailed narrative choices, characters voices, expressions, and overall presence. In many ways, emotions can contribute greatly to the atmosphere of a game, let alone their influence on how a player interacts, responds, or makes choices within an interaction. However, emotions play a more important role than simply conveying an atmosphere. They greatly influence the way that we make decisions. For example, a character is less likely to think if they haven't been experiencing a stressful event or challenge during gameplay, whereas if they have just narrowly escaped a boss and now have to make a fast decision (while a timer is ticking away) about whether to shoot a target or not, chances are there will be a very different thought process behind it. One of the best examples that I have experienced would be while playing Spec Ops: The Line (spoilers ahead). After having spent most of the game killing influxes of enemies, you finally reach a level where you have them cornered, but they then begin to "flee". Switching to an aerial view via helicopter, you can see that they appear to be converging into a corner with no way out. Perfect! Right? So, naturally, caught up in the moment, you spam the button to unleash fury onto them, trying to destroy every last one. However, that illuminated group of people isn't running. They're trapped—they're not fighting back. Well, needless to say, after being caught up in the moment to bring down hell onto your enemies, you have inadvertently failed your mission—to save the innocents. At this point, you're mentally drained and from here on out, in every dialogue option, you start to think more carefully about your choices and how they impact others—more so if you hadn't already.

# Building better AI through psychology

To make something inhuman (the AI) act human, you need to keep in mind that humans don't always act rationally—we can often be unpredictable. There are so many different things that humans consider before making choices (even in games) about what to do next. For example, they may take social information, such as the rank (status, level, etc.) of a player, into account before deciding to attack them. This is most likely to impact the narrative. In addition, players are likely to use mental shortcuts in their decision-making, which, depending on their own mental models, may lead to all kinds of unpredictable behavior. This can be further influenced by the game's environment and previous experiences. Therefore, how can you teach a computer to emulate, let alone respond in a believable way?

Developers need to design AI, and in doing so they also need to consider the psychology behind it. For example, should the AI respond to a player the way that he/she may be expecting (like that of a normal human being)? Perhaps the developer has created a fantasy where conventions exist and therefore the AI must respond accordingly (which may be out of the conventions of reality). In all cases, there are always points related to the psychology of the player, which the developer needs to keep in mind for the design of AI behavior. Therefore, as a developer, you need to consider *how* the AI interacts with the game environment in a convincing way. You need to make the AI aware of its environment, confine to the game's conventions, and respond/behave accordingly. Having the player trigger the AI by walking into a collision box to trigger an immediate response is a sure way to break the immersion. The AI needs to consider its current situation and be contextually aware.

Another consideration is the kinds of relationships that players are likely to form with **non-player characters** (**NPCs**). In games where there is a dynamic and branching narrative that the player influences, the idea is that you want players to feel connected to the game—to the characters within it. Ultimately, you want players to "feel" for the other characters and how do you do that, that is, with a convincing AI that was developed to connect with the human psyche. This can be done in such a way that it begins to feel like an interactive Turing test. At this point, you can see that there are at least several ways that you can use psychology to influence the design of AI.

In addition to branching narratives, another important aspect is the ability to incorporate emotion into the AI's interaction with the player. For example, if a player is interacting with different NPCs in a negative way, then this will influence the way that the AI will respond. This isn't necessarily in terms of narrative, but also in terms of attitude toward the player. For example, an NPC, in the beginning, may be willing to help you—perhaps even offer you a discounted rate during a trade. However, based on your relationships with other NPCs (e.g. negative attitudes), your actions may inevitably influence the attitudes of NPCs that you haven't behaved in the same way toward (e.g. those with a previously positive attitude toward you).

The irony is all of this is that to make AI believable is to make it imperfect. Humans are not perfect—we are far from it in many cases—so AI should be as well. For example, if an AI is chasing a player—even shooting at them—it doesn't make sense for the AI to hit the player with every bullet, just like human players; it would be reasonable that the AI misses. It should be a situation where the AI *barely* wins/loses. In this way, even if it is, to some level, a false sense of security for the player, it makes them feel like he/she is achieving something. It far outweighs a "God mode" scenario where the player can destroy everything with minimal effort or, in contrast, where he/she struggles to move forward because the AI is simply too powerful. Of course, this balance can be influenced depending on the difficulty setting that the player has set. By doing this, you're able to contribute to the player's immersion, that is, to make the game environment believable and that the player is interacting with another "person" rather than just a scripted character within a game.

Along the same lines of "believability" is the reaction time of AI. Just as much as you don't want to make them more powerful than the abilities that a player possesses, they too need to react with the same speed in terms of processing events as a player would. For example, players (a.k.a. humans) have an average reaction time of 0.2 seconds (vision) and 0.15 seconds (audio) (www.humanbenchmark.com). What this means is that if we were to stand inside of a room, if another person was to open the door, it would take us 0.2/0.15 seconds to react to it, whether that is to turn our head to see who is at the door or to block the door from opening or even hide. Therefore, AI needs to behave the same, albeit handicapped, in terms of reaction time in order to avoid having an advantage to that of a human player. However, this extends to many other things, such as comprehending an event (e.g. was the explosion a bomb or a car backfiring?) and then responding (e.g. look for enemies, ignore, investigate). Keep in mind that for each of these types of events, the necessary reaction times *and* responses need to be implemented.

By using psychology to drive the design of AI, we have a framework that helps us create believable narratives, characters, and environments so that we can create more immersive game environments. In addition, the consideration of psychology doesn't specifically relate to the design of AI—we can build upon this in terms of in-game events. For example, NPCs that move around the environment may have their own stories, their own "psychology", that drives their movement and even their interaction with the player. For example, NPC characters may encounter each other, some sort of altercation occurs, and as a result, this impacts the player's future interaction with them. This is likely to occur if there are characters within the game that the player can interact with and either does (but in a particular way) or does not interact with at all, which can influence the AI's interaction with the player at later parts within the game experience. Randomization is another aspect that can help improve the realness of AI within a game environment. Of course, to some extent, NPCs are likely to follow the same path when they walk, especially in a situation where there are guards protecting an area. However, every now and then, allowing the NPC to deviate on their path, perhaps to go around the front of a fountain instead of behind it, can all contribute to the authenticity of the environment.

Lastly, before we wrap up this chapter, *testing* your AI is essential to its success. Just like how human behavior is unpredictable, so can the behavior of your AI. This is particularly prevalent when it comes to pathfinding. For example, when a player is supposed to follow a path, but should another NPC cross it, or even the player, it may result in the AI acting in a strange way. As a result, it may break the immersion of the player or worse, disrupt the game mechanics and/or balance because of a glitch.

As we reach the end of this chapter, one piece of advice that I can recommend to you is that even though you don't need to get a degree in psychology to create convincing AI, it helps if you truly want to create AI that connects to your players on a deeper level.

# Machine learning

Artificial intelligence on its own is not enough to "genuinely" connect with players. More complicated and elaborated ways are necessary for the technology to align with us in more intimate ways. Therefore, machine learning provides us with a body of knowledge that can be used to find out what users like, don't like, to track their interactions and behavior, and adapt systems accordingly—of which includes instructing the AI on what to do next. Simply put, machine learning is a sub-domain of AI. This is very important to remember because, in many cases, people often confuse not only the definition of AI and machine learning, but also what they achieve. Machine learning allows a system to autonomously learn from data rather than the developer providing the data—or *hardcoding* it into the interaction.

One last thing to keep in mind before considering AI and psychology is not to overestimate what either is capable of. Each have their limits, and we have limited (albeit growing) knowledge of their respective domains and how they can used together. Therefore, make sure that you do your research when you consider using them as part of your own project.

# Uses of AI and machine learning in games

There are instances where you might and can use AI in games, but in these cases, it will differ from instances when you will use machine learning. However, it is very important to know the difference between the two, as we have already discussed, but also to know the differences in terms of their application and implementation within a game context.

## Uses for AI in games

Game designers might consider the use of AI within a game if there is a need to have autonomous characters. For example, if you want to have enemies that run around chasing the player if he/she shoots at them or to detect the player if he/she gets too close.

## Uses for machine learning in games

On the other hand, the use of machine learning in games would require a slightly different approach and set of considerations. Like our example with AI, you may implement machine learning in a game environment if you want the game to "learn" the habits of a player.

# Adaptive behavior

A practical use of AI for gameplay is the ability to adapt a game's environment (and all that it contains) in ways that respond to a player's input. For example, if players are constantly failing at a certain part of a level, then the player spawns closer to it or the enemies become easier to attack. This process of adapting difficulty is known as dynamic difficulty adjustment, and it is great because it allow players to progress through a game where some parts are particularly more challenging than others. The game Crash Bandicoot is an excellent example of a game that implements this mechanic, and allows you to enjoy a challenging yet playable game experience.

# What we haven't covered in this book

Well, pretty much everything!

Despite the many pages within this book, we have only just scratched the surface of this wonderful topic of AI in games. How many times did I say in this book "*Unfortunately, this [insert topic] is outside the scope of this book*"? Too many to remember. This is just for the built-in AI Framework of Unreal (for instance, we haven't covered how to properly extend Generators and Tests for EQS, or how to create a custom AI Sense). However, I strongly believe that this book gave you some solid foundation to iterate upon and keep learning the Unreal AI Framework. Hopefully, you will be able to use this book as a reference for your work in Unreal.

As much as I hope that this book has been helpful to set the first stone, the intention of this section is to indicate that the path is made of thousands of stones. By randomly pointing toward the main ones, I hope to inspire you to keep going on this path. We will discuss some of these "stones" in more detail in the following sections.

## Motion and navigation (low level)

In Chapter 3, *Navigation*, we explored the navigation system that comes within Unreal. However, we didn't talk about motion, which comes down in the AI schema we presented in Chapter 1, *Making the First Steps in the World of AI*.

Motion deals with the acceleration and velocity of the character, including the avoidance of obstacles and other agents. Of course, we looked at *avoidance* in Chapter 7, *Crowds*, and acceleration and low-level movement is within the Movement components in Unreal. However, there is a whole part about *steering behaviors* that deals with controlling the acceleration of the agents to create more realistic behaviors, which we haven't explored.

## Racing games

Racing games are definitely a case on their own. In fact, we will need an AI that is able to perform Continuous Pathfinding (which is still an unresolved problem in its general form) and compete with different gameplay mechanics. Many other AI algorithms play a role there, such as those for balancing the game (e.g. creating a "virtual spring" among all the cars).

# Agent awareness

Agent awareness deals with the capacity to give senses to the AI agents—in particular, sight, which is the most common and widely used, but also hearing and smelling. Moreover, we can start to explore how this data will be used in higher level structures so that the agent can act accordingly.

# Environment Query System

The **Environment Query System (ESQ)** can gather information from the environment surrounding the agent, allowing the agent to make decisions accordingly. This book dedicates a whole chapter to this system. In fact, it lies between *Agent Awareness* and *Decision-Making*, and it is a great resource that's already built into Unreal.

# Decision-making and planning

Once the agent can perceive the world around it and move into it, it is time to act by making decisions, which have consequences. Some decision-making processes might become so complicated that the agent needs to come up with a proper plan to successfully achieve a goal.

We have just explored Behavior Trees, but there are many decision-making algorithms and systems that are worth exploring, from FSMs to Utility Functions, and Multi-Agent Systems to Planning Algorithms.

# Discrete games/board games

Sometimes, the world around the agent is not continuous, but discrete and potentially turn-based. As such, the agent cannot always use the algorithms that we have explored in this book. Game theory and the maths behind discrete games are important for many game applications, from turn-based games to the strategic allocation of resources for combat systems.

# Learning techniques

Even if, when you think about AI in games, agents are the first thing that comes to mind, a game might contain many other AI algorithms. Although learning techniques are not widely used in games due to the fact that they don't always lead to coherent results, and most of the time they are not required by the game, this topic starts to become appealing to the game industry.

# Procedural Content Generation (PCG)

**Procedural Content Generation** (PCG) is another example of an AI algorithm that isn't tied to an agent, but rather it is the whole world in the game that generates content for the player. These techniques are used both by level designers to create worlds and artists to customize meshes or textures, but also at runtime, while the player is playing, to create an infinite world, usually in arcade games.

# Search and optimization

Search and optimization are fundamental tools for any AI Developer, since these are important techniques that are used widely in AI in general, but which might come in handy when working on AI systems for games. Although these techniques are not used in front of the player, they are used under the hood by the game engine.

# Multi-Agent Systems

Often, AI agents in video games are not alone, but they need to collaborate to achieve a common goal. Multi-Agent Systems are uncommon in video games because they are sometimes hard to implement, but if they're well-combined, they can achieve greatly realistic behaviors. For this reason, most of the time, the collaboration is faked, but this problem can be solved with Multi-Agent Systems, especially if the design of the game requires a more advanced interaction between agents. In addition, these systems are suitable to achieve realistic behaviors in online games with many agents, where computational power can be distributed on many machines.

# AI and psychology

This chapter explains the broader role of AI within the workflow of game development, and how it should be integrated with Game Design to get the best out of the different systems. The aim of this section is to introduce you to different common and less common situations in which an AI algorithm is more suitable than another. Moreover, this section will give you an insight into the relationship between AI and psychology, and how the former affects the latter. In fact, the end user of an AI system is the player, and how he/she feels comfortable or believes in an AI system is a crucial element.

# Going beyond classical AI

There are plenty of exciting ideas and innovations currently going on in the world of AI, and you should always be inspired by inner curiosities to continue your wonderful journey. Being aware of new technologies and algorithms is key to always being up to date.

# Much, much, much more!

This list is in no way exhaustive since there is so much more than you can explore!

# Some useful resources

If you are thirsty to learn more, I can completely understand. Finding good materials on the subject is hard, despite the community being very wild, friendly, and very nice.

For sure, the first place to look is the ***Official Documentation*** (`https://docs.unrealengine.com/en-us/`), which needs to be integrated with the ***Forum*** and ***Answerhub***.

Secondly, participating in events is a great way to connect with people and share knowledge. Did you know that Unreal Engine has official meetups around all the globe? Check it out: `https://www.unrealengine.com/en-US/user-groups`.

Other events include ***Unreal Fest***, ***GDC***, and ***Gamescom*** (among many others).

If you are looking for more traditional resources instead, such as books and blogs, there are a few resources about Unreal Engine (especially related to AI in some way) that I found particularly useful. These are personal blogs, but they contain very useful information. I wish I could state them all, and maybe we should do a list, because there are great people around doing amazing stuff. These are just a few:

- *Tom Looman's blog* (`https://www.tomlooman.com`): You can find a bit of everything, especially about C++. An interesting article is about *Utility AI* here: `https://www.tomlooman.com/journey-into-utility-ai-ue4/`.
- *Orfeas Eleftheriou's blog* (`https://orfeasel.com`): A rich blog about very interesting topics. What's particularly interesting is the article about how to extend the AI perception System, which can be found here: `https://orfeasel.com/creating-custom-ai-senses/`. Honestly, I was going to add a whole section to this book about extending the AI perception System, but unfortunately, I didn't have the time. I hope that this blog article can put you on the right path.
- *Vikram Saran's blog* (`https://www.vikram.codes`): This is a small blog at the moment, but you can find some nice additional information about the *Navigation System*.

# AI and philosophy

Finally, I want to conclude this book with some thoughts about AI that you may find interesting.

The crucial questions to ask if we are considering the philosophical side of artificial intelligence are: how do minds work? Is it possible that machines act intelligently in the way people do? Can machines be conscious?

These simple questions have sparked a great deal of controversy over the past century (and they still do). The aim of this section is not to discuss them thoroughly, but to provide very general ideas about the interesting dialogue around these issues and to stimulate your interest in reading more literature on them.

Gödel's incompleteness theorem states that, for any formal axiomatic system, F, that's powerful enough to do arithmetic, it is possible to construct a sentence, G (F), with the following properties:

- G (F) is a phrase of F, but cannot be proved within F
- If F is coherent, then G (F) is true

Some philosophers maintain that Gödel's theorem shows that machines are inferior to humans because they are formal systems that are limited by the theorem, while humans have no such limitation. Or do we?

It seems impossible to prove that humans are not subject to Gödel's theorem, because any rigorous proof would require a formalization of human talent declared non-formalizable, and would, therefore, be rejected.

Humans are known to be inconsistent in everyday reasoning, and this may leave us unable to prove our superiority.

The *weak AI hypothesis* implies that machines can act as if they are intelligent. In 1950, Alan Turing suggested that instead of asking if machines can think, we should ask ourselves if machines can pass a behavioral intelligence test, which has become known as the Turing test. The test makes a program have a conversation (via messages typed online) with an interrogator for five minutes. The interrogator must, therefore, guess whether the conversation is with a program or a person; the program passes the test if it deceives the interrogator 30% of the time. Turing speculated that by the year 2000, a computer could be programmed well enough to pass the test.

Today, internet chatbots like Natachata have repeatedly deceived their correspondents, and the Cyberlover chatbot can cause people to disclose sufficient personal information that their identity can be stolen.

The *strong AI hypothesis*, on the other hand, claims that machines can really think, not just simulate thought.

Can machines be aware of their mental states and actions? Can they really feel emotions? Turing himself opposed these questions, arguing that in ordinary life, we never have direct evidence of the internal mental states of other humans. Do the other humans that surround us think, or are they simulating?

Can we imagine a future time when realistic conversations with machines are the order of the day, and it becomes customary not to make linguistic distinctions between real and simulated thinking? Turing thought that these problems would eventually disappear by themselves once the machines reached a certain level of sophistication, thus dissolving the difference between strong and weak AI.

Another important issue is consciousness, which is often divided into aspects of understanding and self-awareness.

Turing admitted that the question of conscience was difficult, but denied that it was important for artificial intelligence. Human beings can create thinking machines, but whether consciousness arises it is far beyond our current knowledge.

An important debate concerns the physical composition of minds and bodies and the separation between them.

How can the mind control the body if the two are really separate?

A theory called *physicalism* asserts that the mind is not separate from the body, but it is not yet necessary to explain how the biochemical processes in our mind can generate mental states (such as fear or anger) and emotions.

The theory of functionalism holds that a mental state is an intermediate causal condition between input and output. Artificial intelligence could have the same mental states as a human being in the right conditions. The basic assumption is that there is a level of abstraction, below which the specific implementation does not matter.

A strong challenge to functionalism is posed by *biological naturalism*, according to which mental states are high-level characteristics that emerge from low-level physical processes in neurons.

The Chinese Room is a thought experiment that demonstrates this vision. It consists of a human, understanding only the English language, equipped with an English grammar book, and several piles of sheets. The system is inside a room with a small opening.

Undecipherable symbols appear on paper through the opening. The symbols are checked by the human in the rules book and instructions are followed. These instructions may include writing symbols on new sheets of paper, looking for symbols in the stacks, reordering the stacks, etc. At the end, the instructions will cause one or more symbols to be transcribed on a piece of paper that is returned to the outside world.

From the outside, we see a system that is taking the input in Chinese sentences and generates answers in Chinese that makes perfect sense.

Does the Chinese room system speak Chinese? At what level does the interpretation of the language occur? Does it really happen?

 For more information, visit `https://en.wikipedia.org/wiki/Chinese_room`

I will conclude with some brief ethical considerations. Okay, we might be able to create intelligence... but should we? Do we have moral responsibilities?

Many engineers and scientists have addressed ethical considerations on the technologies they were dealing with. Just think of nuclear fission, or even cars, which cause a huge number of deaths each year.

The AI raises many questions, ranging from the possibility that people lose their jobs to the fear of losing our privileged place on Earth, from military uses of robots as tools of death to moral questions about the relationships between human beings and artificial beings. But probably the most common ethical objections to AI concern the possibility that the advent of artificial intelligence could mean the end of the human race.

Countless science fiction films have been produced by Hollywood studios on cyborgs or smart networks that go to war with humans. More recently, the debate has shifted to different aspects, such as autonomous cars causing accidents that could kill occupants, or a missile defense system that could mistakenly launch a counterattack, leading to the death of billions.

The correct way to mitigate these risks is to include the controls in these systems so that a single error does not spread to unplanned consequences.

But the rules to be imposed on AI (starting from Asimov's laws for robots) are probably the core of ethical implications. We must be very careful about what we ask!

Humans sometimes use their intelligence in aggressive ways because of natural selection. The machines we build must not be intrinsically aggressive, unless they emerge as the end product of a mechanism that encourages aggressive behavior.

The most important risk is the evolution of AI that leads to unexpected behavior. The desire not to harm humans can be designed from the beginning, but engineers should recognize that their designs might be imperfect and that the system will learn and evolve over time. So, the real challenge is to implement a project for evolving artificial intelligence systems within a system of checks and balances and to giv e the systems utility functions that will remain friendly in the face of such changes.

*We need to hope that artificial intelligence will find it tolerable to share this planet with us!*

# Goodbye

I hope you enjoyed this journey with me, and hopefully, our paths will cross again.

Until then, I wish you the best of luck with your journey into *AI Game Development*.

If you feel like dropping a line, you can always contact me. You can find my details on my website: www.francescosapio.com.

# Other Books You May Enjoy

If you enjoyed this book, you may be interested in these other books by Packt:

**Mastering Game Development with Unreal Engine 4 - Second Edition**
Matt Edmonds

ISBN: 9781788991445

- The fundamentals of a combat-based game that will let you build and work all other systems from the core gameplay: the input, inventory, A.I. enemies, U.I., and audio
- Manage performance tools and branching shaders based on platform capabilities in the Material Editor
- Explore scene or level transitions and management strategies
- Improve visuals using UE4 systems such as Volumetric Lightmaps, Precomputed Lighting, and Cutscenes
- Implement audio-to-animation timelines and trigger them from visual FX
- Integrate Augmented Reality into a game with UE4's brand new ARKit and ARCore support
- Perform almost any game logic needed via Blueprint Visual Scripting, and know when to implement it in Blueprint as opposed to C++

## Unreal Engine 4.x Scripting with C++ Cookbook - Second Edition
John P. Doran

ISBN: 9781789809503

- Create C++ classes and structs that integrate well with UE4 and the Blueprints editor
- Discover how to work with various APIs that Unreal Engine already contains
- Utilize advanced concepts such as events, delegates, and interfaces in your UE4 projects
- Build user interfaces using Canvas and UMG through C++
- Extend the Unreal Editor by creating custom windows and editors
- Implement AI tasks and services using C++, Blackboard, and Behavior Trees
- Write C++ code with networking in mind and replicate properties and functions

# Leave a review - let other readers know what you think

Please share your thoughts on this book with others by leaving a review on the site that you bought it from. If you purchased the book from Amazon, please leave us an honest review on this book's Amazon page. This is vital so that other potential readers can see and use your unbiased opinion to make purchasing decisions, we can understand what our customers think about our products, and our authors can see your feedback on the title that they have worked with Packt to create. It will only take a few minutes of your time, but is valuable to other potential customers, our authors, and Packt. Thank you!

# Index

Printed in Great Britain
by Amazon